Reconcilable Differences?

United States–Japan Economic Conflict

C. FRED BERGSTEN

MARCUS NOLAND

INSTITUTE FOR INTERNATIONAL ECONOMICS
Washington, DC
June 1993

C. Fred Bergsten is Director of the Institute for International Economics, Chairman of the Competitiveness Policy Council, and Chairman of the APEC Eminent Persons Group. He was Assistant Secretary for International Affairs of the US Treasury (1977-81); Assistant for International Economic Affairs to the National Security Council (1969-71); and a Senior Fellow at the Brookings Institution (1972-76), the Carnegie Endowment for International Peace (1981), and the Council on Foreign Relations (1967-68). He is the author or editor of 22 books on a wide range of international economic issues including *Pacific Dynamism and the International Economic System* with Marcus Noland (1993), *America in the World Economy: A Strategy for the 1990s* (1988), *Trade Policy in the 1980s* with William Cline (1982), *American Multinationals and American Interests* (1978), *The Dilemmas of the Dollar* (1976), and *World Politics and International Economics* (1975).

Marcus Noland was until recently a Research Fellow at the Institute for International Economics and Visiting Assistant Professor of Economics at The Johns Hopkins University. Currently he is a Senior Economist for the Council of Economic Advisers. He was formerly Assistant Professor at the University of Southern California, Visiting Professor of Policy Science at Saitama University in Japan and a Visiting Scholar at the Korea Development Institute. He has written many articles on international economics and is the coeditor of *Pacific Dynamism and the International Economic System* (1993) and the author of *Pacific Basin Developing Countries: Prospects for the Future* (1990) and *Japan in the World Economy* with Bela Balassa, (1988).

INSTITUTE FOR INTERNATIONAL ECONOMICS
11 Dupont Circle, NW
Washington, DC 20036-1207
(202) 328-9000   FAX: (202) 328-5432

C. Fred Bergsten, *Director*
Christine F. Lowry, *Director of Publications*

Printed in the United States of America
96 95 94 93   4 3 2 1

Library of Congress Cataloging-in-Publication Data

Reconcilable differences? : United States—Japan economic conflict / C. Fred Bergsten, Marcus Noland
   Includes bibliographical references and index.
   1. United States—Commerce—Japan.
   2. Japan—Commerce—United States.
   3. United States—Commercial policy.
   4. Japan—Commercial policy.
   I. Bergsten, C. Fred, 1941–
   II. Noland, Marcus, 1959–
HF1456.5.J3I77   1993
382'.0973052—dc20   93-13689
               CIP

ISBN 0-88132-129-X (paper)

The views expressed in this publication are those of the authors. This publication is part of the overall program of the Institute, as endorsed by its Board of Directors, but does not necessarily reflect the views of individual members of the Board or the Advisory Committee. This book was written while Dr. Noland was at the Institute and the views contained herein do not represent the official position of the Council of Economic Advisers or the United States Government.

Marketed and Distributed outside the USA and Canada by Longman Group UK Limited, London

Contents

Preface   **v**

Acknowledgments   **ix**

1 Introduction   **1**

What Is the Problem?   4

How Different Is Japan?   7

Management of the Relationship   12

Previous Policy Initiatives   14

The Current Policy Framework   18

Plan of the Book   21

2 The Macroeconomic Context   **23**

US–Japan Trade in a Global Perspective   23

Saving, Investment, and the Trade Balance   36

Macroeconomic Policies in the United States and Japan   43

Conclusions   55

3 Structural Access Barriers   **59**

The US-Japan Pattern of Trade   60

Industrial Policy   67

Trade Policy   69

Nontraditional Access Barriers   73

US-Japan Rivalry in High Technology   85

Tactical Implications   96

4 The Sectoral Impact   **99**

  Primary Products   100
  Manufactures   104
    Automobiles   104
    Computers   124
    Semiconductors   127
    Supercomputers   144
    Computer Software   149
    Telecommunication Services and Equipment   150
    High-Definition Television (HDTV)   156
  Services   158
    Retailing   159
    Construction   161
    Financial Services   167

5 Assessment and Lessons   **179**

  Assessment of Market Access Barriers   179
  Lessons   190

6 Conclusions and Policy Recommendations   **199**

  Analytical Findings   199
  The Trade Imbalances   203
  Structural Differences   210
  Sector-Specific Issues   219
  Cooperative Leadership of the Global Economic System   233
  Implementing the Strategy   242

References   **249**

Index   **259**

Preface

The Institute has devoted extensive attention to Japan, and to economic relations between the United States and Japan, throughout the life of its research program. William Cline and I published *The United States–Japan Economic Problem* in 1985 (revised in 1987). Bela Balassa and Marcus Noland prepared *Japan in the World Economy* in 1988. Major components of United States–Japan policy have been included in a number of other publications including Jeffrey Frankel's *The Yen/Dollar Agreement: Liberalizing Japanese Capital Markets* (1984), Edward M. Graham and Paul Krugman's *Foreign Direct Investment in the United States* (1989, revised 1991), Paul Krugman's *Has the Adjustment Process Worked?* (1991), and Laura Tyson's *Who's Bashing Whom? Trade Conflict in High Technology Industries* (1992).

This new volume attempts to provide a comprehensive assessment of the United States–Japan economic relationship, and to suggest a course of action to deal effectively with the wide range of problems it encompasses, as the two governments begin a new set of negotiations in mid–1993. It divides the conflict into four elements: the trade imbalances, structural differences between the two economic systems, specific sectoral difficulties, and the countries' responsibilities for managing the world economy. In light of the reductions in the aggregate imbalances and the increased prominence of structural and sectoral issues since the mid–1980s, when William Cline and I prepared the Institute's previous overview of the United States–Japan problem which stressed the former, this new book places particular emphasis on the latter.

As with all major projects at the Institute, the authors were assisted by comments received on an early draft at discussion meetings held at the Institute and attended by a large number of governmental, corporate, academic and other experts. The study was also informed by the discussions at several meetings of the United States–Japan Economic Policy Group, a small group of leading American and Japanese economists chaired by the Institute and sponsored by the United States–Japan Foundation. I also derived considerable benefit from two conferences on United States–Japan economic issues held at the Aspen Institute in August 1992, especially comments by the participants on my presentations to both and on a paper that Paula Stern and I prepared for one of the sessions.

The Institute for International Economics is a private nonprofit institution for the study and discussion of international economic policy. Its purpose is to analyze important issues in that area, and to develop and communicate practical new approaches for dealing with them. The Institute is completely nonpartisan.

The Institute is funded largely by philanthropic foundations. Major institutional grants are now being received from the German Marshall Fund of the United States, which created the Institute with a generous commitment of funds in 1981, and from the Ford Foundation, the William and Flora Hewlett Foundation, the William M. Keck, Jr. Foundation, the C. V. Starr Foundation, and the United States–Japan Foundation. A number of other foundations and private corporations also contribute to the highly diversified financial resources of the Institute. About 14 percent of the Institute's resources in our latest fiscal year were provided by contributors outside the United States, including about 6 percent from Japan. Partial support for this study was provided by a generous grant from The Rockefeller Brothers Fund.

The Board of Directors bears overall responsibility for the Institute and gives general guidance and approval to its research program—including identification of topics that are likely to become important to international economic policymakers over the medium run (generally, one to three years), and which thus should be addressed by the Institute. The Director, working closely with the staff and outside Advisory Committee, is responsible for the development of particular projects and makes the final decision to publish an individual study.

The Institute hopes that its studies and other activities will contribute to building a stronger foundation for international economic policy around the world. We invite readers of these publications to let us know how they think we can best accomplish this objective.

C. FRED BERGSTEN
Director
June 1993

Acknowledgments

The authors gratefully acknowledge the research assistance of Chongshan Liu, Pamela Winston, and Chang-Tai Hsieh.

We also thank the following for providing valuable comments on the early drafts of the manuscript: Raymond Ahearn, Thomas O. Bayard, Lawrence Brusa, William Cline, Stephen Cohen, Richard N. Cooper, Charles Dallara, I. M. Destler, Rimmer De Vries, Neil Dunay, John T. Eby, Kimberly Ann Elliott, Michael Farren, Robert Fauver, Kenneth Flamm, John Goodman, Edward M. Graham, Eiichi Hasegawa, Noboru Hatakeyama, Elizabeth Hoffman, Gary Clyde Hufbauer, Mariko Ikehara, Takatoshi Ito, Mordechai Kreinin, Allen J. Lenz, Edward Lincoln, Kazuo Matsunaga, G. Mustafa Mohatarem, Seiichiro Noboru, Peter Petri, Timothy Regan, J. David Richardson, Jane Rossetti, Gary R. Saxonhouse, Jeffrey J. Schott, Michael Smith, Paula Stern, S. Linn Williams, Alan Wm. Wolff, Masaru Yoshitomi, and Robert Zoellick.

We are indebted to Coleen McGrath and Alda Seubert for their assistance in typing the many drafts; Michael Treadway for his meticulous editing; and Faith Hunter, Valerie Norville, and Christine Lowry for ensuring timely publication.

1

Introduction

The economic relationship between the United States and Japan is both the most important and the most complex in the world. The two countries together account for 30 to 40 percent of global output, and their wealthy populations make them the world's largest national markets. Their firms compete aggressively for world leadership in numerous high-technology sectors, such as electronics, and in many other industries, such as automobiles, that employ large numbers of workers. America is the world's largest debtor nation and Japan the largest creditor (figure 1.1). America's current account deficits, representing trade in both goods and services, have cumulated to about $1 trillion over the past decade, and Japan's current account surpluses have accounted for about two-thirds of that total (figure 1.2).

It is plausible to argue, and many do, that the United States and Japan are on a collision course. Japan's global trade surplus is soaring, to a succession of record levels, while virtually every other country in the world, including the United States, is in deficit and experiencing at best sluggish growth. The similar industrial composition of output in the two economies virtually ensures continued conflict, as we show in chapters 3 and 4, because they compete frontally across a wide range of manufacturing and services industries and protect some of their own markets against the other's most successful producers. Despite two decades of intense negotiation, problems remain across an array of sectors. Failure of the Uruguay Round of global trade negotiations could sharply intensify the pressure for unilateral and protectionist trade initiatives in the United States, and around the world, many of which would inevitably be directed at Japan.

Figure 1.1 United States and Japan: net international investment position, 1981–92[a]

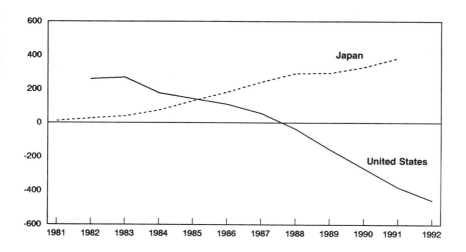

a. Market values at year-end.
Source: Economic Report of the President, various issues; Bank of Japan, *Balance of Payments Monthly,* various issues.

Figure 1.2 United States and Japan: global current account balances, 1981–92[a]

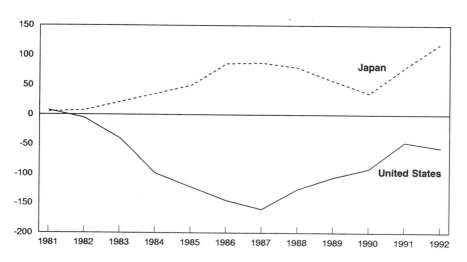

a. The 1991 balances are adjusted for Gulf War transfers.
Source: International Monetary Fund, *International Financial Statistics,* various issues; Organization for Economic Cooperation and Development, *OECD Economic Outlook,* various issues.

On the political front, many Americans—including a number of politicians, businesspeople, and labor leaders—view Japan as a major threat to America's economic future. Many see Japan as an international "free rider" that fails to pay its way, let alone exercise the leadership responsibility that its economic success permits, but instead depends on others (notably the United States) for defense of its strategic interests and for maintenance of the open international economic system that is so crucial to its economy. Japan has become a global economic superpower, increasingly able to resist American demands, but its political system continues to require foreign pressure (or *gaiatsu*, to use the increasingly familiar Japanese term) to galvanize constructive responses to legitimate criticism. The end of the Cold War has removed at least part of the security blanket that required previous leaders in both countries, in the interest of maintaining their anticommunist alliance, to resolve their economic problems cooperatively.

Perhaps most important, a very different administration has assumed office in the United States. The Clinton administration intends to focus on restoring American economic strength, including the ability to compete internationally.[1] It believes in active government intervention in the economy, including through trade and other international economic policies. It has publicly declared that it will seek concrete and measurable results from its economic negotiations with Japan.

At the same time, there are reasons to believe that US-Japan economic tensions will ease in the near future. The US economy has been growing faster than the Japanese since early 1992, and that trend seems likely to continue for a while. Japan's vaunted economic machine and many of the most powerful Japanese companies (including its automakers and its banks) have been severely weakened by the bursting of the "bubble economy" of the late 1980s. Key American industries that have been sources of major concern, such as semiconductors and computers, have made substantial strides, and some of their firms again lead the world (and their Japanese competitors). Corporate alliances between American and Japanese firms have become pervasive, and this too could reduce the prospects for conflict.

Moreover, policy measures are already in place or planned that should moderate the conflict. The economic program of the Clinton administration, including its effort to cut the budget deficit substantially by 1997, would if faithfully implemented begin to improve American competitiveness. Japan, for its part, enacted two huge fiscal stimulus programs in late 1992 and 1993, with an advertised total of about $200 billion, to expand domestic demand and cut the external surplus. The yen has

---

1. In so doing it will pursue the first half of the strategy of "competitive interdependence" recommended for the United States in Bergsten (1988). Most of this study addresses the international part of that strategy.

risen to a record high—about 106 to the dollar at this writing—that if maintained virtually guarantees a substantial fall in the Japanese surplus by 1995 (see chapter 2). Trade in many sectors, including many of the most sensitive politically, is already "managed" by the two countries to a great degree. The countries' external imbalances fell to around 1 percent of their GDPs as recently as 1990–91, demonstrating that some of the conventional tools of adjustment work effectively when applied consistently and cooperatively.

It is exceedingly difficult to predict which of these two tendencies— toward escalation of conflict or away from it—will prevail. A critical determinant will be the future course of the American economy. Restoration of satisfactory economic growth and international competitiveness in the United States itself would go far to defuse tension with Japan, as much of the hostility toward that country reflects frustration with America's own performance and the resulting tendency to look for scapegoats abroad. Japanese behavior will also be critical, however, as Japan will continue to engender negative reactions in the United States (and elsewhere) as long as it retains the image of a closed and exclusionary society that fails to play an international role commensurate with its wealth and capability.

For the next few years, it is clear that the United States and Japan will continue to face significant problems. Under the best of circumstances, it will take some time to restore adequate growth in the United States. Japan's economic problems, while perhaps tempering American fears of its competitive capability, may also limit its ability and its willingness to make concessions to the United States. Even a successful conclusion of the Uruguay Round would leave many trade problems unresolved, especially those centered on Japan. Hence it is clear that the two countries need to launch new initiatives to deal effectively with the economic problems that they confront.

What Is the Problem?

These economic problems are very real. They have both macroeconomic and microeconomic dimensions. On the macroeconomic side, with the United States at less than full employment, continued large American current account deficits represent a net transfer of American production and jobs to the rest of the world. Increases in the deficit increase American unemployment unless domestic demand is rising by an offsetting amount. Adjustment of the deficits usually requires depreciation of the dollar, which reduces the wealth and income of the United States, or some other mechanism that depresses domestic absorption (consumption and investment) in order to achieve the needed transfer of resources through the trade balance (i.e., to other countries). Financing the accumulated foreign debt requires a further transfer of resources abroad.[2]

To be sure, there can be offsetting benefits from external deficits. The net inflow of foreign capital that mirrors a current account deficit can, if used constructively, supplement domestic saving to generate higher national investment and faster productivity growth. The net influx of foreign products helps restrain inflationary pressures.

At the present time, however, the primary economic problem facing the United States—and the world economy as a whole—is sluggish economic growth. Inflationary risks remain modest. As just noted, it will be some time before the economic program of the Clinton administration, even under the best of circumstances, will be able to correct the American budget deficit and have an impact on the country's other underlying problems. Hence renewed reductions in the trade deficit, as in fact occurred to a substantial extent from 1987 through 1991 but began to reverse again in 1992, would be highly desirable and could make an important contribution to the country's overall prospects.

Japan's large and growing global surplus represents a major problem in this context. Japan is now the only surplus country in the G-7 and is running the only large surplus in the world. Hence Japan is maintaining domestic output and employment at the expense of other countries, whose external deficits have risen as a counterpart to the increase in the Japanese surplus.

As Japan's major trading partner, the United States has of course experienced such an impact directly. America's bilateral deficit with Japan has only increased by about $10 billion, however, while Japan's global surplus has soared by about $100 billion. But the United States has also suffered indirectly from the sharp increase in Japan's surplus with other countries, such as those in Europe and East Asia, because those countries are as a result less able to buy from (or become more aggressive in selling to) the United States. Hence the high level and sharp rise of Japan's global surplus is levying significant costs on the United States and on other countries. This multilateral pattern of trade relationships indicates both that we should not focus excessively on the US-Japan bilateral balance, despite its salience in the US political debate, and that we should, particularly in periods of slow growth like the present, be concerned about the level and especially the sharp increase in Japan's global surplus.

Even in the absence of such macroeconomic problems, however, the United States and Japan would face potential economic conflict at the microeconomic level. Some degree of tension is inherent between any pair of large trading partners, such as the United States and Canada, as problems inevitably arise over specific products and even entire sectors.

---

2. See Lawrence (1988) for an excellent analysis of these relationships.

But, as we have already noted, the unique composition of trade between the United States and Japan virtually ensures continuous conflict.

In particular, denial of access to the Japanese market—the world's second largest and its most sophisticated in many high-technology sectors—can significantly hamper individual American (and other foreign) industries. It reduces their ability to achieve economies of scale and scope. It slows their progress down the learning curve, which can be very steep (and critically important to success) in some cutting-edge sectors.

These adverse effects on individual American firms and sectors can in turn carry significant costs for the economy as a whole. Some of them affect industries that create large numbers of jobs, such as automobiles. Some emerge in high-technology (and perhaps services) sectors, which convey important externalities and spinoffs to the rests of the economy. Thus they may have disproportionately important effects on the United States, both quantitatively and qualitatively.

The microeconomic dimension must therefore be considered along with the macroeconomic in assessing the overall US-Japan economic conflict. We will emphasize the microeconomic issues in this book, for three related reasons. First, the macroeconomic questions are much more tractable. These problems are not always easy to resolve, and they are quantitatively much larger, but the terrain in this area is well-plowed. In contrast, the contemporary microeconomic issues are both newer to the policy arena and much more controversial. Detailed analysis of key structural components of the two economies, and particularly of individual sectors, is necessary to provide useful guides for policy action. The most contentious debates, such as that over the desirability of more "managed trade," arise in this area.

Moreover, the politics of the "Japan issue" within the United States tilt heavily toward the sectoral dimension. This is partly because the problems of individual industries are easier to discern, lending themselves to anecdotes and outcomes that are far more comprehensible to the broad public than saving-investment balances and other central elements of the macroeconomic problem. It is also partly because sectoral complaints are the direct source of constituents' appeals to their governmental representatives, delivery on which demonstrates the ability of those representatives to "do something."

Some sophisticated producers recognize the critical importance to them of macroeconomic conditions; for example, the automobile companies have continually emphasized the importance of achieving an equilibrium yen-dollar exchange rate. But the macroeconomic phenomena, particularly the bilateral trade balance, are more often used as arguments for action than as sources of direct concern for most participants in the policy debate.

Hence we will direct the bulk of our analysis to the structural and sector-specific issues in chapters 3 through 5. We will summarize the more familiar macroeconomic terrain much more briefly, but we will do so first, in chapter 2, because it is essential to understand the aggregate context within which the sectoral disputes take place if the latter are to be seen in the proper light.

How Different Is Japan?[3]

A major new issue has come to influence and perhaps dominate all of these disputes, namely, the systemic differences between the two countries. Orthodox economics held that such differences either were not large or did not matter—mechanisms existed to accommodate whatever untoward effects any differences might have, and trade and other economic relations with Japan could be pursued just as with any other country.

"Revisionists" to this traditional view, however, argue that these differences are so fundamental in the case of Japan that it must be treated differently from all other countries. They believe that normal market-oriented, process approaches to trade and economic policy will not work with Japan. While acknowledging that macroeconomic adjustment must be pursued, they conclude that some form of "results-oriented" managed trade is essential. The issue is not Japan's alleged unfairness, as often charged in the past, but rather its unique brand of capitalism. Throughout this book, we will thus focus on the differences between the American and Japanese economies and their policy implications.

There is now widespread recognition of important differences between the Japanese and American brands of market economy. Over a decade ago, Chalmers Johnson (1982) portrayed Japan in the earlier postwar period as a "developmental state" akin to mercantilist nations of a previous era. More recently, Clyde Prestowitz, Jr. (1988), has called attention to Japan's emphasis on production, which contrasts sharply with America's emphasis on consumption. Eisuke Sakakibara (1992) portrays his country as a "noncapitalist market economy." Iwao Nakatani (1992) makes a useful distinction between American "market capitalism" and Japanese "network capitalism." The late Saburo Okita (1992) labeled Japan's model, which he regarded as very useful for developing and emerging market economies, "catch-up capitalism" or "the capitalism of the latecomer."

These differences between the Japanese and American economies relate primarily to methods of corporate governance, financial markets, labor-management relations, interactions between government and the

---

3. Much of this section was originally prepared by Bergsten and Stern (1993).

private sector, and linkages among companies—the famous *keiretsu* system.[4] Japanese companies respond to the interests of a wide array of stakeholders (notably employees, suppliers, and affiliated firms) rather than mainly to the interest of shareholders as US firms tend to do. Many of these stakeholders, including the "main banks" and other members of financial *keiretsu*, take a long-term view of the firm, provide "patient capital" that emphasizes long-term market shares rather than immediate profits, and block attempted takeovers. Japanese labor, thanks largely to the promise of lifetime employment and extensive (compared with their US counterparts) participation in corporate decision making, has been enormously supportive in raising corporate productivity. The Japanese government, particularly in earlier periods but still to an important if disputed degree (as analyzed in chapters 3 and 4), has provided systematic and sustained support (including protection against external competition) for important domestic industries, both sunrise and sunset.

Thus, the debate today is not about the existence of these differences but rather over the following:

- How much of a difference do the differences make?

- Which set of arrangements is superior?

- Are the differences likely to converge sufficiently and in the right directions, within a reasonably short time (the next decade or so), so that they can be viewed as essentially temporary phenomena?

- If some key differences are not likely to converge, can ways be found to live with them? Is "mutual recognition" of permanent differences, as within the European Community, a viable option in some cases?

This is where the serious debate begins. One view holds that Japan and America are so set in their ways that "special approaches" (usually implying at least some degree of managed trade) are needed toward Japan. Japanese business, labor, and government, it is argued, will continue to emphasize production, while their counterparts in America continue to emphasize consumption. Japan will maintain opaque protection of its markets, while America will maintain its relatively transparent openness. Japan will remain an international outlier on certain critical economic measures, importing less (especially of manufactured products) and hosting much less foreign direct investment than other industrial countries.

---

4. The *keiretsu* is a uniquely Japanese form of business organization consisting of separately organized firms linked together through product market, labor market, and financial market ties (see Aoki 1987, 1990, 1991; Yoshitomi 1990). *Keiretsu* and their various manifestations will be an important focus of the analysis in this book.

On this view, Japan will continue to catch up with—and perhaps ultimately pass—the United States, achieving higher real standards of living and global domination in an increasing number of leading-edge industries. Japanese per capita income is already about 50 percent higher than that in the United States when market exchange rates are used to compare the two (although in most studies that adjust for actual purchasing power, American per capita income remains about one-third higher, because of the generally higher level of consumer and other prices in Japan; *Fortune*, 27 July 1992, 68; see also Summers and Heston 1991). Even in terms of total GDP, measured at market exchange rates, Japan could catch and pass the United States early in the 21st century if it resumes sustained growth of 3½ to 4 percent while American growth remains at its 2 to 2½ percent average of the last two decades. This would be a stunning result since the Japanese population is only about half that of the United States.

The alternative view is that the differences between the Japanese and American systems are already declining steadily and are likely to erode fairly rapidly over the coming decade or so. As a result, the countries' economic performances are likely to converge substantially. Japan will suffer from an increasingly acute labor shortage, an aging population, and its unwillingness to import labor. Its national saving rate, particularly in the private sector, has been declining steadily for almost two decades (although it has risen again of late). Its society will increasingly demand a higher standard of living and more consumption, channeling resources into nontradeables (like housing and leisure) and cutting hours from the work week. Political competition to exploit these changes will inevitably emerge.

Japanese business, in keeping with the Maekawa Report (Advisory Group on Economic Structural Adjustment for International Harmony 1986) and recent proposals by Sony Corp. Chairman Akio Morita (1992), will in this view ease off at least a bit as employees and suppliers demand better treatment, and as the imperative of globalization induces Japanese firms to harmonize their practices with the rest of the world.[5] Globalization of financial markets will meanwhile weaken the financial *keiretsu* and equalize the cost of capital across countries; access to cheap capital has been a major advantage for Japanese companies in the past. Japan is beginning to apply antitrust policy more aggressively and has started to liberalize its distribution system; both of these initiatives can also erode the *keiretsu* system over time. The bureaucracy will steadily lose its ability to guide the economy as a result of globalization and the inexorable increase in the economy's complexity and market orientation.

---

5. For evidence see Aoki (1990, especially p. 24). Japanese public opinion polls, which revealed support for the US position in the 1989—90 Structural Impediment Initiative talks (discussed below), also support this view.

Table 1.1 United States, Japan, and Europe: growth rates of labor productivity in manufacturing, 1960–90 (percentages)

Period	United States	Japan	Europe
1960–73	3.3	10.2	5.8
1973–79	1.2	5.0	4.1
1979–85	1.9	3.9	3.5
1985–90	3.1	4.3	2.8

Source: US Bureau of Labor Statistics, as reported in Shigehara (1992, table 3).

This view also foresees convergence from the American side. It is clear that a number of American firms—in a wide array of sectors, including the most advanced—have sharply improved their quality, productivity, and competitiveness (table 1.1). Some of the American gains have reflected conscious adaptation of Japanese management practices—including worker empowerment, just-in-time inventory practices, "total quality" manufacturing processes, and even a few customer-supplier and financial *keiretsu*-style arrangements. Some Japanese firms are contributing directly to this process through their investment in the United States.

The American government is also contributing to convergence. The Reagan and Bush administrations, even while maintaining most of their anti-interventionist rhetoric, and the Congress initiated a number of steps during the second half of the 1980s to help America compete. These included adjustment of the overvalued dollar, reductions in the proconsumption bias of the tax code, considerable increases in civilian research and development (R&D) spending, authorization for research consortia (used most notably so far in the case of Sematech, the semiconductor R&D consortium, which counts most of the major US semiconductor firms among its members), and more aggressive trade policies, including a number of instances of managed trade as described below.

The economic program of the Clinton administration aims to move much further in this direction. It seeks to increase national saving substantially by cutting the annual budget deficit by over 2 percent of GDP by 1997. Private investment is to be spurred by the lower interest rates that should result and perhaps by new tax incentives. Public infrastructure investment is to be increased. Human capital is to be improved by investments in worker training and reform of the education system. The shift of federal technology support to civilian and dual-use purposes is to be accelerated. Sweeping changes in the health care system will seek to redirect national resources into more productive uses. This strategy, if successful, could significantly reduce the gap between US and Japanese economic policies over the next five to ten years.[6]

6. Two blueprints for going even further can be found in Competitiveness Policy Council (1992, 1993).

It is evident that convergence is occurring. It is likely to continue and will probably accelerate with the increasing internationalization of both economies. Business, labor, and government on both sides of the Pacific are all participating in the process. Some of the problems posed for America (and the world) by Japan's differentness will diminish as a result.

But two key questions remain. First, will convergence go far enough to resolve the problems and conflicts that now afflict the relationship?[7] Second, in which direction should policy push convergence? Should we be seeking harmonization around American standards in such areas as antitrust policy (so that the *keiretsu*, while maintaining their efficiency advantages, become more transparent and open to outsiders[8]), higher education, and government procurement practices? Should we be promoting Japanese norms in areas such as customer-supplier relations (vertical *keiretsu*, including just-in-time inventory practices and "design-in" R&D collaboration), patient long-term investment (financial *keiretsu*, including the main bank system), and job security and worker training?[9]

Are there some issue-areas where the countries should converge toward some middle ground—such as housing policy, where the United States still subsidizes too much and Japan (for example, through its land use policy) discourages too much, and national saving, which Japan has promoted excessively while US policy remains proconsumption? Are there some areas where the differences are so great that convergence is impossible and other remedies are required? Conversely, are there differences that are likely to remain but whose effects are sufficiently innocuous that "mutual recognition"—live and let live—should be agreed?

The postwar economic policies of the United States and Japan suggest that they have pursued two very different sets of economic priorities. The United States set out to create the world's greatest consumer society and, within a single generation, attained a standard of living for most of its people beyond anything history had seen before. Japan, in contrast, set out to create a production machine that would restore both its eco-

---

7. A negative answer was offered several years ago by Kozo Yamamura (1990), who makes an interesting distinction between "market school optimists," "structural optimists," "structural pessimists," and—his term for those who share his view—"market school realists."

8. This is the view advocated both by Nakatani in his analysis of Japanese corporate practices (Nakatani 1992) and, in a separate paper on Japanese government-industry relations, by Okuno-Fujiwara (1992).

9. The positive impact on productivity of Japanese practice in these areas is documented in Aoki (1990, 24). Many US firms, in contrast, are reportedly reluctant to train their workers because they fear that the workers, once trained, may leave the firm—perhaps even to be hired by its competitors.

nomic security and its respectability in the family of nations. It too succeeded beyond all historical precedent—the formidably competitive manufacturing sector that emerged is the envy of the world.

While both countries achieved their intended goals in spectacular fashion, their policymakers never dreamed that realization of these fundamentally different national purposes would bring them into frontal conflict. This conflict in turn is now exposing the gaps and shortcomings within each country's economy. In the United States, the emphasis on consumption and the discouragement of saving have retarded growth in productivity, ultimately slowing the growth of per capita income (and consumption). In Japan, the rapid growth of income and wealth has not been fully translated into greater welfare for its citizens[10]—and meanwhile its production juggernaut may now have begun to falter. Hence both countries need to broaden the targets of their economic policy, and both are beginning to recognize that need.

The need is more self-evident for the United States. Its economic weaknesses, which have been building over twenty years and are now widely recognized, call for extensive reforms. This includes emulation of foreign models, notably Japan's, where these point to better outcomes (as in the areas just cited). But many Japanese also recognize the need for convergence from their side. One reason is that Japanese consumers simply want a higher quality of life. But many Japanese also favor convergence to avoid worsening hostility from America (and the rest of the world) and to make the Japanese brand of market economics more acceptable to other countries and thus more exportable.

Management of the Relationship

To those primarily interested in dealing with the economic problems, management of the relationship is simply a question of which means— multilateral negotiations, bilateral pressures, or unilateral actions—will most effectively achieve each country's economic objectives. But the US-Japan economic relationship, important as it is, must be seen in the broader context of overall relations between the countries.[11] These relations comprise crucial security and political, as well as economic, dimensions.

"Managing the relationship" has two distinct but related aspects. The more prominent is the bilateral contact between the countries across the entire range of economic and other topics. The other, whose significance

---

10. As captured in a prescient editorial in the *Nihon Keizai Shimbun* entitled "Rich Country, Poor People."

11. An excellent recent analysis is that by Nye (1992—93).

is growing with Japan's continuing rise to global prominence, is their interaction on global issues—avoiding currency misalignments and promoting trade liberalization on the purely economic side, but also cooperating in efforts that involve political objectives, such as sharing the costs of the Gulf War and mobilizing aid to Russia.

There are two polar views on managing the relationship. The traditional "foreign policy school" has sought to minimize the economic problems and avoid tensions that could disrupt the broader relationship. This runs the risk, however, that the economic difficulties will grow rather than decline and create even greater problems in the future. The opposite school would argue that, even from the standpoint of managing the relationship, the superior course is to address the real problems head-on to avoid their further escalation.

All elements of the US-Japan relationship—including the economic element—are affected by recent historic transformations in the global setting (Bergsten 1990). The end of the Cold War has reduced both America's global security clout and its need for allies at distant points around the globe. The advent of tripolarity, with Japan and the uniting European Community joining the United States as economic superpowers, has weakened America's economic dominance. Each country's pursuit of its economic objectives with the other now takes place in a very different global environment than just a few years ago—one that requires much more extensive collective action on both the economic and the security fronts than in the past.

There is widespread agreement in both Japan and the United States, however, that America's ability to pursue its economic objectives with Japan is now greater than at any time in the recent past. One reason stems from the asymmetrical impact of the end of the Cold War: Japan continues to need American support—in light of its ongoing dispute with Russia over the Kurile Islands, but more broadly in responding to the uncertain future course of a dynamic China and events on the Korean peninsula—more than America needs its Japanese ally in the absence of a hostile military and ideological superpower rival. Hence Japan is more likely than the United States to make future concessions on economic issues to preserve trans-Pacific security ties.

A second element in the equation is Japanese domestic politics. With Japan now an economic superpower, the need for *gaiatsu* as a prod to Japanese policymaking appears increasingly anachronistic, yet it continues to be essential to forging sufficient domestic consensus in Japan to respond positively to American (and other foreign) proposals for economic reform. Thoughtful Japanese leaders recognize this and occasionally say so publicly.[12] Hence the United States, as Japan's leading foreign

---

12. See "Japanese Invite Trade Hard Line: Tough U.S. Stance Could Spur Change, Prime Minister Says" (*Washington Post*, 13 April 1993, A-1).

ally and economic partner, can—and almost must—play a pivotal role in Japanese decision making by exerting pressure on Japan to change its ways. In doing so, the United States can maximize its chances for success by finding, and working with, domestic forces in Japan that share its views. The Japanese public strongly supported aspects of America's Structural Impediments Initiative (SII), for example, but probably opposes most "managed trade" proposals.

Even in purely economic terms, however, the United States remains at least for now the stronger partner. Its economy is still considerably larger than Japan's. Japan depends much more heavily on the United States, particularly as a market but also as a supplier, than the United States depends on Japan.[13] Japan would lose more from closure of the American market to its exports than from liberalizing its imports in response to American demands (Lee and Roland-Holst 1993). Financially, Japan with its huge portfolio of US investments is at least as exposed to economic difficulties in the United States as the latter is threatened by the risk of a withdrawal of Japanese funds—at least as long as the American current account deficit remains at a modest level.

Hence the United States is in a strong position to aggressively pursue its economic interests with Japan, and many in Japan acknowledge this. However, some Japanese now believe in a "Japan that can say 'no' " (Ishihara 1989) and indeed believe that Japan *should* say "no" to future US demands, at least if the United States pursues indefensible objectives or overplays its hand tactically. Moreover, there is always the risk of miscalculation. There is also the danger of a confrontation in which capitulation would be too dishonorable for Japan to contemplate, even if objectively correct (just as prior to World War II some Japanese leaders recognized that the United States would probably win a war but still did not oppose the attack on Pearl Harbor).

We will discuss alternative methods for the United States to pursue its objectives in chapter 6, after analyzing the substance of the issues and suggesting a course of policy action. But it should be remembered throughout that the United States must constantly seek the correct balance between exercising its considerable negotiating clout and tipping the Japanese response in a negative or even dangerous direction. America's objectives and its tactics must be logical and sensible if they are to pursue US national interests effectively.

Previous Policy Initiatives

The United States and Japan have of course been addressing their economic conflicts for some time. As the centrality of their relationship has

---

13. Exports to Japan account for 11 percent of US exports, while exports to the United States account for about 30 percent of Japanese exports. Conversely, the United States supplies about 24 percent of Japanese imports, while Japan supplies less than 19 percent of US imports.

grown over the past decade, and as the intensity of the conflict has ebbed and flowed, the variety of policy responses has grown apace. We will briefly summarize these efforts here and evaluate them where relevant in later chapters.

There have been three types of responses to the macroeconomic issue. The most prominent has been *management of the exchange rate*. In 1971, the United States insisted on a substantial revaluation of the yen as part of the Smithsonian Agreement that encompassed the first postwar devaluation of the dollar (and attempted to restore the Bretton Woods system of fixed exchange rates). In 1977, the United States insisted that Japan stop intervening to avoid yen appreciation (under the system of flexible exchange rates that then prevailed).[14] In 1985–87, massive yen appreciation was a central part of the Plaza Agreement to restore the dollar to a more competitive level. In early 1993, the United States successfully "talked up" the yen as part of the effort to reverse the renewed growth of Japan's surplus.

Some of these episodes of currency management have been accompanied by efforts to *improve international monetary arrangements*, with the goal of avoiding renewed currency misalignments in the future. Most notably, the United States and Japan agreed in October 1986 to try to stabilize the yen-dollar rate by adopting a system of "reference ranges" for their currencies. That agreement was accepted by the rest of the Group of Seven (G-7) major industrial countries at the Louvre in February 1987. However, the dollar-yen range had to be "rebased" in April 1987, and the whole stabilization effort was premature, because the misalignment that preceded it had not yet been fully corrected; consequently it did not prevail for long.[15]

Some of the currency episodes have also been accompanied by efforts on either side to alter the course of the partner country's *macroeconomic policy*, or even to coordinate the two. At the Bonn economic summit in 1978, Japan accepted a quantitative target for expanding its domestic demand, to bring down its external surplus and help correct the American deficit—thus accepting the "locomotive theory" that the surplus countries (Germany as well as Japan at that time) had a responsibility to become engines of world growth. In the Plaza Agreement in September 1985, the United States promised to cut its budget deficit and Japan again agreed to expand domestic demand. The countries cut their interest rates together on several occasions in 1986–87. During the SII talks of 1989–90, discussed briefly below and again in later chapters, the United States reiterated its budget pledge and made several other commitments to raise its national saving rate. On the same occasion, Japan agreed to

---

14. As called for in Bergsten (1976).

15. The complete story is contained in Funabashi (1989).

a long-term increase in public works spending in order to raise its level of national investment and help curtail its external surpluses.

As their name suggests, a wide array of *structural issues* were also addressed in the SII talks. For example, the United States agreed to improve its education system and to seek to lengthen the time horizons of its private investors. Japan agreed to strengthen its antitrust enforcement to limit *keiretsu* collusion, and to amend its Large Scale Retail Store Law to open its distribution system to more efficient volume merchants (such as Toys 'R' Us).

Sector-specific initiatives have also been frequent. Some have been handled in clusters, such as the market-oriented, sector-specific (MOSS) talks initiated by the United States in 1985–86, which covered telecommunications and other electronics products, forest products, and medical equipment and pharmaceuticals. Most, however, have been handled individually. The United States has sought both restraints on Japanese sales into the American market (in automobiles, machine tools, and steel in the 1980s) and better access to the Japanese markets for a very wide range of products (recently including semiconductors and auto parts). Some of these initiatives have been pursued under explicit or implicit American threats of market closure if Japan failed to cooperate. The most prominent example has been the so-called Super 301 provision of the 1988 trade act, which obliged the US administration to designate "priority foreign countries" whose trading practices it found to be "unfair" and to set a deadline for remedial action, under threat of retaliation.

As a result of these past negotiations, a significant portion of trade between the United States and Japan is already managed with the use of quantitative indicators. Some of Japan's most successful exports to the United States have been limited by so-called voluntary export restraints (VERs) for considerable periods: Japanese exports of automobiles, machine tools, steel, and textiles and apparel have been subjected to such restraints. Some of America's exports to Japan are now promoted by voluntary import expansion schemes (VIEs): Japan has committed itself to import specific quantities of semiconductors, and the relevant Japanese industries have set targets for their imports of auto parts and of automobiles themselves.[16]

There have also been a few efforts by the United States and Japan to exercise joint leadership to *improve the functioning of the international economic system.* Most of the macroeconomic initiatives mentioned above,

---

16. Over 20% of Japanese exports to the United States, and more than 15 percent of US manufactured exports to Japan, are now covered by such arrangements. These numbers of course understate the impact of the restrictions, since trade would presumably be higher in their absence—for example, Japan's zero quota on rice eliminates that sector from the entire calculation. (These figures ignore quantitative restrictions in agriculture.) VIEs are discussed in detail in chapters 4 and 5.

such as the Bonn summit package in 1978 and the Plaza-Louvre episode in 1985–87, took place in a broader G-5 or G-7 context. In a few instances, "G-2" efforts by the United States and Japan were aimed at galvanizing the European countries to proceed likewise; notable examples, both eventually successful, were the reference ranges of October 1986 and the Brady Plan approach to Third World debt in 1989.

In tactical terms, the United States has deployed an extensive array of techniques for *managing the relationship* across these several issue-areas. Some initiatives have been pursued multilaterally: these include the exchange rate realignments in the G-5 and G-7 (and earlier in the G-10) and efforts to improve access to the Japanese market through negotiations on tariffs, government procurement, subsidies, and other trade issues in the Kennedy, Tokyo, and Uruguay rounds of the General Agreement on Tariffs and Trade (GATT). Other initiatives have been pursued in the bilateral mode: in this category on the trade side are the MOSS and SII talks as well as virtually all of the sector-specific efforts, including those that produced the VERs and VIEs, while financial examples include the G-2 efforts cited above and the yen-dollar talks (Frankel 1984). The United States has also taken unilateral measures toward Japan, mainly in implementing its domestic trade laws (notably on antidumping) and, in 1987, retaliating against Japanese noncompliance with the 1986 Semiconductor Trade Agreement (STA). (Retaliation has been threatened in many other instances as well.) Yet another mode of dialogue, a regional one, could become available in the future if the recently established Asia Pacific Economic Cooperation (APEC) evolves into a major forum for trade and broader economic negotiations.

Thus, over the past decade, the US-Japan economic agenda has been pursued through initiatives that have ranged far and wide in terms of both substance and tactics. We have seen multilateral, bilateral, and unilateral approaches to the macroeconomic, structural, sector-specific, and systemic components of the conflict. As we will document in the next three chapters, there have been notable successes: negotiations at the macroeconomic level have produced sizable reductions in both countries' global current account imbalances, both in the 1970s and from 1987 to 1991; many American (and other foreign) firms now enjoy enhanced market access as a result of negotiations on Japan's structural barriers; and significant increases in US exports of a number of products have been the direct result of sector-specific negotiations.

On the other hand, there have been numerous disappointments. Japan's global current account surplus has again soared to new highs. The bilateral imbalance has resisted decline even as the global imbalances of both countries have dropped sharply. Most analyses suggest that Japan remains an international outlier in terms of foreign suppliers' (and especially foreign investors') access to its market. Japan has done little to obviate the adverse effects of the *keiretsu* system on outsiders. *Gaiatsu* still seems a necessary catalyst to Japanese public decision making, and Japan has shown few signs of exercising constructive international leadership.

For its part, the United States has yet to significantly reduce its budget deficit. On a number of indicators, America has yet to improve its international competitiveness substantially. Its national saving and investment rates remain a fraction of those in Japan. Its external deficit is rising again and will probably exceed $100 billion again in the near future.

The Current Policy Framework

Five significant changes mark the US-Japan policy environment within which these issues will be addressed during the foreseeable future. First, the coming to office of the Clinton administration has altered the posture of the United States in several key respects. The most important is that the administration's domestic economic proposals offer the prospect of enhancing the US competitive position. By proposing to sharply reduce the budget deficit and improve America's performance in such key areas as technology and worker training, the new administration hopes to improve America's fundamental ability to compete with Japan. If realized, these reforms should noticeably reduce the intensity of the US-Japan economic conflict. Indeed, a restoration of American competitiveness—and thus of national self-confidence—is essential for any lasting and satisfactory resolution of that conflict.

The Clinton administration's economic program also strengthens the negotiating credibility of the United States. It clearly seeks to implement most of the commitments made to Japan (and America's other international partners), but ignored in practice, by previous administrations. This not only enhances the US bargaining position but provides the basis to ask for greater cooperation from Japan in return.

The Clinton administration, as already noted, is also likely to pursue sector-specific policies much more actively than its recent predecessors. The United States has always had, has now, and always will have policies to promote particular industries—mainly conducted under noneconomic rubrics such as "national defense" and "the space program." Some have produced spectacularly successful commercial results, for example in agriculture (which has seen major government involvement for over a century) and commercial aircraft (where the very existence of the modern industry is due largely to defense investment). President George Bush was conducting sector-specific policies when he negotiated VIEs with Japan on auto parts or extended the VERs on machine tools.

The issue is not whether the United States will have sectoral policies. It is rather whether the United States will have *intelligent* sectoral policies.

This usually requires anticipatory efforts rather than the all-too-common reactive approaches, which have regularly produced useless (or even counterproductive) trade restrictions.

The Clinton administration's more active pursuit of sector-specific approaches to economic problems could cut either way with respect to Japan. Its sectoral trade initiatives might add more VERs or VIEs to the agenda. Alternatively, its willingness to deploy domestic policy instruments to support key industries could reduce America's reliance on trade measures. More timely attention to the problems of individual industries, particularly those (such as aircraft and most of electronics) that are still very competitive, should reduce the likelihood of situations where pressure for import relief becomes intense. The Clinton program, over time, thus should reduce the level of trade conflict with Japan through its microeconomic as well as its macroeconomic components.

On the other hand, the Clinton administration will also pursue its activist program in part through levying additional costs on the private sector. This is partly ascribable to the budget deficit, as the scarcity of public funds leads to calls for both higher corporate taxes and more corporate spending for such programs as health care, worker training, and environmental cleanup. Some industries, particularly those that are already in trouble and are exposed to heavy international competition, may seek a governmental *quid pro quo* in the form of import protection and/or stronger efforts to expand their access to markets abroad.

The administration has also begun its tenure with extremely tough talk and calls for "results-oriented" outcomes with Japan—albeit calls that have aimed wholly at opening Japan's market rather than closing America's and that seek access to Japan for all foreign exports rather than American exports alone. It has been encouraged in this attitude by the private-sector Advisory Committee on Trade Policy and Negotiations, which has called for "temporary quantitative indicators" (TQIs, the new euphemism for VIEs) where necessary to "simulate what both sides expect would happen in a particular sector if Japanese businesses and consumers made purchase decisions on the sole basis of commercial considerations" (ACTPN 1993). Previous administrations, particularly in their first few months in office, have also used tough rhetoric to try to establish their credibility with the Congress and other constituency groups. But Japan is clearly worried by the prospect for tougher action. The net impact of the Clinton administration on the conflict is thus unclear for the coming year or so.

A second and closely related change in the US-Japan policy environment derives from the apparent success of the STA in raising the share of foreign semiconductor firms in the Japanese market. This success has spurred interest in similar approaches in other sectors. So has the apparent success of the new VER that limits sales of Japanese automobiles throughout the European Community, including those produced by the transplants of Japanese firms in Europe itself. Possibilities for additional "managed trade" arrangements are numerous but include at least computers and supercomputers, construction contracting, and telecommunications equipment. The activism and emphasis on "results" on the part of the Clinton administration reinforce the likelihood that it will resort to this approach at least on some occasions. Japan, however, has adopted a strongly negative position toward any new arrangements of this type. Sector-specific conflict could intensify as a result.

The third new development is the renewed surge, to record levels in absolute terms, of Japan's global current account surplus. That surplus reached almost $130 billion in Japan's fiscal year 1992 (which ended March 1993) and will probably climb even higher in fiscal 1993. It may even approach the previous record of 4.3 percent of Japan's GDP, set in 1986. Although the bilateral imbalance with the United States has risen much less rapidly, the renewed increase in that measure of Japan's surplus could revive interest in earlier proposals, such as those by House Majority Leader Richard A. Gephardt (D-MO) and more recently by Senator Donald W. Riegle, Jr. (D-MI), to "require" Japan to eliminate its bilateral surplus with the United States over five years or face across-the-board retaliation, such as an import surcharge or a comprehensive import quota. (We evaluate these proposals in chapter 6.)

As noted above, Japan's surplus this time around is very different from its past surpluses in one key respect. In all previous episodes, including its previous highs in the mid-1980s, the Japanese surplus was only one among many worldwide. Then Germany, some other European countries, and some other Asian nations (such as Korea) were also running trade surpluses. The outlier was almost always the United States, whose deficits mirrored most of the surpluses of the rest of the world—clearly indicating that an "America problem" was at the heart of the international imbalances. This time, however, Japan is the only G-7 country in surplus. The other surplus countries of the 1980s—including Germany, Europe as a group, and Korea—are now all in deficit. The "Japan problem" is clearly the heart of the matter on this occasion.

The fourth key difference in the policy environment is the possible failure of the Uruguay Round of multilateral trade negotiations in the GATT. The round has been the chosen instrument of the major trading countries, including the United States and Japan, to strengthen the global trading system in terms of both its coverage (e.g., adding agriculture and services to the GATT's jurisdiction) and its ability to resolve disputes effectively. Japan, in particular, has appealed to GATT rules and procedures in preference to bilateral negotiations with the United States.

As of this writing in mid-1993, however, the prospects for the Uruguay Round are quite unclear. Its failure would almost certainly unleash a series of unilateral trade initiatives by the United States to resolve problems that had been assigned to the round (such as Japan's ban on rice imports). It might also trigger new protectionist measures, as the entire case for trade liberalization would be weakened. Both sets of pressures would inevitably fall on Japan to an important extent.

The fifth and final difference is the increased focus on the structural element of the conflict. As discussed above, there is now widespread agreement that "Japan is different" and that the difference has a significant impact on the United States. Hence this aspect of the conflict will underlie all future negotiations and is a primary topic of this book.

Plan of the Book

We turn in the chapters that follow to an analysis of the several dimensions of US-Japan economic conflict and possible steps to resolve them. Chapter 2 will assess the macroeconomic dimension: the global and bilateral imbalances of the two countries, their underlying macroeconomic positions and policies, and the record of past experiences with adjusting these policies in an effort to correct the imbalances. Chapter 3 will address the structural issues in a similar manner. Chapter 4 will do the same for a wide range of specific sectoral problems. Chapter 5 will assess the quantitative impact of these structural and sectoral policies and practices and draw lessons for US policy. Chapter 6 will then summarize our analytical conclusions, seek to answer the questions posed in this introduction, and propose a comprehensive policy response to the US-Japan conflict.

2

The Macroeconomic Context

Much public discussion in the United States of US-Japan economic relations centers on the large and continuing US merchandise trade deficit with Japan, which was $50 billion in 1992 (see table 2.1). A widely held premise is that much of that deficit is due to trade barriers in Japan. As we will argue in later chapters, the level of the bilateral imbalance is indeed importantly affected by such barriers.

Few if any, however, would ascribe the wide swings in the bilateral imbalance over the past decade—its sharp rise in the first half of the 1980s, its subsequent narrowing between 1987 and 1990, or its renewed widening thereafter—solely or even significantly to changes in Japanese (or US) trade policy. Most observers would rightly attribute most of these changes to fluctuating macroeconomic conditions in the two economies. So, while the bulk of this book is devoted to the examination of specific US-Japan trade conflicts and their resolution, we must first examine the macroeconomic environment within which they occur.

US-Japan Trade in a Global Perspective

It is essential to place the bilateral merchandise trade imbalances between the United States and Japan in the context of each country's global position—its trade deficit or surplus with all other countries (tables 2.1 and 2.2)—and of broader measures of international competitiveness such

Table 2.1 United States: geographic composition of merchandise trade, 1985–92

	1985	1986	1987	1988	1989	1990	1991	1992	Change, 1985–92[a]
Exports									
Total (billions of dollars)	213.1	217.3	252.9	319.4	363.8	393.1	421.8	448.2	235.1 (110.3)
Japan									
Billions of dollars	22.6	26.9	28.2	37.6	44.6	48.6	48.1	46.9	24.3
Percent of total	10.6	12.4	11.2	11.8	12.3	12.4	11.4	10.5	(107.5)
Other developed countries									
Billions of dollars	108.2	111.6	133.4	162.4	185.5	202.6	210.2	217.2	109.0
Percent of total	50.8	51.4	52.7	50.8	51.0	51.5	49.8	48.5	(100.7)
China									
Billions of dollars	3.9	3.1	3.5	5.0	5.8	4.8	6.3	7.5	3.6
Percent of total	1.8	1.4	1.4	1.6	1.6	1.2	1.5	1.7	(92.3)
Other Asia									
Billions of dollars	23.9	25.5	31.4	45.1	50.3	154.1	59.4	68.2	44.3
Percent of total	11.2	11.7	12.4	14.1	13.8	13.8	14.1	15.2	(185.4)
Oil exporters									
Billions of dollars	12.0	10.4	10.6	13.3	12.7	13.0	18.3	20.7	8.7
Percent of total	5.6	4.8	4.2	4.2	3.5	3.3	4.3	4.6	(72.5)
Other non-oil-exporting LDCs									
Billions of dollars	39.6	38.3	44.1	52.7	60.0	65.9	75.3	78.7	39.1
Percent of total	18.6	17.6	17.4	16.5	16.5	16.8	17.9	17.6	(98.7)
Imports									
Total (billions of dollars)	361.6	387.1	424.1	459.8	493.3	517.0	509.3	535.5	173.9 (48.1)
Japan									
Billions of dollars	72.4	85.5	88.1	93.1	97.1	93.1	95.0	96.9	24.5
Percent of total	20.0	22.1	20.8	20.2	19.7	18.0	18.7	18.1	(33.8)

									Change[a]
Other developed countries									
Billions of dollars	156.4	165.4	174.1	189.6	198.9	211.0	203.6	218.7	62.3
Percent of total	43.3	42.7	41.1	41.2	40.3	40.8	40.0	40.8	(39.8)
China									
Billions of dollars	4.2	5.2	6.9	9.3	12.9	16.3	20.3	25.7	21.5
Percent of total	1.2	1.3	1.6	2.0	2.6	3.2	4.0	4.8	(511.9)
Other Asia									
Billions of dollars	52.1	59.8	74.0	81.9	84.6	84.2	84.7	95.1	43.0
Percent of total	14.4	15.4	17.4	17.8	17.1	16.3	16.6	17.8	(82.5)
Oil exporters									
Billions of dollars	21.6	19.7	24.2	23.6	31.0	38.8	33.7	33.5	11.9
Percent of total	6.0	5.1	5.7	5.1	6.3	7.5	6.6	6.3	(55.1)
Other non-oil-exporting LDCs									
Billions of dollars	54.4	50.7	56.2	61.4	67.9	72.1	71.0	65.6	11.2
Percent of total	15.0	13.1	13.3	13.4	13.8	13.9	13.9	12.3	(20.6)
Balance (billions of dollars)									
Total	−148.5	−169.8	−171.2	−140.4	−129.5	−123.9	−87.5	−87.3	61.2
Japan	−49.8	−58.6	−59.9	−55.5	−52.5	−44.5	−46.9	−50.0	−0.2
Other developed countries	−48.2	−53.8	−40.7	−27.2	−13.4	−8.4	6.6	−1.5	46.7
China	−0.3	−2.1	−3.4	−4.3	−7.1	−11.5	−14.0	−18.2	−17.9
Other Asia	−28.2	−34.3	−42.6	−36.8	−34.3	−30.1	−25.3	−26.9	1.3
Oil exporters	−9.6	−9.3	−13.6	−10.3	−18.3	−25.8	−15.4	−12.8	−3.2
Other non-oil-exporting LDCs	−14.8	−12.4	−12.1	−8.7	−7.9	−6.2	4.3	13.1	27.9

LDCs = less developed countries

a. Numbers in parentheses are cumulative percentage change from 1985 to 1992.

Sources: International Monetary Fund, *Direction of Trade Statistics Yearbook*, various issues; US Department of Commerce, *Survey of Current Business*, various issues.

Table 2.2   Japan: geographic composition of merchandise trade, 1985–92

	1985	1986	1987	1988	1989	1990	1991	1992	Change, 1985–92[a]
Exports									
Total (billions of dollars)	177.2	210.7	231.3	265.0	274.6	287.7	314.9	339.7	162.5 (91.7)
United States									
Billions of dollars	66.7	81.9	85.0	90.2	93.9	91.1	92.2	95.8	29.1
Percent of total	37.6	38.9	36.7	34.0	34.2	31.7	29.3	28.2	(43.6)
Other developed countries									
Billions of dollars	36.1	49.2	57.6	69.9	71.9	77.4	83.1	89.0	52.9
Percent of total	20.4	23.4	24.9	26.4	26.2	26.9	26.4	26.2	(146.5)
China									
Billions of dollars	12.6	9.9	8.3	9.5	8.5	6.1	8.6	11.9	−0.7
Percent of total	7.1	4.7	3.6	3.6	3.1	2.1	2.7	3.5	(−5.6)
Other Asia									
Billions of dollars	32.0	40.3	51.3	64.8	70.8	78.9	91.7	n.a.	59.7
Percent of total	18.1	19.1	22.2	24.5	25.8	27.4	29.1	n.a.	(186.6)
Oil exporters									
Billions of dollars	13.6	11.7	11.5	11.6	10.9	13.9	16.9	n.a.	3.3
Percent of total	7.7	5.6	5.0	4.4	4.0	4.8	5.4	n.a.	(24.3)
Other non-oil-exporting LDCs									
Billions of dollars	12.0	13.8	14.4	15.1	15.0	17.4	20.0	n.a.	8.0
Percent of total	6.8	6.5	6.2	5.7	5.5	6.0	8.4	n.a.	(66.7)
Imports									
Total (billions of dollars)	130.5	127.7	150.9	187.5	209.6	235.3	236.6	233.0	102.5 (78.5)
United States									
Billions of dollars	26.1	29.4	32.0	42.3	48.3	52.8	53.6	52.2	26.1
Percent of total	20.0	23.0	21.2	22.6	23.0	22.4	22.7	22.4	(100.0)
Other developed countries									
Billions of dollars	25.6	31.2	37.9	50.4	56.5	65.3	61.5	61.7	36.1
Percent of total	19.6	24.4	25.1	26.9	27.0	27.8	26.0	26.5	(141.0)

China									
Billions of dollars	6.5	5.7	7.5	9.9	11.1	12.1	14.2	17.0	10.5
Percent of total	5.0	4.5	5.0	5.3	5.3	5.1	6.0	7.3	(161.5)
Other Asia									
Billions of dollars	20.8	23.1	31.2	39.4	42.9	43.3	47.5	n.a.	26.7
Percent of total	15.9	18.1	20.7	21.0	20.5	18.4	20.1	n.a.	(128.4)
Oil exporters									
Billions of dollars	39.6	25.5	28.2	28.5	33.1	43.3	41.2	n.a.	1.6
Percent of total	30.3	20.0	18.7	15.2	15.8	18.4	17.4	n.a.	(4.0)
Other non-oil-exporting LDCs									
Billions of dollars	10.2	10.4	11.2	13.6	14.2	14.7	14.8	n.a.	4.6
Percent of total	7.8	8.1	7.4	7.3	6.8	6.2	6.3	n.a.	(45.1)
Balance (billions of dollars)									
Total	46.7	83.0	80.4	77.5	65.0	52.4	78.3	106.7	60.0
United States	40.6	52.5	53.0	47.9	45.6	38.3	38.6	43.6	3.0
Other developed countries	10.5	18.0	19.7	19.5	15.4	12.1	21.6	27.3	16.8
China	6.1	4.2	0.8	-0.4	-2.6	-6.0	-5.6	-5.1	-11.2
Other Asia	11.2	17.2	20.1	25.4	27.9	35.6	44.2	n.a.	33.0
Oil exporters	-26.0	-13.8	-16.7	-16.9	-22.2	-29.4	-24.3	n.a.	1.7
Other non-oil-exporting LDCs	1.8	3.4	3.2	1.5	0.8	2.7	5.2	n.a.	3.4

n.a. = not available; LDCs = less developed countries.

a. Numbers in parentheses are cumulative percentage change from 1985 to 1992. Where 1992 data were not available, comparisons are with 1991.

Sources: International Monetary Fund, *Direction of Trade Statistics Yearbook*, various issues; Bank of Japan, *Balance of Payments Monthly*, various issues.

as the current account.[1] The global trade balances of the two countries are presented in figure 2.1. The two balances have followed virtually opposite paths: the US trade deficit grew rapidly from $26 billion in 1980 to a peak of $160 billion in 1987, fell back to $73 billion by 1991, and began to rise again thereafter. Japan's trade account meanwhile soared from near balance in 1980 to surpluses of over $90 billion in 1986 through 1988, declined sharply to about $63 billion in 1990, but then rose again to about $140 billion in 1992.[2]

Movements in a country's overall trade balance are a function of differences in income growth rates between the country and its trading partners, and of the exchange rate of the country's currency. Changes in relative growth rates have fairly immediate effects, while exchange rate changes produce their effects with a lag on the order of two years (Noland 1989; see figure 2.2 and figure 2.3). Indices of real effective exchange rates (which are trade-weighted averages of each country's bilateral exchange rates, adjusted for national price levels) for the United States and Japan as well as trade volumes and prices are reported in table 2.3.

The real effective exchange rates are key. In the first half of the 1980s, the real value of the dollar increased enormously. From that point it declined sharply until the end of the decade. These exchange rate movements are reflected in US export and import volumes. Global US export volumes—the actual quantities of exported goods—fell from 1980 to 1985 after the dollar appreciated, then surged in the latter part of the decade as the exchange rate fell. In contrast, import volume grew rapidly in the first part of the decade and then slowed as dollar depreciation drove import prices up.

The movement of trade volumes is critical, as it is they, not the dollar values of exports and imports, that determine the level of output and employment in the traded-goods sector. This in turn drives much of the pressure for government action to restrict imports and promote exports. The experience of the United States in the 1980s can be summarized in two stages. Real overvaluation of the dollar obtained in the first half of the decade, with a resultant fall in global export volume, rise in import volume, shrinkage of output in the traded-goods sector, and surge in political pressure for protection of import-competing sectors. In the sec-

---

1. The US bilateral deficit with Japan is now considerably smaller on a current account basis than when simply limited to merchandise trade: in 1993, $38 billion instead of $50 billion. (The even larger difference in 1991, $23 billion as opposed to $44 billion, was distorted by Japan's contribution to the United States to help finance the Persian Gulf war.) As argued in the text, current accounts are more relevant than trade balances for most macroeconomic purposes.

2. These figures are taken from the International Monetary Fund, *International Financial Statistics*, various issues. They differ somewhat from the numbers in tables 2.1 and 2.2 because of how freight and insurance costs are valued, differences in timing, and the like.

Figure 2.1 United States and Japan: global balances of merchandise trade, 1980–92

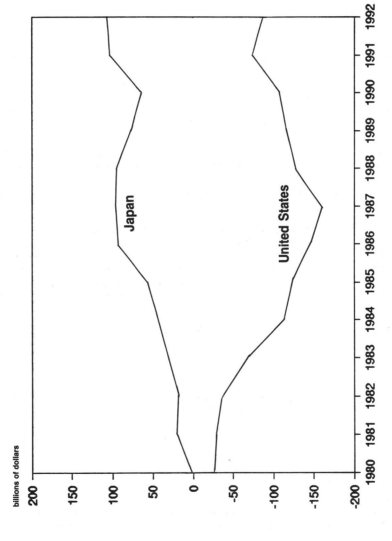

billions of dollars

Source: International Monetary Fund, International Financial Statistics, various issues.

Figure 2.2 Japan: current account and real exchange rate

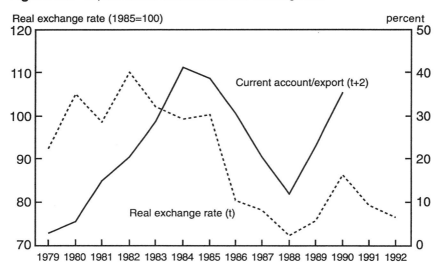

Real exchange rate (1985=100)

percent

Source: International Monetary Fund, *International Financial Statistics,* various issues.

Figure 2.3 United States and Japan: real dollar-yen exchange rates and bilateral trade balances, 1978–92

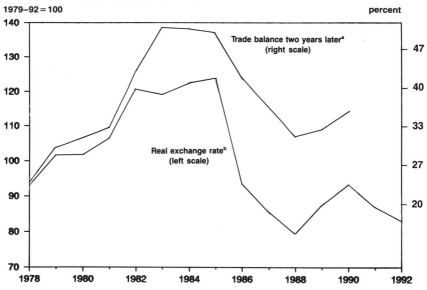

1979–92 = 100

percent

a. US–Japan bilateral balance as a share of total US–Japan trade.
b. Yen-dollar rate adjusted for inflation in both countries.

Source: calculations by William R. Cline from International Monetary Fund data in *International Financial Statistics* and *Direction of Trade Statistics,* various issues.

Table 2.3 United States and Japan: global merchandise trade balance, exchange rates, and export and import volumes and prices, 1980–92[a]

	1980	1981	1982	1983	1984	1985	1986	1987	1988	1989	1990	1991	1992
United States													
Trade balance (billions of dollars)	−25.5	−28.0	−36.4	−67.1	−112.5	−122.2	−145.1	−159.6	−127.0	−115.7	−108.8	−73.4	−96.3
Real effective exchange rate	71.8	80.6	91.0	93.1	98.4	100.0	79.4	68.4	64.5	66.7	61.3	60.0	57.0
Export volume	118.3	114.5	101.1	95.5	102.0	100.0	99.5	112.5	132.7	147.4	157.9	168.1	177.8
Import volume	69.0	70.8	67.2	74.2	92.0	100.0	110.5	113.4	117.7	125.7	127.3	125.4	135.3
Export prices	89.1	97.3	98.4	99.2	100.8	100.0	101.0	102.7	109.9	112.8	113.9	114.8	115.0
Import prices	101.3	106.8	105.1	100.8	102.6	100.0	96.6	103.6	108.6	111.9	115.6	115.6	116.6
Japan													
Trade balance (billions of dollars)	2.1	20.0	18.1	31.5	44.3	56.0	92.8	96.4	95.0	76.9	63.6	103.1	137.0
Real effective exchange rate	94.8	102.5	91.4	97.2	100.6	100.0	123.6	128.4	136.1	129.9	115.5	125.0	132.7
Export volume	70.0	77.5	75.7	82.3	95.3	100.0	99.4	99.7	104.8	108.8	114.8	118.2	117.7
Import volume	91.9	89.9	89.4	90.5	100.0	100.0	109.5	119.7	139.7	150.6	159.3	164.0	162.4
Export prices[b]	102.0	103.2	107.3	100.8	101.5	100.0	84.9	80.6	78.8	82.3	84.0	81.1	79.0
Import prices[b]	105.0	106.7	115.1	106.1	102.5	100.0	64.2	58.9	56.2	60.5	65.7	60.5	56.2

a. Exchange rates and trade volumes and prices are stated as index values with 1985 = 100.
b. Nominal yen index.

Source: International Monetary Fund, *International Financial Statistics*, various issues; *OECD Economic Outlook*, December 1992.

ond half of the decade, dollar depreciation produced a reversal in trade flows, some diminution in the pressure for protectionism, and new interest in obtaining better access to foreign markets (including Japan) because the firms had again become price-competitive.

The story for Japan is nearly a mirror image of that of the United States. The real exchange rate of the yen remained relatively stable during the early 1980s; the yen then appreciated sharply in 1985–88, although thereafter it partly reversed its earlier rise. Japanese global export volumes increased rapidly in the early part of the decade, generating a growing trade surplus and foreign pressure on Japan to change both its macroeconomic policies and its trade policies and practices. The surge in the yen during 1985–88 pushed the prices of both imports and exports down. There was a significant slowing of the rate of export growth, and import volume exploded, growing by more than 65 percent between 1985 and 1990.[3]

The weakening of the yen in real terms after 1988 suggested that a renewed increase in the Japanese global surplus could be expected to appear, with a lag, as indeed has occurred since 1990. That surplus had risen to a record level by 1992 and is expected to increase substantially further.

Moreover, today it is Japan's global trade surplus rather than the US global deficit that stands out in international comparisons. None of the other Group of Seven (G-7) countries is in surplus. Previous surplus countries such as Germany and Korea are now in deficit. In the entire world apart from Japan, only China and Taiwan are running sizable surpluses. The yen had become undervalued against virtually all other currencies by the late 1980s, and its surplus with most other developed countries has risen accordingly—by more with the EC countries and the rest of Asia (excluding China) in fact than with the United States. The Japanese surplus thus clearly represents the major international imbalance at this time.

In contrast, Japan's surplus of the mid-1980s was simply one among many that mirrored the huge American deficit. The US deficit was clearly the major international imbalance of that period, indicating that the dollar had become substantially overvalued against all other major currencies. Just as the major responsibility for corrective action at that time rested with the United States, today that responsibility rests with Japan.

---

3. The stronger yen meant that the dramatic changes in trade volumes were not immediately reflected in the dollar value of Japan's surplus. This was due to the J-curve effect, in which a currency appreciation initially leads to an increase in the trade surplus before reducing it in the long run, because the value of exports denominated in dollars rises immediately while the dimunution of export volumes in response to the change in relative prices occurs only gradually.

Tables 2.1 and 2.2 report the *bilateral* pattern of trade for the United States and Japan, respectively.[4] As shown in table 2.1, between 1985 and 1992 US exports to Japan grew at more than three times the growth rate of US imports from Japan: exports more than doubled over the period, while imports grew by only a third. However, US imports from Japan were already more than three times as large as US exports to Japan by 1985. Hence US exports had to grow more than three times as fast as US imports just to keep the trade deficit from widening in absolute terms. As a consequence, the bilateral imbalance shrank only modestly, from $60 billion in 1987 to $45 billion in 1990. Moreover, with the weakening of Japan's real exchange rate after 1988 (figure 2.3) and the slowdown of growth in Japan after 1991, the trade imbalance slowly began rising again in 1991 and had reached $50 billion by 1992. Meanwhile the US trade balance improved significantly with virtually all other countries except China and the oil-exporting countries.[5]

The relative inflexibility of the US-Japan bilateral imbalance presumably also has to do with the composition of their bilateral trade. The Long Term Credit Bank of Japan (1993) identifies two possible factors. First, an increasing amount of bilateral trade between the two countries consists of price-inelastic high-technology products. Second, $4.5 billion of the imbalance consists of products such as compact disc players, video cameras, and numerically controlled machine tools that are simply not produced in the United States.

The most recent rise in the US deficit with Japan marks the beginning of the fourth cycle in the US-Japan bilateral trade imbalance in the past twenty-five years. The US deficit rose sharply during 1967–72 and 1977–78 as well as the early 1980s, falling after each rise. These changes correlated closely with major exchange rate shifts, and the level of overall US-Japan economic tension has also tracked fairly closely these fluctuations in the bilateral imbalance.[6]

It is sometimes argued that these data on US-Japan bilateral balances are misleading because Japanese firms have "shifted" some of their surplus with the United States to Southeast Asian export platforms (see, e.g., Schlesinger 1993). But Japanese firms have shifted production there because the sharp appreciation of the yen in the mid-1980s permanently

---

4. The figures for US-Japan trade in tables 2.1 and 2.2 differ slightly due to differences in timing, whether freight costs are included, and other minor technical factors.

5. China now exports to the United States over three times as much as it imports from the United States. US exports to China would thus have to grow more than three times as fast as US imports from China just to keep *this* imbalance—already at about $18 billion per year—from growing further.

6. An assessment of the earlier swings is given in Bergsten (1982).

changed the relative costs of production, making it attractive to locate labor-intensive operations in these countries. This is simply comparative advantage at work. US firms have done the same thing. Moreover, as Urata (1993) points out, the Asian affiliates of Japanese firms increasingly sell into their local markets or ship their products back to Japan, rather than export to third-country markets such as the United States. Indeed, the available evidence suggests that Japanese affiliates in Asia are *less* export-oriented than the Asian affiliates of American firms.

In any event, the data in tables 2.1 and 2.2 do not support the "shifting surplus" story. The US trade deficit with the developing countries of Asia (excluding China) has remained essentially flat. Japan's surplus with these countries has risen substantially. Japan thus appears to have shifted its trade (and a considerable share of its rapidly increasing global surplus) away from the United States and toward the rapidly growing economies in the rest of Asia, unaccompanied by a significant increase in the US deficit with these countries.

Two significant events dominate all these data: the rapid deterioration of the US trade balance in the early 1980s and its subsequent partial recovery, and the emergence of a structural surplus in Japan. These events are clearly tied to the dramatic exchange rate changes that occurred during the 1980s, which were in turn caused by macroeconomic developments in the two countries. We examine these domestic developments in the next several sections of this chapter.

These changes in the US and Japanese trade balances also need to be viewed in the larger context of the countries' global current account positions. Trade in services together with unilateral transfer payments are combined with merchandise trade to make up this comprehensive gauge of a country's international competitive position. The United States runs a sizable surplus in services trade because of its sizable tourism surplus, the earnings of its manufacturing firms from royalty and other payments from abroad, and its continuing net earnings on foreign (especially direct) investment despite becoming the world's largest debtor country. Japan, in contrast, has traditionally run a sizable services deficit because of its huge foreign expenditures for tourism and transportation, though the sharp rise in its foreign investment portfolio is now producing enough income to convert that deficit into a surplus in the near future. Each country's services balance has thus partly offset its merchandise trade deficit or surplus, both globally and bilaterally, and hence both countries' current account imbalances have been considerably smaller than their trade imbalances.

Changes in the current account, however, are dominated by changes in merchandise trade (services trade is of considerably small magnitude). Thus, the broader current account measure tends to reveal the same basic posture as the narrower merchandise trade measure in terms of both secular and cyclical shifts. Since this book is mainly about merchandise trade issues, we will focus more heavily here on the trade balance than on the current account, although the latter should be used in assessing the countries' overall global financial positions.

It should be noted that there is no reason to expect zero balance in either the global merchandise trade account or the current account of the two countries. Balance in their bilateral trade is even less likely. The key issue is the appropriate level of capital flows and current account balances, which raises a range of questions concerning the sustainability of the financial movements as well as the economic impact of the corresponding trade surpluses and deficits. Judgments on these variables must be made in the context of the global position of the two countries, and indeed of the outlook for the world economy as a whole.

In attempting to construct a consistent and desirable set of national current account positions, Williamson (1985) suggested that the United States should aim for a zero current account balance and Japan should run a surplus of 1 to 1½ percent of its GDP.[7] Since that time, however, a number of major changes have transpired in the world economy. As a result of reunification, Germany (and perhaps Europe as a whole) has moved from external surplus into deficit. Some Latin American and other developing countries, as exemplified by Mexico and Chile, have overcome their debt crises and can again attract (and responsibly finance) sizable imports of capital. The United States, after reducing the magnitude of its external deficit substantially, has demonstrated that it can sustain modest levels of capital inflow. A feasible international equilibrium can probably now be maintained with the United States running current account deficits of as much as 1 percent of its GDP ($60 billion at current prices) or even a bit more and Japan running surpluses as high as 1½ to 2 percent of its GDP (about $65 billion to $85 billion at current prices).

Even if both the United States and Japan were to achieve zero global current account balance, however, Japan would almost certainly continue to run a bilateral surplus with the United States. Japan's trade pattern is triangular. It imports vast amounts of primary products from countries such as Saudi Arabia (oil), Australia (coal), and Brazil (soybeans). To pay for these net imports it must export large amounts of manufactured products to higher-income countries in North America, Europe, and the rest of East Asia. Hence we should expect a sustained bilateral trade (and current account) imbalance between the United States and

7. The Maekawa report (1986) recommended a Japanese current account surplus of 1½ percent of its GDP.

Japan even if their overall external positions adjust in fully satisfactory fashion.[8]

Saving, Investment, and the Trade Balance

The trade balance is the difference between what a country produces and what it consumes. When a country consumes more than it produces, the excess consumption must come from abroad in the form of imports. If a country produces more than it consumes, it disposes of the excess output in the form of exports.

This story changes only a little when one allows for saving and investment. Current income can be divided into consumption and saving. What is not consumed domestically can be used for domestic investment or exported abroad. A country that saves more than it invests will export that excess in the form of capital outflows and goods, while a country that invests more than it saves must import savings and goods from abroad to make up the shortfall.

Thus, the aggregate trade imbalance is intimately related to saving and investing behavior. The surplus of national saving over national investment equals the trade (or, more precisely, the current account) surplus. High-saving societies tend to run trade (current account) surpluses, and low-saving societies tend to run trade (current account) deficits.

Saving and investing are done by three sectors of the economy: the household sector, the corporate sector (these two together make up the private sector), and the public or government sector. Each sector both saves (or dissaves—that is, consumes more than its income) and invests. In Japan the national accounts report these phenomena separately. The same is true in the United States, except that all government expenditure is (incorrectly) treated as current consumption. Data on saving and investment in both countries as shares of GDP are reported in table 2.4. These are gross rather than net figures (that is, they ignore depreciation of the capital stock), and they are reported according to the US national accounts convention for purposes of comparability.

Two things stand out. First, Japan appears to maintain rates of saving and investment roughly twice those of the United States. Second, the United States (the low-saving country) is forced to rely on foreign saving to finance its investment needs, while Japan (the high-saving country) is a supplier of capital to foreign countries.

These data have two shortcomings. First, US and Japanese accounting conventions differ. The Japanese accounts mistreat capital depreciation. The US accounts, as already noted, do not distinguish between public

---

8. For a detailed analysis, see Bergsten and Cline (1987, 32–41 and appendix A).

Table 2.4 United States and Japan: saving and investment, 1980–91 (percentages of GDP)

	1980	1981	1982	1983	1984	1985	1986	1987	1988	1989	1990	1991
United States												
Domestic investment	16.7	18.0	16.2	15.8	19.3	18.0	16.8	17.0	16.8	15.8	14.4	12.3
Domestic saving	17.1	18.3	16.1	14.7	16.8	15.1	13.5	13.6	14.4	14.1	13.0	12.5
Foreign saving[a]	−0.4	−0.3	0.1	1.0	2.5	2.9	3.3	3.4	2.4	1.7	1.4	−0.2[b]
Japan												
Domestic investment	32.2	31.1	29.9	28.1	28.0	28.2	27.8	28.7	30.6	31.8	32.8	32.2
Domestic saving	31.2	31.5	30.5	29.8	30.8	31.8	32.1	32.3	33.4	33.8	34.0	34.4
Foreign saving[a]	1.0	−0.4	−0.6	−1.8	−2.8	−3.7	−4.3	−3.6	−2.7	−2.0	−1.2	−2.2

a. Equals the inverse of net domestic saving.
b. 1991 CA includes gulf war transfers. After adjustment for gulf war transfers, foreign saving is 0.8% of GDP.

Source: International Monetary Fund, *International Financial Statistics,* various issues.

consumption and public investment, but instead treat all government expenditure as current consumption. Attempts to rectify these differences have reached significantly different conclusions. Dekle and Summers (1991) argue that, on a consistent accounting basis, Japanese net national saving is 15 to 30 percentage points higher than that of the United States, and the gap has widened since 1985. Hayashi (1991, 1992), in a response to Dekle and Summers, counters that the gap is smaller than that—on the order of 10 to 15 percentage points for recent periods.

Second, there are conceptual inadequacies (as distinct from accounting differences) in both countries' national accounts that probably overstate the true difference between Japanese and US saving behavior. Three important adjustments—reclassifying expenditures on consumer durables from consumption to saving (since this represents households' investment in real assets), similarly reclassifying private research and development expenditures as investment (and hence saving), and standardizing for differences in tax regimes—together reduce the gap by half, but by no means eliminate it (Balassa and Noland 1988). So, while Japan may not truly save twice as much as the United States, it undoubtedly saves considerably more.

This appears to be a purely post–World War II phenomenon. Data from the prewar era indicate that Japanese saving rates were not unusual by international standards, and indeed appear to have been lower than those of the United States, whereas Japan's postwar saving rates appear to be higher than those of all other major industrialized countries (table 2.5). Although it is undoubtedly true that the war destroyed much of Japan's national wealth, the extraordinary postwar accumulation of savings put Japan's national wealth well above the prewar trend line (Hayashi 1992).

Why has the Japanese saving rate been so high in the postwar period? A large part of the answer must lie in the behavior of Japanese households. The household sector accounted for the bulk of saving (64 percent) during the period 1970–90, while business contributed 15 percent and the government 21 percent. Since households account for most of saving and ultimately hold claim to profits in the business sector, it is analytically convenient to disregard the difference between households and firms and focus on household behavior as the main determinant of private saving.[9]

---

9. In theory, government saving could be treated in the same way, since households ultimately are responsible for government liabilities and arguably take these into account when making saving decisions. But it is unclear to what extent this proposition, commonly referred to as the Ricardian equivalence doctrine, actually holds. Given the magnitude of government saving, its fundamentally different determinants, and its role in short-run demand management, it will be treated separately.

Table 2.5 Historical gross domestic saving rates in 10 industrialized countries

Country	Rate (percentages of GNP)[a]			Ratio to pre–World War II rate	
	Pre–World War II	1950–59	1960–84	1950–59	1960–84
Australia	12.4 (1861–1938)	26.2	22.7	2.12	1.84
Canada	14.0 (1870–1930)	22.4	21.2	1.61	1.52
Denmark	10.1 (1870–1930)	18.9	19.6	1.87	1.94
Germany	20.0 (1851–1928)	26.8	23.7	1.34	1.19
Great Britain	12.3 (1860–1929)	16.2	18.1	1.32	1.47
Italy	12.0 (1861–1930)	19.8	21.0	1.65	1.75
Japan	**11.7 (1887–1936)**	**30.2**	**32.5**	**2.59**	**2.79**
Norway	11.5 (1865–1934)	27.5	27.1	2.40	2.36
Sweden	12.2 (1861–1940)	21.4	21.4	1.75	1.75
United States	**18.7 (1869–1938)**	**18.4**	**18.0**	**0.99**	**0.96**

a. All figures are annual averages for the period.

Source: Balassa and Noland (1988, table 4.2).

Although the Japanese household saving rate has been declining more or less steadily since its peak in the early 1970s, Japanese households still maintain one of the highest rates of saving among the industrialized countries (figure 2.4 and table 2.6). In contrast, the US household saving rate has been relatively low and declining: among the OECD countries US households outsave only Spain, New Zealand, Great Britain, and three Nordic countries with very high proportions of children and retirees in their populations (and hence low expected saving rates).

Explanations for these divergent outcomes have focused on the role of taxes, pensions, specific saving targets, life-cycle considerations, intergenerational transfers, and, in Japan, the practice of giving large semiannual bonuses to corporate employees. In both the United States and Japan, research suggests that factors related to optimizing allocation of consumption over time—for life-cycle, bequest, and dynasty motives— are quantitatively the most important determinants of household saving. In the simple life-cycle model, households' saving rates exhibit a "humped" pattern: saving rises during early adulthood, peaking during the high-earning period of middle age, and then declines as saving is disbursed during retirement. The bequest and dynasty hypotheses extend this analysis to take into account agents' various incentives to leave bequests to heirs.[10] As a consequence, pensions (including the provision of health care), demographic factors, and, in Japan, the availability of housing are all likely to have significant impacts on the national saving rate, by affecting the saving and bequest behavior of the retired population.[11]

Horioka (1992a) summarizes 10 studies that attempt to model the implications of changing demographic and social welfare policies on Japanese saving behavior (and ultimately Japan's current account position). These studies, which employ a variety of modeling approaches, all reach the same qualitative conclusion: that the rapid increase in Japan's dependency ratio (the combined proportion of children and retirees in the population), possibly reinforced by the provision of more lavish social welfare benefits, will reduce Japan's saving rate. All the studies indicate that the Japanese household saving rate should fall to single-digit or even negative levels by 2015–30.

These studies do not, however, necessarily indicate that the Japanese external surplus will decline, since, as we have seen, the current account

---

10. See Balassa and Noland (1988) and Horioka (1989, 1990, 1991b) for detailed surveys of this literature, and Horioka (1991a, 1992c, 1992d) and Ohtake (1991) for elaborations. Dekle (1989), in an interesting dissent, argues that intergenerational transfers are not an important explanator of Japanese postwar saving behavior, although he acknowledges that demographic changes will make this factor more important in the future.

11. See Balassa and Noland (1988, chapters 4 and 5) for an analysis of the link between housing and saving in Japan.

Figure 2.4 United States and Japan: gross household saving rates as a share of disposable income, 1972–91

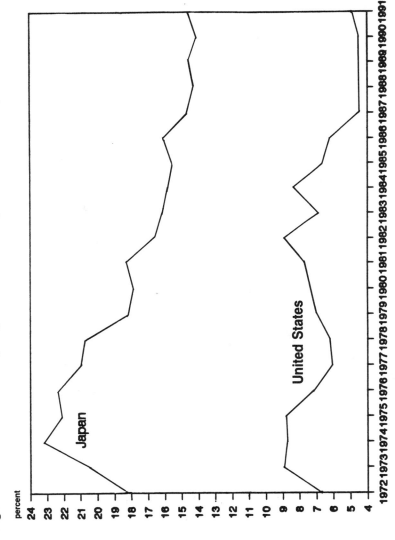

Source: Organization for Economic Cooperation and Development, *OECD Economic Survey*, various issues.

Table 2.6 Household saving rates in 18 countries, 1989

Country	Rate (net saving as share of net national income)	Rank
Australia	6.7	12
Austria	14.1	5
Belgium	13.3	7
Canada	11.1	9
Finland	−0.0	17
France	7.7	10
Germany	12.5	8
Great Britain	1.9	14
Greece	23.7	1
Italy	16.4	3
Japan	**14.3**	**4**
Netherlands	14.0	6
New Zealand	1.6	15
Norway	1.0	16
Spain	5.3	13
Sweden	−4.0	18
Switzerland	17.9	2
United States	**6.7**	**12**

Source: Horioka (1992b).

is the counterpart not of domestic saving by itself but of the excess of domestic saving over domestic investment. Japan had a very high saving rate in the 1950s and 1960s yet consistently ran current account deficits, because investment was even higher. (The United States likewise ran current account surpluses when its investment levels were even lower than its low saving rate.) Therefore, the current account surplus will not shrink, no matter how much national saving declines, if investment falls at the same rate or faster.

Three studies address this issue directly. Noguchi (1989) develops a simulation model in which Japan's current account surplus (the excess of domestic saving over domestic investment) declines between 1985 and 2000 and then rises between 2000 and 2015 before falling to zero in 2020 and becoming negative thereafter. Auerbach et al. (1989), using similar simulation techniques, find that Japan's current account surplus will widen until 1990 (reaching a peak of 5.6 percent of GNP) and subsequently decline, becoming negative in 2030. Masson and Tryon (1990), in a multicountry simulation, find that Japan's current account surplus becomes negative in 2000 and declines further until 2015.

The common conclusion of these studies is that demographic changes will eventually eliminate Japan's current account surplus, although the surplus will not decline as rapidly as the saving rate, since the rate of investment will also fall, and elimination of the surplus will come in 2000 at the earliest. Auerbach and Kotlikoff (1989), applying a similar demographically driven model to the United States, predict that the United States will begin generating current account surpluses in the

1990s, which should persist for another three decades. On the basis of these models, demographic factors should in the long run reduce the trade imbalance between the United States and Japan by driving down the Japanese surplus and reducing the US deficit.

There are, however, good reasons to believe that these results may not be achieved. Japanese saving may not fall as fast as predicted by these models because of four factors: reductions in the value of public pensions and/or continued increases in life expectancy, either of which would reduce dissaving by the elderly; changes in the tax system, including possible increases in the consumption tax; and large falls in asset prices (more on this below). At the same time, several factors could accelerate the decline in the saving rate and hasten the decline in the external surplus. These include further slowdowns in the rate of growth, reform of the property tax system, increases in pensions and/or raising of the retirement age, shortening of the work week, increased availability of credit cards, and a generational shift in cultural values away from frugality (Horioka 1992a). Analogous arguments could be used to qualify the predictions for the United States.

Even if the results of these demographically driven simulation models come to pass, they will be of little comfort to today's policymakers, who face more years of political conflict emanating at least in part from the confluence of Japanese surpluses and US deficits. Indeed, the single most important cause of the shifts in each country's saving-investment balance in recent years has been its own macroeconomic—and in particular fiscal—policies. As Hayashi (1992) has observed, the more than 7 percent of GDP increase in public saving has been the driving force in the increase in total Japanese saving in the late 1980s. This rise has more than fully offset the decrease in Japanese private saving (figure 2.5). In contrast, public *dis*saving has been in the norm in the United States, where public-sector deficits increased from less than 3 percent to more than 6 percent of GDP in the early 1980s and remain at about 5 percent now; changes in private saving did not offset these shifts. We summarize and evaluate each country's current macroeconomic policies in the section that follows.

Macroeconomic Policy in the United States and Japan

Japan: The "Bubble Economy" and the Policy Response

The implications of recent exchange rate movements and shifts in the saving-investment balance can be seen in table 2.7, which decomposes real growth in both the United States and Japan into its constituent parts.

Figure 2.5 United States and Japan: general government balances as a share of GDP, 1980–91

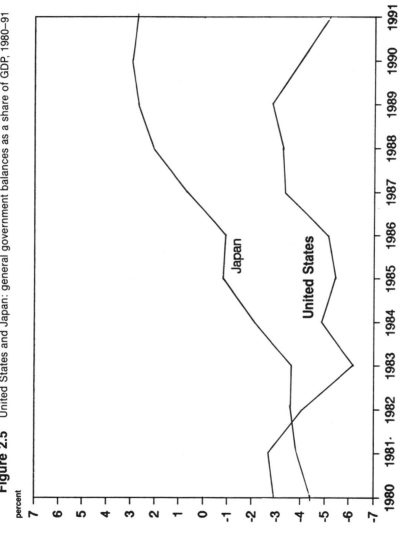

Source: Organization for Economic Cooperation and Development, OECD.

44

Table 2.7 United States and Japan: contributions to total output growth, 1985–92[a] (percentages of GDP)

	1985	1986	1987	1988	1989	1990	1991	1992
United States								
Domestic demand	3.6	3.1	2.7	3.0	1.8	0.4	−1.8	2.5
Private	2.5	2.1	2.1	2.8	1.5	−0.2	−2.0	2.5
Public	1.1	1.0	0.6	0.1	0.4	0.5	0.2	−0.1
Net exports	−0.5	−0.2	0.3	0.8	0.6	0.4	0.6	−0.4
Total	3.1	2.8	3.0	3.8	2.5	0.8	−1.2	2.1
Japan								
Domestic demand	4.0	3.6	4.9	7.4	5.8	5.1	2.7	0.6
Private	4.3	2.9	4.5	6.9	5.7	4.6	2.3	−0.4
Public	−0.3	0.7	0.4	0.5	0.1	0.5	0.4	1.0
Net exports	1.2	−1.0	−0.6	−1.2	−1.0	−0.3	1.4	0.9
Total	5.2	2.6	4.3	6.2	4.8	4.8	4.1	1.5

a. Numbers may not sum to totals because of rounding.

Sources: Economic Report of the President, various issues; Bank of Japan, *Economic Statistics Monthly*, various issues.

In the case of Japan, net exports provided much of the impetus to growth in the first half of the decade, while domestic demand remained weak (Balassa and Noland 1988, table 1.4). The contribution of net exports turned negative in the second half of the decade, as export volume growth slowed and import volume rose dramatically in response to the yen's appreciation; meanwhile domestic private demand more than doubled its contribution to growth, from 2.9 percentage points in 1986 to 6.9 percentage points in 1988. The subsequent collapse of private domestic demand, combined with the lagged effects on net exports of a lower real exchange rate at the end of the decade, contributed to a resumption of net export expansion in 1991–92. The contribution of public demand was relatively flat throughout this period despite the repeated promulgation of "domestic stimulus packages."

In contrast, the United States, which had experienced substantial trade drag during the period of dollar appreciation at the beginning of the decade, witnessed a burst of net export expansion from 1987 to 1991. Indeed, as private demand weakened between 1989 and 1991, the increase in net exports accounted for about three-quarters of US growth. This contribution turned negative in 1992, as the domestic economy pulled out of recession while the economies of major trading partners (including Japan) weakened and the lagged effects of dollar appreciation were felt.

Thus, macroeconomic adjustments in the United States and Japan during most of the 1980s and the early 1990s were dominated by major movements in each country's real exchange rate in the mid-1980s and their partial reversal during the second half of the decade, along with recessions caused by declining private demand—first in the United States and then in Japan. In Japan, the rapid rise in private demand between 1986 and 1990 and its subsequent fall in the 1990s has been termed the "bubble economy."

Economists use the term "bubble" to refer to extreme increases in asset prices based on expectations of future price increases, unsupported by economic fundamentals and typically followed by a reversal in expectations and a collapse in prices. The Dutch tulip mania of 1646 and the London South Sea stock bubble of 1719–20 are the archetypical speculative bubbles. In the case of Japan, allegations of a bubble have been most frequently made with respect to stock and land prices in the late 1980s. Analysts have faced the difficult problem of sorting out two discrete phenomena: first, why stock and land prices in Japan are (or appear to be) very high by international standards, and second, why these asset prices increased and then fell dramatically during the late 1980s.

Japanese asset prices in the late 1980s were indeed high by international comparison. Japanese stocks, even taking into account extensive cross-shareholding among firms and different accounting standards, appeared to have high price-to-earnings ratios relative to stocks on other national exchanges. (Indeed, in the late 1980s the Tokyo stock market had the largest capitalization of any in the world.) Likewise, the price of land in Japan appeared remarkably high by international standards: Boone and Sachs (1989) report that, at late-1980s prices, the land under the Imperial Palace in Tokyo was worth as much as all the land in California, or all the land in Canada, or all the land, houses, and factories in Australia!

It turns out there are good fundamental reasons to expect Japanese asset prices to be high. A high expected rate of growth and a low rate of time preference (high saving rate), together with low taxation of income from capital and land, could be expected to boost stock and land prices. Agricultural protectionism and regulations impeding the rational allocation of land among alternate uses could further boost land prices.[12] Indeed the data in figure 2.6 show that asset prices have increased for prolonged periods.[13]

Within this almost unbroken climb, however, there have been periods of more rapid asset price increases followed by significant slowdowns or, occasionally, actual declines (figure 2.7). In the case of land there have been three such episodes: around 1960, in the early 1970s, and in the late 1980s and early 1990s. Indeed, the most recent episode has been the mildest of the three. In each case, specific economic factors were invoked to explain the rapid price increase: the first episode was associated with increased demand for land for industrial use at the beginning of Japan's high-growth period, the second related to the outset of Prime Minister Kakuei Tanaka's "reconstruction plan for the Japanese archipelago," and the third occurred with the *endaka* ("high yen") boom of the late 1980s (Asako 1991). Although Asako maintains that fundamentals alone cannot explain these price movements, he goes on to observe that the "three land price hikes occurred during loose monetary policy and

---

12. See Balassa and Noland (1988, chapters 4 and 5) and Takagi (1989) for more complete discussions of Japanese land use policies.

13. The stock price index in figure 2.6 is the Topix index, which differs from the more familiar Nikkei index in that it is broader and is capitalization-weighted (the Nikkei includes a much smaller number of stocks, all given equal weights). The land price index is for all land. There are slight differences between the indexes for residential, commercial, and industrial land, as well as between indexes based on the major cities and those for the rest of the country. (In particular, price increases have tended to start in the major cities and emanate outward.) For our purposes the national index is adequate. The indices are based on actual trades; as a consequence of the government intervention described below, disequilibria have developed in the markets (especially for land), so that these price data probably do not exactly equal the prices that would have been market clearing in the absence of government intervention.

Figure 2.6 Japan: indices of land and corporate stock prices, 1955–92[a]

natural logarithm

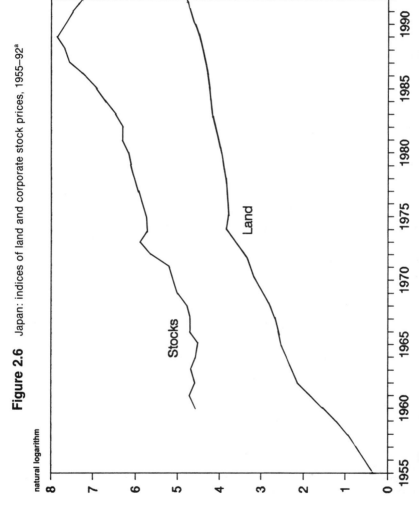

a. The stock index used is the Topix index; the land price index is that for all Japanese land.

Sources: Japanese Statistical Monthly, Economic Statistics Monthly, various issues.

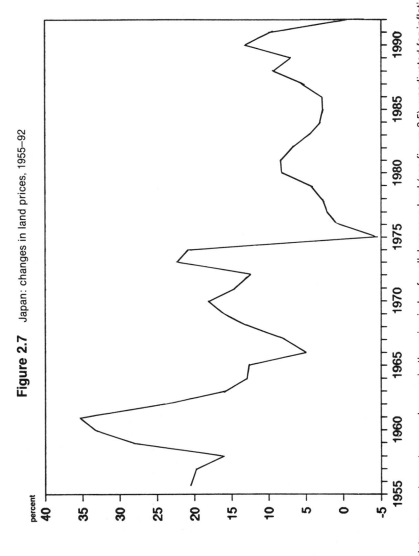

Figure 2.7 Japan: changes in land prices, 1955–92

a. The data represent year-to-year changes in the price index for all Japanese land (see figure 2.5), unadjusted for inflation.

Sources: Japanese Statistics Monthly, various issues; Office of Prime Minister, *One Hundred Year Statistics of the Japanese Economy.*

came to an end with changes in the stance of monetary policy" (Asako 1991, 169).[14]

The latest episode had its origins in macroeconomic policies and the attendant exchange rate misalignments of the mid-1980s (Marris 1987). By 1985 the dollar had become significantly overvalued, and in September of that year the major industrial countries began a concerted effort to reinforce the depreciation of the dollar that had begun earlier in the year (Funabashi 1988). The yen then began a rapid appreciation, which greatly impacted the traded-goods sector, as we have seen. On the domestic economy, the high yen had two effects: there was a substantial positive wealth effect, as with a stronger currency Japanese now could command more international resources, and there was a fall in the rate of return in the traded-goods sector both absolutely and with respect to the nontraded sector. The wealth effect and the shift toward nontradeables set off a land price increase, initially felt in Tokyo in 1986.

The authorities, concerned about slumping growth in 1986, undertook stimulatory measures. However, the unwillingness of the Ministry of Finance to countenance serious fiscal expansion forced an overreliance on monetary stimulus (Balassa and Noland 1988, chapter 6). The discount rate was halved in slightly more than a year, from 5 percent on 29 January 1986 to its all-time low of 2.5 percent on 23 February 1987, and the money supply grew by nearly 50 percent in the next four years. Much of this liquidity was absorbed by a land market distorted by a variety of government regulations and policies, and land prices rose through 1987 and 1988 (Balassa and Noland 1988, chapters 4 and 5). The Japanese authorities, concerned about the price increases, inaugurated a variety of measures designed to curb speculation. These measures, which initially applied only to Tokyo but were later extended to the entire country, included monitoring of all large transactions, instructions to financial institutions to restrain lending to the property sector, an increase in the capital gains tax on land held less than two years, and a freeze on sales of publicly held land. The effect, rather than dampening the land boom, was to spread it to areas not initially subject to the regulations (Miyao 1991).

Moreover, since many of the major industrial firms were also major landholders, they were able to collateralize these "hidden assets" into loans.[15] These loans, together with funds raised through the issue of equity-linked warrants in the Euroyen market made possible by the rising

---

14. There is a sizable literature that attempts to determine econometrically how much of recent Japanese land price changes can be ascribed to the bubble phenomenon, with estimates ranging from roughly half (from a paper by Yukio Noguchi cited by Ito 1989a) to "very small, if any" (Ito 1989a, 54), with intermediate estimates provided by Boone and Sachs (1989) and Okumura (1991).

15. Indeed, according to Miyao (1991) the spatial pattern of land price increases coincided with increases in domestic demand.

stock market, set off a boom in both domestic and foreign investment. Domestic investment's share of GDP rose above 30 percent between 1989 and 1991, exceeding investment in the United States even in absolute terms, and outward foreign direct investment surged by nearly $27 billion between 1987 and 1990.[16]

The monetary authorities, now worried that the economy was growing overheated, raised the discount rate three times in 1989 and twice in 1990, to a peak of 6 percent, in an effort to rein in the boom. They eventually succeeded in bringing down both stock and land prices. However, Japanese banks, which are large holders of corporate stock, had by now also become highly extended in the domestic property market. There was increased talk of Japanese banks being saddled with nonperforming property loans, and of possible difficulties in their meeting the Bank for International Settlements' capital adequacy guidelines scheduled to go into effect in 1993.[17] It appeared that Japanese government authorities were willing to go a long way to prevent Japanese financial institutions from failing, including using the deposit insurance system, forced mergers, and ultimately general tax revenues.

Such government intervention in asset markets can have unanticipated effects on the "real" economy. If firms believe that the government can and will ensure the solvency of the financial system indefinitely, then government intervention may have no impact on the timing of firms' investment decisions. If, however, firms believe that the government lacks the will or the resources to hold the line indefinitely, a credit contraction is possible. In this circumstance, the optimal behavior for firms is to bring investment plans forward, raising outside capital while it is still available. This intertemporal shift in investment demand can generate a pattern of investment boom followed by financial collapse (Brock 1992).

In the case of Japan, the investment boom lasted until well after asset prices had begun their steep fall (figure 2.8). Moreover, it appears that households treated their unrealized capital gains as wealth, so that when asset prices began falling, households were led to reduce consumption and increase saving (Horioka 1992e, Dekle 1992). Thus, when investment

---

16. Foreign investment issues are taken up in the next chapter.

17. The Bank for International Settlements (BIS) is a bank for central banks. In response to concerns over the stability of the international banking system, the BIS issued capital adequacy guidelines for commercial banks, which went into effect in March 1993. National bank regulators are empowered to restrict the activities of banks not adhering to the BIS rules. Under these rules, a portion of a bank's stock holdings may be counted toward its capital base. With their large stock holdings, Japanese banks saw their capital base as measured under BIS rules grow rapidly in the late 1980s when the Tokyo stock market rose, then shrink precipitously as it fell. They have not run afoul of the BIS rules thus far, however.

Figure 2.8 Japan: changes in land and corporate stock prices and in real investment, 1984–92

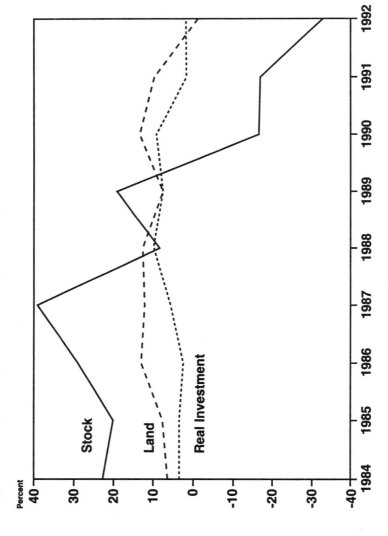

Percent

Sources: Economic Statistics Monthly, various issues; International Monetary Fund, *International Financial Statistics,* various issues; Nomura Research Institute.

demand collapsed in 1992, consumption growth had already slowed, so that total private demand actually shrank in 1992. The rate of economic growth slowed significantly from 4.1 percent in 1991 to a paltry 1.5 percent in 1992.

With private demand shrinking and the economy going into recession, the Bank of Japan cut the discount rate five times in a little more than a year, from 6 percent on 1 July 1991 to 3¼ percent on 27 July 1992. In March 1992 the government brought forward planned public investments. Further fiscal stimulus measures were announced in August of that year. These included increases in public investment, additional tax incentives for business investment, more-liberal lending rules for the public housing loan authority, a proposal to establish an organization to purchase real estate, and the diversion of postal saving system funds to the stock market. The advertised size of this stimulus package was ¥10.7 trillion ($85 billion at the then-prevailing exchange rate), but as in previous supplementary budget proposals, this overstated the true expansionary impact of the package: much of the money consisted either of purchases of land (thus simply reallocating assets between public and private hands), shifts among public expenditure categories, or previously planned expenditures that were merely brought forward. Contemporary observers calculated that, of the total package, only around ¥4 trillion to ¥6 trillion would represent additional demand stimulus (Long Term Credit Bank of Japan 1992; Japan Research Institute 1992–93; *Nikkei*, 19 April 1993). VanDenBerg (1993) argues that, when the plan was implemented, spending cuts in the general budget actually offset all of the additional spending in the package, and that the net effect was to *reduce* public expenditure by ¥200 billion.

The economy continued to falter, and once again the monetary authorities cut the discount rate, to 2.5 percent on 4 February 1993. Under mounting domestic criticism for the recession and foreign criticism for the rising trade surplus, in April 1993 the ruling Liberal Democratic Party announced plans for another supplementary spending package. The advertised size of this package was ¥13.2 trillion ($110 billion), and again a debate ensued as to how much of this was actually additional spending. An analysis in the 19 April 1993 *Nikkei* put the net impact at slightly more than ¥5 trillion, while VanDenBerg (1993) estimated that the effective increase in public demand would be less than ¥4 trillion.

The United States: Confronting the Fiscal Deficit

In the United States, meanwhile, fiscal retrenchment issues dominate macroeconomic policymaking. The current Congressional Budget Office (CBO) baseline forecast (which does not take into account the Clinton administration's budget reduction package) predicts that the consolidated federal government deficit, inclusive of Social Security and other trust fund surpluses, will reach $320 billion, or 5 percent of GDP, in 1993. The deficit as a share of GDP then is forecast to fall slightly for several years before rising to 5.8 percent of GDP ($513 billion nominal) by 2001. Much of this increase is driven by a projected $566 billion increase in health care expenditures, whose share of federal expenditures is projected in the baseline forecast to rise from 16 percent in 1990 to 27 percent in 2000.

The Clinton administration estimates that its initial budget proposals (i.e., not including health care reform) would cut the deficit in 1997 as a share of GDP from the CBO's baseline of 4.5 percent to 2.7 percent. The deficit could then begin rising again, however, in the absence of fundamental reforms in the national health care system or other new measures. The rest of the Clinton program consists of additional government investments in education, worker training, public infrastructure, and technology. It can be expected to increase the productivity and competitiveness of the economy, but only by modest amounts and only over an extended period of time.

The Trade Impact of Current Policy in Both Countries

A number of studies have assessed the impact on the external balances of the recent and prospective changes in both countries' macroeconomic policies, as outlined in the last two sections. Studies by the Bank of Japan and the Federal Reserve Board find that fiscal contraction in the United States and fiscal expansion in Japan push both countries' external accounts toward balance (Balassa and Noland 1988, chapter 6). For example, the studies indicate that a sustained cut of 1 percent of GDP in the US government budget deficit would shrink the US current account deficit by about half that amount in the long run.

For Japan, the central bank studies indicate that a ¥3 trillion fiscal stimulus would lower the global Japanese trade balance from $1.5 billion to $5.9 billion in the long run. If the effective size of the two recent stimulus plans taken together is assumed to be ¥9 trillion, their impact on the global Japanese surplus would thus be on the order of $5 billion to $15 billion.

With regard to the bilateral balance, these studies found that a ¥3 trillion expansion package would reduce Japan's surplus with the United States by $500 million to $900 million in the long run. Extrapolating these figures suggests that a ¥9 trillion package would reduce the bilateral imbalance by $1.5 billion to nearly $3 billion.

Using a different methodology, Noland (1991) found that the bilateral deficit tends to increase over time, with the imbalance reaching nearly $60 billion by 1993. (This is consistent with more recent work by Cline 1993, which incorporates recent exchange rate movements and finds that, with substantial appreciation of the yen, the bilateral imbalance remains relatively constant in absolute terms at about $40 billion to $50 billion in the medium run, while falling as a share of GDP and total trade turnover.) In the Noland model, each 1 percent of GDP reduction in the US budget deficit reduces the bilateral imbalance by just over $3 billion from its starting point. (This is due to a slowing of growth in the United States and a depreciation of the dollar.) These figures suggest that deficit reduction of the scale envisioned in the Clinton plan could reduce the bilateral imbalance by about $10 billion from its starting point of $50 billion in 1992.

The prospective Japanese stimulus plan would have a far smaller effect, according to the Noland estimates, which use a fundamentally different technique than do the other models. Indeed, the plan would not be enough to reverse the increase in the imbalance embodied in the baseline forecast. The bilateral imbalance would continue to rise from 1992 levels and would decline by only $1 billion relative to the baseline forecast.

Taken together, these studies indicate that US fiscal contraction and Japanese fiscal expansion are complementary policies that should contribute to the reduction in the external imbalances of both countries. In quantitative terms, the promised deficit reductions in the United States are far more important than the fiscal stimulus packages recently announced in Japan. Another important implication of these studies is that, even if both countries undertake macroeconomic policy adjustments and reduce their *global* imbalances to equilibrium levels, the *bilateral* imbalance would remain substantial. The United States would continue to run a bilateral deficit with Japan—the result both of the triangular pattern of trade discussed earlier and the impact of trade restrictions in the two countries (which are taken up in chapters 3 and 4).

One effect of these fiscal policy shifts in the United States and Japan would be to raise interest rates in Japan relative to US rates and thereby contribute to further appreciation of the yen. The fiscal policy changes and the attendant exchange rate rise would encourage a shift toward domestic demand–led growth, and away from a reliance on increasing net exports in Japan, and have the opposite effect in the United States. A sustained real exchange rate realignment would have a significant impact (with the requisite lags) on trade flows. According to Cline (1993), each 1 percent fall (rise) in the trade-weighted real exchange rate of the yen increases (reduces) Japan's global current account balance by about $4 billion, with a lag of two to three years. The linkage between the yen-dollar rate and the bilateral imbalance is even closer, as shown in figure 2.3: every 1 percent fall (rise) in the real value of the yen against the dollar eventually produces an increase (decrease) of about $1 billion in Japan's bilateral surplus with the United States.

Conclusions

The bilateral merchandise trade balance between the United States and Japan, is a political lightning rod for trade tensions. Of more fundamental importance are the global trade balances of the two countries, which are largely a product of their domestic macroeconomic conditions and the exchange rates that result. The bilateral trade balance generally moves in the same direction as the global balances of the two countries, but not on a one-for-one basis: in recent years the bilateral imbalance has shown less volatility than either country's global imbalance.

Each country's saving-investment balance is key, for it, together with the real exchange rate, determines the aggregate trade surplus or deficit. Recent research suggests that long-run demographic changes in the two countries, which determine the relative proportions of high and low savers in the two countries, will ultimately push the trade positions toward balance. In the short run, however, the trade balance will be affected most directly by the macroeconomic policies undertaken in each country.

The two countries begin from very different starting points. In the United States the public accounts are in chronic deficit, and the task is straightforward: government deficit reduction. This would reduce government dissaving and free up more private saving for investment purposes. It would also allow the United States to relax monetary policy and encourage a further reduction in interest rates. This in turn would lead to a depreciation of the currency and an enhancement of international competitiveness. In terms of the trade accounts, econometric models suggest that the current Clinton budget plan and associated changes in monetary policy, if faithfully implemented, could substantially cut the United States' global deficit and reduce the bilateral deficit with Japan by about $10 billion.

In Japan, the general government accounts are in substantial surplus. Given the cyclical weakness of the economy and the condition of public infrastructure, which has not kept pace with Japan's remarkable growth over the last forty years, it would be desirable to pursue a policy of gradual fiscal expansion. This would improve living standards in Japan, avoid the Japanese authorities' tendency to rely too heavily on monetary stimulus, and, through impacts on interest rates, encourage appreciation of the yen. This last effect would, in turn, shift the composition of output toward satisfying domestic demand and away from net exports, reducing Japan's external surplus without reducing overall growth. Indeed, the enactment of recent Japanese stimulus proposals, together with an attendant appreciation of the yen, could reduce the Japanese global surplus substantially, and its bilateral surplus with the United States by a more modest amount.

These macroeconomic policy changes—fiscal contraction in the United States, fiscal expansion in Japan, associated changes in monetary policy, and a permanent change in the real exchange rate—if implemented and sustained, could move the United States toward global current account balance, would contribute to a substantial reduction in Japan's global surplus, and would put a considerable dent in the bilateral imbalance. (Indeed, there is some evidence that these macroeconomic adjustments taken together would have even a bigger impact than the summed effects of each country's changes considered separately ([Noland 1991]). The target would be to reduce the global US deficit to a position of no more than 1 percent of GDP (and preferably balance) and Japan to a surplus of 1½ to 2 percent of GDP. Under current world conditions this would represent a satisfactory outcome from the standpoint of macroeconomic balance.

The United States would still run a large bilateral deficit with Japan, however, because of triangular trade and the structure of trade barriers in the two economies. With global accounts in equilibrium, the size of particular bilateral balances should be of little importance in and of themselves. However, the United States would undoubtedly still want to address the issue of trade barriers, which present a problem in their own right, regardless of the size of the trade imbalance. It is to this issue that we now turn.

3

Structural Access Barriers

The economic relationship between the United States and Japan goes far beyond the aggregate trade and financial relationship analyzed in the previous chapter. The issue of the composition of output—whether a country produces potato chips or computer chips—and the attendant issues of how a government promotes or restricts production in particular sectors are issues for microeconomic analysis. This chapter analyzes the policies and institutions in both countries that affect the sectoral composition of trade. Chapter 4 then examines these issues in the context of selected sectors.

Available technology, the quantity and quality of productive factors, and institutional organization all impact the composition and competitiveness of the US and Japanese economies. Yet the US-Japan trade pattern is not solely a function of these market fundamentals. Both countries' governments intervene in the market in a variety of ways and with myriad motives, and thereby affect the pattern of trade. Government involvement in the market tends to generate rents, and with them a set of incentives for firms to pursue these rents and the relevant bureaucracies to enlarge them. Government intervention can also encourage oligopolies.

While the specifics of these trade and industrial policies differ across sectors, variations on certain leitmotifs recur. In primary products and in mature, non-high-technology manufacturing, both Japan and the United States intervene in fairly transparent ways to protect politically influential declining industries. In high-technology manufacturing and in services, government intervention takes the form of industrial support or regulatory control, and the relationship between business and government creates a far more complex political and economic terrain in which trade competition is played out.

In these sectors, trade disputes typically take the form of complaints by US producers that Japanese public policy and private practices exclude them from what are essentially cartelized markets. These firms then enlist the US government to assist them in prying open the market, and this foreign pressure or *gaiatsu* inevitably becomes entangled with the politics of regulatory reform in Japan.

Understandably, the response in Japan is often to co-opt the complaining foreign firm or firms, to minimize disruption to the status quo. This often suits the interests of the new entrants, since they too come to enjoy the benefits of Japan's cartelized markets. This sets up a dynamic in which the US government is used as a lever to gain market entry, but as soon as entry is achieved, the government is encouraged to cease its liberalization pressures. This "privatization" of US trade policy poses important questions as to how the United States should define and prioritize its national interests in its relationship with Japan. Are US interests adequately served when a few US firms succeed in seizing a share of these rents, or only when the US government pursues true liberalization to the point of opening markets to all firms?

This chapter begins by examining the pattern of trade between the two countries and the conventional explanations for this pattern. Trade and industrial policies as well as differences in economic institutions alleged to contribute to disputes over market access are analyzed in turn. The chapter concludes with an overview of policies in the high-technology sector.

The US-Japan Pattern of Trade

The law of comparative advantage holds that a country's pattern of specialization is determined by the *relative* productivity rankings of its various industries. Table 3.1 reports two alternative rankings of manufacturing industries according to differences in productivity between the Japanese and the US industry. The first column of the table reports the percentage differences in *frontier* efficiencies (best-practice efficiency) for a group of 14 manufacturing industries (a positive number indicates that the US industry is more efficient by the stated percentage), while the second column reports percentage differences in *average* efficiencies for a somewhat more aggregated set of 6 industries. The two sets of rankings are more or less consistent: the United States is relatively more efficient than Japan in natural resource–based manufacturing, and relatively less efficient in the machinery industries.

Table 3.1 United States and Japan: relative efficiencies in selected industries, 1977

Industry	Relative frontier efficiency[a]	Industry	Relative average efficiency[b]
Food products	64.6	Food products	138.6
Wood products	24.8	Textiles	46.2
Chemicals	22.5	Other manufacturing	35.7
Textiles	16.0	Chemicals	8.3
Building materials	6.0	Basic metals	0.9
Rubber and plastic products	−1.5	Machinery	−15.7
Fabricated metals products	−3.0		
Petroleum products	−4.5		
Miscellaneous manufactures	−16.3		
Nonelectrical machinery	−18.7		
Primary metals	−20.2		
Instruments	−23.6		
Transport equipment	−25.6		
Electrical machinery	−30.6		

a. Percentage differences in best-practice efficiency for a group of 14 manufacturing industries. (A positive number indicates that the US industry is more efficient.)
b. Percentage differences in average efficiencies for an aggregated set of 6 industries.

Sources: Relative frontier efficiency, Torii and Caves (1992, table 11.8); relative average efficiency, McKinsey Global Institute (1992, exhibit 1–14).

These relative efficiencies are in turn determined by a number of factors: available technology, the quantity and quality of inputs, the degree of competition prevailing in the sector, openness to international trade, and so on. For Japan, technological catch-up was particularly important until the mid-1970s, when opportunities for easy appropriation of foreign technology were largely exhausted (Dollar and Wolff 1993).

Once opportunities for technological catch-up are exhausted, factor accumulation becomes the main driving force of productivity advance. Table 3.2 reports estimates of human and physical capital per worker for the United States and Japan. Already by 1980, Japan's stock of physical capital per worker exceeded that of the United States by a considerable degree, and the margin widened over the course of the decade. (Indeed, these figures do not reflect the "bubble economy" investment boom in Japan—more recent figures would exhibit an even larger gap.) At the same time, Japan's human capital per worker was catching up to that of the United States. Furthermore, since Japanese workers work longer hours than their US counterparts (about four additional hours a week, or 200 hours a year), Japan's physical and human capital has been applied more intensively than the United States' capital. Moreover, Balassa and Noland (1988) found that the rate of total factor productivity growth (the

Table 3.2   United States and Japan: capital per worker, 1980 and 1988

	1980	1988
Physical capital per worker (purchasing-power-adjusted 1985 dollars)		
United States	29,072	33,147
Japan	36,249	52,470
Human capital per worker (educational expenditure units)		
United States	3,206	3,859
Japan	2,816	3,431

Sources: Physical capital, Summers and Heston (1991); human capital, Noland (1990b, appendix).

increase in overall productivity, taking increases in factor inputs into account) in Japan has been more than twice that of the United States. This finding is undoubtedly due, at least in part, to Japan's continued exploitation of opportunities for technological catch-up and the more recent vintage of its capital stock.

These developments are reflected in the trade patterns of each country. The econometric analysis of Balassa and Noland (1989) demonstrated that Japan has transformed itself from a country specializing in labor-intensive manufactures in the 1960s to one specializing in physical and human capital–intensive manufactures in the 1980s. This process continued through the 1980s, as Japan maintained high rates of physical and human capital accumulation. This is manifested in the indices of revealed comparative advantage shown in figure 3.1. This measure is defined as the ratio of a country's share in world exports of a particular commodity category to the country's share in total world exports. A value greater than one for a particular industry indicates revealed comparative advantage in that industry, and a value less than one disadvantage. The index is useful for illustrative purposes because it does not include imports and is broadly unaffected by the idiosyncrasies of national protection (although it will continue to reflect the influence of trade partners' policies). The measure is also unaffected by the overall level of the trade balance and thus is useful in making intertemporal comparisons.

In 1970, Japan's highest indices were in electrical machinery, miscellaneous manufactures (which include toys, sporting goods, and office supplies), and rubber and plastic products. The lowest indices were in natural resource–based industries such as food, beverages, and tobacco, and wood and cork products. Japan's pattern of specialization changed dramatically over the next two decades. By 1990, Japan's highest revealed comparative advantage indices were all in engineering-based sectors such as electrical machinery, transportation equipment, and precision

Figure 3.1 Japan: revealed comparative advantage in exports, all industries, 1970–90

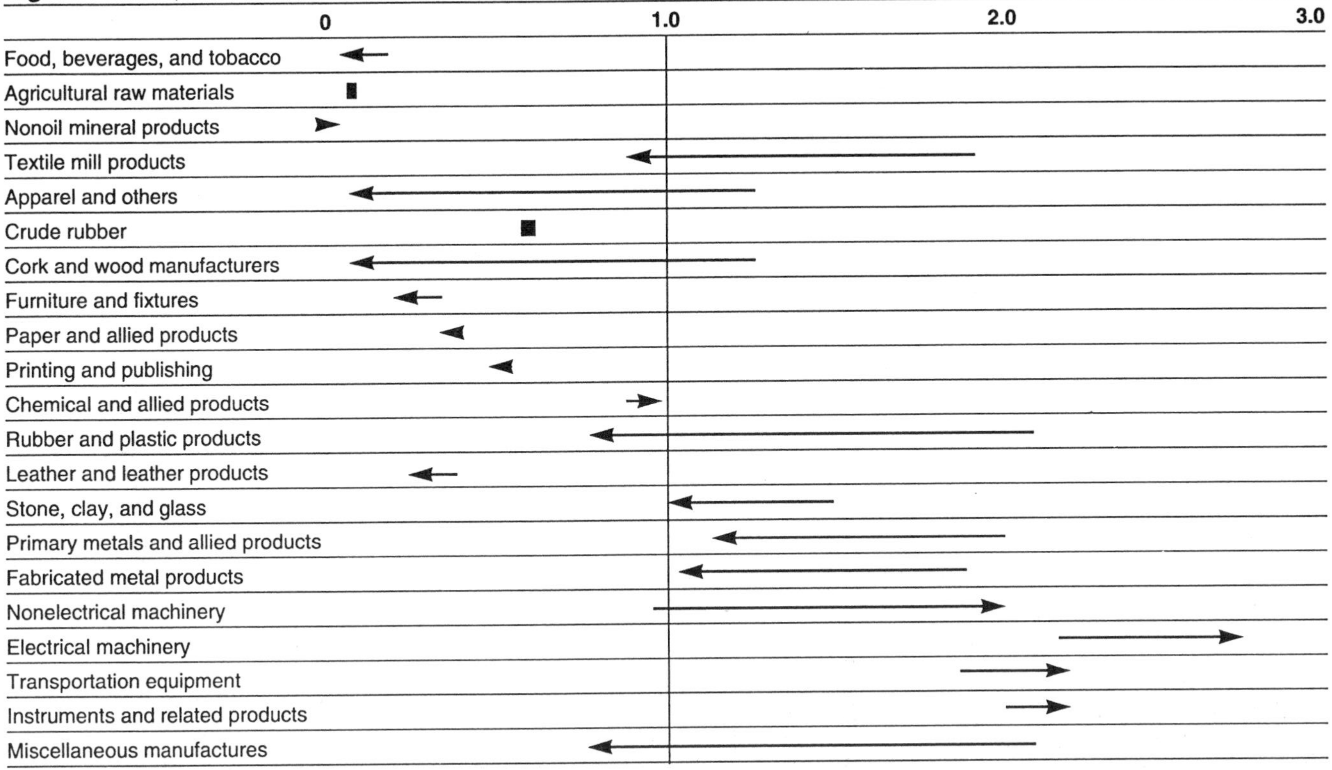

Source: Based on data from United Nations, *Commodities Trade Statistics* and *International Trade Statistics Yearbook.*

machinery. Likewise, the largest *increases* in the index were all in engineering-based sectors (as indicated by the long arrows from left to right in figure 3.1), and the biggest declines (right to left arrows) were all in labor-intensive manufacturing sectors.

The pattern of specialization and change shown for the United States in figure 3.2 is considerably different. The United States has a much broader natural resource base than Japan, and consequently the degree of specialization is less in the United States. In 1970, the United States appeared to have comparative disadvantage in labor-intensive sectors, and comparative advantage in most resource- and human and physical capital–intensive sectors. Changes in the pattern of specialization over the subsequent twenty years appear to be less systematic than in the Japanese case.

There are several explanations for the apparently more rapid change in the Japanese pattern of specialization. One is that the existence of substantial natural resources in the United States exerts a "resource pull," which constrains the employment of factors in non-resource-based segments of manufacturing. Consequently, an economy such as that of the United States will exhibit a less rapid transformation of its manufacturing sector as it develops.[1]

A second possibility is that the existence of large conglomerates and *keiretsu* (affiliated business groups) in Japan, combined with the institution of lifetime employment, facilitates redeployment of productive factors from declining to emerging sectors. For one thing, workers in declining sectors do not fear loss of employment, wages, or seniority because they expect to continue to be employed within the firm or its family. As a consequence, there are fewer demands for public policies to retard the downsizing of declining sectors (although the Japanese government has often pursued policies of creating "recession" and "rationalization" cartels). Second, large firms and the *keiretsu* have relatively good information about conditions across manufacturing sectors. This too helps smooth the movement of factors from one sector to another.

A third possibility is that industrial policies in Japan have been more effective than those in the United States in promoting the expansion of emerging sectors and the contraction of declining ones. The role of industrial policy will be taken up in a later section of this chapter.

Another interesting aspect of the Japanese trade pattern, identified by a number of researchers (e.g., Scott 1987, Lawrence 1987, Balassa and Noland 1988, Lincoln 1990, Noland 1990a), is the relatively low level of intraindustry trade. The term "intraindustry trade" refers to the two-way trade in differentiated manufactures within a given industry. This trade tends to increase as economies develop and the demands of firms

---

1. See Leamer (1987) for a rigorous exposition of this argument.

Figure 3.2 United States: revealed comparative advantage in exports, all industries, 1970–90

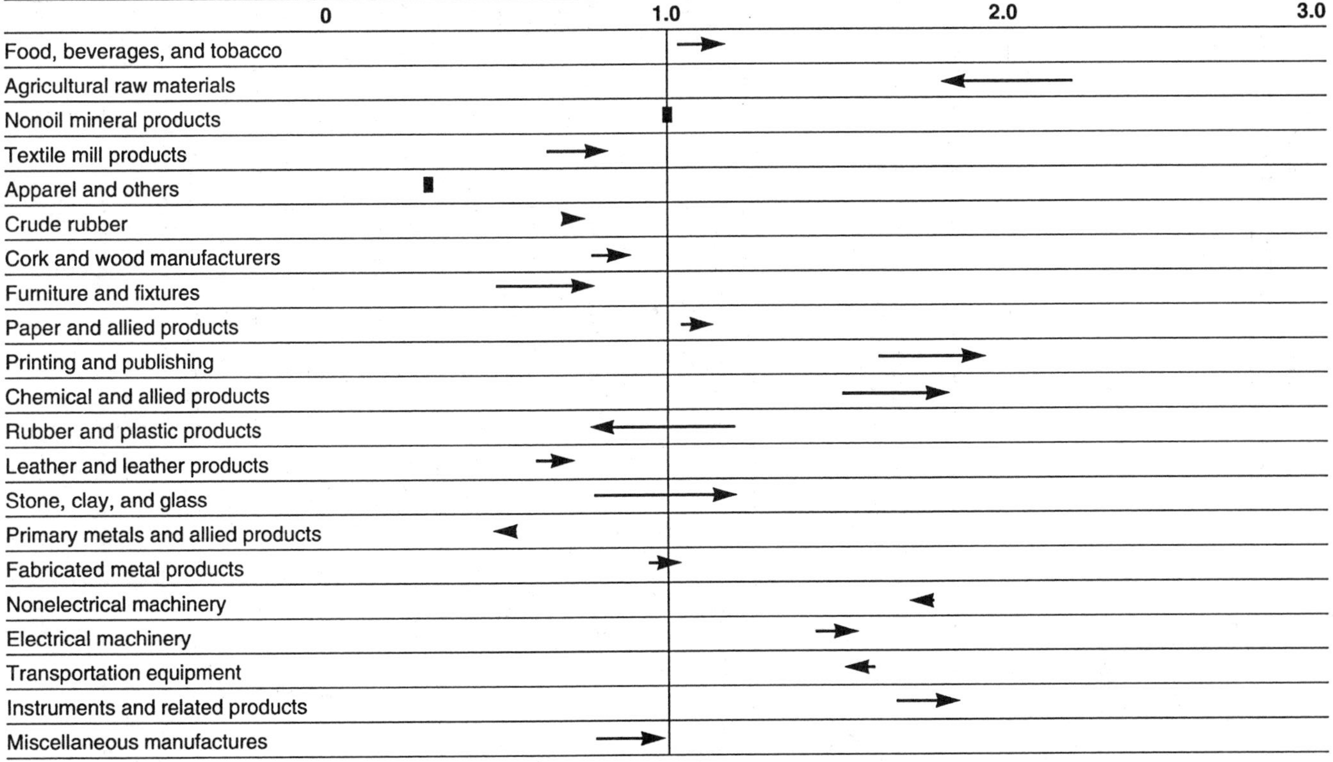

Source: Based on data from United Nations, *Commodities Trade Statistics* and *International Trade Statistics Yearbook.*

Table 3.3 Selected trade indicators for six industrialized countries[a]

Indicator	Japan	United States	Germany	Great Britain	France	Italy
Intraindustry trade index, 1990	0.58	0.83	0.73	0.79	0.77	0.67
Import share of domestic consumption of manufactures, 1990 (percentages)	5.9	15.3	15.4	17.7	13.7	12.6
Foreign firms' share of domestic sales, 1986 (percentages)	1	10	18	20	27	n.a.

n.a. = not available

a. intra-EC trade has been purged from the intraindustry trade and import share calculations.

Sources: Intraindustry trade indices calculated from United Nations *World Commodity Trade Statistics;* import shares calculated from World Bank, *World Development Report;* foreign firms share of sales, Julius and Thomsen (1988).

and consumers become more complex, so that no individual firm is able to produce a sufficiently broad range of products to satisfy all demands. (An example of intraindustry trade would be cross-border trade in different makes and models of automobiles.)

As shown in table 3.3, Japan's intraindustry trade appears to be somewhat lower than that of comparable industrial countries. One interpretation (figuring most prominently in Lincoln 1990) is that this relatively low level of intraindustry trade in manufactures reflects a relatively closed Japanese market. According to this view, once Japanese firms begin producing a good, competing imports are excluded from the market either through public policies or through private arrangements. While this certainly may be the case, analytically it is difficult to determine if the observed low degree of intraindustry penetration reflects the exclusion of imports or the hypercompetitiveness of the domestic industry.

As the second line of table 3.3 makes clear, relatively few manufactured imports make it into the Japanese market. The share of imports in Japanese consumption of manufactures is less than half that in other major industrial countries. Moreover, unlike in the other countries, which have experienced considerable increases in this import penetration ratio, the Japanese imported manufactures share has remained essentially flat, never rising above 6 percent since at least 1975 (cf. Balassa and Noland 1988, table 3.2; Dornbusch 1992, table 8; Advisory Committee for Trade Policy and Negotiations 1993). Again, interpretation of these raw statistics is problematic: it is unclear whether the low level of imports in domestic manufactures consumption reflects protection or the comparative advantage of a capital-abundant country with few natural resources, far from other developed countries.

The Japanese trade pattern appears distinctive in at least two other dimensions. The first is the unusually high share of intrafirm trade. Lawrence (1991a) reports that, while around half of US trade with Europe is intrafirm trade, around three-quarters of US trade with Japan is intrafirm. Furthermore, while in the case of US trade with Europe the ratio of exports from the United States controlled by the US parent firm to exports controlled by the European parent firm is more than 3:1, in the case of Japan the ratio is reversed. That is, whereas American firms control most of the intrafirm US exports going to Europe, Japanese firms control most of the US exports to Japan. Lawrence attributes this to the prominent role of giant trading companies in Japanese trade, and he argues that this pattern of trade is consistent with imperfectly competitive Japanese domestic markets.

The flip side of this phenomenon, reported in the final line of table 3.3, is that foreign firms account for a minuscule fraction of sales in the Japanese market. This reflects the low level of imports, the predominant control of those imports that do enter by Japanese firms, and the low level of inward foreign direct investment.

These distinctive characteristics do not prove that the Japanese market is completely closed to foreigners or their goods. Indeed, a number of US firms such as Schick (safety razors), Coca-Cola Japan (soft drinks), and Johnson & Johnson (adhesive bandages) dominate their markets in Japan (Morgan and Morgan 1991, table 6.1). Nevertheless, the aggregate figures do establish that the role of foreigners and foreign-made goods is unusually low in the Japanese economy, and point toward the exercise of market power by domestic firms and industrial policies as a possible explanation for this distinctiveness.

Industrial Policy

The patterns of trade in both Japan and the United States are affected by trade and industrial policies undertaken in both countries. Indeed, commentators as diverse as Johnson (1982), Shinohara (1982), and Tyson (1992) have put Japan's industrial and trade policies at the heart of explanations of Japan's economic success. These policies contain both domestic and trade components and have been applied to both emerging infant industries and declining senescent ones.

Domestic support policies in Japan have included direct subsidies, preferential tax treatment, preferential access to credit, government procurement preferences, establishment of producer cartels, and public subsidization of research and development (R&D) consortia. External policies have included trade protection, restrictions on inward foreign direct investment, and control over high-technology trade.

The conventional wisdom among economists is that direct subsidies have played little role in fostering changes in Japan's industrial composition. More than 90 percent of on-budget subsidies go to the declining sectors of agriculture, forestry, fishing, and coal mining (Ogura and Yoshino 1988, table 1), and one study by the Japanese government found that only one sector, food processing, received direct subsidies exceeding 0.1 percent of GDP originating in that sector (Saxonhouse 1983).

Indirect subsidies through the tax system and off-budget finance may play a greater role. The primary source of subsidized capital is the Fiscal Investment and Loan Program (FILP), controlled by the Trust Fund Bureau of the Ministry of Finance (MOF). The FILP is an off-budget program around half the size of the general accounts budget. This second, shadow budget has been a powerful policy tool, allowing bureaucrats to address priorities not met in the general accounts budget.

Funds for the FILP come mainly from the postal savings system. In addition to financing the activities of public corporations, private-sector investments are financed through public financial institutions such as the Japan Development Bank, the Export-Import Bank, and the Housing Loan Corporation. Although early in the postwar period much of FILP finance went into strengthening industry, the share of FILP funds going to industry has since fallen steadily, while housing, regional development, and other activities have received larger shares.

One source of indirect subsidy is the public financial institutions that offer loans at interest rates below the prevailing market rate. A second source of implicit capital subsidy is the tax system.[2] In computing corporate income for tax purposes, corporations are allowed to deduct the acquisition cost of machinery and equipment from their annual incomes over a number of years, depending on the stipulated asset life (this is similar to the accelerated depreciation provisions in the US tax code). This system spreads the tax reductions over a certain period, but does not take into account interest costs and inflation over the relevant period. Hence, the longer the stipulated asset life, the longer the period over which the tax saving arising from depreciation is spread, and the lower the present value of the tax reduction. The corporate tax burden with respect to investment goods can thus be reduced by shortening stipulated asset lives, even without changing the tax rate.

Calculations reported in Noland (1992a) indicate that the low-interest-rate loans have generally been of greater quantitative significance than

---

2. This discussion follows that of Ogura and Yoshino (1988). Special depreciation schemes have existed in Japan throughout the postwar period. The most important of these had the effect of subsidizing certain classes of investment goods. In addition, an export-based special depreciation system existed from 1961 to 1972.

the special depreciations. With the exception of mining, where investment has been weak and the involvement of public financial institutions strong, the implicit capital subsidy–to–investment ratio has been low, usually less than 5 percent. After mining, the greatest beneficiary of the reduced interest burdens has been the transportation machinery sector, which includes shipbuilding, motor vehicles, and aerospace.[3]

Serious analyses of Japanese industrial policies indicate that in total these policies have probably been welfare-reducing: on balance, they shifted resources from high- to low-productivity uses and have not been targeted sufficiently narrowly within the manufacturing sector to capture rents effectively. Japan's industrial support policies could thus be regarded as compensation for the negative net transfer from the Japanese manufacturing sector (cf. Krugman 1987, Lee 1989, and Noland 1992a).

The United States, too, has undertaken a set of policy interventions with indirect consequences for trade composition, which collectively could be termed an industrial policy. Cooper (1986) lists a number of such policies. They include tax policies that have in practice subsidized capital investment or production; foreign aid tied to the procurement of US products and military sales credits; input subsidies, such as the provision of cheap power or water for irrigation purposes; government R&D expenditures; large-scale government purchases that effectively create a market (for example, avionics, ground tracking stations for satellites); government procurement codes that tilt purchasing toward US suppliers (the "Buy American Act"); and government regulations that implicitly change the relative cost structures across industries. Unfortunately, direct estimates of these policies' effects on US trade structure are unavailable.[4]

Trade Policy

Both Japan and the United States maintain trade policies that interfere with cross-border commerce. In the case of the United States, post–Tokyo Round tariffs average 3.3 percent in agriculture and 5.0 percent in indus-

---

3. Japanese policymakers also have access to off-budget funds for industrial promotion through the revenues of quasi-public organizations such as the Motor Boat Racing Association and the Japan Bicycle Rehabilitation Association (Prestowitz 1988). The amounts in these funds do not appear particularly large, however. Saxonhouse (1983) cites the *Wall Street Journal* to the effect that no more than $500,000 a year from these sources was made available to the Japan Machine Tool Builders Association.

4. Richardson (1993), however, estimates that US policies, most prominently export controls and foreign policy sanctions, have *reduced* US exports by $10 billion to $30 billion, especially in such manufactures as chemicals, equipment, and instruments.

trial goods.[5] The United States maintains formal quotas in a number of agricultural products including dairy products, sugar, peanuts, and cotton. The United States is also a participant in the Multi-Fiber Arrangement, a global system of bilateral quotas in textiles and apparel.[6] The United States has negotiated voluntary export restraints on a number of products, including several with Japan; the most notable ones have covered steel, machine tools, color television sets, and automobiles (VERs are analyzed elsewhere in this volume). Their current impact is questionable, however: the VERs on color televisions and steel have been removed, that on machine tools is scheduled to be phased out, and that on automobiles is no longer binding.

US firms have made extensive use of antidumping and countervailing duty provisions in US trade laws to limit trade between the United States and Japan. Between 1979 and 1991, US firms filed a total of 5 countervailing duty and 58 dumping suits against Japanese exporters, 43 of these (69 percent) resulting in restrictions on trade (Destler 1992). While the disposition of these cases is justifiable under US trade law, the widespread and arguably indiscriminate use of countervailing duty and dumping suits clearly has a protective effect.[7] The United States also maintains a variety of sanitary regulations, standards, testing and certification requirements, and other practices that could be classified as

---

5. Some tariffs, such as those on woolen fabrics, glassware, and pottery exceed 20 percent. In addition, certain imports such as tuna in water are subject to tariff-rate quotas (quantities that exceed the quota are subject to a higher tariff).

6. Hufbauer et al. (1986) estimated that the annual cost to US consumers of dairy product protection was $5.5 billion, and Cline (1990a) estimated that the net welfare cost of textile and apparel protection was more than $8.1 billion annually.

7. The emphasis on dumping actions is fundamentally flawed from a national welfare standpoint. First, in perfectly competitive markets, firms may choose to price below marginal cost in the initial stages of production, in the expectation that costs will eventually fall; indeed, it was Texas Instruments Inc., an American firm, that pioneered "forward pricing" in the semiconductor industry. Second, perfectly competitive firms may temporarily price below costs if production or sales distribution is characterized by quasi irreversibilities or hysteresis. This may occur frequently in a floating exchange rate system as a result of temporary exchange rate misalignment. Dumping rules make no provision for this. Third, dumping may arise even under competitive market conditions because of market segmentation due to transport costs or other trade impediments (cf. Brander and Krugman 1983, Weinstein 1992). Lastly, there are severe problems with cost-based methods of ascertaining dumping as practiced under US law. (For detailed analyses see the essays in Boltuck and Litan 1991.)

Perhaps most important, though, the emphasis on dumping effectively creates a price floor policy, making the United States a high-cost production location, when antidumping duties are imposed on inputs. During any cyclical weakening of demand, foreign firms will be tempted to cut domestic prices, since their ability to compete on price is restricted abroad. This means that downstream users of a product (manufacturers of computers and telecommunications products in the case of semiconductors, for example) in net importing regions will be put at a competitive disadvantage. Tyson (1992) reaches similar conclusions.

nontariff barriers (General Agreement on Tariffs and Trade [GATT] 1990; Ministry of International Trade and Industry [MITI] 1993).[8] Recent research by Trefler (1993) indicates that, when both the direct effect of reduced trade due to nontariff barriers and the indirect effects through intimidating prospective foreign exporters are taken into account, nontariff barriers in 1983 reduced total US manufactures imports by $49.5 billion, or nearly one-quarter of US manufactures imports. Unfortunately, a breakdown of incidence by trade partner is unavailable.

The United States also maintains a Generalized System of Preferences (GSP), which provides duty-free access to the US market for some imports from developing countries, as well as a broader set of preferences for countries of the Caribbean Basin. The United States also has free trade agreements with Canada and Israel and is in the process of extending the Canadian agreement to include Mexico through the North American Free Trade Agreement (NAFTA).

Japan, like many other countries in the immediate postwar period, operated a tightly controlled import trade regime justified as a response to severe balance of payments constraints. The main policy tool for controlling imports was foreign exchange allocations, but the government also maintained high tariffs and extensive systems of quotas and import licensing. The government supported producers in preferred sectors with subsidized loans and special tax treatment.

In 1955, with the support of the United States, Japan became a contracting party to the GATT and began a gradual period of import liberalization. Most quotas in the manufacturing sector had been eliminated by the beginning of the Kennedy Round of GATT trade negotiations in 1964, but manufactures tariffs remained high by European or American standards and involved considerable escalation by degree of processing.[9]

This tendency toward gradual relaxation of border measures in manufactures continued through the 1970s and 1980s, so that by the mid-1980s tariff levels in Japan were comparable to (if not somewhat lower than) those maintained by the United States and the European Community, and quotas had been largely eliminated.[10] In addition, Japan intro-

---

8. US firms have also made use of Section 301 of the 1974 trade act, initiating 13 such cases against Japan since 1975, and Japan was the primary target of the Super 301 provision of the 1988 trade act. These policies are not directly protective, however, since the stated aim is to increase US access to foreign (in this case Japanese) markets, not to protect the US market.

9. See Komiya and Itoh (1988) for further discussion.

10. There were, and continue to be, a few exceptions, however. High tariffs on semiconductors, computers, and numerically controlled machine tools (which were classified as computers) were maintained until 1979, when they were reduced as part of the Tokyo Round agreement. Quotas on leather and leather footwear products were converted to a tariff-quota scheme in 1986, and since then imports have grown rapidly. Orderly marketing agreements have been negotiated covering raw silk, and a prior confirmation system exists

duced in 1971 a Generalized System of Preferences for developing countries. As of 1989, the applied simple average tariff rate for industrial products (excluding petroleum) was 5.3 percent, and the weighted average 1.9 percent (GATT 1990).

In Japan there is scant evidence of significant tariffs or quotas outside of agriculture.[11] Nevertheless, it is widely believed that the Japanese market is effectively closed to manufactured imports. The methods of import control include discriminatory networks of affiliated firms (*keiretsu*); administrative guidance on the part of government officials to intimidate importers; misuse of customs procedures and product standards, testing, and certification requirements to discourage imports; incomplete enforcement of patent and trademark rights; government procurement procedures that advantage domestic suppliers; and restrictions on the distribution channels for imported products, to name a few.[12]

Moreover, close examination of individual industry case studies (such as those in the next chapter) indicates that these regulatory barriers tend to emerge in industries where domestic producer lobbies are strong: either primary-product sectors where there are well-established producer lobbies, or highly concentrated or cartelized manufacturing and service sectors where the small number of producer firms facilitates the organization of industry lobbies. This confluence of public and private barriers inhibits entry by newcomers, whether foreign or domestic.

---

for the importation of silk fabrics. In 1989, a voluntary export restraint was negotiated with Korean knitwear producers, which expired in 1991, and in 1993, Japan imposed its first antidumping duties, against Chinese producers of ferro-silicon manganese, a steelmaking material.

11. Indeed, the Japanese government has undertaken a number of policies to *increase* the amounts of imports in Japan. These have included the establishment of special import promotion areas, more-generous public financial institution support for the importation of manufactured goods, tax breaks for the importation of manufactured goods, administrative guidance, and supplementary budget allocations earmarked for imports.

In addition, a proposal was floated, but never acted upon, to use the consumption tax rebate on exports (more than ¥1 trillion) to promote imports.

12. Well-known anecdotes provide grist for the mill. In one case, a plan to import gasoline came to naught when government officials successfully pressured the prospective importer's bank to withdraw financing. In another case, small fiberglass boats were kept out of the Japanese market by subjecting them to inappropriate testing procedures designed for concrete boats (such as dropping them). Standards introduced for ski equipment, purportedly to fit the "unique" Japanese snow, excluded foreign-made equipment and foreign manufacturers who were not apprised of the standard-setting process, although at the time they supplied about half of the skis sold in Japan. Particularly intriguing was the long-standing Japanese customs practice (now discontinued) of slicing Dutch tulip bulbs in half to check for insects. In the words of Jagdish Bhagwati (1988, 69), once the bulbs were severed, "even Japanese ingenuity could not put them together again." For additional examples and documentation, see Balassa and Noland (1988) and Lincoln (1990).

Nontraditional Access Barriers

The existence of nontariff barriers in Japan is indisputable: data compiled by Leamer (1991) for 1983 (the only year for which data are available) show that a simple average of 46.7 percent, or a trade-weighted average of 61.7 percent, of US exports to Japan encountered some form of nontariff barrier, indicating that not only are these barriers ubiquitous, but they are erected disproportionately in sectors of US specialization.[13] What is controversial is their significance. To understand how they work, we first examine the regulatory framework, and then investigate industrial structure, barriers to inward investment, and problems of intellectual property protection.

Product Liability and Regulation

In Japan, where product liability law is very weak, product safety is ensured through a bureaucratic standards, testing, and certification system. In practice that system is susceptible to capture by producer interests and can act as a nontariff barrier to trade. Numerous cases exist in which Japanese standards were written or changed to exclude imported products, often after imports had begun to significantly penetrate the market, or in which foreign producers encountered extreme difficulty in obtaining certification (Balassa and Noland 1988).

Japan deliberately uses bureaucratic control as a substitute for the tort system. Plaintiffs must not only prove that a product was defective and caused injury, but that the manufacturer was negligent. As a consequence of this stiff burden of proof, and the relative lack of access to legal counsel for redress, product liability suits in Japan are rare: a recent survey of 194 big Japanese manufacturers found that only 24 had ever faced a product liability suit in Japan, and only 7 had lost (*The Economist*, 18 July 1992).[14]

---

13. Conversely, a simple average of 9.9 percent, or a trade-weighted average of 34.9 percent, of Japanese exports to the United States in 1983 (when the auto VER was binding) encountered nontariff barriers, indicating that Japanese exports also disproportionately face such barriers in the US market. These nontariff barrier data were originally collected by the United Nations Conference on Trade and Development (UNCTAD). See Laird and Yeats (1990) for a description of the UNCTAD methodology. See Lawrence (1992) for a very useful survey of the issues covered in this section.

14. Japanese citizens have far less access to the legal system generally than their counterparts in other developed countries. The incidence of lawyers to the general population in 1 per 8,569 in Japan, compared with 1 per 1,286 in Germany and 1 per 356 in the United States. In addition, Japan does not have a contingency fee system, so that plaintiffs must pay considerable advance fees. Moreover, the courts are understaffed to the point that the average civil case takes more than two years to resolve; complicated cases can take far longer.

Recently, however, an unusual coalition of foreign firms and trade ministries, some domestic firms, the Japan Federation of Bar Associations, the nascent consumer and "green" movements, and some political parties have been calling on the government to revise the product liability law. Japan's Economic Planning Agency has coordinated a review of the system and has released a report recommending that Japan move to a product liability system more similar to the European Community's. Like that in the United States, the EC system does not require proof of negligence on the part of producers. Unlike the US system, however, the EC system does not permit decision by jury or punitive damages. It is hoped that movement toward a strengthened product liability law would permit the dismantling of those parts of the regulatory structure that at times act as a nontariff barrier. Reform of product liability law along the EC model, combined with a reform of administrative guidance law, would be a desirable policy reform for Japan. Movement toward the EC model of product liability law should also be considered in the United States.

Industrial Structure and Competition Policy

The standards, testing, and certification barriers just described are often encountered in concentrated or cartelized industries. Much of Japanese industry is highly concentrated: three firms account for all domestic production of glass, and the top four firms account for 98 percent of beer production and 100 percent of soda ash production, to name a few.[15] Highly concentrated industries tend to be linked (as are these three examples) and to be associated with significant government intervention.

Industrial structure issues are further complicated by the existence of *keiretsu*.[16] These networks of affiliated firms typically have long-standing financial, managerial, and product market interlinkages. A *keiretsu* might consist of a group of large core firms horizontally linked across markets, together with their vertically linked input suppliers, and possibly a captive distribution network.[17]

---

15. The equivalent four-firm concentration ratios for the United States are 82 percent for glass, 87 percent for beer, and 72 percent for soda ash. Comparisons of Herfindahl indices (a less well-known but preferable measure of concentration) yield similar results: the indices for the Japanese beer, glass, and soda ash industries are 3,342, 3,648, and 2,821, respectively; the comparable figures for the United States are 2,089, 1,968, and 2,328.

16. See Aoki (1987 and 1991) and Gerlach (1989) for descriptions of the *keiretsu*.

17. For example, the Mitsui *keiretsu* consists of 24 major companies: Mitsui Bank (the group's main bank), Mitsui Trust (also a bank), Mitsui Life (insurance), Taisho F&M (insurance), Mitsui Bussan (a trading company), Mitsukoshi (a retailer), Mitsui Construction, Sanki Engineering, Mitsui Real Estate, Toray (textiles), Mitsui Toatsu (chemicals), Mitsui Petroleum, Mitsui Mining, Hokkaido Coal, Onoda Cement, Oji Paper, Japan Steel Works, Mitsui M&M (nonferrous metals), Toyota Motors, Mitsui Shipbuilding, Toshiba (electronics), Mitsui OSK (shipping), Mitsui Warehouse, and Nippon Flour. Cross-share-

Keiretsu are inherently exclusionary. Firms within the group receive preference over those outside. This discrimination may apply equally to foreign and domestic firms outside the group. There are two salient issues. First, do the possible efficiency gains through better information exchange, coordination, and monitoring outweigh the implicit costs of maintaining in-group preferences? Second, even if *keiretsu* are on balance efficiency-enhancing, how can this system, developed under what were essentially closed-economy conditions, be broadened to include non-Japanese firms, and made both more politically palatable and even more economically efficient?

Analyses of the *keiretsu* have sometimes distinguished three roles. First are the financial links. It is sometimes argued that the cross-holding of shares among *keiretsu* firms, in contrast to the more open "Anglo-American" stock market model, allows managers to adopt longer time horizons because of reduced fear of takeover. At the same time, the heavier reliance on main-bank loan finance and the pattern of cross-shareholding better facilitates monitoring of management decisions than would more diffuse ownership. The effects of *keiretsu* in the financial sphere are discussed in the section on foreign direct investment below.

It is claimed that the vertical integration of major firms and component suppliers through *keiretsu* relationships may also be efficiency-enhancing.[18] Product development is enhanced by firms' greater willingness to exchange information in the context of a long-standing relationship. It has been argued that the vertically organized *keiretsu* are an efficient halfway house between complete vertical integration within a single firm (with its attendant costs) on the one hand, and arm's-length transactions on the other, by balancing reliability and control against some degree of competition among suppliers.[19] The impacts of vertical *keiretsu* are discussed in the context of the semiconductor and other industries in chapter 4.

A third aspect of the *keiretsu* is their distribution function: many of the major Japanese consumer-goods producers have captive distribution networks, sustained by practices that would be illegal in the United States. Few seriously argue that these practices are efficiency-enhancing: they simply act as a barrier to entry and a means to gouge consumers.

The Japanese distribution system is of relevance to US-Japan trade relations for two reasons. First, it is alleged to act as an impediment to

---

holding accounts for more than half of all the shares of these firms, and the main bank finances around one-fifth of all their borrowing (Gerlach 1989).

18. Torii and Caves (1992), for example, find that the extent of subcontracting is a robust explanator of increased industrial efficiency in Japan.

19. For example, American automobile producers reportedly source around 50 percent of their parts internally, while for Japanese automakers the figure is around 25 percent (Womack et al. 1990).

imports. Second, the regulation of the system has hindered the entrance of US retailers into the Japanese market (an issue that will be addressed in the next chapter).

Importation of foreign goods into the Japanese market is alleged to be impeded by the distribution system in three ways. First, the Japanese government requires licenses to retail many products. To the extent that these regulations disproportionately affect imports, the volume of imports will be depressed: import prices will be higher, reflecting both the costs of obtaining a license and the reduced number of outlets that will obtain the license and offer the product. The reduced-outlet effect would presumably also reduce volumes directly.

A second source of discrimination against imports is vertical foreclosure within the distribution system.[20] This occurs both in consumer and in capital goods. Vertically integrated firms refuse to carry products of competitors, and product return and rebate systems are used to tilt retailer incentives toward domestically produced products. Sophisticated econometric research by Ariga et al. (1991) points to administered prices in sectors where there are strong vertical relationships or *keiretsu*, suggesting that control of the distribution system acts as an effective barrier to entry.[21] Although recent reforms have narrowed the scope of permissible vertical restraints, enforcement remains lax.

Both of these problems are worsened by the preponderance of small, poorly capitalized stores in the Japanese retail system. The relative weakness of the retailers increases both the discriminatory impact of government regulations and the likelihood of capture by large manufacturers.[22] The numerous small shopkeepers also act as the primary domestic pressure group to maintain regulations that impede the establishment of large retail stores.

---

20. See Flath (1989) for a description of vertical restraints in Japan.

21. For example, the three glass firms that own or control 100 percent of output also own or control 99 percent of the distribution system for glass in Japan, keeping prices 30 to 400 percent above world prices. When Guardian Industries, a major US firm, began selling in Japan, Asahi Glass, a Japanese rival, reportedly scolded the customer, then bought back the American glass and substituted its own product. It is also claimed that excess profits from the cartelized Japanese market have been used to buy up potential competitors abroad (Robert Keatley, *Wall Street Journal*, 19 March 1993).

Another recent source of conflict is the automobile sector, where Japanese automakers can restrict marketing of foreign competitors' cars at their affiliated dealers. Such practices are illegal in the United States.

22. Of related interest are papers by Sato (1990), Ito and Maruyama (1991), Itoh (1991), and Nishimura (1991), which examine the efficiency of the Japanese distribution system. Cheng (1993) develops a theoretical model to show how inefficiency in the distribution system could give rise to higher consumer prices of an exportable good at home than abroad, and nonequivalence of distribution costs and tariffs.

Two changes could ameliorate these problems in the distribution system. First, changes in the structure of the system, in particular the spread of chain convenience and discount stores, the rise of mail-order marketing, and the entry of foreign retailers into the market may all serve to reduce the power of domestic manufacturers vis-à-vis retailers in consumer goods, making the system more hospitable to imports. Second, the government could more aggressively enforce existing competition laws.

Not surprisingly, competition policy has become a major issue in bilateral relations between the United States and Japan, leading to action by both governments. Under US pressure as part of the Structural Impediments Initiative (SII) talks, Japan began a process of strengthening its competition laws and their enforcement in 1990. The Japan Fair Trade Commission drafted guidelines on anticompetitive practices, especially in the distribution system, clarifying which practices are illegal and therefore subject to criminal sanctions and levies. The commission also issued new guidelines restricting the use of cross-ownership of stock as a condition of doing business or as a means of limiting third-party transactions. New rules also forbid a firm with more than 25 percent market share of a product from becoming the sole distributor of a similar imported product. Some commentators, however, have criticized these new guidelines as excessively vague.

Penalties have also been increased: the surcharge that can be levied on firms for engaging in illegal cartels was raised from 2 percent of sales to 6 percent (the United States had originally requested 10 percent); this surcharge is the chief financial deterrent to illegal cartelization. The maximum criminal fine was raised from ¥5 million to ¥100 million, an impressive increase, but still far below comparable limits in the United States or the European Community.[23] The budget of the Fair Trade Commission was expanded, and the number of investigators was raised considerably, although the agency is still far smaller than its US counterparts (the Federal Trade Commission and the Department of Justice's Antitrust Division).

The result has been a significant increase in the number of antitrust actions in Japan, although the degree of activity remains well below that observed in the United States. New guidelines were issued in some industries, and investigations were launched in others, including the financial, automobile, auto parts, paper products, and glass industries.

---

23. A Japan Fair Trade Commission Advisory Council had recommended a higher ceiling on corporations, but this was opposed by business interests and politicians. The council had also recommended raising the ceiling on criminal fines for individuals, but this was left unchanged. These recommendations were of debatable importance in any event: in only one case up until that time had criminal penalties been imposed during the postwar period.

Punitive surcharges have been running significantly higher than in the past, criminal charges were brought against firms in 1991 and 1993 (after only a single case in the preceding 17 years), and for the first time criminal charges were brought in a bid-rigging case.[24] (Ironically, some of the firms involved in these cases were the Japanese subsidiaries of US firms.) The US government has expressed satisfaction that reforms of the Large Scale Retail Store Law, which was alleged to have hindered both the importation of goods and the entrance of foreign retailers into the Japanese market, are being implemented.

Action has also been attempted in the United States. In April 1992, during the presidential primary campaign in which incumbent President George Bush was taking a drubbing from both Democrat and Republican opponents for allegedly being soft on trade in general, and Japan in particular, the US Justice Department announced that it would revive the rarely used policy of applying US antitrust laws extraterritorially. (The policy had been abandoned by the Reagan administration.) This meant that US exporters could take foreign firms to court if actions undertaken anywhere in the world that would be illegal under US law restrained US exports.

This decision was widely criticized in Japan and elsewhere for its unilateral nature. Foreign governments could retaliate, either by adopting a similar stance or by enacting "blocking statutes" that prohibit or restrict firms from complying with US court rulings, as several did during earlier episodes of this type. Indeed, internal opposition within the Bush administration, and a Japanese threat to block, effectively killed the Bush administration proposal.

It would be preferable to reach multilateral (or even bilateral) agreement on competition policy. The United States already has a comity agreement with the European Community that facilitates cooperation between their competition policy authorities. The United States also has had success in prosecuting Japanese firms for bid rigging in contracts for services to US military bases in Japan. In one such case, the Justice Department reached an out-of-court settlement with 99 Japanese construction firms for bid rigging at the Yokosuka Naval Base; the firms agreed to pay fines of $32.4 million, or 24 percent of the billed costs. In another case involving bid rigging at the Yokota Air Force Base, 11 Japanese electronics firms agreed to pay $36.7 million in fines, or nearly 36 percent of the value of the $103 million in contracts. Although these cases represent victories for US antitrust authorities, it would be desirable to more fully internationalize Japanese competition policy through either

---

24. The Fair Trade Commission angered the public, however, when it declined to press criminal charges in a Saitama prefecture *dango,* or construction bid-rigging case, which reportedly involved 66 construction firms (including Taisei, Japan's largest) and as much as $700 million in public contracts. *Dango* is discussed further in chapter 4.

bilateral agreements (see chapter 6) or a broader agreement involving the European Community and perhaps other OECD countries as well.

Restrictions on Foreign Direct Investment

One explanation for the small role of manufactured imports in the Japanese economy is that restrictions on foreign direct investment (FDI), both historical legal restrictions and private impediments in the form of oligopolies and the *keiretsu*, have impeded manufactured imports, especially of complex capital goods. For most of the postwar period, the Japanese government discouraged inward FDI. In the early postwar years, this was accomplished mainly through restrictions on converting domestic profits to foreign exchange for repatriation; later an extremely restrictive approval system for FDI served the same purpose.

As a result, FDI in Japan was much lower than in other industrialized countries. Encarnation (1992) reports that in 1960, for example, Japan hosted less US FDI than the Philippines, or than any of the eight largest Latin American economies. Mason (1992) likens Japanese policy at this time to a "screen door," designed to encourage inward technology transfer while discouraging inward FDI. Borrus et al. (1986, 96) similarly describe the government's role as that of a doorkeeper, "determining under what conditions capital, technology, and manufactured products enter and leave Japan."

Put in another way, the Japanese government has used its various policy levers to bargain with foreigners from a monopsonist's standpoint. Goto and Wakasugi (1988, 190) provide the example of royalty payments on the importation of a particular Austrian steel production technology: these payments were "held down to 1 cent per ton for Japan through an agreement between MITI [the Japanese Ministry of International Trade and Industry] and the industry, while the U.S. firms paid up to 35 cents per ton for the import of the same technology." What is common in the cases of steel, numerically controlled machine tools, microelectronics, and now possibly aircraft is a pattern of selective protection, strict regulation of inward FDI and technology transfer, and preferential tax treatment and access to capital until the industry has achieved international competitiveness. Rosovsky (1985) has called this pattern "the denial of the profits of innovation."

In 1967, Japan began liberalizing its investment regime, and in 1980 the remaining legal obstacles were removed. Nonetheless, foreign firms continue to play an extraordinarily minor role in the Japanese economy (table 3.3). Strikingly, whereas in bilateral comparisons US and Japanese multinational firms exhibit similar behavior in third-country markets, their positions in each other's markets are very different (table 3.4). Even though the US firms' global stock of foreign investment is larger than Japanese firms', their stake in the Japanese market is only a quarter that

Table 3.4   United States and Japan: stock of foreign direct investment, 1991 (billions of dollars at book value)

United States	
Outward foreign direct investment stock, 1991	
All countries	450.2
In Japan	22.9
Inward foreign direct investment stock, 1991	
All countries	407.6
From Japan	86.7
Japan[a]	
Outward foreign direct investment stock	
All countries	352.4
In United States	148.6

a. The Japanese data are on an "approvals" basis and will overstate the actual stock of foreign direct investment because they included projects approved but not actually undertaken, and they do not include remittances back to Japan. Data are for fiscal 1991 (April to March).

Sources: Survey of Current Business, August 1992; Japan, Ministry of Finance.

of Japanese firms in the United States, according to US data; Japanese MOF data show the US firms' relative share to be even smaller.

Foreign direct investment through merger, or acquisition of existing firms, is limited by the extensive cross-holding of shares through the main bank and *keiretsu* systems. A market for corporate control does not exist in Japan in the same way it does in the US. An alternative to investment through merger and acquisition would be through the establishment of new greenfield operations. In a 1991 survey of US firms operating in Japan, conducted for the American Chamber of Commerce in Japan by the consulting firm A. T. Kearney, respondents cited the high cost of doing business in Japan (largely high land costs), difficulties in locating and hiring qualified personnel, general complexities in doing business in Japan, multitiered distribution systems, exclusionary business practices by the *keiretsu*, and bureaucratic practices that discriminate against foreign firms as the main barriers to investment. The respondents indicated that some problems on the US side—management short-termism, inability or unwillingness to modify products for the Japanese market, and quality problems—also impeded the US presence in Japan.

Encarnation (1992) argues that the relatively small presence of US firms in the Japanese market, and the atypical scarcity of majority subsidiaries in particular, mean that US firms are denied in Japan the same degree of managerial control, especially over sourcing, that they enjoy in other developed-country markets.[25] As a result, US firms are disadvantaged

---

25. Indeed, Encarnation reports that the share of US intrafirm manufactured exports to Japan in all manufactured exports is only approximately half as large as in other industrialized-country markets.

Table 3.5   Mergers and acquisitions involving Japanese firms, 1988–92

Year	Total	Japanese firms acquiring Japanese firms	Japanese firms acquiring non-Japanese firms	Non-Japanese firms acquiring Japanese firms
1988	438	161	270	7
1989	590	172	408	10
1990	801	341	450	10
1991	655	386	257	12
1992	584	387	165	32

Source: Nomura Research Institute, *Quarterly Economic Review*, various issues.

in the Japanese market by being unable to implement the full range of management strategies that are available in other markets, and that are, indeed, available to Japanese firms in the US market. This asymmetry has facilitated the creation of bastion markets in Japan, and thus aided Japanese firms in international competition in industries characterized by scale economies or significant learning curves (i.e., any industry where the relevant portion of the long-run marginal cost curve slopes downward).

There is some evidence that this situation is easing. With the collapse of the Japanese bubble economy, the number of takeovers of Japanese firms by foreigners increased dramatically in 1992, although this was from a low base and remained far below the number of Japanese takeovers of foreign firms that same year (table 3.5).

Indeed, in the American Chamber of Commerce in Japan survey most respondents thought that the climate for trade and investment in Japan was improving. A bare majority (52 percent) indicated that the current climate was favorable or somewhat favorable, while 18 percent thought that it was unfavorable. Fifty-five percent of the respondents thought that the investment climate had improved in the previous five years, while 40 percent saw no change, and 5 percent sensed deterioration. Two-thirds of the respondents expected continued improvement in the trade and investment climate over the next five years.

The improvement in the investment climate may be in part due to policies of the Japanese government. The government has expanded public financial institution lending and loan guarantees for inward FDI and has introduced tax incentives for foreign investors.[26] MITI has established an organization to offer consulting services to firms investing in

---

26. Subsidiaries of US firms receiving Japan Development Bank loans have included Mead Paperboard Japan KK, GE Plastics Japan Ltd., Corning Japan KK, LSI Logic KK, Procter & Gamble Far East Inc., Applied Materials Japan Inc., and AMP (Japan) Ltd. The new tax law permits foreign affiliates to carry forward losses in the first three years to be set off against taxable income for seven years—two years longer than the carryforward period allowed to Japanese companies.

Japan. The Japan Federation of Economic Organizations (Keidanren), the most influential business lobby, fearing an increase in investment-related tensions, has called for the government to go further and expand the scope of tax breaks and public financial institution loans for inward FDI. The Keidanren has also proposed the liberalization of legal services to facilitate inward FDI.

Ultimately, this issue is of considerable economic and political importance. The fact that foreign firms have a relatively small presence in the Japanese market means that there is relatively weak political pressure in the home countries of multinationals to moderate their governments' policies toward Japan. Japan, in essence, holds few hostages. The development of a more symmetrical set of interdependencies would undoubtedly temper economic conflict between Japan and other countries.

This would be encouraged by expanding existing programs to increase FDI as well as adopting the Keidanren proposal to liberalize legal services. (This would have the additional benefit of resolving the sectoral conflict over the provision of legal services and could also dovetail with product liability reform.) Trade policy and competition policy reforms would also tend to increase inward FDI.

Reforms to reduce the costs of entering the Japanese market should also be considered. These could include measures to facilitate foreign investment in existing firms (raised by the US side during the Structural Impediments Initiative talks) to improve shareholders' rights and reduce the ability of *keiretsu* from discouraging foreign investment through cross-shareholding. Indeed, this may be a particularly propitious time to act in light of depressed stock prices in Japan.

As for greenfield investments, although the difficulties new entrants face in recruiting skilled workers are probably beyond the government's purview, the high cost of land is not. As analyzed in detail by Balassa and Noland (1988) the natural scarcity of land in Japan is greatly exacerbated by land use policies that discourage its rational use. The primary beneficiaries of land use reforms would undoubtedly be residents of Japan. The impact on prospective foreign investors should not be overlooked, however.

Intellectual Property Rights

An alternative means of entering a foreign market, besides exporting or investing in subsidiaries, is to license or lease firm-specific assets to producers in that market. This strategy is contingent on the existence of an enforceable system of intellectual property rights. Intellectual property consists of valuable but intangible assets such as inventions, technology, technical information, brand names, identifying symbols, and distinctive styling of products. Property rights to these assets are usually protected by exclusive and enforceable patents, design registrations, trademarks and service marks, copyright laws, and trade secret laws.

Intellectual property rights disputes between the United States and Japan fall into two interrelated categories. In the first category are disputes arising from systemic differences in the two countries' intellectual property regimes. The second category of disputes stem from simple conflicts over property rights, driven by technological rivalry.

The United States has a "first-to-invent" patent system. This system is centered on the notion that the economy as a whole benefits from protecting the property rights of innovative entrepreneurial inventors. Patents are granted on the basis of which claimant is first to invent (rather than first to file an application), and technical information supporting the patent application is guarded closely during review. Foreigners have complained that the evidentiary rules effectively discriminate against foreign inventors (MITI 1993).

In contrast, Japan (along with nearly every other country in the world) has a "first-to-file" system. Under these rules, the patent is awarded to the applicant who files first, regardless of who actually made the innovative discovery. This system is alleged to give an advantage to large firms, which can more easily routinize and finance the patent application procedure. Unlike under the "first-to-invent" system, information on the application is more readily available, and indeed, one can argue that the system is essentially designed to accelerate the diffusion of technological advance throughout the economy.

Japan's intellectual property rules have been widely criticized and were taken up in the context of the SII negotiations. The major complaint of foreign firms is that the Japanese implementation of its "first-to-file" system is inadequate. The average time required for a patent to be granted is five to six years, with some applications taking a decade or more. (In the United States the average time is 19 months.) Reasons for the long delays include too few inspectors, the practice of allowing firms to file oppositions to the patent before it is granted, and the requirement that applications be filed in Japanese (but with later correction of translation errors not permitted).[27] As a result of the protracted process, Japanese firms can gain access to information on foreign technological developments before foreign firms have been able to secure their property rights. Moreover, since protection is granted from the date of filing, the

---

27. The United States has 1,500 patent office officials, who handle 150,000 annual applications; the European Community has 1,300 officials to handle 50,000 applications; Japan, meanwhile, has fewer than 1,000 officials, who attempt to process 720,000 applications yearly. Japan is virtually alone among developed countries in allowing pregrant challenges to patents; the European Community discontinued this process because it was being abused by firms to delay the issuance of patents to rivals.

delays can substantially erode the period of exclusivity that the innovating firm eventually enjoys.[28]

Trademark registration is similarly slow. In the United States, the right to a trademark belongs to the firm that first used it commercially, but in Japan, foreign trademarks may be registered by Japanese firms to preempt their subsequent introduction by the originating firm.[29] Until recently, foreign firms have also encountered difficulty in securing copyright protection for recorded material.

Intertwined with these systemic problems are patent infringement cases (table 3.6). Some of these cases would have undoubtedly occurred under any policy regime, but their number and prominence serve to highlight the inadequacies in the Japanese and the US systems. In the United States, legislation sponsored by Sen. Dennis DeConcini (D-AZ) would move the United States to the first-to-file system, open patent applications to public inspection after 18 months, and change the term of the patent from 17 years from the date of issue to 20 years from the date of filing. In Japan, a centralized photocopying royalty clearinghouse has been established, trade secret protection was formalized in 1990, copyright service marks were introduced in April 1992, and new rules have strengthened property rights in sound recordings.[30] A proposal

---

28. In one case, it took Corning Glass Works (now Corning Inc.) nearly a decade to obtain a fiber optics patent. In the meantime, Japanese rivals developed competing products. Corning sued, and Sumitomo Electric eventually paid the US firm $25 million in an out-of-court settlement.

The most celebrated case, however, is the Texas Instruments Inc. (TI) Kilby '275 patent for the integrated circuit. TI applied in Japan for the patent in 1960, but it was not granted until 1989—nearly three decades later! TI subsequently engaged nearly 30 firms in negotiations over licensing and royalty fees, which are estimated to now bring the company $250 million annually. The firm is still locked in a suit with Fujitsu Ltd. over whether to interpret the Kilby '275 patent narrowly or broadly.

29. Balassa and Noland (1988) give several examples of this practice. A more recent (1991) example comes from Texas, where, upon liberalization of the Japanese ice cream market, a Japanese firm tried to preemptively register the trademark of the locally beloved Blue Bell Dairy. The attempt was foiled by the high-level political intervention of then-Sen. Lloyd Bentsen (D-TX).

30. On 1 January 1992 changes in Japan's copyright law went into effect that extend copyright protection for recorded materials to 50 years and protect foreign recordings created between 1968 and 1978, which had previously not been protected. (Japan refused to extend copyright protection to recordings made prior to 1968, when Japan introduced its first copyright law for sound recordings. As a consequence, recordings by such popular foreign artists as Frank Sinatra and Elvis Presley remain largely unprotected. Bruce Springsteen and the surviving Sex Pistols should be pleased, though.)

A loophole in the earlier Japanese law permitted unrestricted reproduction of foreign recordings. A booming business in renting compact discs for taping developed, with foreign recordings (on which no copyright fees were paid) accounting for about 30 percent of the market. Foreign observers estimate that the rental shops cost foreign firms around $1 billion annually in lost sales. The recent accord allows foreign firms to prohibit the

has been endorsed by the Japan Patent Office to create a global arbitration panel under the auspices of the World Intellectual Property Organization.

As a consequence of these reforms Japan has been moved from the list of "Special 301" intellectual property rights "priority watch countries" where it had been since 1989, to the lower-priority "watch country" list in April 1993. In light of past difficulties in obtaining intellectual property rights in a timely fashion and securing their enforcement in Japan, it remains to be seen whether these new legal rights will represent a major step forward. A key may be the changing interests of major Japanese firms: as these firms become relatively more important innovators, their own political interests will increasingly lie with strengthening intellectual property rights protection. It would be desirable for the United States and Japan to move closer to the European Community standard in this area. This would involve bringing the United States into conformity with the first-to-file patent system used elsewhere in the world. For Japan it would mean speeding up the patent approval process (as it pledged in the SII negotiations) and discontinuing the practice of allowing pregrant patent challenges.

US-Japan Rivalry in High Technology

Patent infringement disputes are only one indicator of the increasing US-Japan rivalry in high-technology sectors, which account for an increasing share of bilateral trade. Research by Balassa and Noland (1989) indicated that both the United States and Japan had comparative advantage in R&D-intensive activities, a result confirmed for Japan by Grossman (1990). Indicators of revealed comparative advantage in high-technology products are shown in figures 3.3 and 3.4. As in the broad sectors shown in figures 3.1 and 3.2, the pattern of Japanese revealed comparative advantage displays a "spikier" pattern than that of the United States: Japanese revealed comparative advantage is high in office equipment and in telecommunications equipment, but low in aircraft, pharmaceuticals, agricultural chemicals, and steam engines and turbines. US revealed comparative advantage, in contrast, is by far the highest in aircraft, followed by medical equipment, and steam engines and turbines.

One possible explanation of this apparently complementary pattern of high-technology specialization is that the United States tends to specialize in science-based industries, which are dominated by large firms capable of financing the basic research necessary for innovation, while Japan fares better in industries in which research is more product-specific

---

rental of their recordings for a period of up to one year from date of release and entitles them to remuneration for rentals thereafter.

Table 3.6 Recent patent disputes between US and Japanese companies

Year	Complainant	Defendant(s)	Dispute	Outcome
1991	Genentech	Toyobo	Pharmaceutical patent infringement	Japanese court ruled in favor of Genentech.
1991	Iowa State University	Several Japanese electronics firms	Fax machine patent infringement	Unresolved.
1992	Wang Laboratories	Numerous Japanese electronics firms	Microprocessor patent infringement	Thirty-four firms signed licensing agreements with Wang. Wang-Mitsubishi dispute unresolved.
1992	Gilbert Hyatt	Several Japanese electronics firms	Microprocessor patent infringement	Unresolved.
1992	Honeywell	Minolta	Autofocus patents infringement	US court ruled in favor of Honeywell. Minolta agreed to pay Honeywell $127.5 million to license technology (including $96.35 million in damages ordered by the court).
1992	Honeywell	Eastman Kodak, Konica, Kyocera, Canon, Nikon, Matsushita, and Premier	Autofocus patents infringement	Defendants agreed to pay Honeywell $124.1 million to license technology.
1992	Honeywell	Olympus, Asahi, and Ricoh	Autofocus patents infringement	Unresolved.
1992	Loral Fairchild	Several Japanese electronics firms	Camcorder patents infringement	Unresolved.
1992	Corning	Sumitomo Electric	Optical fiber patent infringement	US court ruled in favor of Corning; Sumitomo agreed to pay Corning $25 million.
1992	Jan Coyle	Sega	Video game patent infringement	US court ruled Sega must pay Coyle $12 million. (Nintendo and Atari had previously settled out of court for undisclosed terms.)

Year	Company	Defendant	Issue	Details
1992	Texas Instruments	Sharp, Ricoh	Kilby '275 patent infringement	Sharp and Ricoh joined Toshiba, NEC, Oki Electric, Matsushita, Hitachi, and Samsung of Korea in reaching licensing agreements with TI. Suit and countersuit between TI and Fujitsu remain unresolved.
1993	International Business Machines	Kyocera	Unauthorized use of basic input-output system (BIOS)	IBM demanded $149.6 million in first civil action of this type filed in Japan; currently unresolved.

Source: press reports

Figure 3.3 Japan: revealed comparative advantage in high-technology exports, 1971–90

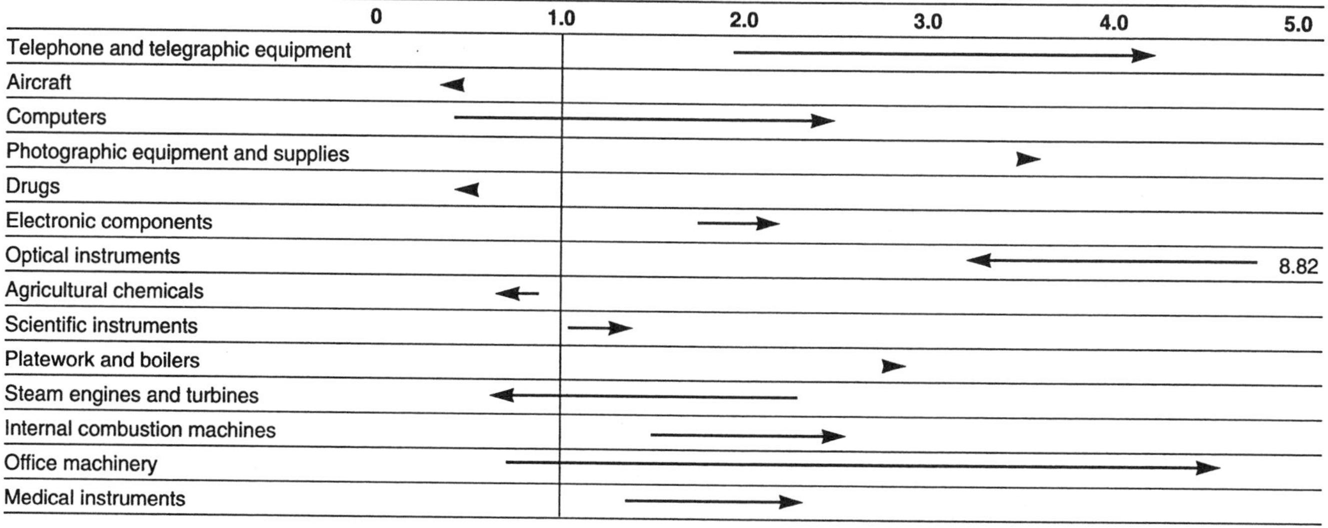

	0	1.0	2.0	3.0	4.0	5.0

Telephone and telegraphic equipment

Aircraft

Computers

Photographic equipment and supplies

Drugs

Electronic components

Optical instruments — 8.82

Agricultural chemicals

Scientific instruments

Platework and boilers

Steam engines and turbines

Internal combustion machines

Office machinery

Medical instruments

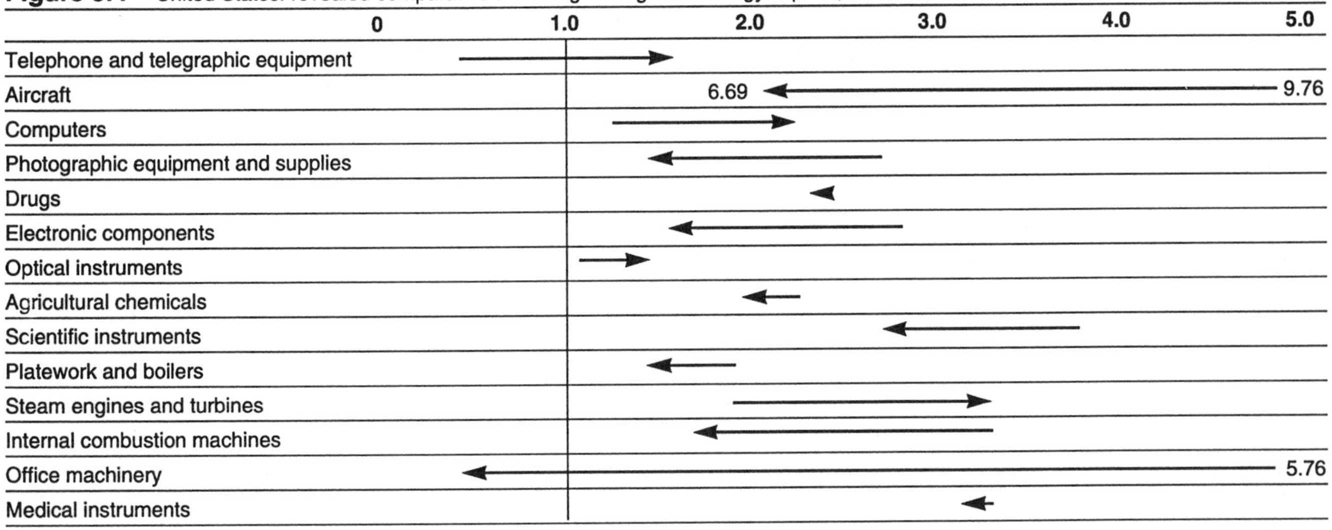

Figure 3.4 United States: revealed comparative advantage in high-technology exports, 1971–90

and the management of research activities is more important (Kodama 1986). This view has received some support from research by Noland (1992d), who disaggregated R&D activities into basic, developmental, and applied components. He found that Japan has a comparative disadvantage in basic R&D-intensive activities, but a comparative advantage in developmental R&D-intensive activities, and an even larger comparative advantage in applied R&D-intensive activities. These results reinforce the notion that at present Japanese comparative advantage lies in applied, rather than fundamental, research activities. This has obvious implications for technology policy, since the primary source of US comparative advantage (the university system) is relatively open, while the primary locus of Japanese activities (private firms) is relatively closed, creating an asymmetry. Current bilateral science policies attempt to increase US researchers' access to Japanese corporate laboratories; private corporate alliances and additional foreign direct investment may be more efficient complementary strategies.

Noland also found that public funding of R&D activities in a particular industry is strongly associated with large net exports in that industry. Indeed, the effect was so large as to suggest that the public R&D variable might be capturing the influence of not only public R&D subsidies, but other types of public support for high-technology industries as well. In addition to the subsidies discussed earlier, certain tax and budgetary provisions have been used to promote high-technology sectors in Japan. There are special depreciation rules for the purchase of numerically controlled machine tools, computers and terminals, computer-aided design equipment, and industrial robots. Additional tax incentives exist for the use of these products by small businesses, although the amounts of funds involved appear to be relatively small. Other special tax provisions exist for the software industry.[31] The Japanese computer and robotics industries have also been assisted by Japan Development Bank and Small Business Finance Corporation funding, including the establishment of special corporations to encourage the leasing of Japanese computers and robots, especially by small firms.[32]

The Japanese government has also promoted high-technology sectors through direct subsidies to R&D activities, as mentioned earlier, as well

---

31. The tax benefits are not contingent on the origin of the purchased software or equipment, so the impact of these provisions has been to expand the Japanese market for these products, not to assist Japanese producers per se. Likewise, special provisions that allow computer manufacturers to deduct expected losses on the return of equipment offered to users on a trial basis do not discriminate by origin, and thus in principle could be used by domestic manufacturers, local subsidiaries of foreign manufacturers, or importers.

32. Unlike the tax provisions, which are justified on the grounds of promoting the diffusion of new technologies and do not discriminate between domestic and foreign products, the leasing schemes specifically apply to Japanese-made equipment. The amounts of money involved appear relatively small, however.

as special tax deductions for R&D costs, and reduced interest burdens through the provision of low-interest loans by public financial institutions. Tax preferences are provided through a variety of schemes. The most important channel in quantitative terms, however, has been the system of research contracts on large-scale industrial technology R&D, established in 1966. Of particular significance were subsidies to promote the development of computers in the 1970s, and research contracts on so-called next-generation industrial technology, including new materials, biotechnology, and new electronic devices, in the 1980s.

Private R&D also has been subsidized through the provision of low-interest loans by public financial institutions for "financing the development of new technology." Private R&D activities are provided indirect support by a number of government-supported institutions. These include national and public research institutes, private nonprofit research organizations, special public corporations, and the mining and manufacturing technology research associations such as the Very Large Scale Integration Research Association.

In quantitative terms, the direct subsidies are the most important component of government R&D support, running about twice as large as the tax provisions in recent years. Implicit subsidies through the provision of low-interest-rate loans have been relatively unimportant. Government support for research organizations is of approximately the same scope as direct subsidies. Altogether, the government finances around 20 percent of R&D expenditures.[33]

The United States also pursues policies designed to support its high-technology sectors. Such policies have included special tax credits for R&D expenditures, as well as direct federal government expenditures on R&D, through contractual research, the system of national laboratories, and industry-administered federally funded R&D centers such as the semiconductor R&D consortium Sematech. Altogether, the federal government accounts for 44 percent of all R&D expenditures in the United States, more than double the figure for Japan. Most of this funding is carried out through the Defense Department, which accounts for 53 percent of federal-government R&D expenditures, followed by the Department of Health and Human Services (14 percent), the National Aeronautics and Space Administration (12 percent), and the Department of Energy, which maintains the nation's nuclear weapons laboratories (11 percent). (All figures are for 1991 and come from the National Science Board, *Science and Engineering Indicators*.)

---

33. Assessing the sectoral pattern of this support is difficult. Indirect subsidies and special R&D tax deductions are reported only at the aggregate level. The amount of sector-specific indirect support through the research associations is difficult to ascertain, partly because individual associations frequently encompass more than one sector, and partly because the budgets of these organizations include private as well as government funding.

Table 3.7 **United States, Japan, and Germany: central-government R&D appropriations by mission, 1988** (percentage of total R&D budget)

	US	Japan	Germany
Industrial development	0.2	4.8	14.5
Defense	65.6	4.8	12.5
Health	12.8	2.6	3.6
Energy	3.9	22.3	7.8
Advancement of research	3.8	7.6	13.3
General university funds	0.0	43.7	30.8
Infrastructure[a]	1.8	1.8	1.8
Agriculture	2.0	3.9	2.1
Civil space	7.4	6.1	5.4
Environmental protection	0.5	0.5	3.4
Other[b]	1.8	2.0	4.8

a. Includes transport, telecommunications, and rural and urban planning.
b. Includes social development and services, earth and atmosphere, and R&D not elsewhere classified.

Source: Council on Competitiveness (1991).

As may be inferred from these figures, federal support for R&D is heavily oriented toward defense-related work, which accounts for more than 60 percent of the federal R&D budget. And virtually all incremental federal R&D expenditures during the 1980s went into defense-related R&D. In this regard, the pattern of governmental support for R&D is far different in the United States than in its major industrial competitors (table 3.7), with industrial development receiving a relatively small share. Moreover, because as Noland (1992d) showed, R&D expenditures tend to have long-lasting, persistent effects on industrial composition, the pattern of economic expenditures in the past could be expected to have significant ramifications well into the future.

Lastly, the greater prominence of governmental support for R&D has contributed to the development of a more easily accessible, less proprietary system of R&D activities in the United States, with its characteristic emphasis on university research and training, labor mobility, and small entrepreneurial firms in comparison with Japan. R&D in Japan tends to be carried out by large corporations with their tradition of lifetime employment; as a result, knowledge generated within the organization tends to stay there. This, in turn, has led to concerns in the United States about "leakage" of technological advances abroad; much of this concern has focused on the acquisition by foreign firms of small US high-technology firms.[34]

Indeed, cross-investment between the United States and Japan in R&D activities has grown considerably in recent years. According to Graham

---

34. The US and Japanese governments have also begun negotiations to increase the access of American researchers to Japanese corporate laboratories.

(1992), total annual R&D undertaken by the US affiliates of Japanese firms rose from $300 million in 1987 to approximately $750 million in 1989, the most recent year for which data are available. This accounted for 1.1 percent of total company-funded R&D in the United States in that year. Graham estimates that perhaps one-third of the increase in expenditures by foreign-owned affiliates was due to the establishment of new operations or the expansion of existing operations, and around two-thirds was due to takeovers of existing domestically owned operations. Survey evidence suggests that the main Japanese motivations are to develop products for the US market and to tap into the US basic science base (Peters 1993).

Graham argues that expansion of Japanese R&D operations in the United States is probably beneficial to the extent that it adds to the amount of R&D activity performed in the United States. The takeovers are harder to justify, in that they simply represent a change in ownership without any addition to R&D activity; hence the "leakage" concern may be more relevant in this case. Mowery and Teece (1992) point out that the main cause of these takeovers is that small entrepreneurial firms in the United States lack access to capital; hence the obvious solution is to pursue policies to enhance that access. At the same time, Mowery and Teece note that the relevant externalities may be very local in scope: they point to the persistence of high-technology activities in areas such as California's Silicon Valley, Massachusetts's Route 128, and North Carolina's Research Triangle Park, and question the ability of international capital flows to displace such concentrations of activity.

Conversely, a report prepared for the National Science Foundation (Bloom 1991) estimates that US firms operating in Japan employ 5,200 scientists and engineers and spend more than $500 million annually on R&D operations in Japan.[35] These firms do not appear to have encountered significant barriers to making R&D investments in Japan, and a large majority express the belief that the investments are worthwhile and intend to expand them in the next five years.

Survey responses indicate that the main motivations of US firms doing R&D in Japan are to develop new products for Asian markets and to play a more aggressive role in assimilating Japanese manufacturing and product technology and transferring this expertise back to the United States. In light of these motivations, it is unlikely that R&D activities in Japan substitute for investment that would have been made in the United States.

A number of groups have identified certain "critical technologies" that they believe will drive technological and economic development in the

---

35. Somewhat different figures are reported by Mowery and Teece (1992), who refer to a MITI study that in 1990 identified 83 R&D laboratories operated by US firms in Japan at a cost of nearly ¥ 83.5 billion, or approximately $700 million, per year.

future. There appears to be a considerable overlap in these lists (e.g., Council on Competitiveness 1991, National Critical Technologies Panel 1991). Whether this overlap reflects genuine scientific consensus or merely authorial risk aversion is unknown, nor is it possible to assess the predictive power of these lists. Nevertheless, both groups have attempted to evaluate US competitiveness in these fields.[36] The Japanese share of patents granted in the United States has risen in all high-technology sectors (Mowery and Teece 1992, table 1), and Japanese firms receive more US patents than do firms of any other foreign country (Mowery and Teece 1992, table 2). Although Japanese productivity tends to be lower than in the United States in most manufacturing industries, total factor productivity has been rising at a more rapid rate (Fecher and Perelman 1992). This suggests that the Japanese investment in R&D is indeed paying off.

An issue distinct from relative technological capability is the access of American firms to high-technology products produced in Japan. The US General Accounting Office (1991) surveyed 59 companies in the semiconductor, semiconductor materials, and computer industries as well as two government research laboratories. Fifty-two respondents (85 percent) said they purchased state-of-the-art products from Japanese suppliers. Around half of these firms did not report any problems. Twenty-two (42 percent) provided specific examples of instances in which Japanese suppliers had refused orders or delayed delivery for more than six months. A number of firms indicated that the implicit costs, in terms of delays or inability to bring products to market, were significant. Seven firms (12 percent) reported being pressured into buying other products in order to obtain the requested product.

US company representatives indicated that the reasons given by their Japanese suppliers for not fulfilling orders were lack of service facilities

---

36. The private-sector Council on Competitiveness classified US commercial (not laboratory) performance in each of the technologies it listed as either strong (US technological superiority), competitive (US performance roughly even with world best), weak (US behind or falling behind world best), or losing badly or lost (US not important or likely to be important). As might be expected, US performance is mixed, with relative strengths in biotechnology, environmental technology, information technology, and propulsion, and relative weakness in electronic components. The report reviewed public policies in the United States, Japan, and Europe and made recommendations for the United States but did not discuss US-Japan rivalries.

Similarly, the Presidential National Critical Technologies Panel identified 22 technologies as critical on the basis of their importance to industrial competitiveness, national defense, energy security, quality of life, improving productivity, and reducing vulnerability. Unlike the Council on Competitiveness, the National Critical Technologies Panel did not publish a succinct evaluation of the US international competitive position in each technology. It did, however, discuss the relative positions of the United States and other countries, and in all 22 technologies Japan was a factor, sometimes leading the United States, sometimes lagging behind.

in the United States and need for product testing. Japanese firms interviewed for the report denied withholding products. US respondents did not believe the Japanese firms' practices to be illegal and did not advocate punitive sanctions.

Several things should be kept in mind when assessing this report. First, both the Council on Competitiveness and the National Critical Technologies Panel have identified the semiconductor industry as one in which the United States lags well behind Japan. Thus, the experience of the semiconductor industry may not be at all representative of the experiences of the US high-technology sector as a whole. Indeed, a survey of Japanese firms in a sector in which US firms are the dominant suppliers might reveal similar problems of access. Second, the cases cited of firms being pressured into purchasing other products dated from 1987 and 1988, when a worldwide shortage of computer chips created a seller's market. The exploitation of market power under such circumstances presumably is not unusual.

Alarm has been expressed that foreign acquisitions, especially Japanese takeovers in the electronics industry, are eroding the US defense industry base and rendering the Pentagon increasingly dependent on foreign firms for important military parts and components.[37] Congress added a provision to the 1988 omnibus trade act intended to respond to these concerns. This provision, commonly known as the Exon-Florio amendment (after its sponsors Sen. J. James Exon [D-NE] and then-Rep. James Florio [D-NJ]), gives the President authority to review foreign acquisitions of US firms and, if a takeover threatens US national security, to block it.

Day-to-day administration of Exon-Florio is handled by the interagency Committee on Foreign Investment in the United States (CFIUS). Since the law's enactment, a number of cases have been subject to formal investigation, and the record with regard to Japanese firms does not appear unusual.[38] Indeed, the most controversial case has been the proposed sale of the missile division of LTV Corp. to the French firm Thom-

---

37. The *cause célébre* was Fujitsu Ltd.'s proposed takeover of Fairchild Industries, at that time a division of Schlumberger NV, which was opposed by the Department of Commerce on national security grounds. The offer was eventually withdrawn. Fairchild was taken over by National Semiconductor Corp. and no longer exists as a separate operation.

38. Some takeovers have been approved without condition; some were approved after foreign firms agreed to certain performance requirements; one required more extensive restructuring before approval (the domestic firm's subsidiary supplying nuclear triggering devices to the Department of Energy was spun off before the acquisition); one proposed takeover was withdrawn; and in the case of China National Aero-Technology Import and Export Corp.'s acquisition of Mamco Manufacturing Co., the President ordered divestment. In the case of Japanese robotics firm Fanuc's offer to take a minority stake (40 percent) in Moore Special Tool Co., the CFIUS investigation was not completed before the original law lapsed (it was later extended), and the Fanuc offer was ultimately withdrawn.

son-CSF. In response to this case, the law was amended in 1992, so that foreign government–controlled firms are prohibited from purchasing US firms meeting certain defense procurement or top-secret information access criteria. The revised statute also makes formal CFIUS investigations mandatory in certain instances and broadens the definition of national security to include the impact on US technological leadership in weapons of mass destruction and involvement by foreign countries in supporting terrorism.

Tactical Implications

This chapter has examined the pattern of trade specialization in the United States and Japan. The United States increasingly specializes in natural resource–based products and high-technology manufactures, while Japan specializes in a broad range of manufactures, with a growing concentration in high technology. Barriers to trade are ubiquitous. In the United States these primarily take the form of transparent border measures that restrict manufactured imports. In Japan, border measures are largely confined to agriculture, while nonborder measures restrict trade in other product areas.

Lee and Roland-Holst (1993) have recently attempted to assess the prospective impact of alternative trade policies in the two countries, using a sophisticated computable general equilibrium model. Their results are quite interesting. Imposition of optimal tariffs on bilateral trade between the United States and Japan would raise welfare in the United States while reducing it in Japan. However, the welfare gains to the United States from bilateral liberalization are much larger than those obtainable though a trade war—nearly nine times as large, in fact. Liberalization is found to be welfare-enhancing for Japan as well.

The problem is one of incentives. Although the United States would gain from unilateral liberalization, it would gain even more from mutual liberalization. Japan as a big country would suffer a terms of trade loss, so it has no independent incentive to reciprocate US actions. The solution to this incentive problem is the threat of market closure by the United States. Since the United States gains regardless of Japan's response, and Japan loses in the case of a trade war, it is in Japan's interest to act cooperatively and engage in mutual liberalization, or, if the United States refuses to liberalize, unilateral liberalization. Even though Japan would suffer a terms of trade loss, it would lose less than if the United States closed its market.

Lee and Roland-Holst are quick to note the stylized nature of their model and the practical difficulty of designing optimal policies. Nonetheless, their work points to two themes that recur in the chapter on sectoral trade issues that follows. First, credible threats of US market closure may be essential in securing any opening of the Japanese market. Second, implementing such a strategy may be problematic for the United States. As soon as the United States begins to formulate a more aggressive policy, the process will become subject to political pressure that may drive the outcome far from the optimal set of tariffs that one would derive from a model such as that of Lee and Roland-Holst. It is to these issues of the sectoral impact of trade impediments and the formation of US policy that we now turn.

4

The Sectoral Impact

The previous chapter examined structural access limitations in the US and especially the Japanese markets. We will now analyze how these problems affect the pattern of trade in primary products, manufacturing, high-technology goods, and services. This analysis is made concrete by examination of the experiences of specific industries: automobiles in manufacturing, a wide range of high-technology electronics, and retailing, construction, and banking and securities in the service area. These case studies are meant to be illustrative, not comprehensive; other sectors in which US-Japan trade conflict occurs are not discussed in detail. The main purpose of the case studies is to flesh out general leitmotifs and themes.

One pattern in particular emerges, most apparently in high-technology and services, in which innovative US firms possessing some competitive advantage encounter a concentrated and regulated Japanese industry. The firms enlist the US government as an ally in their effort to penetrate the barriers they face in the Japanese market. The government adopts a policy of negotiating procedural changes aimed at dismantling the barriers, combined with monitoring of outcomes and threats of retaliation. The Japanese respond by attempting to co-opt the foreign firm or firms, inviting them into the domestic oligopoly, so as to cause minimal disruption to the status quo.

US public policy faces a dilemma at this point. It may no longer be in the interests of the US firms, now that they have joined the cartel, to see it dissolved. Hence, the US government must weigh the gains to these of its firms (in the form of shares of the oligopoly rents) against the potential gains of other US entrants to this market if the cartel is broken up. Essentially the government has three options: it can accept co-optation, go for a voluntary import expansion that opens the market to other foreign firms (albeit still on a limited basis), or attempt to negotiate genuine liberalization. Indeed, this is the crux of the problem that US policymakers face: they must prioritize among the competing demands of numerous industries and identify which policy option—co-optation, voluntary import expansion, or liberalization—to pursue.[1]

Primary Products

Domestic agricultural production in Japan is protected from foreign competition through tariffs, quotas, state trading monopolies, and, when formal barriers are insufficient, informal barriers to imports.[2] The degree of distortion in product markets due to these policies can be summarized in terms of producer subsidy-equivalents (PSEs) and consumer subsidy-equivalents (CSEs), which measure the overall price wedge created by border and domestic policy interventions. Although distortions in the Japanese market were of similar magnitude to those observed in the European Community as late as 1960, the heavy reliance on quantitative restrictions in Japan has increasingly distorted the market over time, with Japanese agricultural PSEs and CSEs now among the highest in the world. As seen in the first column of table 4.1, government policies generate more than two-thirds of agricultural incomes, at a cost to Japanese consumers of more than $1,000 annually for a family of four.

Moreover, Japan, unlike the small European countries that maintain comparably distorting agricultural policies, is a large country whose agricultural policies could reasonably be expected to have significant effects on world trade. Table 4.2 reports results from two multicountry, multiproduct partial equilibrium models of world agriculture trade based on mid-1980s data (Anderson and Tyers 1987, Roningen and Dixit 1991).

---

1. This problem of disentangling national and firm interests is a subtle example of the phenomenon of "directly unproductive profit-seeking activities," originally analyzed in the pioneering work of Bhagwati (1982) and Krueger (1974).

2. Until 1988, the quotas covered 22 products, while trade in 6 more was monopolized by official or quasi-official organs. In 1987, the United States brought a complaint to the General Agreement on Tariffs and Trade (GATT) about 12 of these quotas; the following year a GATT panel ruled that 10 of the 12 were fundamentally at odds with Japan's commitments under the GATT. Japan acceded to the panel ruling and agreed to a liberalization schedule involving the phaseout of the quotas and their replacement with high tariffs, to be reduced over time. Japan subsequently acquiesced to US demands to eliminate its beef and citrus quotas, which were similarly replaced with high tariffs. US beef exports, in response, have nearly doubled from $531 million in 1987 to more than $1 billion in 1992. Citrus exports rose from $280 million in 1987 to $388 million in 1992. See Hillman and Rothenberg (1988, 68–69) for examples of Japanese informal barriers to trade in agriculture.

Table 4.1 Agricultural producer and consumer subsidy-equivalents in selected industrialized countries, 1990

Country	Producer subsidy-equivalents		Consumer subsidy-equivalents	
	Percentages[a]	Billions of dollars	Percentages[b]	Billions of dollars
Australia	11	1.3	8	0.4
Austria	46	2.4	45	2.2
Canada	41	6.5	26	3.5
European Community	48	81.6	41	63.8
Finland	72	5.3	71	3.5
Japan	**68**	**30.9**	**48**	**32.8**
New Zealand	5	0.2	7	0.1
Norway	77	3.1	64	1.7
Sweden	59	3.4	63	2.8
Switzerland	78	5.0	56	5.5
United States	**30**	**35.9**	**19**	**19.3**

a. Percentages of total producer incomes accounted for by government policy.
b. Percentages of total consumer expenditures accounted for by government policy.

Source: Organization for Economic Cooperation and Development (1991).

According to these results, liberalization of Japanese agricultural policies could have a large impact on world prices and trade volumes in a number of specific product areas, including rice, beef, and pork. The potential impact on the trade balances of Japan and its trading partners is reported in table 4.3. Working from a mid-1980s base, these models suggest that complete agricultural liberalization would lead to a fall in Japan's agricultural trade balance of about $6 billion to $7 billion. (Japan's agricultural trade deficit in 1987 was nearly $21 billion.) According to the models summarized in table 4.3, a major beneficiary would be the United States, whose agricultural net exports could rise between $1.3 billion and $4.6 billion annually. Applying these results to 1992 data and adjusting for sectors such as beef and citrus that have been liberalized, the potential gain to the United States would be on the order of $1.2 billion to $5.9 billion.

Table 4.4 summarizes the results of a general equilibrium study of Japanese agricultural liberalization, again calibrated to mid-1980s data (Vincent 1988). The model was employed under two alternative sets of assumptions. In scenario A, nominal wages and domestic demand were fixed, and the trade balance was assumed to adjust; in scenario B, wages and domestic demand were assumed to adjust to maintain a fixed trade balance. These simulations illustrate the important point that, although agricultural liberalization would generate increased agricultural imports, it is also likely to be accompanied by increases in nonagricultural exports as resources move into the manufacturing sector.[3]

---

3. It should be noted, however, that another general equilibrium model of Japanese agriculture calibrated to 1980 data generated a 6 percent increase in agricultural imports and no apparent rise in nonagricultural exports (Ichioka and Tachibanaki 1989).

Table 4.2 Alternative estimates of the impact of complete Japanese agricultural liberalization on world trade

	Beef	Pork	Dairy	Wheat	Coarse grains	Rice	Sugar	All
Change in world prices (percentages)								
Anderson and Tyers	10.0	4.0	10.0	2.0	1.0	6.0	2.0	
Roningen and Dixit	1.8	2.3	4.5	2.5	0.6	19.6	6.4	3.6
Change in world trade volumes (percentages)								
Anderson and Tyers	40.0	30.0	18.0	1.0	−3.0	12.0	1.0	
Roningen and Dixit	7.0	38.0	5.0	1.0	−4.0	40.0	7.0	19.0
Change in Japanese net exports								
Anderson and Tyers (percentage of total volume)	−3.4	−2.4	−14.5	0.5	6.2	−4.2	−0.5	
Roningen and Dixit (billions of dollars)	−0.9	−1.5	−0.7	−0.2	0.3	−2.3	−0.2	−5.9

Sources: Anderson and Tyers (1987), Roningen and Dixit (1991).

Table 4.3   Alternative estimates of the impact of complete Japanese agricultural liberalization on Japanese and partner-country trade balances

Study	United States	Japan	European Community	Australia	New Zealand	Canada	Less developed countries
Anderson and Tyers[a]	4.6	−6.5[b]	0.7	0.4	0.4	n.a.	0.3[c]
Roningen and Dixit[d]	1.3	−5.9	1.3	0.3	0.2	0.2	2.0

a. In billions of 1985 dollars.
b. Calculated as the sum of foreign exchange losses to trading partners.
c. Refers to Thailand only.
d. In billions of 1986–87 dollars.

Sources: Anderson and Tyers (1987), Roningen and Dixit (1991).

Table 4.4   Projected general equilibrium effects of complete Japanese agricultural liberalization[a] (percentage changes)

	Scenario A	Scenario B
Aggregate exports	3.2	6.1
Major exports		
Chemicals	19.3	26.2
Machinery	2.1	5.0
Transport equipment	2.2	4.7
Aggregate imports	5.4	5.6
Agricultural crops	93.5	93.1
Livestock and meat	22.6	21.1
Other food	−4.5	−7.0
Mining	0.3	0.9
Oil	0.0	0.7

a. In scenario A, nominal wages and real domestic aggregate demand are assumed to remain fixed, and the trade balance adjusts in response to liberalization; in scenario B, the trade balance is assumed to remain fixed, and nominal wages and real domestic aggregate demand adjustment.

Source: Vincent (1988).

All of these results should be viewed as benchmarks of the potential stakes involved in Japanese agricultural liberalization, not precise predictions of any likely eventuality. No plans under consideration either in multilateral or bilateral forums would involve complete liberalizations such as those modeled in this research. Nevertheless, these studies do point out that the impact on the rest of the world economy of liberalization in Japanese agriculture could be quite large.[4]

---

4. As noted in chapter 3, the US also maintains agricultural trade barriers in goods such as sugar, dairy products, and peanuts. These are inconsequential in the context of US-Japan trade.

Similarly large trade barriers exist in other primary products. US fish products exports are subject to quotas in 12 categories, covering about one-quarter of all US fish exports to Japan. Wood products exports are impeded by escalating tariffs and a variety of regulatory barriers and standards, testing, and certification requirements. In the fuels sector, an import quota on coal was eliminated in 1992, although Japan continues to provide subsidies to domestic producers. Petroleum imports are subject to a tariff-quota and a prior confirmation system, and Sazanami et al. (1993) estimate that the tariff-equivalent for gasoline is 489 percent. Verleger (1993) calculates the annual cost of protectionism in the petroleum sector to Japanese consumers to be $19.2 billion, or more than $600 annually for a family of four. The United States, which used to maintain tight import controls, now imposes *export* controls in this sector: US law bans the exportation of Alaskan oil, a portion of which might otherwise be shipped to Japan.

Manufactures

Trade disputes between the United States and Japan in primary products strongly reflect the fact that the United States has an overwhelming comparative advantage in these sectors relative to Japan. In manufactures the situation is different. In the past, trade disputes have involved both Japanese penetration of declining manufacturing industries in the United States (e.g., the textile wrangle of the 1960s) and problems encountered by US firms seeking to penetrate Japanese industries characterized by concentration and public targeting (e.g., computers). However, with Japan's rapid accumulation of physical and human capital, detailed in the previous chapter, Japanese comparative advantage has rapidly shifted to more capital- and technology-intensive sectors. As a consequence, the old labor-intensive sector disputes have dropped off the agenda, to be replaced by conflicts in more sophisticated manufacturing sectors such as steel (now declining as a bilateral issue), machine tools, and automobiles. At the same time, the United States faces a range of access problems in high technology. In this sense, the issues in the automobile sector, the most important of these industries in terms of sheer trade volume, are typical of the import-competing sectors, while access problems in sophisticated electronics are representative of the issues in high-technology manufacturing. We now take up each of these industries in turn.

Automobiles

Background

During the immediate postwar period, the US automobile industry was characterized by extreme concentration, with the so-called Big Three producers—General Motors Corp. (GM), Ford Motor Company, and Chrysler Corp.—accounting for 95 percent of the market. At least as far as GM, the largest of these firms, was concerned, this situation arguably discouraged innovation, as further significant growth in market share might well be blocked by antitrust authorities. To paraphrase Nobel Prize winner Sir John R. Hicks, American producers led the quiet lives of oligopolists.

The situation in Japan evolved quite differently. Although small craft producers began manufacturing automobiles soon after the turn of the century, by the late 1920s the market was dominated by GM and Ford. The military government introduced legislation in 1936 to encourage Japanese-owned production, and by 1939 the American firms had been driven out of Japan.

With much of the capital stock destroyed, automobile production at the end of the war was virtually nil, and what production was possible was controlled by US General Headquarters (GHQ) occupation authorities. As GHQ withdrew its direct control over the economy, a debate ensued within the Japanese government over the future direction of the automotive industry. MITI proponents of infant-industry-style nurturing won out.

Subsequent policy toward the industry had two main thrusts. First, local producers were protected from foreign competition through high tariffs, internal taxes that discriminated against imports, restrictions on inward foreign direct investment, and, in the early postwar period, restrictions on the availability of foreign exchange for automobile importation. At the same time that the government protected domestic producers from foreign competition, it supported them through subsidized loans and preferential tax treatment. These policies were maintained to a varying extent through the 1960s (Mutoh 1988).

A large number of firms entered (or reentered) the automobile market, competing largely on equal footing. At Toyota Motor Corp., which had been established in 1937, Eiji Toyoda and Taiichi Ohno began introducing a series of production innovations, including continuous improvement circles (*kaizen*), the just-in-time (*kanban*) delivery system, and *keiretsu*-style relationships with suppliers. These innovations, collectively dubbed "lean production," revolutionized the Japanese automobile industry (Womack et al. 1990).

By the 1960s, MITI had come to regard the Japanese industry as too fragmented, and observing the giant firms in the United States and the experience of Volkswagen in Germany, it attempted to force consolidation of the industry by encouraging mergers and discouraging new entries (Johnson 1982). This policy was a failure, however, and eight producers today maintain a significant presence in automobiles.

Competition and innovation spurred the development of a very efficient domestic industry, and Japanese producers began exporting a significant number of small, low-cost cars in the late 1960s. The Japanese export drive was given an enormous boost by the first oil shock in 1973, which prompted a worldwide shift in demand toward fuel-efficient cars. Japanese exports of passenger cars nearly doubled from 381,338 in 1970 to 695,573 in 1975.

Eventually the real price of gasoline began to fall, and demand shifted back toward larger, less fuel-efficient cars. Then, in 1979, OPEC oil producers once again raised prices. The subsequent economic slowdown and the shift in demand back toward small fuel-efficient cars greatly reduced the demand for the Big Three's products. In contrast, Japanese producers, which had (unintentionally) built up large inventories, were perfectly positioned to meet demand. The Japanese assemblers' competitiveness in the United States was reinforced by a substantial strengthening of the real exchange rate of the dollar (the automobile trade balance is highly correlated with the real yen-dollar exchange rate with a two-year lag; figure 4.1).

Ford and the United Auto Workers union responded in 1980 by filing a Section 201 case with the US International Trade Commission (ITC). The ITC rejected the case on the grounds that import competition was not the predominant cause of the industry's distress. Political pressure intensified to provide relief to the automobile industry, and several bills were introduced in Congress to put quotas on Japanese car imports. Under pressure from the industry, the US Congress, and especially the new Reagan administration, the Japanese government immediately announced voluntary export restraints (VERs) on automobiles to the United States.[5]

What followed was a textbook example of the self-defeating nature of VERs. Japanese producers initially responded to the VER by raising prices on their cars, which now had an additional scarcity value due to their limited supply. With the prices of Japanese cars going up, American and European producers were free to raise prices as well. All told, an estimated $5.8 billion to $10.3 billion in quota rents were transferred annually from US consumers to the world's automobile producers.[6] Most of these rents were captured by Japanese producers, and for several years in the 1980s Toyota was the most profitable firm in Japan. These excess profits were plowed back into investment in new plants, equipment, and research and development (R&D), making the Japanese firms even more formidable.

---

5. The Carter administration rejected Detroit's plea for a VER during the election year of 1980, opting to provide trade adjustment assistance to auto workers instead. The Reagan administration quickly reversed course upon entering office.

6. For alternative estimates see Dinopolous and Kreinin (1988), Tarr (1989), and deMelo and Tarr (1992).

Figure 4.1 United States and Japan: trade in automobiles and the real dollar-yen exchange rate, 1981–91

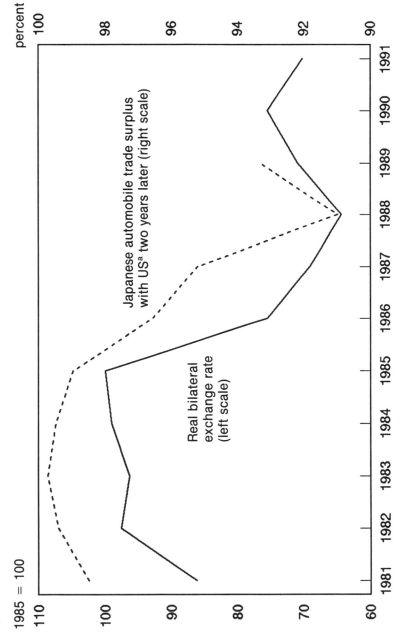

a. As a share of total US–Japan bilateral trade in automobiles.

107

Moreover, since Japanese producers were limited in the number of cars they could sell in the US market, they attempted to maximize profit margins on each unit by upgrading into the luxury car market, previously an exclusive American and European preserve. Three of the Japanese firms ultimately established separate luxury brands: Lexus (Toyota), Infiniti (Nissan), and Acura (Honda). With the Japanese moving up-market, new entrants, notably producers based in Korea and Yugoslavia, were drawn into the market to service its low-end niche.

Fortunately, the next step was for the Japanese assemblers to circumvent the VER restrictions by establishing assembly operations in the United States (the so-called transplants). Honda Motor Co. was the first, establishing a plant at Marysville, OH, in 1982. It was followed by Nissan Motor Co. (Smyrna, TN), Toyota (the NUMMI joint venture with GM in Fremont, CA, and later its own plant in Georgetown, KY), Mazda Motor Corp. (Flat Rock, MI), Mitsubishi Corp. (the Diamond-Star joint venture with Chrysler in Normal, IL), Subaru-Isuzu (Lafayette, IN), and the Nissan-Ford joint venture (Avon Lake, OH). Output from these plants reached 1.7 million vehicles in 1992 and is expected to rise to more than 2 million in 1995. Observers have credited these developments with accelerating the diffusion of Japanese management and production techniques in the United States.

The most in-depth study of the automobile industry ever undertaken was that of the International Motor Vehicle Program (IMVP) at the Massachusetts Institute of Technology (summarized in Womack et al. 1990). An unmistakable conclusion of this research is that a key to the current situation in automobiles is the significant competitive advantages that Japanese firms possess.

With regard to manufacturing prowess, the MIT researchers found considerable divergences among producers and plants in Japan, the United States, and Europe. Nonetheless, both Japanese firms and plants located in Japan appear to hold significant productivity and quality edges over their competitors (table 4.5), although "the best U.S.-owned plants in North America are now nearly as productive as the average Japanese plant—and are nearly equal in quality" (Womack et al. 1990, 86). Japanese transplants in North America achieved levels of quality similar to plants in Japan, but were around 25 percent less productive. Interestingly, the firms that ran the most efficient plants in Japan also maintained the most efficient transplants in North America, suggesting that firm-specific management quality is a significant determinant in variations in performance across plants.

Japanese competitive advantages are apparent in product development as well. The IMVP researchers found that a totally new Japanese car required 1.7 million hours of engineering effort on average and took 46 months from first design to customer deliveries (table 4.6). In contrast,

Table 4.5 Characteristics of automobile plants in Japan, North America, and Europe, 1989[a]

	Japanese plants in Japan	Japanese plants in North America	US plants in North America	All European plants
Performance				
Productivity (hours per vehicle)	16.8	21.2	25.1	36.2
Quality (defects per 100 vehicles)	60.0	65.0	82.3	97.0
Layout				
Space (sq. ft. per vehicle per year)	5.7	9.1	7.8	7.8
Repair area (as percentage of total area)	4.1	4.9	12.9	14.4
Inventories (days' supply for 8 sample parts)	0.2	1.6	2.9	2.0
Work force				
Percentage of work force in teams	69.3	71.3	17.3	0.6
Job rotation[b]	3.0	2.7	0.9	1.9
Suggestions received per employee	61.6	1.4	0.4	0.4
Number of job classes	11.9	8.7	67.1	14.8
Training for new workers (hours)	380.3	370.0	46.4	173.3
Absenteeism	5.0	4.8	11.7	12.1
Automation (percentage of direct steps automated)				
Welding	86.2	85.0	76.2	76.6
Painting	54.6	40.7	33.6	38.2
Assembly	1.7	1.1	1.2	3.1

a. All figures are averages for the year.
b. On a scale where 0 = no rotation and 4 = frequent rotation.

Source: Womack et al. (1990).

Table 4.6 Characteristics of automobile product development in Japan, North America, and Europe, 1989

	Japanese producers	North American producers	European producers Mass producers	European producers Specialty producers
Average engineering hours per new car (millions)	1.7	3.1	2.9	3.1
Average development time per new car (months)	46.2	60.4	57.3	59.9
Number of employees in project team	485	903	904	
Number of body types per new car	2.3	1.7	2.7	1.3
Average ratio of shared parts to total parts (percentages)	18	38	28	30
Supplier share of engineering (percentages)	51	14	37	32
Engineering change costs as share of total die costs	10–20	30–50	10–30	
Ratio of delayed products	1 in 6	1 in 2	1 in 3	
Die development time (months)	13.8	25.0	28.0	
Prototype lead time (months)	6.2	12.4	10.9	
Time from start of production to sale (months)	1	4	2	
Return to normal productivity after new model (months)	4	5	12	
Return to normal quality after new model	1.4	11	12	

Source: Womack et al. (1990).

comparable US and European efforts took 3 million hours and 60 months on average.

It is also striking to note (in table 4.6) the differences in shares of supplier-engineered parts used in Japanese and US cars. This reflects the far greater vertical integration of the US firms, versus the *keiretsu*-style vertical relationships of the Japanese firms. The IMVP researchers found that US firms do detail engineering on 81 percent of their parts, while the Japanese assemblers detail-engineer only 30 percent of their parts. Indeed, the IMVP researchers found that, of the total cost of materials, tools, and finished parts needed to make a Toyota, work done within Toyota itself accounted for only 27 percent, while for GM the corresponding figure was 70 percent.

Keiretsu organization also affects the financial structure of the Japanese firms. When Mazda ran into severe difficulties following the 1973 oil shock (unlike the other Japanese firms, its products were at that time based on the fuel-hungry Wankel engine), its rescue was organized by the Sumitomo group, which provided new management, a guaranteed customer base, and a massive infusion of capital. The contrast with the government-led rescue of Chrysler could not be more striking.

The US automobile industry has a much smaller direct presence in Japan than the Japanese industry has in the United States, in part because of the historical prohibition on direct investment in the Japanese industry. US and Japanese producers maintain a number of joint ventures, however, and US firms have significant stakes in several Japanese producers (Ford owns 25 percent of Mazda, and GM 38 percent of Isuzu and 4 percent of Suzuki; Chrysler once owned 24 percent of Mitsubishi but has since reduced its stake to less than 6 percent). US firms also use joint venture plants in Japan and elsewhere to ship cars to both the US and the Japanese market. These "captive imports" contribute to the profitability of the firm, although not to production or employment in the home country. The result of all these arrangements is a truly confusing plethora of intercorporate connections in which the same car produced at the same plant may be sold under different manufacturers' nameplates, and what at first appears to be an American or a Japanese car can turn out to be neither.[7]

Most observers believe that the transplants have had a positive impact on the US industry by increasing the diffusion of innovative Japanese practices. Partly this is done through the establishment of research and design operations in the United States. Perhaps more important, Japanese transplants have been instrumental in bringing more-cooperative

---

7. For example, Ford, which owns a stake in the Korean manufacturer Kia Motors Co., ships Ford Festivas to both the United States and Japan from the Kia plant. Indeed, one of the authors had the experience of visiting a dealer and finding identical model cars produced in three different countries.

models of management-labor relationships to the US industry. The high productivity at the transplants indicates that problems of low productivity in the US-owned plants are not due to poor US workmanship.

Similarly, competition from Japan is pushing US producers toward components procurement practices similar to the Japanese model, involving greatly intensified interdependence between the assemblers and their first-tier suppliers and between those suppliers and their vendor networks. GM shocked the auto parts industry in June 1992 by announcing that it was reopening contracts to new bids and would seek cost savings of at least 10 percent, with much of the savings expected to come at the expense of its internal parts divisions, which would no longer receive preference with regard to supply contracts. GM is seeking to establish two types of supplier relationships: long-term and lifetime contracts. Under long-term contracts, companies would supply parts for several GM programs but could be replaced by other suppliers. The lifetime contracts would include a "no divorce" clause whereby GM agrees to stay with the supplier as long as GM produces the particular car or truck platform in question. GM is also reportedly proposing insourcing arrangements, in which certain high-quality parts producers would set up operations inside GM plants and employ workers from GM's job bank.

With the shifting of Japanese production to the United States, the sourcing of auto parts has become an increasingly contentious issue. A number of critics complain that Japanese assemblers are importing the *keiretsu* system to the United States and discriminating against established US parts suppliers. The parts issue is particularly sensitive, as employment in the parts industry (565,000 in 1991) is considerably greater than that in assembly (351,000).[8]

A second dimension of this problem is the issue of US exports of parts to Japan. US sales have been hindered by Japanese assemblers' tendency to source through their own long-standing supplier networks. Contracts are specified in such a way that assemblers effectively guarantee the fixed payment that will cover the sunk costs of their suppliers. This encourages high-volume procurement and discourages assemblers from switching suppliers, since they are already committed to a fixed payment regardless of the volume of parts they procure. Assemblers will change suppliers if cost differences become large enough. But the structure of the contract discourages switching in response to small cost differences. In addition, access to the Japanese after-sales market has been retarded

---

8. At the same time, there is some evidence that the *keiretsu* have begun to fragment in the United States. Nissan, concerned about the trade friction over auto parts, and unable to source fuel pumps from one of its own affiliates in the United States, has procured them from a joint venture between a US maker and Nippondenso, Toyota's largest affiliated parts producer.

Table 4.7 United States: auto parts sales to Japanese assemblers, actual 1990 and targeted 1994 (billions of dollars)

	Actual purchases, FY1990	Original target, FY1994	Revised target, FY1994
Toyota	2.6	4.6	5.3
Nissan	1.3	3.3	3.7
Honda	2.8	4.5	4.9
Mitsubishi	0.7	1.4	1.6
Mazda	1.2	2.2	2.3
Other companies (approximate)	0.5	n.a.	1.2
Total	9.1	16.0[a]	19.0

a. Total does not include other companies.
Source: Japanese assemblers' public statements.

by the disinclination of Japanese assemblers to certify US manufacturers' parts as "genuine parts," without which certification dealers, garages, and other repair operations are reluctant to use them.[9] "Genuine parts" comprise more than half of the Japanese after-sales service market.

At the time of President George Bush's January 1992 trip to Japan, Japanese automakers revised upward to $19 billion their self-imposed targets for the purchase of American auto parts, 80 percent of which will be procured for the transplants (table 4.7). Toyota, which had earlier agreed to work with six US semiconductor firms on component development, announced that it would begin sourcing parts from Chrysler and Ford. Under US Commerce Department pressure, MITI agreed to monitor the implementation of the targets on a semiannual basis.[10] At the same time, US firms have stepped up their efforts in Japan. GM, for example, has opened a new parts development and design center in Japan and plans to triple its sales of parts in Japan by 1996.[11]

Penetrating the market for finished cars may be more difficult. As noted earlier, access to the Japanese market was restricted by border measures until these were reduced in the 1960s. Despite zero import duties, access to the market continued to be impeded until the late 1980s by discriminatory internal taxation, difficulty in obtaining safety and environmental certification, costly and time-consuming customs procedures, insurance rates that discriminated against foreign cars, and lack

---

9. Nissan announced in November 1991 that a contract clause requiring dealers to use Nissan-designated "genuine parts" for repairs and maintenance would be eliminated.

10. Other foreign producers, notably European and Australian ones, have complained that the increases in sales of US parts have come at their expense. Japanese automakers have denied these allegations of trade diversion.

11. GM has received a ¥550 million subsidized loan from the Japan Development Bank (JDB) under a special JDB program designed exclusively for foreign automakers operating in Japan. The JDB has also received applications from Ford and Chrysler.

Table 4.8   Japan: Imports of automobiles by country of origin, 1991

Source	Vehicles
Germany	119,048
United States	30,128
Big Three	13,711
Transplants	16,417
Great Britain	17,130
Sweden	12,363
France	10,854
Italy	5,754
Korea	688
Others	1,219
Total	197,184

Source: Japan Automobile Manufacturers Association, *Motor Vehicle Statistics of Japan, 1992.*

of access to existing distribution networks. Moreover, this is a sector of expected Japanese comparative advantage, confirmed by Japanese producers' worldwide competitiveness. Not surprisingly, imports make up a minuscule share of domestic consumption, less than 3 percent in 1991.

Given the barriers to entry to the Japanese market and the Japanese producers' fundamental competitiveness, most foreign firms have not made a major commitment to selling in Japan, the exceptions being some European luxury car producers that are able to sell into a niche market with, until recently, little domestic competition. Nevertheless, it is striking how poorly the Big Three have fared (table 4.8). Big Three exports to Japan from the United States are only now reattaining levels reached in the late 1970s (when the dollar was weak in real terms) and are exceeded by exports from Germany and Great Britain, and nearly by those from France and Sweden.[12] Indeed, the Europeans' share of the Japanese market is comparable to their share in the US market; in contrast, exports to Japan by the Big Three have now been surpassed by exports by the Japanese transplant operations in the United States. The similarity of European shares in the US and Japanese markets could be interpreted as indicating similar degrees of openness in the two markets. The real puzzle is the low US producer share in Japan.

American producers have cited the expense of establishing dealer networks as an obstacle to increasing sales in Japan. (Unlike that in the United States, competition policy in Japan permits the maintenance of exclusive dealer arrangements.) Questions remain, however, as to the seriousness of the Big Three's commitment to selling finished cars in the

---

12. It should be noted that the German export figure in table 4.8 includes a small number of GM Opels, and that the Korean figure includes Fords produced by Kia.

Japanese market. Current Big Three vehicles are somewhat ill suited for the Japanese market, given the lack of space and far higher gasoline prices in Japan. Perhaps most revealing is that none of the Big Three yet produces right-hand-steering cars in the United States, although GM does ship a small number of right-hand-steering Opels from Germany.[13] Only Ford uses its Japanese partner to produce cars for sale in Japan rather than for export to the United States.

During President Bush's trip to Japan, Japanese automakers announced fiscal 1994 targets for imports of American cars, with Toyota announcing it would import 5,000 GM vehicles, Mazda 4,500 Fords, Nissan 3,000 Fords, Mitsubishi 2,000 Chryslers, and Honda 1,200 Chryslers. The vice president of sales and services at GM Japan subsequently branded the Toyota pledge as "very political" and observed that his company expected little cooperation from the Japanese firm. At the same time, observers have surmised that GM may be wary of getting too close to Toyota and thereby offending Yanase, Japan's largest car importer and distributor of nearly all GM cars in Japan (*Nikkei*, 22 August 1992). Nissan also announced that it would permit its dealers to sell foreign cars, but three months after the announcement the director of public affairs at Nissan observed that, "Since we publicly announced the revision of our contracts with the dealers none of them have so far shown any intention to buy American cars. No American carmaker has asked Nissan to use our dealer network to sell their cars. There seems to be a large gap between Detroit and Washington" (quoted in *Nikkei*, 7 December 1991). Even if one accepts that the Japanese producers' pledges to import small numbers of Big Three automobiles are purely a function of political arm twisting, it is striking that the Big Three are apparently willing to allow their competitors to control the distribution of their products rather than seeking to fundamentally undermine their competitors' control of the Japanese distribution system. Indeed, some have argued that the Big Three have no real interest in penetrating the Japanese market—that the actual goal of these complaints is to justify protection at home.

At the same time, the importation of significant numbers of Big Three cars by the major Japanese firms could act as a seal of approval, signaling to Japanese consumers that Big Three quality problems have been resolved. Importation of cars produced in US transplant factories could similarly signal the quality of American workmanship.

But cracking the Japanese market under any circumstances may prove increasingly difficult. Coming demographic changes mean that the growth of the Japanese market is expected to slow. Most families already

---

13. Ford has announced that it will begin shipping right-hand-steering Ford Probes from its Mazda joint venture plant at Flat Rock, MI, in late 1993. GM has announced that it may begin producing right-hand-steering vehicles for the Japanese market in the mid-1990s.

own one car, and given the lack of parking space, congested roads, and relatively extensive public transportation systems, the Japanese market may be approaching saturation. Any slowdown will be moderated by regulations that restrict the used car market and encourage the rapid turnover of cars, however.

Trade Policy in Motor Vehicles

"The harsh fact is that the recession that we are witnessing here is being made in Japan."
—Rep. John D. Dingell (D-MI)
(Washington Post, 21 December 1991)

"I am for managed trade. If the market share is fixed, the Big Three would have nothing to fear from Japanese automakers. Car prices for both American and Japanese manufacturers could rise, and all automakers would be able to take a breather."
—A senior Nissan official
(Nikkei, 9 March 1992)

"[The EC quota on Japanese vehicles] has a lot of merit. . .because it makes the ground rules very clear, very simple, easy to understand and easy to monitor. It covers cars. It covers trucks."
—Harold A. Poling, Chairman and CEO, Ford Motor Co.
(Nikkei, 7 December 1992)

With transplant production in the United States substituting for exports from Japan, with the yen appreciating in real terms, and with the ceiling on automobile exports slowly being raised, by the late 1980s the VER on automobiles had become nonbinding. The Reagan administration, with its public espousal of free trade ideology, was embarrassed by the VER and did not request its extension after 1985. The VER is useful to the Japanese government, however, as it prevents export surges in automobiles, and it facilitates MITI's administrative control of the Japanese industry. In April 1992 the government of Japan unilaterally reduced the VER from 2.3 million to 1.65 million automobiles.

In addition to protection under the VER, the US industry has filed antidumping cases against Japanese producers in profitable segments of the industry where Japanese producers have not established transplant production, namely, off-road vehicles (1988) and minivans (1992). Although the Japanese exporters were found to be dumping, the US International Trade Commission declined to impose antidumping duties because the US industry did not prove sufficient injury. Given the ubiquitous tie-ups between US and Japanese producers, the antidumping cases made for some strange politics—Ford, for example, was producing sport utility vehicles for Mazda at the same time that it was accusing Mazda of dumping minivans.

Auto parts have also been prominent in US trade policy: they were one of the focuses of the mid-1980s market-oriented, sector-specific (MOSS) negotiations and the Bush trip to Japan in January 1992. Indeed, some in the industry supported making auto parts a Super 301 case in 1989, but industry lobbying groups were split over the proposal, and trade officials were uneasy about the mandatory retaliation provisions of the Super 301 legislation. Instead, the Commerce Department has pursued a strategy of developing long-term relationships between Japanese companies and US parts makers. At the same time, the Federal Trade Commission has initiated investigations into whether the practices of Japanese assemblers have violated US antitrust laws. The recent agreement in auto parts, in which 80 percent of purchases by Japanese assemblers of US parts are for their US transplant operations, could be regarded as disguised domestic content policy.

Controversy over the procurement practices of the transplants has also arisen in the context of the Canada-US Free Trade Agreement (FTA) and the proposed North American Free Trade Agreement (NAFTA).[14] In the short run, these disputes have been resolved in a bilateral side agreement to the proposed NAFTA; in the long run, however, the NAFTA rules of origin appear to be even stricter than those of the Canada-US FTA (Hufbauer and Schott 1993).

Distressed conditions at the Big Three and their traditional suppliers have led to renewed congressional calls for protection. The Orwellian-titled Trade Enhancement Act introduced in 1992 by House Majority Leader Richard A. Gephardt (D-MO) mandates 20 percent annual reductions in the US-Japan bilateral trade deficit for a period of five years. If these targets are not reached, the number of Japanese cars sold in the United States (including output from transplants) would be reduced.[15] Section 301 and antidumping cases would be initiated against Japan's "toleration of systematic anti-competitive practices" in auto parts. Certain specialty vehicles would be reclassified as trucks, thus raising tariff rates on them by a factor of 10. Tariffs would be raised on Japanese cars

---

14. US Customs officials claim that less than 40 percent of the content of Canadian-assembled Honda Civics is North American; hence they do not qualify for duty-free treatment, and Honda owes the US government $16.5 million in back duties. The main source of contention is the Ohio-produced engine block. Customs claims that it is only 10 to 15 percent North American, and therefore under the rounding rules of the FTA does not count toward North American content. Both Honda and the Canadian government dispute this. The case has worsened relations with Canada, where some interpret the Customs action as a move to encourage the location of future assembly activities in the United States rather than Canada. (The exclusion of the Canadian press from the Customs press briefing did not help matters.) Indeed, Honda claims it is the only automaker making small automobile engines in the United States, since the Big Three source theirs from Asia. A similar case involves the GM-Suzuki joint venture.

15. Other provisions would permit Japanese automakers to increase sales in the United States by the amount of increase in US car sales in Japan and the increase in the US-made car parts content of cars produced in Japan.

unless auto parts sales to Japan increase. The transplant-inclusive VER idea, minus the trade balance targets, has also been proposed by US automakers.

Research by Elliott and Hufbauer (1992) indicates that implementation of the transplant-inclusive VER proposals would cause significant welfare losses in the United States. Lost consumer surplus would be between $3.5 billion and $8.0 billion, depending on the modeling assumptions. Most of this would be lost in the form of transfers to US and foreign producers. The net national welfare loss would be $3.0 billion to $6.0 billion, of which $0.5 billion to $1.1 billion would be a deadweight efficiency loss to the US economy.

These proposals would have deleterious impacts beyond the simple economic losses. Domestically, they would be completely at odds with a US antitrust tradition that almost never impedes internal competition or permits markets to be carved up. Moreover, these proposals would create a fundamental clash of interests between employees of transplant factories and Big Three plants, setting off potentially explosive domestic politics, with region set against region, state against state, and locality against locality. Internationally, these proposals would violate the proposed NAFTA, and would call into question the treatment of inward foreign investment in the United States, with unforeseeable consequences for future capital inflows.

Automobile Policy Recommendations

The US economy has clearly benefited from the entry of Japanese producers into the automobile market. Increased competition in what was previously a largely sheltered market has led to improvements in product design, performance, safety, and price. The Big Three have made strides in quality, reliability, and fuel efficiency. They still lag the Japanese producers on all three criteria (Economic Strategy Institute 1992), although some have argued that Big Three fuel efficiency is comparable once differences in product composition are taken into account. It is hard to imagine that the Big Three would have made these strides without pressure from the Japanese producers.

How future trade in automobiles plays out will depend on the relative competitive positions of Japanese and American firms. Financing advantages that Japanese producers achieved during the "bubble economy" of the late 1980s have disappeared. (During that period Toyota, for example, issued $6.2 billion worth of convertible bonds at interest rates of 1.2 to 4.0 percent—a cost of capital far below that faced by its foreign competitors. Even weaker firms such as Isuzu and Subaru were able to obtain low-cost financing in this way.) The disappearance of capital cost advantages and the development of excess capacity could be expected to alter the Japanese corporate emphasis from pursuit of market share to profitability. Already Toyota and Nissan have made announcements of this sort. This change in focus can be seen most immediately in moves to reduce the number of models offered and to prolong the intervals between model changes.

The development of worldwide excess capacity in automobiles suggests that some current assemblers may shrink or leave the market altogether. (Isuzu has already announced plans to pull out of the passenger car market, and Nissan recently announced plans to close one of its Japanese plants.) One researcher (Smitka 1993) argues that excess capacity, combined with high and rising costs and a stagnant domestic market, will force a significant downsizing of Japanese production operations. Smitka goes so far as to say that within a decade the US bilateral trade deficit with Japan in automobiles will shrink to insignificance. The Japanese firms' share of the US market has indeed fallen from its peak of 30 percent, to 27 percent in 1992.

Under these circumstances, what should policy toward the automobile sector be? Automobile policy should be geared toward the maintenance of open markets and the enhancement of competitiveness. Here the United States faces three big issues: whether to emulate the European Community and restrict Japanese firms' sales (inclusive of transplant production); whether to pursue a policy of so-called voluntary import expansion (VIE) along the lines of the US-Japan Semiconductor Trade Agreement (STA, discussed below); and whether to support the domestic industry through a variety of other actions such as socializing Big Three healthcare and pension costs or raising the tariff on minivans.

With regard to the first issue, the recommendation is straightforward: resist self-destructive quota proposals. As noted earlier, implementation of proposed quotas on the US sales of Japanese firms (inclusive of both imports and transplant production) would impose a national welfare loss of $3.0 billion to $6.0 billion annually. They would set off domestic political strife, violate the proposed NAFTA and US antitrust precedent, and discourage other foreign investors, and could be used against US producers in foreign markets. Similarly, proposals to tighten the existing VER, exclusive of the transplant production, should be resisted for the reasons indicated earlier. Solutions of these types should be avoided at all costs.

The United States and Japan will also have to come to terms with EC rules on automobiles. Under the recent Japan-EC deal, the Japanese share of the EC market is to grow from 11 percent to 16 percent by 1999, with direct exports from Japan frozen at 1.2 million vehicles. (Japanese transplants in Europe accounted for 260,000 vehicles in 1990; this is expected to rise to 1.2 million vehicles by 1999.) After 1999, the limits are supposed to be removed, although a certain degree of skepticism is in order. The key issues from the US perspective are how Japanese firms' exports from the United States will be treated, and how much Japanese production will be diverted to the United States. The answer to the first question is that Japanese assemblers' exports from the United States will not be counted as part of the quota. The US government should remain vigilant, however, as even the exports by Japanese transplants in Great Britain to the Continent are treated as part of the quota. Potential restrictions by the Community on exports of cars from Japanese firms in the United States would be a useful target for extraterritorial antitrust activism on the part of US authorities if this unfortunate eventuality were to transpire.

To the extent that Japanese firms' ability to sell in Europe is limited, there will be downward pressure on prices in the United States. Although this would be desirable, from the standpoint of US consumers, it would put additional pressure on US firms and limit the expansion of transplant facilities in North America. Diversion of exports from the Community to the US market would have a similar effect but would in principle be limited by the VER that remains in effect. In all likelihood this effect will not be large: Japanese firms are scaling back production in Japan, and Southeast Asian markets are booming. Again, the US tactic should be to export production from the United States to the Community and other markets, not to limit Japanese firms' activities within the United States.

The task in Japan is more complicated. As Peter J. Woods, Chairman of the European Community Automobiles, Power Units, and Components Committee, has observed, "The market is basically open now. But having kept out imported cars for so long, it must surely be possible to think in terms of what we call affirmative action to compensate." The Japanese government has begun to do this by providing Japan Development Bank funds to help foreign automobile firms expand operations in Japan, and by pressuring Japanese firms to increase their importation of foreign cars and parts. It could do more: it could specify environmental and safety regulations in terms of performance, not design, for example, and a more aggressive, proactive stance on the part of the Japanese government could be useful in reinforcing the desirability of trade-expanding solutions.

This raises the issue of the VIEs. In general, skepticism is in order. VIEs are likely to be captured politically; there is only a weak scientific basis for setting quantitative targets; to the extent that actual outcomes may in large part be generated by fundamental economic forces beyond any government's control (i.e., changes in the composition of demand, and technological innovations), enforcement of these agreements is problematic. (These issues are addressed comprehensively in the following chapter.) Nevertheless, with the apparent success of the STA (analyzed later in this chapter) and the recommendation of the Advisory Council on Trade Policies and Negotiations (ACTPN) that the United States consider a policy of "temporary quantitative indicators" (TQIs), proposals to set market shares for imports by Japan have received increased attention. Much of this interest centers on the auto parts market, where, under prodding from the Japanese government, Japanese automakers announced foreign parts procurement targets during the Bush visit in January 1992 (see table 4.7 above).[16]

The January 1992 import targets are specified in terms of purchases by Japanese firms of US firms' parts. Eighty percent of these purchase goals involve purchases by Japanese transplants in the United States; less than 20 percent will involve sales to operations in Japan. In effect, as already noted, this VIE was largely domestic-content policy in disguise, motivated by the difficulty of US parts producers in penetrating the long-term contract networks of the Japanese assemblers.

If the problem is breaking into the *Japanese* market, then the United States should negotiate the removal of practices (such as the "genuine parts" certification system) that act as a trade impediment. However, the emphasis on *domestic* procurement in the agreement suggests that the problem is primarily within the United States. If this is the case, the United States has *domestic* competition policies that can be brought to bear if, for example, the Japanese assemblers' practices violate US vertical foreclosure laws. If they are illegal, the assemblers should be prosecuted. If the practices are not illegal and simply represent an efficient way of organizing business, then US firms should emulate them (as some are now doing). This leaves open the question of how to get US suppliers into the long-term contract markets that have been historically closed to them. The VIE is a risky second-best to these approaches.

Lastly, the United States must also come to terms with proposals such as those to socialize Big Three pension obligations and to increase the tariffs on minivans. The first issue speaks to the relative costs of production in Japan and in the United States, and within the United States between the Big Three and the transplants. The argument in its simplest form (e.g., as presented in Economic Strategy Institute 1992) is that health care is socialized in Japan, while in the United States private firms bear much of their employees' health costs. Within the United States, the transplants employ younger, healthier workers than the Big Three and thereby incur lower health care costs. Similar arguments can be made with regard to pensions.

Proponents of socialization ignore the fact that Japanese firms pay higher corporate taxes than do US firms to pay for their system. It is unclear whether US firms actually bear a larger financing burden. In any event, it is important to recognize that Big Three health care costs reflect

---

16. Unlike the STA, there is no bilateral agreement formalizing either the auto parts procurement targets or their enforcement—a point made repeatedly by the Japanese government.

both inefficiencies in the overall US health care delivery system and private arrangements between the Big Three and their employees. There is an obvious case for reforming the US health care system to eliminate distortions and inefficiencies, as is currently being contemplated. The case for industry-specific measures is much less obvious, as are the solutions.

The most far-reaching ideas would involve socializing all or part of the Big Three's health and pension costs. These proposals, which would delink the level of benefits from their financing, are horrendous: they would encourage the Big Three and their employees to collude to take compensation in the form of the socialized benefits (since the taxpayer, not the firm or its employees, would ultimately foot the bill), and they would encourage emulation by firms in other industries, running up unsustainable health care and pension obligations that the government would then have to absorb. The ESI recommends taxing the transplants to pay for Big Three pensions and health care. This is preferable to socialization, since it limits the scope for emulation, but it still faces the problem of delinking the setting of benefit levels from their financing. (Indeed, under the ESI proposal, the Big Three would have an even greater incentive to increase employee compensation in the form of health care and pension benefits, since their rivals, not society at large, would be paying for it.) A less objectionable solution would be to tax all domestic automobile production and imports and apply the tax to financing all pension and health care obligations for all domestic automobile workers. This again would be subject to the moral hazard problems identified above, and would in effect tax US consumers to defray the costs of Japanese firms. In the end, all of these proposals should be rejected.

A final issue relates to the US tariff on minivans. In 1989 the US Customs Bureau reclassified minivans from cars to small trucks, thereby increasing the tariff 10-fold, from 2.5 percent to 25 percent. The Treasury, in keeping with international classification norms, ordered Customs to reverse its decision. Legislation has been introduced in both houses of Congress to reclassify minivans as small trucks and again raise the tariff to 25 percent. President Clinton has criticized the Bush administration's handling of the issue, noting that the United States "got nothing" in return for keeping the tariff at 2.5 percent. In mercantilist terms (or in the "enlightened mercantilist" terms of GATT-speak), it is correct to say that the Bush administration did not push its tactical advantage to the maximum with regard to the tariff setting. It should be noted, however, that imports make up less than 10 percent of the minivan market, and the ITC did not find any evidence of injury to the domestic industry in its investigation.

The real issue, however, is why the United States has a tariff of 25 percent on small trucks (or any other product for that matter). The answer is that the tariff was raised to 25 percent in 1963 to retaliate against the European Community in the so-called chicken war, when the Community raised the tariff on chickens to a level far higher than the previous German tariff. (That the US-Japan dispute is in part an artifact of a US-EC fight over chickens 30 years earlier is support for Thomas O. Bayard's quip that, with regard to TQIs and VIEs, the 'T' is to temporary as 'V' is to voluntary.) Raising the tariff on minivans would reportedly increase consumer costs by $1,300 to $3,700 per vehicle, implying a transfer of millions of dollars to domestic producers (who control more than 90 percent of the market) and the US Treasury. There is no justification for any developed country to maintain tariffs of this magnitude, and indeed the administration has offered to cut the tariff as part of the Uruguay Round package.

The fundamental point that should not be lost in this welter of detail is that, although the Japanese market has been historically closed, this does not explain why Germany and Great Britain export more cars to Japan than the Big Three, and France and Sweden nearly as many. In the long run, competitiveness will determine trade performance as long as markets are open. From a US perspective, the fortunes of the domestic industry will hinge on economywide factors, such as the cost of capital, the quality of the labor force, and the real exchange rate, and on the firm-specific reforms that are already occurring to varying degrees. Special proposals, such as to provide tax breaks for the purchase of Big Three cars, or to socialize Big Three pensions, might help the Big Three, but at the cost of harming the rest of the economy and setting dangerous precedents. They should therefore be avoided.

Rather, emphasis should be put on improving the quality of productive factors that would help the US automobile industry and other medium-technology manufacturing industries. This means first and foremost reducing the cost of capital investment through reductions in the government budget deficit and perhaps directly through an investment tax credit. In parallel, the quality of labor must be raised through enhanced worker training and education. Technological capability should also be strengthened, preferably through an economywide R&D tax credit.

Sustained exchange rate realignment would further cement these gains. As figure 4.1 shows, automobile trade closely tracks (with a lag) the real yen-dollar exchange rate. Maintenance of a strong yen would boost the relative competitiveness of both US assembly plants and US-based parts producers. Ironically, policy actions to widen the Japanese assemblers' supplier networks to include US firms, and boosting US parts exports to Japan, could thereby make the assemblers' Japanese plants even more competitive.

The Japanese automobile firms face the challenge of becoming truly global firms. This will involve the difficult task of genuinely incorporating foreign nationals in management and foreign firms in supplier networks. *Keiretsu* with weak car firms might consider incorporating a non-Japanese firm into their ranks. Likewise, Honda, the largest Japanese assembler not part of a *keiretsu*, might consider forming an international *keiretsu*, especially given that it now sells more cars in North America than in Japan. Steps such as these in such a key industry could significantly accelerate the overall convergence process.

Computers

The modern computing age can trace its origins to the invention of the transistor at AT&T's Bell Laboratories in 1947. In 1956, however, an antitrust consent decree prohibited AT&T from entering markets other than telecommunications and required that all patents controlled by AT&T at that time be licensed to others upon request. The effect was to grant new entrants to the fledgling semiconductor industry access to the basic technology at low cost (Steinmuller 1988).

Soon thereafter, transistors were first combined to form early integrated circuits. The big breakthrough came in 1959, when two engineers—Jack Kilby of Texas Instruments Inc. (TI) and Robert Noyce of Fairchild—independently discovered planar technology, the basis of modern integrated circuits. This represented a giant leap in semiconductor technology and spurred the development of the computer industry, for which the integrated circuit became the basic building block. The computer industry came to be dominated by one giant, International Business Machines Corp. (IBM), and a fringe of competitors. The semiconductor industry, in contrast, was made up of a number of undiversified merchant semiconductor producers. ("Merchant" producers are those who sell their products to other firms for use as inputs rather than build them into their own end-user products.)

The situation in Japan was considerably different. In the early 1950s, relatively primitive computers were constructed through the joint efforts of Toshiba, Tokyo University, and the R&D laboratory of the telecommunications monopoly Nippon Telegraph and Telephone Corp. (NTT). The first commercial Japanese computers were introduced in the late 1950s. The goal of Japanese industrial policy was to create a viable domestic industry (Shinjo 1988). The government followed a two-pronged strategy to accomplish this goal.

First, the government pursued policies to subsidize production and develop the domestic market. Direct fiscal incentives were extended through the provision of small direct subsidies, larger subsidized loans through government-controlled financial institutions, and preferential tax treatment (Shinjo 1988, table 4-7; Office of Technology Assessment [OTA] 1991, table 6-7). At the same time, the government established the Japan Electronic Computer Company (JECC) to provide subsidized leasing finance to potential users of Japanese systems and provided tax breaks to encourage the installation and use of computers.[17]

These policies encouraged expansion of the market by stimulating demand and subsidizing supply. They not only provided direct support to the industry, but by reducing the risk associated with investment, induced domestic private capital inflows into the sector at more favorable rates. Moreover, policies to support expansion of the computer industry clearly induced expansion of demand for semiconductors, a major input to computers. The OTA (1991) estimates that the value of these subsidies over the period 1961 to 1989 was $12.6 billion.

The second thrust of Japanese government policy was to protect the upstart domestic industry from foreign competition. Foreign firms' access to the Japanese market was restricted by high tariffs, control by MITI of foreign exchange allocations for the importation of products and technology licensing, discriminatory government procurement policies, and a prohibition on foreign direct investment.[18] The last of these was possibly the most important. Because computer systems are complex capital goods, support services were deemed essential. The restrictions on their domestic presence forced foreign firms to compete at a severe disadvantage.

The preeminent computer firm in the world at the time was IBM. In the prewar years it had maintained a small importing operation in Japan. In the mid-1950s, the company petitioned the Japanese government to allow it to establish a subsidiary that would be 99 percent owned by the parent company. (The remaining ownership would reside with its Japanese board of directors.) Negotiations were finally concluded in 1960. IBM was permitted to establish the only wholly foreign-owned

---

17. The tax benefits have not been contingent on the origin of the purchased software or equipment, so that in theory the impact of these provisions has been to expand the Japanese market for these products, not to assist Japanese manufacturers per se. Likewise, special provisions that allow computer manufacturers to deduct expected losses on the return of equipment offered to users on a trial basis do not discriminate by origin, and thus in principle could be used by domestic manufacturers, local subsidiaries of foreign manufacturers, or importers. In reality, however, the lion's share of the benefits of these provisions have undoubtedly gone to Japanese firms. Unlike the tax provisions, the leasing schemes apply only to Japanese firms. OTA (1991) estimates the implicit subsidy to demand for Japanese computers through the JECC between 1961 and 1989 to have been $451 million.

18. Starting in 1964 (when IBM-Japan began shipments), the government permitted purchasers using public funds to specify bidders, thus permitting foreign firms to be excluded prior to bidding. (According to the American Electronics Association, nearly two-thirds of government procurements are through single tenders.) NTT, a major public purchaser, purchased Japanese firms' computer systems exclusively, and indeed would not buy any domestic products containing foreign semiconductors. These practices were harbingers of recurrent disputes about foreign access to the Japanese public market.

computer manufacturing subsidiary in Japan and to freely remit profits, but the *quid pro quo* was that IBM had to license valuable technology patents to its Japanese rivals, submit to MITI controls on production and market share, and agree to export performance requirements.[19]

Pressure from the United States later forced a liberalization of the market, which, however, was delayed as long as possible and accompanied by compensatory policies to improve domestic firms' competitiveness.[20] First, in 1971, trade in products was liberalized, and at the same time the Japanese government greatly increased fiscal supports and began initiating publicly supported large-scale cooperative research ventures among domestic firms. Joint ventures were permitted beginning in 1974, and investment was fully liberalized in 1976, but meanwhile the government again increased its support of the domestic industry. By 1976, Japanese firms had developed their own proprietary operating systems, thereby making it extremely costly to users to switch systems. As a consequence, liberalization did little to change the status of foreign firms in the Japanese market. The big three Japanese makers, Fujitsu Ltd., NEC Corp., and Hitachi Ltd., still account for more than 60 percent of the Japanese mainframe market, but only 3 percent in the rest of the world.

Two other factors aided the development of the Japanese industry. First was the fact that the major computer makers were large, vertically integrated firms, which permitted them to cross-subsidize among different products. Second, *keiretsu* relationships provided stable financing and customer bases.[21]

Foreign firms account for less than 10 percent of the public computer systems market in Japan (compared with 35 to 40 percent of the private market), with IBM-Japan capturing a mere 3.5 percent. Government procurement accounts for about a fifth of the total market, and Japanese firms get around 30 percent of their revenues from the government market. Public-sector purchases totaled $9 billion in 1990 and are expected to increase more than 10 percent a year through 1995.[22] If

---

19. See Anchordoguy (1989), Mason (1992), and Encarnation (1992) for more complete descriptions of the IBM experience.

20. Interestingly, as in the case of the automobile industry, MITI in its near-pathological pursuit of scale economies attempted to orchestrate the consolidation of the industry through a series of mergers. Luckily for Japan, this was as unsuccessful in computers as it was in cars.

21. See Imai (1990) and OTA (1991) for conflicting quantitative assessments of the importance of *keiretsu* relationships in providing a customer base.

22. Government procurement has been a continuing source of friction between the United States and Japan. The 1991 edition of the Office of the US Trade Representative's *National Trade Estimates* for the first time cited public computer procurement as a significant barrier to US exports to Japan. Cited practices include computer leasing, computer service contracts (which may involve hardware procurement), and procurement by prefectural and local

foreign firms could capture a share of the public market equal to their present share in the private market, their sales could rise by more than $2 billion per year. What share of this increase would be met by US exports is unclear. Bergsten and Cline (1985) cite Department of Commerce estimates of just over $1 billion. A market access agreement in computers was negotiated as part of the January 1992 Bush visit to Japan; the jury is still out on the agreement's impact.

The situation has begun to change considerably with the introduction of personal computers (PCs) into the Japanese market. Initially, the Japanese firms (with the notable exception of Toshiba) attempted to do in PCs what they had more or less successfully done in mainframe computers: use proprietary operating systems to create a captive consumer base. The IBM disk-operating system (DOS) had already become the *de facto* world standard, however, and the preponderance of DOS-based software, together with the development of a Japanese-language version of DOS, opened up the market for relatively cheap and powerful imported IBM-compatibles. Meanwhile Apple Computer, Inc., whose Macintosh computers are the principal challengers to IBM-compatible dominance of the PC market, developed its own Japanese-language operating system and pushed hard into the Japanese market. By 1991 the foreign firms' share of the market was 15 percent and rising.

Semiconductors

Background

In several respects, the development of the semiconductor industry in the United States and Japan parallels that of the computer industry. The US semiconductor industry began its development in the mid-1950s and has always had a major independent merchant presence. Of the top 10 US semiconductor firms, only IBM (which produces for its own use), Motorola, Inc., and RCA are significantly diversified. The industry's dynamism has reflected labor mobility and the entry of new start-up firms into the market.

US firms attempted to enter the Japanese market in the early 1960s but were rebuffed by MITI, and the Japanese industry was launched in 1963, when Fairchild licensed its process patent to Nippon Electric

---

authorities, both of which fall outside the GATT government procurement code. Examples include three incidents in 1989 when Japanese firms bid 1 yen on contracts to write the specifications for the Saitama and Nagano prefectural library systems, and the Hiroshima municipal water system. Since rival manufacturers maintain incompatible operating systems, once a producer has secured the contract, the user is committed to further purchases from the same producer (in these cases significant software and terminal purchases). The United States has asked Japan to voluntarily extend GATT codes to these practices.

Company (today's NEC Corp.), after being prevented from establishing a presence in Japan itself.

Texas Instruments proved to be a tougher bargainer. TI first applied to establish a wholly owned subsidiary in Japan in 1964 and was refused. The company continued to press its case, however, and made clear that it was serious about bringing a patent infringement suit against any firm, anywhere, importing any product into the United States embodying the Kilby patent technology. Eventually, under pressure from Japanese firms, which wanted to resolve the TI dispute in order to gain access to the company's technology and export to the United States, MITI agreed in 1968 to permit TI to establish its subsidiary. As a face-saving device for MITI, the operation would take the form of a joint venture with Sony Corp., which would sell out its share after three years at an agreed price. More important, TI agreed to license its technology to Japanese firms at concessional rates and to submit to MITI monitoring and limitations on production and market share for a period of three years.[23]

In 1966, the Japanese government began targeting the semiconductor industry. As in the case of computers, Japanese policies combined restrictions on imports and foreign direct investment, restrictions on technology importation and MITI's assumption of the role of monopsonist buyer, and public research support. All of these policies were maintained through the late 1970s.[24] According to Tyson (1992, 98), "Protection allowed Japanese producers to reach minimum scale; promotion reduced their risk in making the big capital investments necessary to enter."[25]

The structure of the Japanese industry that emerged is significantly different from that of the United States. The 10 largest Japanese semiconductor producers are all large, vertically integrated electronics firms with extensive nonsemiconductor businesses. Together they account for more than 90 percent of Japanese semiconductor production, and that share has risen over time (Steinmuller 1988). They also account for a significant share of Japanese consumption, with the top six producers together accounting for more than 60 percent of the total (Tyson 1992). This structure of the Japanese industry has clear implications for international trade in semiconductors.

Because the production of semiconductors is characterized by huge fixed costs and steep learning curves, marginal cost is falling and is less than average cost for most if not all of a product's life. Pricing decisions are consequently extremely complex, and profit-maximizing prices may actually lie below marginal (as well as average) cost at times during the

---

23. See Anchordoguy (1989), Mason (1992), and Encarnation (1992) for more complete descriptions of TI's experience.

24. See Borrus et al. (1983) for a comprehensive discussion of these issues.

25. Tyson notes that this chapter of her book was written in part with David Yoffie.

product's life (Flamm 1993). A vertically integrated firm typically will face strong incentives to source internally and increase production volumes to move down the marginal cost curve, which typically (though not necessarily) lies below the price and is falling, and to minimize uncertainty with regard to price and supply availability. The implication is that merchant producers will have difficulty selling semiconductors to vertically integrated users, regardless of whether those users are IBM or Hitachi. The greater diversification of the Japanese firms and their *keiretsu* links (hence their greater opportunities for cross-subsidization, and greater ability to weather cyclical downturns in the market) simply reinforce this tendency.[26]

The results can be observed in the data: Japanese firms have always supplied more than 80 percent of the Japanese market, where vertically integrated firms predominate, while US firms have dominated markets in the United States and Europe, where they do not. Unfortunately for US producers, Japan is the world's largest market: in 1991 Japan accounted for 38 percent of world semiconductor sales, while the United States accounted for only 28 percent.

The Semiconductor Trade Agreement

Conflict between the US and Japanese industries came to a head in June 1985, when the Semiconductor Industry Association, the US industry's trade association, submitted a Section 301 petition against unfair Japanese trading practices. Shortly thereafter, a US firm, Micron Technology, charged the Japanese with dumping 64K DRAMs. In August of that year, the Justice Department opened an antitrust investigation into possible predatory pricing by Hitachi. The following month, three more American firms filed dumping complaints against Japanese producers of erasable programmable read-only memories (EPROMs). Finally, in December 1985, in an extraordinary move the Commerce Department self-initiated a dumping case in 256K DRAMs.

This flurry of activity alarmed Japanese trade officials, who moved to reach a bilateral settlement that would short-cut these legal actions. After months of negotiations, the United States and Japan announced

---

26. If information availability and capital markets were perfect, US firms could simply borrow in capital markets to weather downturns, and the vertical integration and *keiretsu* links of Japanese firms would confer no advantage. Considerable evidence suggests, however, that monitoring problems may impede the perfect functioning of capital markets. As a consequence, cash flow and *keiretsu* links may have a significant impact on capital budget constraints. This is particularly important as minimum efficient scale in semiconductors has grown quite large. According to Tyson (1992), minimum efficient plant size was approaching $150 million in 1985, and $500 million by 1991. She argues that the Japanese firms' greater access to investment funds was very important in the 1985–86 price war, in which seven of nine US dynamic random access memory (DRAM) producers left the market.

an accord at the end of July 1986. The Semiconductor Trade Agreement (STA) contained eight principal provisions. The Japanese government would monitor costs and prices of semiconductor exports from Japan to the United States and other markets. Japanese firms would submit cost and price data to MITI. If dumping appeared to be occurring, the two governments would have two weeks to pursue consultations before proceeding with the case. The Japanese government would try to prevent dumping by Japanese firms. These first four provisions effectively created a firm-specific price floor for semiconductors.[27]

The next four provisions were aimed at increasing foreign firms' access to the Japanese market. The Japanese government would encourage Japanese producers and consumers of semiconductors to purchase more foreign semiconductors. (A then-secret side letter called for increasing the foreign share to 20 percent.)[28] The Japanese government would establish an organization in Japan to help foreign producers increase sales in Japan. The Japanese government would promote long-term relationships between Japanese and foreign firms. And finally, the Japanese government would ensure full and equitable access for foreign firms to patents generated by government-sponsored R&D.

To implement the agreement, MITI in effect began to establish a production cartel, issuing quarterly "forecasts" of semiconductor demand and production that carried an implicit administrative imprimatur. Prices remained low, however, and the United States warned Japan that it was not adhering to its commitments under the STA—in particular to prevent dumping in third-country markets and to improve access to the Japanese market. In February 1987, MITI began issuing "requests" for production cutbacks, and although there was initially some resistance, by the following month all of the Japanese producers (including TI's Japanese subsidiary) had fallen into line. But by then it was too late: that same month Oki Electric's salesmen were lured into documenting sales at less than fair market value in Hong Kong. In an increasingly tense atmosphere in which both houses of Congress voted to recommend retaliation for

---

27. It should be noted that not all semiconductors were covered under the agreement. Moreover, the "fair market values" whose determination was called for in the agreement were calculated on a firm-specific basis in an attempt to preserve competition.

28. The determination of semiconductor "nationality" raised in stark terms the "Who Is Us?" question posed by Robert B. Reich (1990). In the STA, semiconductor nationality was determined by the nationality of the producing firm, not the location of production, implicitly revealing the trade negotiators' implicit goal of furthering the interests of (internationally mobile) capital rather than (internationally immobile) labor. So, for example, a TI semiconductor produced in Japan counted as American, and a Hitachi chip produced in the United States counted as Japanese for the purpose of calculating market shares. It is apparent that, in negotiating this deal, the US negotiators attempted to satisfy relatively organized and concentrated producer interests more than the relatively less organized and more diffuse interests of labor and consumers.

violations of the price floor agreement, and the Defense Department issued an alarming report on the state of the US industry, the Reagan administration announced the imposition of $300 million in punitive tariffs on Japanese exports to the United States.[29]

The retaliation had two apparent effects. First, the US share of the Japanese market began to rise. Second, the prices of semiconductors began to rise.[30] Indeed, by the fall of 1987 the price increases were beginning to seriously hurt semiconductor users, particularly the computer firms. The US government reversed course and asked MITI to abandon the production controls, and in November 1987 it partially removed the spring sanctions.

MITI complied but continued to impose strict restrictions under COCOM (the international agreement aimed at controlling the diffusion of sensitive technologies to the Soviet bloc). This had the effect of maintaining the system of administered prices. Moreover, MITI continued to provide "opinions" to the Japanese firms as to their investment plans (Flamm 1990). Thus, one effect of the price floor provisions the STA, as with the automobile VER, was to increase MITI's control over the Japanese economy.

Semiconductor prices continued to rise through 1988, with some users reporting that Japanese firms were demanding access to advanced technology as a *quid pro quo* for semiconductor sales (Tyson 1992). Flamm (1990) estimates that semiconductor producers made $3 billion to $4 billion in excess profits on global sales of approximately $45 billion in 1988, the vast majority of these profits accruing to Japanese producers. Again, as in the automobile case, these rents further improved the Japanese firms' competitive position, not only in semiconductors but potentially in downstream products such as computers and telecommunications equipment, through cross-subsidies. Tyson (1992) reports that R&D expenditures in semiconductors in Japan exceeded those in the United States by $2 billion in 1988.

---

29. The European Community meanwhile objected to certain provisions of the STA and filed a GATT complaint against the United States and Japan. The GATT panel struck down the *de facto* production controls (which the US government maintained were outside the agreement) as a violation of GATT Article XI in June 1988, but by this point the Europeans were well on their way to establishing their own agreement with the Japanese. See Flamm (1990).

30. Tyson (1992) argues that the sequence of events does not entirely support the argument that the imposition of production controls in 1987 led to the price increase, and indeed there may have been other factors encouraging prices to rise. Some have argued that the price increase was due to the exercise of monopoly power by Japanese firms. Nonetheless, the semiconductor industry is highly concentrated and characterized by strategic pricing decisions on the part of firms. It is not difficult to imagine that, in the highly politicized environment of the spring of 1987, firms would raise prices for a variety of motives related to anticipated trade policy actions by the US and Japanese governments.

Coincident with the STA was increased activity by US firms to penetrate the Japanese market.[31] This was accompanied by a plethora of tieups involving US and Japanese firms (table 4.9). It is difficult to say, however, how many of these were due to the STA and how many would have occurred anyway in response to business conditions.

With the foreign market share still below 20 percent of the Japanese market, the STA was renegotiated and extended in 1991. The new STA explicitly set a 20 percent target for foreign market share and replaced the "fair market value" calculations with a fast-track dumping procedure. The remaining punitive sanctions were suspended. In the fourth quarter of 1992, the foreign-firm share of the Japanese market exceeded the 20 percent target for the first time.

The original STA was a departure in US trade policy in three ways. First, it sought to expand US access to a foreign high-technology product market, rather than reduce foreign access to the US market. Second, with a target for foreign market share formally enshrined in the 1991 extension, it became the first US example of what Jagdish Bhagwati has called "voluntary import expansion" (VIE). Third, the STA was the first bilateral deal to explicitly involve monitoring of third-party markets.

Given the innovative nature of the STA and the obvious interest in applying this approach to other sectoral disputes, a careful evaluation is warranted. There is a widespread consensus that the price floor part of the STA was a mistake: it harmed non-Japanese downstream users while transferring large rents to Japanese firms. The market access provisions of the STA are more controversial. Whether a VIE is globally welfare-enhancing comes down to whether the initial situation is distorted or not, and if it is, how. If the foreign market is protected and a VIE is implemented on a nonpreferential basis among foreign suppliers, the VIE may be globally welfare-enhancing, although producers in the protected country will lose. If the market is protected and the VIE is administered preferentially, it is possible that both the importing and the exporting countries as a whole may gain at the expense of importing-country and third-country producers. If the market is initially undistorted, the VIE will reduce importing-country welfare and increase exporting-country welfare. Indeed, the exporting country would prefer the VIE over an equivalent export subsidy because of the favorable terms-of-trade effects in the VIE case (Dinopoulos and Kreinin 1990).

---

31. Tyson (1992) reports that between 1986 and 1989 US suppliers added 30 sales offices to 42 already in place; opened 16 new design centers and 6 new test centers to quadruple and triple the US presence, respectively; and added 4 new failure analysis centers to bring the total to 15. Personnel expenditures increased 32 percent, capital expenditures 162 percent, and sales expenses 86 percent between 1985 and 1990. Moreover, US firms have been increasingly included in the design stage of products, with design-ins increasing nearly sixfold between 1986 and 1991.

Table 4.9 Joint activities of US and Japanese semiconductor firms

Japanese firm(s)	US firm	Activity
Fujitsu	Advanced Micro Devices	Flash memory chip production
Fujitsu, Toshiba	Sun Microsystems	RISC chip development
Fujitsu	Hal Computer Systems	RISC chip development
Hitachi	Hewlett-Packard	RISC chip development
Hitachi	Texas Instruments	DRAM development
Hitachi	Wang Laboratories	Marketing arrangement
Matsushita	Solbourne Computer	RISC chip development
Matsushita	Intel	Marketing and production arrangement
Mitsubishi	AT&T	Gallium arsenide chip development
Mitsubishi	DEC	RISC chip development
NEC	AT&T	Marketing and R&D arrangement
NEC	Micron Technologies	Marketing arrangement
NEC, Sony, Toshiba	MIPS Computer Systems	RISC chip development
NMB Semiconductor	Ramtron International	DRAM development
NMB Semiconductor	Intel	Marketing arrangement
Oki Electric	Hewlett-Packard	DRAM development
Sanyo	Micron Technologies	Marketing arrangement
Sharp	Intel	Flash memory chip production
Toshiba	Motorola	Production and marketing arrangement
Toshiba	IBM	DRAM development, flat panel displays, flash memory chips
Toshiba	Mical	Microprocessor R&D
Toshiba	National Semiconductor	DRAM development, flash memory chips

Source: Press reports.

The welfare impact of the STA therefore comes down to whether the Japanese market was initially protected, and whether the agreement facilitated an anticompetitive cartel in semiconductors. Clearly, by 1986 traditional border protection was minimal, so that with regard to the first issue, the case must be made on the basis of private practices that discriminated against imports. As noted earlier, vertically integrated firms will tend to source inputs internally in products such as semiconductors that are characterized by huge fixed costs and significant learning curves over the product cycle, but this is efficient and not a trade impediment per se.

Tyson (1992), however, argues that *keiretsu* links provide considerable scope for trade discrimination. This claim of *keiretsu* barriers has to be examined very carefully. Tyson (1992, 134) asserts that "preferential arrangements both within and between the Japanese suppliers and their *keiretsu* partners acted as an opaque but nonetheless powerful barrier to foreign suppliers." The problem with this argument is that discrimination has a well-known efficiency cost. Firms that do not source from the most efficient suppliers will themselves be put at a competitive disadvantage. The proven ability of the Japanese electronics firms to compete in world markets implies that they are not competitively disadvantaged in any significant way. This suggests that either Tyson's argument is incorrect or that some other barriers in the production system generate rents for the electronics firms, permitting them to indulge in this discriminatory and seemingly self-destructive behavior.

The fact that the electronics firms are highly diversified could create many possibilities of this sort. *Keiretsu* control of the distribution system in consumer electronics, for example, could facilitate the gouging of Japanese consumers and the cross-subsidization of the semiconductor business. Likewise, preferential access to the government market for telecommunications and computers, together with a largely captive private market in computers (due to the incompatible operating systems) could give rise to similar opportunities.

Even so, these possibilities do not appear to be entirely convincing: if a firm can earn rents in protected downstream markets, why dissipate them supporting inefficient suppliers? One possible answer is that vertical integration can capture significant pecuniary externalities in industries where the upstream input market is characterized by significant scale economies. Another is that the *keiretsu* might prefer to source from affiliated companies as part of a kind of profit-sharing or insurance scheme.

The next question, then, is how much the exporting country gains. In the case of the STA, the 20 percent market share appears to have been a lower-bound estimate of what the foreign producer market share would have been if the Japanese market were like markets elsewhere in the world. (In 1986, US firms had a 40 percent share of the European market and a 66 percent share of the world market excluding Japan.) Table 4.10 reports data on sales and exports in the Japanese market disaggregated by product for 1987 and 1991.[32]

Total sales by North American firms grew more than twice as fast as the market in the wake of the STA, from $1.2 billion in 1987 to more than $2.8 billion in 1991. Some analysts have attributed this increase both to shifts in the composition of demand in Japan and to technological innovations by US firms (such as the development of the 486 chip by Intel Corp.). The latter hypothesis is difficult to assess, and the former does not appear to be supported by the data. The segment of the market where the North American presence was greatest in 1987, namely, bipolar digital logic chips, actually shrank between 1987 and 1991.[33] Rather, the striking thing that emerges from the first two panels of this table is that the North American firms' market shares grew most rapidly in MOS memory chips, MOS logic chips, and MOS microcomponents, which all accounted for a growing share of the Japanese market. That is, US firms increased their shares in the most rapidly growing part of the market.[34]

The results for sales by US firms do not necessarily hold for exports from the United States. Recall that, under the STA, the "nationality" of a product was determined by the producer's headquarters, not the location of production. Consequently, semiconductors produced by US firms in Japan or third countries counted as foreign, while products produced by Japanese firms abroad and shipped back to Japan did not.

The third panel of table 4.10 reports data on US semiconductor exports to Japan. Extreme caution is warranted in making comparisons between the data on sales and those on exports; they are from two different sources, product definitions may differ, and only the sales data include Canadian firms. With these caveats, the data indicate that the growth rate of US exports actually exceeded the growth rate of sales by North American firms. The absolute increase in exports was greatest in bipolar devices (accounted for completely by increases in bipolar digital memory devices), while the growth rate was greatest in MOS memory devices.[35]

---

32. Unfortunately, the original data source does not separate US from North American sales. Canadian sales are presumably negligible.

33. Data on sales of bipolar digital logic and bipolar digital memory chips are combined in table 4.10 because of difficulty in matching Dataquest and Department of Commerce data in this sector. Both the total market and the North American share of the market shrank in both of these segments between 1987 and 1991.

34. This can be interpreted as supporting the notion that entry is easiest in expanding sectors, where domestic firms may not be able to meet demand, and in any event where imports do not directly displace *existing* domestic production.

35. Indeed, the measured exports of bipolar devices actually exceed North American sales. This could occur either because exports from Japanese plants in the United States back to

The same enormous increases did not occur in microprocessors, undermining the argument that it has been technological innovations in this market segment that has generated the growth in US semiconductor exports. Taken together, the data on sales and exports do not support the contention that the increase in foreign market share has been due largely to either shifts in demand toward market segments of high foreign penetration or technological innovations in semiconductors.

So how much of this increased foreign activity can be ascribed to the STA? One way of answering this is to ask the counterfactual: what would sales (or exports) have been if the foreigners had merely maintained their market shares? If bipolar devices (where the North American firm share of sales actually declined) are excluded (presumably the STA did not cause a decline in market share) and the North American market shares in 1987 are applied to each segment of the Japanese market in 1991, the predicted sales are $1.4 billion. In fact, sales in those categories were $2.5 billion. The difference, $1.1 billion, could be interpreted as an upper-bound estimate of the impact of the STA. A similar calculation could be done with respect to exports. Thus, if the share of US exports in each product category (including bipolar devices, where their share increased) had remained unchanged between 1987 and 1991, US exports would have been $457 million. In fact, exports in these categories (excluding the "other" category) were $872 million, yielding $415 million as an upper-bound estimate of the STA's effect.

It should be stressed that this is an upper-bound estimate that ascribes all market gains to the STA and not to other factors (such as technological innovation).[36] If accepted, these calculations suggest that the impact of the STA was to nearly double US semiconductor exports between 1987 and 1991. Even so, this would imply that less than half of the increased sales by North American firms were sourced from the United States.[37]

The next issue is whether the implementation of the STA facilitated a cartel in semiconductors, at least in the short run.[38] Even after MITI ended its production guidance and the semiconductor market began to weaken in 1989, Japanese producers openly discussed and implemented

---

Japan are not counted in the North American sales data, or because of incompatibility between the Department of Commerce and Dataquest data.

36. This interpretation assumes that there would not have been any *decline* in US market shares in the absence of the STA. In this case the gains would have been even larger than cited above.

37. Similar calculations to quantify the gains to other countries such as Korea would be desirable, but are beyond the bounds of this study.

38. See Krishna (1989) for a theoretical exposition of how trade restrictions can facilitate cartel behavior.

Table 4.10 Semiconductor sales in the Japanese market, 1987 and 1991 (millions of dollars except where noted)

	1987	1991
Total Japanese market	14,667	22,405
Growth rate, 1987–91		11.2
Bipolar digital logic and memory devices	1,530	1,435
Percentage of total	10.4	6.4
Growth rate, 1987–91		−1.6
MOS memory devices	2.311	4,228
Percentage of total	15.8	18.9
Growth rate, 1987–91		16.3
MOS microcomponents	1,964	3,579
Percentage of total	13.4	16.0
Growth rate, 1987–91		16.2
MOS logic devices	2,284	4,074
Percentage of total	15.6	18.2
Growth rate, 1987–91		15.6
Analog devices	3,188	3,954
Percentage of total	21.7	17.6
Growth rate, 1987–91		5.5
Discrete devices	2,424	3,432
Percentage of total	16.5	15.3
Growth rate, 1987–91		9.1
Optoelectronic devices	966	1,703
Percentage of total	6.6	7.6
Growth rate, 1987–91		15.2
Total North American sales in Japan	1,238	2,833
Percentage of total market	8.4	12.6
Growth rate, 1987–91		23.0
Bipolar digital logic and memory devices	356	276
Percentage of total bipolar	23.3	19.2
Growth rate, 1987–91		−6.2
MOS memory devices	110	470
Percentage of total MOS memory chips	4.8	11.1
Growth rate, 1987–91		43.8
MOS microcomponents	238	815
Percentage of total MOS microcomponents	12.1	22.8
Growth rate, 1987–91		36.0
MOS logic devices	157	495
Percentage of total MOS logic chips	6.9	12.2
Growth rate, 1987–91		33.3
Analog devices	299	618
Percentage of total analog	9.4	15.6
Growth rate, 1987–91		19.9
Discrete devices	57	103
Percentage of total discrete	2.4	3.0
Growth rate, 1987–91		15.9
Optoelectronic devices	21	0
Percentage of total optoelectronic	2.2	0.0
Growth rate, 1987–91		−100.0

Table 4.10 Semiconductor sales in the Japanese market, 1987 and 1991 (millions of dollars except where noted) Continued

	1987	1991
Total US exports to Japan	384	969
Growth rate, 1987–91		26.0
Bipolar digital logic and memory devices	72	298
Growth rate, 1987–91		42.6
MOS memory devices	20	176
Growth rate, 1987–91		72.2
MOS microcomponents	65	102
Growth rate, 1987–91		11.9
MOS logic devices	41	112
Growth rate, 1987–91		28.6
Analog devices	50	162
Growth rate, 1987–91		34.2
Discrete devices	70	22
Growth rate, 1987–91		−25.1
Other devices	65	97
Growth rate, 1987–91		10.5

Sources: Sales, Dataquest Inc.; Exports, US Department of Commerce.

cutbacks in DRAM production to boost prices.[39] Moreover, it is speculated that this will significantly slow the fall in memory prices as new generations of chips are brought to the market. Flamm (1990) estimates that the reduced long-run rate of decline in memory cost could reduce the demand growth for computers due solely to computing power increases from 5.5 percent a year to 3.1 percent a year, with obvious deleterious effects for computer hardware and software producers.

Tyson (1992) argues that in the long run the STA, by stopping dumping by Japanese firms, encouraged the entry of new, non-Japanese producers into the market and ultimately undermined the cartel's cohesion. The entry of new firms in Korea, Taiwan, and Europe is undisputable. The counterfactual—what would have happened in the absence of the STA— is more difficult to answer. Given many governments' desire for local semiconductor manufacture, it is not implausible that national champions might have entered the market without the STA. It is also possible that the threat of retaliation associated with the VIE has encouraged a loosening of exclusionary practices.[40]

---

39. Tyson (1992), for example, cites the simultaneous announcement of production cutbacks in September 1989 by all Japanese producers of 1M DRAMs.

40. After US Trade Representative Carla A. Hills publicly expressed frustration in March 1992 over the slow growth of foreign market share, US and Japanese industry groups agreed that major Japanese semiconductor firms (which are also major consumers) would provide foreign suppliers with lists of planned chip purchases—information that they had previously given only to foreign suppliers with whom they had long-term relationships.

This raises the final issue of implementation. If the ultimate justification for the STA was to keep prices high and encourage entry, and thereby undermine cartel behavior, it is reasonable to ask whether this was the first-best solution. As noted earlier, US antidumping laws are deeply flawed,[41] and their emphasis on dumping effectively creates a price floor policy and makes the United States a high-cost production location. During any cyclical weakening of demand, foreign firms will be tempted to cut domestic prices, since their ability to compete on price is restricted abroad. This means that downstream users of semiconductors (computers, telecommunications) in semiconductor net-importing regions will be put at a competitive disadvantage. In the case at hand, the STA put US and European semiconductor users at a competitive disadvantage relative to their counterparts in Japan.[42]

Unfortunately a similar pattern of development appears to be occurring in liquid crystal displays (LCDs), a type of flat panel display. Flat panel displays are thin, bright, pin-sharp displays that are in the early stages of replacing the familiar television screen-type display in innumerable applications, and indeed the nascent US industry has received promotional subsidies through the Pentagon's Advanced Research Projects Agency (ARPA). The Advanced Display Manufacturers of America, an industry group, brought a successful dumping action against Japanese display manufacturers in 1991. The original dumping suit was against all flat panel displays, but four big users—Apple, Compaq Computer Corp., IBM, and Tandy Corp.—persuaded the Commerce Department that the displays should be treated as four separate products: active matrix LCD, passive matrix LCD, electroluminescent (EL), and gas

41. In perfectly competitive markets, firms may choose to price below marginal costs in the initial stages of production; indeed, it was an American firm, TI, that pioneered the strategy of forward pricing. Second, perfectly competitive firms may temporarily price below costs if production or sales distribution is characterized by quasi irreversibilities, for instance in the face of demand shocks or temporary exchange rate misalignment. US dumping rules make no provision for this. Indeed, since domestic firms cannot, by definition, dump, if domestic firms are price leaders, foreign firms will be forced into dumping. Lastly, there are severe problems with the actual calculation of dumping margins. See Flamm (1993) for a discussion of these issues in the semiconductor context.

42. Recently a dispute has developed in the area of "flash" memory chips. These chips, invented by Toshiba in 1986, retain data in their memory even when the electrical current is cut off. Thus, they are an obvious candidate to replace magnetic disks and other media as computer memory storage. Intel has leapfrogged Toshiba and Hitachi through its superior production technology and now controls 85 percent of the world market for these chips. US semiconductor makers successfully petitioned the Commerce Department in December 1991 to classify flash memory chips as EPROMs, and thus bring them under the STA. As a consequence, there will be upward pressure on flash memory chip prices in the United States as production comes on line in Japan (Intel has signed agreements with NMB Semiconductor and Sharp). This will put US-based computer and electronics makers at a disadvantage vis-à-vis their Japanese competitors.

plasma. The passive matrix investigation was immediately halted, since there were no domestic producers of this product. (Motorola and In Focus Systems have since announced plans to begin jointly producing passive matrix LCDs in the United States). No dumping was discovered in the case of gas plasma, and in the case of EL displays, dumping margins of 7 percent were levied on Japanese producers. In the case of active matrix LCDs, dumping margins of 63 percent were assigned. US-based makers of laptop computers immediately moved production offshore, ironically encouraged by the elimination of tariffs on laptops as part of the extension of the STA.[43] In November 1992, Optical Imaging Systems (OIS), the sole producer of active matrix flat panel displays, asked that the 63 percent dumping margin be cancelled; in January 1993, the Commerce Department announced that it backed the request, noting that the other flat panel producers had no right to object, since they used different technologies. In March 1992, the ITC upheld the 63 percent dumping margin in active matrix LCD panels, but ruled against the dumping finding in EL displays. The results of these rulings must now be reviewed by the Court of International Trade.

Semiconductor Manufacturing Equipment

Parallel to these issues of declining competitiveness in semiconductors have been concerns about the health of the US semiconductor manufacturing equipment industry, which saw its world market share decline from 75 percent in 1980 to 45 percent in 1990, before rebounding to 47 percent in 1991 and an estimated 49 percent in 1992. Over the same period, the Japanese world market share rose from 18 percent to a peak of 51 percent in 1990, before declining to 47 percent in 1991 and an estimated 43 percent in 1992. This raised the specter of US chip makers being dependent on Japanese suppliers for their chip-making equipment. Such concerns were heightened by the actual and possible Japanese acquisitions of US chip-making firms, and charges publicly aired by then-Sen. Lloyd Bentsen (D-TX) that Japanese firms were disadvantaging US equipment users by withholding state-of-the-art technology.[44]

---

43. ARPA has since supported the formation of a domestic consortium, the High-Definition Display Manufacturing Consortium (HDDMC), to encourage the development of flat panel display mass production capability in the United States. Japanese firms have reportedly outspent US firms by more than 20 to 1 in the development of this technology, with one firm alone, Sharp, budgeting nearly $1 billion for flat panel display R&D between 1991 and 1993. Korean firms have also begun to enter the flat panel market. In certain respects this situation resembles the DRAM market in the late 1980s.

44. As noted earlier, the subsequent US GAO (1991) report did not find convincing evidence of illegal or predatory behavior by Japanese firms. A main beneficiary of increased government support for chip-making equipment would be Sematech, located in Texas. The research consortium has been under continual funding pressure.

In reality, the decline in US market share appeared to be intimately tied to the relative decline of the United States as a location of semiconductor production and the exit of US firms from high-volume DRAM production. Semiconductor manufacturing machines are highly complex capital goods, and sales are tied to the seller's ability to work closely with customers. US firms maintain a market share of 70 to 80 percent in the United States, but their market share in Japan has declined from around 40 percent to 15 percent over the course of the 1980s. Some firms, such as Applied Materials, have maintained a strong presence in Japan, and the share of sales in Japan is similar to the Japanese share of the world market.[45]

The relative competitiveness of US and Japanese firms varies significantly across different segments of the industry. US firms, for example, account for 75 percent of the world market for ion implanters, while Japanese firms dominate logic test systems. More troubling than the nationality of competing firms is the degree of concentration in some products: Nikon controls roughly half the market for optical lithography wafer steppers, while Canon has another fifth of the market.

Semiconductor Policy Recommendations

The STA had two parts: one relating to pricing, and the other to market access. While virtually all observers would concede that the floor price aspect of the STA was a failure, less consensus exists with regard to the market access aspects. In 1992, US and Japanese firms were virtually tied for the lead in worldwide semiconductor sales, with each accounting for approximately 43 percent of the total. This represents a significant turnabout from the situation in 1986, when Japanese and American firms held 47 percent and 39 percent of the market, respectively. While it is clear that foreign firms have made considerable gains in penetrating the Japanese market, technological innovations may have played an important role in this process. An upper-bound estimate that ascribes to the STA all increases in foreign-firm market shares would credit the agreement with increasing North American sales in the Japanese market by $1.1 billion and US exports to Japan by $415 million.

These gains are considerable. It is less obvious whether they should be regarded as true welfare gains, however. The answer comes down to whether the STA ultimately reduced or enhanced the efficiency of the

---

45. Indeed, Applied Materials and AMP have been recipients of Japan Development Bank loans to establish operations in Japan. To further facilitate access to the Japanese market, 11 firms of the Semiconductor Equipment Association of Japan, including Nikon and Canon, announced in April 1992 that they would offer their own office space at below-market rents to US firms to help defray high initial start-up costs stemming from high land prices. (Of course, both the office rental market and the chip equipment business were in cyclical decline at this point, so the space might have gone empty otherwise.)

world semiconductor market. It can be argued that the procurement behavior of the integrated Japanese electronics firms prior to the STA reflected the economically rational behavior of vertically integrated firms where an upstream component (semiconductors) was subject to scale economies. In this case the VIE introduced a distortion, which benefited US and other non-Japanese semiconductor firms but arguably reduced the welfare of all other agents, including consumers. If this is the case, the STA reduced welfare in Japan and possibly the rest of the world (including the United States) as well.

Alternatively, one could regard the pre-STA semiconductor market as a distorted one in which large Japanese firms used rents generated from a variety of protected product markets to cross-subsidize the production of semiconductors. In this case the VIE was arguably welfare-enhancing from both a US and a global standpoint, and possibly even from the Japanese standpoint if consumer interests are taken into account. The VIE increased the numbers of suppliers (and thus increased competition, reducing rents and most likely increasing consumer welfare) while at the same time shifting some of those rents to non-Japanese firms. The available evidence does not permit a confident rejection of either interpretation; in the end it is a judgment call as to which characterization best describes the reality of the semiconductor market in the mid-1980s. We believe that the preponderance of evidence points to this latter intepretation.

This does not mean, however, that the VIE was necessarily the best policy option. If the goal of policy is to ensure the access of semiconductors to domestic users at competitive terms, as often claimed on national security grounds, a tit-for-tat countervailing subsidy policy could have also accomplished this—although without the favorable terms-of-trade effects of a VIE. This would have the effect of undermining possible cartel behavior by the Japanese producers, while at the same time keeping prices of semiconductors faced by domestic users competitive. It would also benefit equipment makers by increasing domestic demand for their product. Moreover, acceptance of this proposal would change the political dynamics of policy formation: the cost of the subsidy (as opposed to antidumping measures or a price floor) would be transparent and would be judged against possible alternative uses of the funds. Under the current antidumping-oriented system, aggrieved firms can wrap themselves in the flag, claiming they are being preyed on by unscrupulous foreigners, while the costs of the remedy in terms of reduced competitiveness by users has no similar politically appealing cast, if it is recognized at all. The United States in fact pursued this approach with Sematech.

Indeed, it should be recognized that governments are going to engage in public support for emerging industries for a variety of motives, and attempting to prohibit such support is doomed to failure. Energy would be better spent attempting to negotiate an international code of acceptable subsidies to countervail foreign-government targeting.

A second tack would be to ensure the availability to foreign firms of patents produced by publicly supported activities. In this regard, the STA was on target. In the case of semiconductors and computers, this would mean bringing in foreign firms to participate in MITI-sponsored research consortia in Japan, and publicly funded efforts such as Sematech in the United States and JESSI in Europe. Indeed, given the extent of cross-border corporate alliances and cooperation, and the high cost of R&D, it seems naive to restrict these projects to putatively domestic firms, and allowing the foreigners in has the virtue of making foreign expertise available for capture.[46]

Domestically, the US government could strengthen the competitiveness of the semiconductor and computer industries by undertaking the macroeconomic reforms detailed in chapter 2, which would reduce the cost of capital. The United States could also encourage more cooperative R&D activities along the lines of Sematech and the proposed US Memories consortium. At the same time, the agendas of publicly funded programs should be geared toward increasing the degree of competition in highly concentrated markets such as that for optical lithography wafer steppers, regardless of the oligopolists' nationality.

Lastly, the military budget is sometimes cited as a source of significant support to semiconductors. This is probably exaggerated. According to Tyson (1992, 152), "in recent years as much as 70 percent of Defense Department R&D support for the semiconductor industry has concentrated on developing hardened chip technology capable of withstanding a direct nuclear hit." Moreover, technology is increasingly "spun on" from civilian to military applications rather than "spun off" in the other direction. Indeed, firms have encountered significant difficulty capitalizing on dual-use technologies (those with both civilian and military applications) because of restrictions such as COCOM export controls. The Pentagon has generously supported Sematech, providing it with far greater funding than MITI has for consortia such as the Fifth Generation Computing Project in Japan. Conversely, in cases where the United States runs the risk of dependence on foreign suppliers, the appropriate response is to require inward foreign direct investment by those firms as a condition for sales in the US market, as Graham and Krugman (1991) recommend.

---

46. In addition, at least some of the Sematech development grants to chip equipment firms require the firms to withhold the products from companies that are not Sematech members (including nonmember US chip companies) for one year after they introduced.

Supercomputers

"Japanese machines are much faster and better. If the U.S. market were not closed, Japanese supercomputers would dominate the U.S. market."
> —Kunio Kuwahara, Director, Institute for Computational Fluid Dynamics
> *(Nikkei,* 1 August 1992*)*

"Our sales are good everywhere but the U.S."
> —Toshio Hiraguchi, Managing Director, Fujitsu
> *(Japan Economic Journal,* 6 October 1990*)*

"We are going to stomp on NEC."
> —Carl Diem, Vice President for Marketing Support, Cray Research, Inc.
> *(Los Angeles Times,* 9 April 1991*)*

Supercomputers are extremely fast, powerful computers: the Office of the US Trade Representative defines a supercomputer as a device capable of 300 million mathematical operations per second. There are two basic types of supercomputers. The traditional type relies on a relatively small number of very powerful processing units working in tandem. The first of these machines was built by Cray Research, Inc., in 1976, and these machines make up most of the stock of currently installed supercomputers.

A second approach to supercomputing, called massively parallel processing, was developed in the United States in the 1980s. A massively parallel supercomputer employs hundreds or thousands of microprocessors working together. If the traditional machines are behemoths smashing computational problems, the newer machines could be likened to swarms of ants nibbling away at them. A third strategy is to cluster work stations (single-user computers that are somewhat more powerful than PCs) into loosely coupled, parallel supercomputing systems. Most observers expect that the new approaches will ultimately supplant the traditional supercomputers.

For any of these approaches to work effectively, a variety of tasks— data retrieval and processing, processing unit task assignment, computation itself—must be coordinated. A bottleneck at any stage can nullify efficiencies elsewhere. And, as with any computer, a supercomputer is only as good as the software that can be run on it.

Supercomputers are mainly used in analyzing problems that require enormous numbers of mathematical calculations: weather and earthquake modeling, aerospace design, and crash analysis, to name a few. Supercomputers are also enormously expensive, with a single unit costing millions of dollars. Because of their current applications and their costs, the purchases of most supercomputers either directly or indirectly involve public funding.[47] Consequently, trade disputes between the United States and Japan over supercomputers have a somewhat different emphasis than in the rest of the computer industry, centering on public procurement issues.

At the outset, in the late 1970s, the industry consisted of two firms: Cray Research and ETA Systems, a subsidiary of Control Data Corp. The Japanese government first targeted supercomputers for development in 1981 and purchased its first supercomputer in 1983, when the first Japanese models became available. Through 1986, the Japanese government purchased 22 supercomputers, 21 of them domestically made. The foreign manufacturers complained that they were not notified when procurements were to take place; that Japanese firms bid on the basis of models still under development (so-called paper machines), not actually existing ones; that no performance criteria were specified in the bids, or that, when they were, the specifications appeared to be written for specific Japanese models; and that Japanese manufacturers were giving discounts of up to 80 to 90 percent of cost.

The American machines were clearly superior at this time on the basis of performance and the availability of software. Indeed, the two US firms accounted for 94 percent of the market outside of Japan, and 18 percent of the Japanese private market.[48]

The US government initiated negotiations over the supercomputer market in 1987 as part of the MOSS talks. During the talks, MITI Vice Minister Makoto Kuroda reportedly stated that the American firms would never be able to sell in Japan, and that the United States might have to nationalize Cray Research to save it from the coming Japanese onslaught.[49] The statements attributed to Kuroda galvanized high-level administration attention on the supercomputer issue. NEC announced that it would begin importing semiconductors to be used in its supercomputer, but this had little if any impact on attitudes in the United States. The Japanese government announced that it was including money for two supercomputer purchases in its 1987 emergency supplemental budget. (Perhaps not surprisingly under the circumstances, the US firms each won a bid for these additional purchases.) A formal agreement was concluded that summer that improved the transparency of the bidding process.

---

47. One estimate puts the public funding–dependent share of the US market at over 70 percent (*Electronic Engineering Times,* 19 June 1989).

48. As might be expected, internal demand by the three Japanese producers (Hitachi, Fujitsu, and NEC) and *keiretsu* ties have inhibited US penetration of the Japanese private market. Most US firm sales have gone to private firms with few corporate ties to Japanese producers (OTA 1991).

49. Kuroda's alleged remarks were reported both in the press and in US diplomatic cables, although he denied making them.

Soon, however, it became apparent that these purchases had been largely symbolic, as the foreign manufacturers failed to sell any additional supercomputers the following two years. In May 1989, the US government named public procurement of supercomputers a priority foreign practice for bilateral negotiation under the Super 301 provision of the 1988 omnibus trade act.

In many ways the experience of 1989–90 was a reprise of 1987. With great public fanfare, Cray Research (ETA Systems was by then no longer in the supercomputer business) was awarded the contract to install one of its supercomputers at a national university.[50] The United States held firm, however, and the day before the Super 301 negotiation period was to end, the United States and Japan announced a new set of agreements on supercomputer procurement. The new accord improved upon the old by mandating that performance requirements be stipulated in terms of real rather than peak performance, and discouraging bidding on the basis of paper machines.[51] A Procurement Review Board was established and empowered to reopen bidding if the accord's provisions are violated.[52]

Tyson (1992) rated it only a partial victory, however, as ETA Systems had already left the market, and the Japanese firms had become far more formidable competitors during the period of greatly hindered access. From a world welfare standpoint, this may have been welfare-enhancing since it reduced the degree of concentration in the industry. From a US national standpoint, however, it was almost assuredly a loss. The OTA (1991) estimates that, if the Japanese market had been open, Cray Research would have realized an additional $676 million in revenues, financing an additional $100 million of R&D, between 1980 and 1990.

Cray Research and the US government subsequently expressed dissatisfaction with Cray's ability to penetrate the Japanese public procurement market, and the Office of the US Trade Representative announced in April 1993 that it was opening a review of the agreement. To put it

---

50. It was widely reported that NEC, the expected winner, withdrew from the bidding at the behest of MITI. For its part, NEC claimed that it withdrew because it was bidding on the basis of a new model that might not have been ready by the deadline. Given that eliminating bidding on the basis of paper machines was one of the main topics under negotiation at that time, both explanations may contain an element of truth.

51. As noted earlier, the operation of a supercomputer requires the coordination of several computing tasks, bottlenecks in any of which can slow the actual operation of the machine. Clyde V. Prestowitz, Jr., (personal communication) has likened judging supercomputers on theoretical peak performance to evaluating a car by depressing the gas pedal while in park and reading the rpms off the tachometer.

52. The July 1992 National Institute of Fusion Science's award of its contract to NEC over Cray Research provided the first test case of this grievance procedure. Cray claims that the process was rigged in NEC's favor. The review board rejected Cray's appeal in October 1992.

Table 4.11 World supercomputer market shares, 1990 (percentages)

Market	US firms	Japanese firms
United States	97.9	2.1
Public sector	100.0	0.0
Universities	100.0	0.0
Other	94.1	5.9
Japan	13.1	86.9
Public sector	4.8	95.2
Universities	3.7	96.3
Other	18.3	81.7
Europe	88.0	12.0
Public sector	88.9	11.1
Universities	72.2	27.8
Other	94.9	5.1

Source: US Department of Commerce.

bluntly, the Japanese government had attempted to co-opt Cray, and Cray refused to play the game.

Private procurement presumably reflects at least some economic rationality. Public procurement offers greater scope for pure discrimination, and both countries' public procurement policies appear to discriminate against imported supercomputers. (Japanese firms have sold no supercomputers in the US public market, where an informal "buy American" policy continues even though no formal policy exists; table 4.11.)[53] Thus, not only did the agreement not clean up procurement in Japan, it did little for procurement in the United States as well.

If US and Japanese firms attained market shares in each other's public and university markets equal to their respective shares in Europe, Cray's share of the joint US-Japan public and university market would rise from 67.4 percent to 83.0 percent, and the Japanese firms' share would fall commensurately. Assuming that the US-Japan public and university market will grow by 15 supercomputers annually, this would mean that Cray would sell 2.34 additional supercomputers per year. This would represent more than $30 million per year in additional revenues, funding $4.6 million in additional R&D (applying the OTA figures of $13 million

---

53. There is a formal domestic preference policy in the national security area that is permitted under the GATT. US practice has gone well beyond this, however. In 1987, the Commerce Department in effect pressured the Massachusetts Institute of Technology not to buy an NEC supercomputer, even though it had no statutory authority to exercise such pressure. In 1990, NEC was excluded from bidding on a National Aeronautics and Space Administration (NASA) supercomputer contract. NEC protested, and the General Services Administration subsequently ruled that NEC must be permitted to participate. NEC has since formed a US sales alliance with Control Data, a firm with considerable federal contract experience. In 1991, the National Science Foundation (NSF) stopped Fujitsu from donating a supercomputer to a Colorado environmental research consortium which, although it receives no public funds, is housed in an NSF facility.

per supercomputer and a 15 percent share of revenues going to R&D). This gives a rough magnitude of the stakes.

Moreover, while both countries subsidize supercomputing research, the US subsidies, if anything, appear larger. US firms receive considerable subsidies through ARPA, and the United States has just embarked on a five-year, $1.9 billion program to support supercomputer research and develop a supercomputer electronic data network.[54]

The picture that emerges with regard to supercomputers is strikingly similar to those in semiconductors and computers, except the roles are roughly equalized. The United States and Japan have effectively excluded each other's firms from their respective domestic markets, and firms from both countries compete against each other from bastion markets of protection and subsidy.

From Cray's standpoint, the stakes are important, but the industry is in a state of flux, with the introduction of cheap mini-supercomputers on the one hand, the arrival of massively parallel machines on the other, and clustered work stations on the horizon. It is important, then, that US policy not degenerate into a Cray Research national champion policy. At the bilateral and ultimately the international level, the United States should push for better procurement codes, which would cover leasing, a primary form of supercomputer contracting, as well as purchases. The United States should also abandon its *de facto* buy-American policy except in cases of narrowly defined national security reservations.

Also on the bilateral and eventually the international level, the United States should push for reciprocal access to publicly funded research results, with the goal of gaining access to foreign expertise. Already MITI is reportedly attempting to include IBM, AT&T, and the German company Siemens AG in its Sixth Generation Computing Project, which will involve supercomputer research; the United States should open up its projects to foreign participation as well.

At home, the United States could rationalize its export control process, for example to allow for automatic approvals as new best-practice technologies or suppliers arise. Current restrictions can be particularly onerous for the small and medium-sized firms involved in the production of mini-supercomputers and massively parallel processing machines.

Lastly, the United States must confront the issue of deep-pocket cross-subsidization by the vertically integrated Japanese producers. It is clear that the Japanese producers lose money in providing the massive discounts that they offer to the Japanese public sector. This can be rationalized either as a payoff for public research support or as a kind of leading-edge loss leader. As Tadashi Watanabe of NEC has stated, "We don't

---

54. Not to be outdone, the European Community announced in November 1992 a $4.3 billion program to support its own nascent supercomputer industry.

need to make a profit on our line of supercomputers. Whatever is spun off from our supercomputer R&D helps in other information technology fields" (OTA 1991, 275). Or, as his colleague Michiyuki Uenohara prosaically explained, "The reason Japanese companies are going into the supercomputer business is the same reason that auto companies get into race cars; even though it's a small market, it drives technology" (OTA 1991, 253).

This practice of cross-subsidization could present a considerable obstacle to the smaller, less diversified US firms. Although some of the problem may have been due to the very low cost of capital that Japanese firms faced in the late 1980s, the potential of cross-subsidization by the larger, diversified Japanese firms remains. The current US policy—to discourage deep discounting in the Japanese public market—is flawed. Because public procurement budgets have risen far more slowly than discounts have declined, the result has been to reduce the demand for supercomputers. This does not help US firms trying to crack the market, and at the same time it increases the profitability of Japanese firms in that market. A tit-for-tat subsidy such as that advocated by Tyson (1992) would amount to a transfer from US taxpayers to Japanese public institutions. The United States has enough trouble funding its own universities, let alone theirs.

A preferable policy would be one that attempted to create the conditions of massive discounting in the United States, and capture whatever efficiency gains or externalities are associated with the *consumption* of supercomputer services. This policy would have two parts. The first would be to induce the Japanese companies to participate in the US public market. This means getting rid of the informal "buy American" policies and the threat of self-initiated dumping suits, as was used against NEC in the MIT case. Only then would the United States provide subsidies to the supercomputer users. In this way the United States would induce both the US and the Japanese firms to engage in subsidized competition in the US public procurement market, with the Japanese firms cross-subsidizing from other product lines and the US firms being subsidized publicly.[55] The net result would be a transfer from Japan to the United States, a stronger US supercomputer industry, and more choice at better prices for US consumers.

Computer Software

The United States has traditionally been the world leader in computer software—an area in which Japan conspicuously lags behind. Given the

---

55. Cray could conceivably claim dumping in such a scenario, but as long as it is receiving subsidies and getting contracts, it would not be able to meet the injury test.

US dominance and the fact that software is typically licensed abroad and does not appear in the merchandise trade statistics, software has not figured prominently in US-Japan trade disputes. An exception was the 1988–89 flap over TRON, a developmental operating system that the Japanese government was supporting and planning to purchase for use in the national education and telecommunications systems. (TRON would also require specialized terminals and other equipment, thus adding a major hardware dimension to this dispute.)

The US preeminence in software is likely to erode, however. With the very rapid growth of personal computer use in Japan, there has been an explosion in demand for software, making Japan the second-largest market in the world after the United States. In the past, major manufacturers sold their products through independent vendors, often with very large markups. (This was feasible as there was no significant Japanese product competition, nor were there large-scale domestic retailers.) Rapid increases in demand, along with the high-margin strategy of the major US firms, has created a market opening for Japanese entrants. At the same time, Japanese firms are moving aggressively to tap software engineering resources elsewhere in Asia, particularly in China.

The result is that Japan is becoming both a more important market and a potential source of competition for US firms. As a consequence, US firms are increasingly attempting to establish a presence in the Japanese market, through either greenfield investments or acquisitions. Another implication is that Japanese firms will be increasingly important players in worldwide cross-national software development alliances.

Telecommunications Services and Equipment

"The dispute over approving U.S.-made car phones symbolized anachronistic bureaucratic prerogatives. [Japanese] Ministry of Posts and Telecommunications officials insisted they controlled the radio waves and could regulate car phones, essentially denying market access to an American company. I have a Japanese-made phone in my car that is unreliable. It often goes dead in the middle of a conversation. If a large truck pulls up next to me at a traffic light or I go under the elevated highways that criss-cross Tokyo, the phone does not work. Even the best Japanese phone can be easily monitored. Gangsters reportedly listened in when a certain politician was talking to his mistress and blackmailed him for a princely sum. Eavesdropping is so easy that no one dare discuss a confidential matter on a car phone. U.S. models are supposed to be really good and I wanted to get one, but I was foiled by red tape."
—Shintaro Ishihara, LDP Member of Diet *(1989, 99)*

Like most countries, the United States and Japan long maintained highly regulated telecommunications markets. Opportunities for service provision by foreigners was for practical purposes proscribed, and most equipment was procured domestically. The United States began to deregulate these markets in 1984 with the breakup of AT&T's domestic telephone monopoly. This loosened up the market, and foreign electronics firms rapidly increased their telecommunications equipment sales in the United States.

Japan has consistently lagged the United States in telecommunications deregulation, which in large part explains why there have been trade tensions in this sector for more than a decade. In 1979, Motorola attempted to enter the Japanese market for beeper-pagers, but could not even secure an appointment with NTT, the Japanese public telecommunications monopoly, without the intercession of US government officials. Next, in apparent violation of Japan's GATT obligations, NTT refused to disclose its proposal procedures or specifications. This in turn led to government-to-government negotiations and eventually the NTT Procurement Procedure Agreement of December 1980, the first of a series of bilateral telecommunications accords.[56]

By the mid-1980s, imports made up only 3 to 4 percent of NTT procurements, however, and there was growing dissatisfaction in the United States with the implementation of the agreement. In 1984, the United States designated telecommunications as one of the sectors slated for MOSS talks.[57] According to one participant, the goal of these negotiations was "to obtain an environment similar to that in the U.S. with regard to telecommunication enterprises, equipment standards, and certification" (Prestowitz 1988, 297). The 1985 agreements that resulted from these talks appeared to do just that.[58] These agreements, together with NTT's

---

56. NTT subsequently denied that beeper-pagers fell under the agreement, and only released beeper-pager specifications (which included both performance and design requirements) after the intervention of US Secretary of State George P. Shultz; this was the first of several high-level interventions in telecommunications. NTT then set a *minimum* price that it would accept, so that Motorola could not compete on the basis of price, and thereby minimized the disruption to its existing supplier cartel. Eventually NTT was privatized, loosening traditional supplier bonds, and Motorola emerged as the largest supplier—indicating that Motorola was indeed competitive in beeper-pagers (see Tyson 1992, 66–67).

57. The NTT Procurement Procedure Agreement was subsequently renewed four times, most recently in December 1992. After an initial jump in the early 1980s, import procurement by NTT remained essentially flat from 1983 until 1988, when it began to increase in response to both political pressure and NTT's privatization. Nevertheless, NTT estimates that foreign firms still account for less than 11 percent of its purchases.

58. The MOSS agreement in telecommunications addressed a number of market access issues: self-certification for value-added networks was permitted; technical standards and requirements were reduced to those necessary to protect the network; and the Japanese Ministry of Posts and Telecommunications (MPT) agreed to appoint representatives of US firms to its standards-setting board, established a testing and certification agency independent of domestic manufacturers, and initiated the deregulation of the cellular telephone market. See Tyson (1992) for further details.

partial privatization in 1985, were expected to result in greater foreign access to Japanese telecommunications markets. Significant change was not apparent, however, and even relatively minor issues (such as the voice quality of telephones) still required high-level political intervention (in this case the Undersecretary of Commerce and the National Security Adviser for Japan). The Japanese government apparently reneged on agreements in the provision of value-added networks and foreign participation in international telephone service.[59] In March 1986, the US Senate voted 92–0 to recommend that President Reagan retaliate against Japan for its failure to open its telecommunications market.

This unanimous condemnation apparently shocked Japanese policymakers, and a flurry of activity began across several fronts. One area of contention was cellular telephones.[60] The stakes in this dispute were enormous. In 1986, the Japanese market was the third-largest in the world at $400 million and expected to grow by 40 to 50 percent a year for the next five years. These expectations were subsequently borne out. By 1990, Japan was the second-largest market in the world, with 1.2 million users, and growing at 40 percent annually. MPT predicts that the number of subscribers will rise to between 8.2 million and 8.5 million by 2000.

Motorola had attempted to enter the Japanese market in 1984 but encountered the problem that standards and testing were being performed by Japanese industry groups, which had an incentive to develop standards and testing procedures that favored their own products. The MOSS talks resolved this problem, and in March 1986 the standards board, which had been broadened to include foreign participation, recommended that all protocols (including both those of NTT and Motorola) be accepted. MPT, however, argued that the radio frequencies available

---

59. Although foreign participation in the provision of international telephone services was permitted by law, MPT all but proscribed foreign participation until forced by repeated interventions by President Ronald Reagan and British Prime Minister Margaret Thatcher to relent (Balassa and Noland 1988).

With regard to value-added networks, MPT ruled that foreign firms that had developed proprietary protocols would have to replace them with international ones. This had the effect of giving a relative advantage to the recent Japanese entrants to the market, which had not yet developed their own proprietary protocols. MPT eventually bowed to US pressure in 1988 and permitted firms to maintain their own protocols, provided that they also made software available to make them compatible with the international standard (Tyson 1992).

Foreign firms continue to encounter barriers in this market, however. In 1990, KDD (the traditional and still-dominant supplier of international telephone links) agreed to drop the 20 percent surcharge it was applying to international value-added network users; in 1991, it agreed to end the practice of demanding excessive documentation and paperwork and to limit required documentation to the international standard.

60. Much of this discussion is drawn from Tyson (1992, 66–71). See this source for further detail.

for cellular phones were limited, and urged Motorola and its Japanese partner Daini Denden (DDI) to merge with a rival consortium, IDO (which used the NTT system), and together compete against NTT. When this did not materialize, MPT announced that it was allocating to Motorola and DDI the right to compete against NTT in western Japan (comprising 30 to 40 percent of the market), while IDO was allocated the remainder. Motorola protested to US trade officials, and eventually MPT announced that it would permit the Motorola system to be used throughout Japan, except for the lucrative Tokyo-Nagoya corridor. As a consequence, the NTT system could be used anywhere in the country, whereas the Motorola system still could not be used in the most important market.

In 1988, MPT allocated a radio frequency to a new telecommunications service, belying its claim that there were not enough available radio frequencies. This time the negotiating position of Motorola and its patrons at the Office of the US Trade Representative (USTR) had been strengthened by the 1988 trade act, with its special telecommunications 301 provision, and in early 1989 Motorola submitted a public comment to the USTR recommending that telecommunications be designated under the so-called Special 301 provision of the 1988 act.

MPT maintained that the plan was not a violation of its MOSS commitments, and in any event the problem would resolve itself in a few years when the advent of digital cellular telephones would relax the capacity constraint. Motorola interpreted this as a delaying maneuver to convey infant-industry protection to its Japanese rivals, and in April 1989 the USTR determined that Japan had violated the earlier agreement and announced its intention to retaliate unless the dispute was resolved by 10 July. With the conflict now raised to a new, public level and retaliation a real possibility, MPT agreed in late June 1989 to reallocate frequencies so that the Motorola system could be used throughout Japan. Disputes in the telecommunications area soon recurred, however, and another agreement had to be negotiated; it was signed in August 1990.[61]

Motorola's problems still did not end there. As part of the plan, MPT instructed the rival consortium, IDO, to make the necessary broadcast facilities available to Motorola's partner DDI. As might be expected,

---

61. Motorola was also the central player in a related telecommunications dispute during this same period. Third-party radio systems (also called shared mobile radio systems) are used by taxi fleets, delivery services, police departments, and the like to transmit information from a central dispatcher to units in the field. Japanese radio law created a public monopoly to provide this service. Motorola and the US government successfully lobbied the Japanese government to change the law to permit other service providers to compete in the market. Motorola subsequently entered the market but was disadvantaged vis-à-vis the public agency by MPT's frequency allocation decisions, as well as by the ministry's requirement that Motorola sign up customers in advance to demonstrate full loading.

As in the case of cellular phones, Motorola went to the USTR, and the problems were resolved by the June 1989 agreement. The market has grown rapidly, and Motorola regards the third-party radio experience as an unqualified success (Tyson 1992, 71–73).

IDO's response displayed a noticeable lack of alacrity. In the meantime, IDO's revenues were growing rapidly, and Japanese equipment makers had unimpeded access to the US market, while Motorola's ability to penetrate the Japanese market remained constrained.

In the end, the cellular telephone market was substantially deregulated. The obstacles that Motorola confronted in its attempt to establish a presence in the Japanese market certainly provided Japanese equipment suppliers with temporary protection. What if any permanent advantage this may have conveyed is less clear. The Motorola system can now be used throughout Japan, and additional service providers have entered the market. The actual equipment used in this market was not sourced in the United States, however. A number of foreign equipment suppliers in addition to Motorola have also entered the market, and the cellular phones sold by Motorola, although designed in the United States, are produced in Malaysia.

Another source of contention was the market for optical fibers. As in the Motorola cases, a single, politically well-connected firm, this time Corning Glass Works (now Corning Inc.), was effectively stymied in the Japanese market. Corning's problems in Japan have a long history. The company was initially rebuffed in its attempt to sell optical fiber to NTT, and Japanese authorities delayed approval of Corning's patent for nearly a decade, by which time Japanese firms had begun production. And although Corning was the dominant supplier of fiber optical cable worldwide, NTT, which accounts for approximately half of the Japanese fiber optic market, relied on the three domestic suppliers. Again, the stakes were large, with the Office of the US Trade Representative (1989) reporting industry estimates of a potential $198 million in additional sales if trade barriers were removed, as well as additional future sales in the rapidly growing market.

As in the Motorola cases, action was undertaken in 1989 when the fiber optic cable situation moved up the US policymakers' agendas and it became apparent that retaliation was a realistic possibility. Resolution of this dispute appears to have taken the form of inclusion of Corning into the three-firm suppliers' cartel. The USTR's 1990 *Foreign Trade Barriers* reports that "a U.S. supplier has gone from zero to 4.5 percent in the last three years" and that it is "optimistic that [the supplier's] sales volume to NTT will increase greatly in the coming years. . . . The US supplier anticipates it will be granted treatment 'equal' to that NTT grants its three principal suppliers of cable" (Office of the USTR 1990, 122). Subsequent editions of *Foreign Trade Barriers* do not report any further difficulty in the fiber optic cable market.[62] In point of fact, US exports

---

62. Indeed, Corning Japan KK was a recipient of a Japan Development Bank loan to build its Shizuoka-based factory and technical center for the production of liquid crystal display glass. The JDB loan reportedly financed the maximum 40 percent of the project's total cost allowable under the law.

rose from \$10.7 million in 1987 to \$43.4 million in 1992—a substantial increase, although far below the potential \$198 million cited by the USTR in its 1989 report.

The telecommunications cases illustrate several lessons about trade barriers in Japan and the US response. First, the barriers are easiest to identify when the government has a direct role in the market, either through regulatory functions or as a producer or service provider. This suggests that broad, general agreements may not be successful in resolving the problems, and more-burdensome, down-in-the-trenches negotiations along the lines of the MOSS talks may be necessary.

Second, dispute resolution is easiest where there is a potentially growing market (such as in cellular phones and fiber optic cable), whose growth can cushion the impact of greater foreign penetration. Indeed, domestic and foreign firms may be able to form coalitions to push deregulation schemes that greatly expand the scope of the market. In cases where domestic and foreign firms are in something closer to a zero-sum game, as was the case for much of NTT's equipment procurement, foreign firms have found the going far tougher. In these cases, high-level contacts in Washington and credible threats of retaliation may be an important part of a market-opening strategy.

Agreements must be verified and monitored. The experience of the telecommunications MOSS talks illustrates the metaphor of the onion, in which successive impediments must be removed one at a time like the layers of an onion.

In a number of the cases examined here, there was only one significant US producer or service provider. In such cases US trade policy runs the risk of being effectively privatized. While on the one hand it is important to represent the interests of US firms, it must be recognized that these firms' interests and US national interests may not coincide. An obvious example is when US official pressure leads to a US producer being brought into a Japanese cartel. While this may be optimal from the firm's point of view, it may have been in the US national interest to instead break up the cartel, in order to facilitate entry by additional US firms, or by foreign firms that would source exports to Japan in the United States (as the Canadian firm Northern Telecom does in fiber optics), if they exist.

Lastly, even "successful" trade agreements may not have a favorable impact on US trade statistics if the relevant products are not produced in the United States. The obvious example here is cellular phones. Early agreements to expand the market access of Motorola's affiliate DDI presumably increased Motorola's profitability and the employment of design engineers in the United States, but the phones were actually produced in Malaysia and therefore did not appear in the US-Japan trade statistics.

High-Definition Television

Conventional televisions in the United States operate on the National Television Systems Committee (NTSC) standard. Images are displayed in the form of 483 horizontal lines (42 additional lines carry auxiliary information), only half of which are displayed on each electronic gun pass. This produces visible flicker, for which studios compensate by reducing resolution. Moreover, the nearly square dimensions of the standard image necessitate horizontal cropping of material originally produced for theatrical display (i.e., movies). High-definition television (HDTV), in contrast, uses an image of roughly 1,000 lines, can display 35mm movies without cropping, and has an audio signal of enhanced clarity. The high resolution of HDTV is conducive to large-screen displays, and hence encourages the development of flat panel display media.

Both European and the Japanese governments have publicly supported HDTV efforts. According to Beltz (1991), NHK, the Japanese public broadcasting corporation, has spent more than $700 million on HDTV research since 1970. MITI and MPT have also spent $115 million each on competing HDTV research programs. Private firms have spent another $400 million on HDTV development (Tyson 1992, 238). NHK established a technical standard for Japanese HDTV based on a mixed analog-digital design oriented toward satellite broadcast, and is now airing several hours of HDTV programming daily.[63] Japanese electronics firms have begun producing expensive ($7,000 to $35,000 per unit) HDTV monitors for home use.

Industry proponents of HDTV in the United States argue that this is a fundamental innovation in consumer electronics that will have enormous effects on upstream industries (largely through induced demand for semiconductors). The American Electronics Association released a study that indicated that the United States would need to capture half of the world HDTV market to maintain its current market shares in semiconductors and computers, and that if the United States only captured 10 percent of the market (roughly its current share), the US market share in semiconductors and computers would be halved (Beltz 1991).

In part as a response to these concerns, the US government has allocated public funds to support the development of HDTV. Beltz (1991) estimates that in 1990 the US government spent $120 million on high-resolution imaging technologies, although some of this support was reduced in subsequent budgets.

In contrast, the United States has lagged in the standards-setting process, with the Federal Communications Commission not expected to

---

63. The Europeans originally adopted a different technical standard, but have now dropped it and will probably adopt the US standard (*The Economist*, 27 February 1993, 65).

adopt an HDTV standard for US television until 1994 at the earliest. Ironically, the lack of a broadcast standard and the consequent development of competing technologies may have permitted US firms to leapfrog their foreign competitors through the development of fully digital HDTV technology. Digital HDTV both is superior to analog HDTV in its broadcast properties and, importantly, facilitates the interface of HDTV with a whole range of computer and telecommunications technologies. The development of digital HDTV significantly changes the expected trajectory of product development, with narrow use as a television reception medium of far less importance than a broad range of other possible applications.[64]

As a consequence, the case for supporting HDTV as a final-demand consumer product is greatly weakened. First of all, production of the receivers is likely to be dominated by large multinationals. If the monitor is physically fragile (as any product with a large flat panel display might be expected to be), then production will occur largely in the consuming market (as with color televisions now), regardless of the home of the producing firm.[65] If the product is not fragile, assembly will occur in low-wage areas, as with many audio electronic devices. In either event, the importance of the United States as a production location is more likely to be affected by the physical qualities of the product than the nationality of the producing firm.

The existence of country-specific, appropriable R&D spillovers is also questionable. The complexity of HDTV and its multitude of uses suggest that its production will involve a considerable amount of specialization and corporate tieups, some of which will undoubtedly be cross-border. Already, the development of digital HDTV and the need to reduce the price of existing mixed analog-digital models have put a premium on the development of a powerful microprocessor to decode the broadcast signal. This plays to the United States' strong suit, and predictably there have been numerous tieups between Japanese electronics manufacturers and US computer firms (table 4.12).

It thus appears that, from the US standpoint, American firms and consumers are well-positioned to reap the benefits of technological innovation that foreigners have spent billions of dollars developing. Rather than pursue policies of trade protection that would hurt downstream users, the optimal HDTV policy for the US government is to do nothing.

---

64. Indeed, television broadcasters are showing increasing enthusiasm for enhanced-definition television (EDTV), which requires far less expensive broadcasting facilities and home receivers than does HDTV.

65. More than 60 percent of the color televisions sold in the United States are produced domestically, with domestic value added of more than 70 percent. Yet most of this production is by European and East Asian manufacturers—Zenith, the sole US firm in the industry, controls only 12 percent of the market (Beltz 1991) and is moving production to Mexico.

Table 4.12   Joint activities of US and Japanese firms in HDTV

Japanese firm	US firm	Activity
Fujitsu	Texas Instruments	Microprocessor development
Hitachi	Texas Instruments	Microprocessor development
NEC	National Semiconductor	Microprocessor development
NHK	Texas Instruments	Technology license from NHK to Texas Instruments
Sanyo	LSI Logic	Microprocessor development
Sony	Texas Instruments	Microprocessor development
Toshiba	Motorola	Microprocessor development

Source: Press reports.

Table 4.13   United States and Japan: trade in private services,[a] 1982–92 (billions of dollars)

Year	US exports to Japan	US imports to Japan	Balance
1982	5.1	2.6	2.4
1983	5.2	2.7	2.5
1984	6.4	4.3	2.1
1985	6.5	4.2	2.3
1986	9.8	5.6	4.1
1987	11.7	6.4	5.3
1988	14.0	7.0	7.0
1989	16.9	7.1	9.8
1990	19.0	8.4	10.6
1991	24.2	11.2	13.0
1992	26.1	11.9	14.2

a. Private services include travel, passenger fares, transportation, royalties and license fees, education, financial services, insurance, telecommunications, and business and technical services.

Source: Survey of Current Business, various issues.

Indeed, the general lesson of electronics is that it makes no sense for *one* government to fund technological development that intrinsically spills over to producers or consumers in foreign countries whose governments free-ride.

Services

Although generally receiving less attention than merchandise trade issues, international trade in services is a large and growing part of international commerce. Indeed, in the 1990s, the United States has run a surplus in services with Japan of more than $10 billion (table 4.13). Trade frictions in this area have centered on US access to the Japanese market for retailing, professional services (construction, architectural, engineering, legal, and accounting), and financial services in the banking, securities, and insurance areas. Each country has complaints about the other's international aviation policies. Some other disputes involving intellectual property (such as copyrighted materials) concern payments of fees, and at least from a balance of payments perspective are service transactions.

The services trade disputes exhibit some similarities to the merchandise trade disputes discussed thus far. They typically involve difficulties encountered by US firms in penetrating the Japanese market due to a combination of government regulations, and private cartel behavior. This difficulty, sometimes combined with asymmetrical access to the US market, has spurred fears that Japanese firms could exercise predatory behavior from behind the shelter of a domestic bastion market. These concerns have led the US government to attempt to remove the barriers to US firms' access. This foreign pressure inevitably becomes entwined with the domestic politics of regulatory reform. As in other sectors, Japanese government ministries typically react by seeking to incorporate some foreign firms into the domestic oligopoly, without fundamentally disrupting the structure of their client industries. Once in, the incumbent US firms lose interest in liberalization per se and discourage the US government from continuing its pressure.

The services disputes at the same time differ somewhat from the merchandise trade disputes, in that since the services are being performed in Japan (frequently by Japanese nationals), the direct income, production, and employment effects on US nationals or residents are more difficult to ascertain. Indeed, one can think of services disputes as having a relatively larger impact on returns to capital than on returns to labor as a factor of production. As in the previous sections, these general points are illustrated here by the experiences of particular service industries: retailing, construction (from the professional services area) and banking and securities (in the financial services group).

Retailing

> "It must be clearly understood that what the US was asking for in the SII [Structural Impediments Initiative] talks when it demanded that Japan change the structure of its distribution system was nothing less than a demand that the country also change its culture."
> —*Nikkei*, editorial
> (11 January 1992)

The Japanese distribution system is of relevance to US-Japan trade relations for two reasons. First, as elaborated in the previous chapter, the distribution system is alleged to act as an impediment to imports. Second, the regulation of the system has hindered the entrance of US retailers into the Japanese market.

The establishment of large retail stores is governed by the Large Scale Retail Store Law *(Daiten-Ho)*, which was originally introduced by MITI in 1975 as a notification (not an approval) process. Subsequent revisions of the law greatly increased the scope of stores coming under its provisions, and the implementation of the law was captured by local advisory committees dominated by small shopkeepers. Similar laws were adopted at the local and the prefectural level, with the result that the time required to gain approval to open a large store stretched to a decade.

The principal targets of these laws were large Japanese mass retailers, but the provisions effectively kept foreign retailers out as well. For American trade negotiators, the experience of the US toy retailer Toys 'R' Us became the *cause célèbre*.

Immediately upon the announcement in January 1990 by Toys 'R' Us that it planned to open a store of nearly 5,000 square meters in the city of Niigata, Japanese toy retailers organized national and local protests. The Toys 'R' Us case led to the issue of the *Daiten-Ho* being placed on the Structural Impediments Initiative (SII) agenda. Large Japanese retailers, who were the original targets of the law, formed an alliance with the foreign specialty retailers to push for change. Reforms were enacted, and in April 1991 Toys 'R' Us received permission to open a scaled-back version of its store in Niigata. The first store in Ami, Ibaraki prefecture, was opened in December 1991, and President Bush inaugurated the opening of the firm's second store in Nara in January 1992.

Unlike the case of the distributional system's impediments to merchandise imports, where the impact on the US economy of the trade barriers is straightforward, in the case of retailers in the Japanese market the transmission mechanisms are more subtle. By 1992, Toys 'R' Us had six stores in Japan averaging 3,000 square meters in size, each generating ¥1.5 billion to ¥3 billion in revenue, for a total of ¥12 billion (*Nikkei*, 9 February 1993). Approximately 75 percent of the merchandise sold in the stores is of Japanese manufacture, with the imports coming mainly from China, Taiwan, and Korea, although the firm procures some toys as well as store furnishings from US suppliers. Toys 'R' Us plans to open 100 stores in Japan in a seven- to eight-year period (*Japan Economic Journal*, 13 April 1991). Assuming that future stores generate revenue at the same rate the current stores do, this implies long-run revenues of ¥200 billion annually. Gross profit margins in Japanese toy retailing were reportedly 20 to 30 percent at the time Toys 'R' Us entered the market and the retail price maintenance system collapsed (*Nikkei*, 25 April 1992). After some initial difficulties, Toys 'R' Us has apparently had some success at obtaining discounted prices for its merchandise by dealing directly with the Japanese toy manufacturers. Assuming its profit margin is 20 percent and a real Japanese corporate tax rate of 50 percent, this yields an estimate of long-run annual after-tax profits of ¥20 billion. McDonald's Japan, a

US-Japanese joint venture, owns 20 percent of the Toys 'R' Us Japanese operation. Assuming that the effective non-American ownership of the firm's Japanese operation is 10 percent, this means ¥18 billion in profits to US stockholders, or $150 million at a yen-dollar rate of 120.

This does not appear to be a particularly large number. (For comparison, the increases in US exports to Japan of cigarettes and beef after liberalization were more than $1.2 billion and $500 million, respectively.) However, one could argue that Toys 'R' Us is just the leading edge of a much larger movement of US specialty retailers into the Japanese market. A 50-50 joint venture between Blockbuster Video and Fujita (the Japanese partner in McDonald's Japan) plan to open 1,000 Blockbuster stores by 2000. (Toys 'R' Us plans to open 28 stores by 1994, 25 of them in complexes together with McDonald's outlets, and 7 in complexes with both McDonald's and Blockbuster stores attached.) Tower Records has already opened 14 stores, generating ¥10.2 billion in revenue in 1991. Brooks Brothers is already in Japan, Sears has opened three Tireplus tire stores in a 50-50 joint venture with the Seibu department store chain, and Home Depot, Walgreens, Radio Shack, and Bloomingdales have all expressed intentions to enter the Japanese market. Moreover, there is some evidence that Japanese retailers may have to emulate the techniques of Toys 'R' Us to an important extent, both increasing the likely penetration of imports and adding another chapter to the convergence story.

Construction

"We are not trying to change the Japanese system. Rather, those who are making serious efforts here realized that what we need to do is fit into the system."
> —John Dickinson, General Manager, Schal Associates, Japanese branch
> (*Japan Economic Journal*, 20 March 1991)

Two of the themes of this chapter—problems of foreign market access in Japan due to collusive public and private actions, and the tendency to try to resolve these disputes through co-optation—are particularly evident in the area of construction, engineering, and architectural services. The legal impediments to entry are a complex system of firm licensing and the selection of firms to be designated bidders on particular projects. Experience within Japan is an important part of the approval and selection process, and this creates a Catch-22 situation for foreign firms: they cannot get into the market because they are not licensed, but they cannot get licensed because they don't have any experience.[66] This has the secondary effect of forcing foreign firms to seek Japanese partners for joint venture work in order to gain the experience necessary for licensing and to increase the likelihood of being selected as a designated bidder. The result is an asymmetry in which US firms averaged only $190 million annually in contracts in Japan between 1989 and 1992, while Japanese firms averaged more than $2.5 billion in the United States over the same period (unpublished data, US Department of Commerce).[67]

The primary effect of this institutional arrangement within Japan is to create a cartel of licensed general contractors. This cartel generates rents, and the inability of the cartel to completely deter entry encourages excessive local entry and the existence of a fringe of small, inefficient firms. The need then arises for a mechanism to distribute the cartel rents. This is done through the practice of *dango*, a form of bid-rigging in which firms negotiate with each other as to which firms will participate in bidding on a given project and at what prices. McMillan (1991) estimates that excess profits from collusion in public works projects typically amount to 16 percent to 33 percent of the price. Evidence from the few cases that have been prosecuted supports this range of estimates, the most famous case being the 1989 episode in which the US Department of Justice reached an out-of-court settlement with 99 Japanese construction firms for bid-rigging at the Yokosuka Naval Base; fines levied in that case amounted to $32.4 million, or 24 percent of the billed costs.[68] Adding in the costs of technical inefficiencies due to the major firms living the quiet lives of oligopolists, and the large number of small, inefficient firms, Shintaro Ishihara's (1989, 95) assertion of a 40 percent cost differential does not appear unreasonable. Given that the Japanese government annually awards public works contracts in excess of $100 billion, the implicit costs of Japanese policy are staggering.

---

66. Japanese officials argue that the licensing process acts as a substitute for the institution of bonding contractors in the United States.

67. Some Japanese commentators have argued that this asymmetry is not due to market access problems in Japan, but rather to the fact that Japanese property developers, important buyers of construction services, develop projects in the United States while US developers do not do the same in Japan.

68. McMillan (1991) discusses this and three additional cases: the case of soil brought in to build the Kansai International Airport, in which excess profits due to collusion may have amounted to 9 percent; the 1982 case of Matsuyama City kitchen equipment purchases, in which the bids incorporated a profit margin of 31 percent; and a 1979 river-dredging case in which excess profits due to collusion were 27 percent of the contract price.

The Justice Department subsequently settled another case against 11 Japanese electronics firms for rigging bids at the US Air Force base at Yokota. The firms agreed to pay $36.7 million in fines, or nearly 36 percent of the value of the $103 million in contracts.

The flip side of this, of course, is that the potential returns to efficient foreign firms from penetrating this cartel are equally impressive. Since 1984, the strategy of the United States has been to use the Japanese public works market as the wedge to begin getting US firms into the market; the US government (but not necessarily all US firms) views this as the first step in the larger objective of changing the institutions in Japan. This approach has the obvious attraction of focusing on the segment of the construction market over which the Japanese government has the greatest sway and that is most amenable to government-to-government negotiations.

At the same time, however, this strategy might be expected to encounter particular problems, as the construction industry is the single largest source of Japanese political campaign funds, reportedly supplying up to half of Japanese political donations. The construction industry in effect acts as an intermediary, recycling public tax revenues to politicians for private use through excess profits generated through *dango*.

The US strategy led to years of frustrating bilateral negotiations accompanied by threats of retaliation and counterretaliation. Disillusionment in the United States began to build after three years of negotiation with the Japanese government appeared to yield little if any discernible progress. Sen. Frank Murkowski (R-AK) attached legislation to the continuing budget resolution passed in December 1987 that barred firms of countries not granting reciprocal access to US firms from participating in federally funded public works in fiscal 1988, and in early 1988 the Reagan administration began moving toward the extraordinary act of self-initiating a Section 301 case against Japan in construction. Japanese observers were shocked when the low bid on a Washington, DC, subway project, submitted by a joint venture of Kiewit Construction and Kajima Engineering (which had been implicated in the Yokosuka *dango* case), was rejected on the grounds that the Murkowski amendment barred the participation of Japanese firms. With the Murkowski amendment on the books and the threat of a Section 301 case looming, in May 1988 US and Japanese negotiators were able to reach understandings involving increasing transparency of bidding procedures on the giant Kansai International Airport (KIA) project, as well as a number of other Japanese public works projects under the Major Projects Agreement (MPA).

Congress deemed the agreements inadequate, however, and in November 1988 the USTR began an investigation of construction practices in Japan as mandated by Section 1305 of the 1988 trade act. Talks continued through 1989, with the US government pressing Japan to eliminate the designated bidder system and replace it with an open tender system, or alternatively to maintain the designated bidder system but count project experience outside Japan toward licensing and designation. The United States also insisted that Japan include foreign experts in the development of engineering and design specifications, and extend to local-government-funded public works projects the national government's commitment to making the bidding process more transparent.

In its report to Congress in November 1989, the USTR found that certain Japanese government practices were unreasonable and denied access to Japan's market for construction. US Trade Representative Carla A. Hills, however, counseled against retaliation, on the basis of commitments by Japanese Minister of Construction Shozo Harada to implement steps to prevent *dango*; these were to include banning violators of the Japanese law from participating in future government projects; refraining from interfering in joint ventures between US and Japanese firms; providing overseas contractors with more timely information on upcoming projects (by announcing all purchase plans in the *Kampo*, the Japanese equivalent of the *Federal Register*, and lengthening bid times to 60 days for contracts in excess of $5 million); and clarifying the criteria on designated bid selection with the intention of facilitating attainment of these criteria by foreign firms.

Foreign firms continued to have difficulty becoming designated bidders, however, and tensions rose markedly the following year, when a joint venture by the German firm AEG and Westinghouse Electric Corp. did not receive the contract for constructing the people mover system for the KIA as anticipated.[69] AEG-Westinghouse and Otis Elevator (a subsidiary of United Technologies Corp.) each submitted bids on the KIA internal people mover. AEG-Westinghouse was considered the front runner because of its extensive experience (it had built 14 of the 18 systems in existence worldwide at the time).

KIA officials indicated that they were not bound by MPA guidelines because the contract involved consulting work rather than construction work, and they awarded the contract to a joint venture between Niigata Engineering and Sumitomo Corp. on the basis of "pricing, reliability, and experience."

---

69. The airport project seemed plagued from the start. The plan involved building the airport on a man-made island in Osaka Bay. American firms were excluded from the initial design phase, as Japanese officials were quoted as saying that US firms did not understand the characteristics of Japanese soil. Apparently the Japanese project managers did not either. The engineering consultants hired to estimate sinkage rates predicted that the island would sink 23 to 39 feet over the next 50 years. KIA officials adopted the lower figure and acted accordingly. Unfortunately, the higher figure appears more accurate, and at current sinkage rates the island will be only one meter above the waterline sometime in the next century. Observers jokingly predict that the airport will only be operable at low tides. More seriously, the problem has led to massive cost overruns (exacerbated by *dango*) and concerns about the viability of the airport as originally envisioned.

The US firms Bechtel Group Inc. and Fluor Daniels have since won contracts as part of consortia to build wings of the passenger terminal.

This "consulting work" involved the purchase of 200 tons of equipment.

The winning firms had no experience in this area.

Niigata Engineering was one of the firms implicated in the Yokosuka Naval Base *dango* case.

The reaction in the United States was predictable. Sen. Murkowski stated that the incident would have a chilling effect on future attempts to enter the Japanese market because of the great expense that Westinghouse had incurred in making the bid, and he successfully reintroduced the lapsed reciprocity legislation. Japanese officials responded by pointing out that the winning bid was 40 percent lower than the AEG-Westinghouse bid. But one reason that the Niigata Engineering–Sumitomo Corp. was so low was that development costs were not included, since company officials reasoned that they could apply designs under development for another people mover in Tokyo. AEG-Westinghouse officials complained that this was bidding on the basis of "paper machines" and offered to resubmit a lower bid. KIA officials refused.[70]

In subsequent talks during fall 1990 through winter 1991, US negotiators pressed for expansion of existing agreements to cover all public works funded by the central government; inclusion of subcontracts in cases where the primary contracts were part of the 1988 MPA; elimination of rules and procedures that encourage firms to form joint ventures (essentially the rules that require experience in Japan); provision of more information on a timelier basis (US firms complained that Japanese firms were advantaged by inside information); explanations of decisions under the designated bidder system; and creation of a dispute-settlement mechanism that would be empowered to reopen bids or contracts. (Similar to the agreement in supercomputers, this demand was in response to the AEG-Westinghouse case.)

All along the Japanese side had maintained that these measures were unnecessary—indeed, the agreements were temporary measures intended to facilitate foreign firms qualifying for work under existing Japanese rules and procedures, not permanent changes undertaken to increase foreign-firm market access per se; that is, they were intended to facilitate co-optation, not genuinely liberalize the market. Furthermore, the Japanese side argued, Japanese firms had little access to the US public market.

In February 1991, Sen. Murkowski threatened to withdraw his support of the MPA and to back a Section 301 case if there were no progress, and in April the Economic Policy Council of the Bush administration voted unanimously to authorize retaliation on 1 June if the talks broke

---

70. The low bid by Sumitomo Corp. to supply cars to the Los Angeles County, CA, mass transit system was subsequently rejected by county officials in favor of US producers.

down. The Japanese government then threatened unspecified counter-retaliation, with Cabinet Secretary Misoji Sakamoto reiterating that the MPA was not adopted because the Japanese market was closed, but rather to help "foreign firms which are not fully familiarized with Japanese markets"(*Los Angeles Times*, 1 September 1991).

One effect of the war of words was to reveal disunity on the US side. At least some US construction firms active in Japan lobbied against the pursuit of a 301 case because they feared either being the objects of the threatened counterretaliation or the dissipation of oligopoly rents if the Japanese market were indeed liberalized. According to press reports, US Trade Representative Hills sent a letter to one such firm castigating its officers for lack of support. Keith Bovetti, a commercial counselor in the Tokyo embassy, was quoted in the press as stating that "[The U.S. government] has to reflect the interests of those companies that are not in Japan but would like to be"(*Japan Economic Journal*, 20 March 1991).

Faced with the credible threat of action by the United States, Japanese Prime Minister Toshiki Kaifu pushed Ministry of Construction negotiators to accept a compromise, which they did at 9 p.m. on 31 May 1991. The compromise agreement involved increasing the number of projects covered under the MPA to 40, worth an estimated $26.7 billion; providing more information to foreign firms; creating a dispute-settlement mechanism; creating guidelines for a new category called "design and build" work; and toughening enforcement against *dango*.

Since the original MPA agreement in 1988, 14 US general contractors have obtained licenses to work in Japan, and 8 firms have registered as first-class architect's offices. As of January 1992, US firms had been awarded approximately $375 million in contracts under the MPA and another $245 million in private contracts not covered by the MPA. Nonetheless, one has to question whether the US experience in the Japanese construction industry should be considered a success.

Admittedly, the US firms' access to the market has increased, as measured either by licenses or by earnings. Moreover, certain procedural gains have been attained: improved access to procurement information, and the creation of a dispute-settlement mechanism, to name two. Yet after nine years of high-level negotiations, threats and counterthreats, and actual retaliation on a small scale, the United States has made little progress in breaking into the lucrative private construction market, presumably the ultimate goal of the exercise. Moreover, some of the issues covered under the 1991 MPA agreement (including problems with the designated bidding system and *dango*) are the same problems that the two countries began addressing in 1984.

From a US perspective, the experience of the construction industry underlines three important themes in US-Japan trade relations. First, the market access barriers encountered by foreign firms in Japan are frequently a combination of official policy (the designated bidder system) and private arrangements (*dango*). Second, foreign firms that do successfully penetrate the system will earn a share of the oligopoly rents. This immediately sets off the political dynamic we have observed elsewhere, in which US firms support US government pressure until they are in the market, but once inside oppose further market liberalization measures. Third, negotiations with Japan can be protracted and use up considerable bureaucratic and political resources; hence it is important to carefully identify beforehand the likely costs and benefits (Porges 1991). Given the importance of construction-industry contributions to Japanese politicians, the case of construction runs directly to the heart of the Japanese political system, meaning that reforms are likely to be difficult to obtain. Moreover, since much, if not most, of the labor and materials used in these projects are presumably sourced in Japan, and even most personal expenditures by expatriate US professionals will be in Japan, not the United States, overseas construction activities may not have a large direct impact on the US economy. These considerations suggest that care is warranted in ordering priorities.

Financial Services

> "What we've got to do is broaden the trade debate to include financial services, which I see as a priority. The question we're confronting is 'Will stocks and bonds go the way of automobiles and steel?' "
>
> —Rep. Charles E. Schumer (D-NY)
> (*New York Times*, 21 September 1991)

Differentiation and regulation have characterized the Japanese financial system for most of the postwar period. Regulations separated banks from securities firms; established separate classes of banks specializing in long-term finance, short-term finance, and foreign exchange services; and created specialized institutions to manage pensions and investment trusts (mutual funds) and to service particular market segments such as farmers or small businesses. In addition, Japan has long maintained a government-controlled postal saving system, contributions to which make up a large share of national saving. Interest rates were regulated and the variety of financial instruments available was circumscribed. Domestic and foreign capital markets were kept separate through strict controls. In comparison with similarly developed economies, Japanese financial markets could be described as repressed. Regulatory responsibility was centralized in the Ministry of Finance (MOF).

US financial markets in the immediate postwar period had some of the same characteristics: banks and securities firms were separated (indeed, Article 65 of Japan's Securities Exchange Law was modeled on the US

Glass-Steagall Act), and banking regulations demarcated lines of business and established specialized institutions (such as the savings and loan associations). Rates of return for many instruments were regulated. Unlike in Japan, however, regulatory responsibility was splintered among a number of bodies. Some restrictions (such as those separating banking and securities businesses) were stricter in the United States, while others (such as on the joint operation of bank and trust businesses) were tighter in Japan. Overall, however, the United States could be characterized as having more complete, freely functioning financial markets throughout the early postwar period. These were greatly enhanced in the 1970s with the deregulation of rates of return, the introduction of new instruments such as money market mutual funds, and the liberalization of restrictions on activities such as interstate banking.

The process of deregulation and liberalization began later in Japan, and from a more repressed starting point. By the late 1970s, the domestic banking industry was pushing for relaxation of restrictions on business activity in the face of the growing securitization of Japanese financial markets, which culminated in the Banking Act of 1982. Controls on international capital flows were significantly liberalized in 1980, at least in part because of concerns about the rapid depreciation of the currency. Greater integration of domestic and foreign capital markets in turn forced MOF to reform domestic practices in response to developments in the growing Euroyen market beyond its regulatory reach. Foreign governments began playing an active role in the reform process, both for macroeconomic reasons and to obtain better access to the Japanese market for their own financial services firms.[71]

In terms of market access, the issues confronting the US government and US firms centered on entry barriers created by the symbiotic existence of regulatory restrictions and private cartels. Japan formally grants US firms national treatment (and in some instances better than national treatment), and decade-long negotiations have resolved many of these issues. US firms have been offered seats on the Tokyo stock exchange, access to the government bond underwriting business has been greatly increased, and previously restricted activities have been opened up to US firms. In the banking area, commercial paper (an important alternative source of funding for Japanese firms) has been introduced, and the development of a short-term interbank market and improved access of foreign banks to the Bank of Japan's direct lending program have enhanced US banks' ability to compete in Japan. Nonetheless, US firms still express significant dissatisfaction with their ability to do business

---

71. See Rosenbluth (1989) for a description of the Japanese regulatory framework and its reform through the mid-1980s; see Frankel (1984) for an analysis of its international aspects.

in the Japanese market.[72] Firms complain of delays in regulatory approval of new products; tax measures that place disproportionately high tax rates on new products, thus discouraging their introduction; and a general lack of transparency.[73]

This dissatisfaction has in turn led to the introduction of legislation in the US Congress to replace the concept of national treatment in trade relations in this area with one of national treatment contingent on reciprocity.[74] Having removed many of the explicit regulatory obstacles, the US government has been pushing for more rapid and systemic reform. Conversely, MOF still prefers ad hoc, piecemeal liberalization, because this facilitates the formation of internal political compromises among its competing constituent groups.

As a result, the regulatory environment is in a more or less constant state of change as MOF responds to conflicting pressures. The fragmented and cartelized nature of the Japanese financial markets means that these responses sometimes involve providing selected foreign firms with enhanced access to particular markets with the intent of buying them off politically, rather than engaging in wholesale liberalization that could threaten the existence of entire domestic constituencies. This process of regulatory change accompanied by *gaiatsu* is inescapably intertwined with the domestic politics of Article 65 reform.

---

72. Hartzell (1990) reports results from an extensive Japan Center for International Finance survey of market participants, which indicates a far higher degree of dissatisfaction with regulatory practices in Tokyo than in New York or London.

73. For example, enacting legislation to allow firms to trade on overseas futures and options exchanges was delayed for 13 months, until the launch of a domestic financial futures exchange (Hartzell 1990). Citibank has made similar complaints about delays in MOF regulatory approval to market credit card loan–backed securities in Japan. US banks also protest the government prohibition of forward rate agreements (FRA), elsewhere a common off-balance-sheet transaction, on the grounds that they constitute gambling under the penal code!

74. One provision of the 1988 omnibus trade act would have barred foreign firms from the US primary government securities market unless US firms were extended the "same competitive opportunities in the underwriting and distribution of government debt instruments issued in that country as it accords to domestic companies"; the law went on to list seven barriers that US financial firms faced in the Japanese market. The law specified that, if these obstacles were not eliminated by 23 August 1989, "neither the Board of Governors of the Federal Reserve System nor the Federal Reserve Bank of New York may designate, or permit the continuation of any prior designation of, any person of a foreign country as a primary dealer in government debt instruments." On 21 August 1989, the Federal Reserve committee charged with implementing the provision voted 5–1 to accept a staff report that found no "discrimination against U.S. firms in the laws and formal regulations applicable to the government debt market."

At the beginning of the following session of Congress in January 1990, Sens. Donald W. Riegle, Jr. (D-MI), and Jake Garn (R-UT) introduced the Fair Trade in Financial Services Act, which would have amended the 1988 legislation to specify that national treatment includes "effective market access," thus replacing a *de jure* standard with a *de facto* one.

Banking

> *"Recently, a number of banking experts have strongly hinted that the Japanese are dumping financial services in the United States. By selling products or services at below the cost of production, and using subsidies from the home market, dumping is an anti-competitive strategy designed to buy market share. . . . We must make sure that the playing field is level, competition is fair, and that domestic financial institutions are not losing market share as a result of illegal foreign practices."*
> —Rep. Frank Annunzio (D-IL),
> letter to Secretary of Commerce,
> Robert A. Mosbacher, 15 May 1990

Foreign banks face three basic problems in competing with Japanese banks. First, controls on deposit interest rates have acted as an implicit subsidy to Japanese banks.[75] (The banks undoubtedly engage in nonprice competition, but this does not completely erode the rents they receive as a regulated cartel.)[76] Second, foreign firms face a lack of transparency in regulatory procedures, especially in regard to the introduction of new products and services. Third, foreign firms have encountered difficulty developing a Japanese client base. In the retail sphere this results from the regulatory barriers to, and high startup costs of, greenfield operations on the one hand, and MOF's unwillingness to allow foreign takeovers of Japanese banks on the other. In the corporate sphere, long-standing *keiretsu* affiliations, along with a shift away from loan finance, inhibit foreign bank penetration.

These factors have contributed to a considerable asymmetry in the degree of cross-penetration in the US and Japanese banking sectors. The role of foreign banks in Japan actually *declined* during the 1980s, and foreign banks account for less than 2 percent of bank deposits in Japan (US Department of the Treasury 1990). In contrast, Japanese banks alone account for 12.1 percent of assets and 16.0 percent of lending in the United States (*JEI Report*, 8 June 1990). This asymmetry has lead to concerns that regulatory practices and *keiretsu* in Japan are creating the same sort of bastion market in banking that US firms have faced in other businesses.

The situation in Japan is undergoing considerable change, however. Deposit interest rates have been largely deregulated, eliminating whatever advantage to the Japanese banking industry they previously conveyed. Moreover, recent scandals in banking may contribute to consider-

---

75. Regulation Q had a similar effect in the United States prior to 1978.

76. Cozy cartel arrangements manifest themselves in a variety of ways. Checks are not widely accepted in Japan. Instead, wire transfers are the conventional means of settling accounts. Japanese consumers pay extremely high service charges on these transfers.

able change in the status quo.[77] The weakness of several institutions in the wake of financial scandals means that they will need new infusions of capital. MOF has already raised securities firms' permissible stakes in banks from 5 percent to 50 percent. Permitting foreign mergers and acquisitions would be a logical counterpart.

One non-Japanese firm figures prominently in all of this. Citibank has made penetrating the Japanese market a high priority. It was blocked in 1986 from taking over Heiwa Sogo, a troubled 100-branch mutual bank. In 1987, Citibank made a deal to provide foreign remittance services through 2,000 Japanese post offices. It subsequently formed an alliance with Mitsubishi Bank, thereby obtaining access to a nationwide automatic teller machine network. In this regard it has been assisted by MOF, which waived its rule on banks sharing premises. MOF has proved less acquiescent in Citibank's desire to market credit card loan–backed securities in Japan. This would require amending the Securities Law and is opposed by the Japanese banking industry, which fears the marketing of such instruments by Japanese nonbank financial institutions. Yet the reported difficulty of some Japanese banks in meeting the recently promulgated capital adequacy requirements by the Bank for International Settlements in Basel would suggest that a revision of securitization provisions (which would help them shrink their outstanding loans) could be in order. Citibank, which has sought the assistance of the US Treasury in its lobbying effort, could find itself allied with undercapitalized Japanese banks. At the same time, a number of bills have been introduced in Congress to replace a *de jure* standard of national treatment with a *de facto* reciprocity standard, under the threat of restrictions on foreign banks' activities in the United States. The Treasury appears to have used the existence of these bills as a bargaining lever in its negotiations. Indeed, many commentators believe that MOF is being relatively supportive of Citibank because its needs a foreign "success story."[78]

---

77. In July 1991, Fuji Bank disclosed that managers at three branches had forged certificates of deposit (CDs) worth ¥260 billion for 23 clients, who in turn had used the CDs as collateral for speculative loans. When the holders of the fake CDs were unable to make payments, their creditors forced the scandal into the open. Tokai and Kyowa Saitama banks soon admitted to similar breaches amounting to ¥60 billion.

The following month it was revealed that a branch manager at Toyo Shinkin (a credit association) had forged ¥342 billion in CDs (roughly equal to the entire asset base of Toyo Shinkin) for one customer, Ms. Nui Onoue, an Osaka restaurateur with reputed ties to gangsters, who used them to raise another ¥370 billion in loans for speculative purposes. The Industrial Bank of Japan (IBJ) was caught up in this, inasmuch it had lent ¥240 billion of the total. The Bank of Japan was forced to step in with an emergency loan to prop up Toyo Shinkin, and the Bank of Japan together with MOF encouraged the IBJ to absorb the failing credit association.

Ms. Onoue ultimately declared bankruptcy with a reported ¥400 billion in outstanding debts, and two senior officials of the IBJ were forced to resign their positions.

78. Typical are the comments of Yukihiko Endo, a senior researcher for the Nomura Research Institute: "Japan is afraid that the U.S. government would show reciprocal

Thus, the banking sector appears to follow in many respects the patterns of other industries: asymmetrical cross-penetration is observed, as smaller though arguably technologically more advanced US firms encounter regulatory and *keiretsu* barriers in the Japanese market. The US firms enlist the US government in their lobbying efforts, and Japanese government and industry respond by attempting to buy off well-placed firms, with minimal disruptive effects to the status quo. The foreign pressure is then used by competing domestic interest groups to further their own agendas.

Securities

US concerns about the securities market are remarkably similar in outline to those in several of the high-technology fields: innovative US firms are kept out of the Japanese market until Japanese competitors can replicate their technological advances; once this is achieved, the Japanese firms use superprofits from cartelized markets at home to cross-subsidize their expansion abroad. This view was expressed clearly in the US Treasury Department's National Treatment Study (US Department of the Treasury 1990, 238):

> American firms, in particular, feel that their competitive advantage lies in their ability to offer new innovative financial products and a wide range of financial services. Some are frustrated, however, because they feel unable to exploit this strength in Japan due to their inability to offer many of these products and services there. On the other hand, Japanese firms are seen as having the ability to experiment, innovate, and imitate in the open and competitive markets outside Japan. The U.S. firms feel that by the time new products and techniques are permitted in Japan, Japanese firms have caught up with their foreign counterparts and the foreign firm no longer has any advantage over a Japanese firm. Meanwhile Japanese firms have been able to compete aggressively for market share internationally, supported financially by their dominance of the Japanese market.

Initially, many of the obstacles encountered by foreign firms took the form of regulatory prohibitions. Foreign exchange transactions, for example, were funneled through MOF-licensed securities firms and foreign exchange banks. This prevented US firms from offering swaps and hybrid risk management products that they offer in other major financial markets. In 1992, MOF granted the Japanese subsidiaries of Salomon Brothers, Morgan Stanley, Goldman Sachs, and Merrill Lynch permission to begin all types of foreign currency trading; this amounted to the exten-

---

discrimination to Japanese banks if Citibank's breakthrough failed. The Finance Ministry is trying to bring up Citibank as a successful example of a foreign company to reduce trade frictions" (*Los Angeles Times*, 10 October 1990). Indeed, President Bush is reported to have requested to Prime Minister Kaifu at the June 1990 Palm Springs summit that Citibank not be blocked from taking over another Japanese bank.

sion of better than national treatment to the four American securities firms, a move that angered Japanese banks and securities firms alike.

Likewise, US firms were initially kept out of government bond underwriting by a system of syndicating that kept the foreign-firm share to just over 1 percent. At the same time, the syndicate system, restrictions on the short selling of bonds, and infrequent settlements all discouraged the development of a liquid secondary trading market, in which the US firms excel.[79] Starting in 1987, the Japanese government began increasing the foreign share of the syndicate and increasing the share of underwriting allocated through auctions, with the stated goal of eventually allocating all of the business on an auction basis. Now able to compete on more equal footing, the foreign (largely American) firms have raised their share of the government bond underwriting business to more than 30 percent (*The Economist*, 2 December 1990).

A turning point perhaps was the selection of Morgan Stanley Group Inc. to lead-manage with Nomura Securities Co., Ltd., a ¥50 billion bond issue for NTT. This was noteworthy for two reasons. First, it was the first time a foreign firm was chosen to be the lead underwriter. Second, it marked the introduction into Japan of Morgan Stanley's negotiated fixed-price system, which was expected to increase the transparency of pricing and thereby contribute to the development of a liquid secondary market. In the past, Japanese bonds had typically been placed by the underwriter agreeing to underwrite the issue at a high price in return for a fee. The bonds would then be sold to clients at varying (and sometimes large) discounts. The purchaser, unsure about the true underlying value of the bond, was encouraged to hold it to term rather than sell it on a secondary market. In the Morgan Stanley approach, the firm polls potential buyers in advance and forms a consensus as to underlying demand for the bond. Then the bond is priced at a differential to some existing benchmark issue (typically a government issue). This means that all purchasers are buying the bond at the same well-understood price, and the existence of the benchmark issue facilitates the development of a secondary market. MOF reportedly supported the selection of Morgan Stanley in part because of embarrassment over recent financial scandals, discrimination among customers, and concerns of foreign investors about lack of transparency in bond pricing.

The Japanese stock market has been characterized by large fixed commissions, which place a premium on trade volume and large retail networks. The rents created by the fixed commission system and the Big Four's inability to completely deter entry have encouraged excessive

---

79. Another effect of this regulatory structure was to put a big premium on the maintenance of inventories, in effect creating scale economies, with the obvious beneficiaries being the Big Four (Nomura, Daiwa, Yamaichi, and Nikko) Japanese brokerages (Kleidon and Singleton 1989).

entry of firms into the market and, in turn, hidden price competition through the practice of guaranteeing losses. These practices were the subject of scandals that emerged in 1991.

Foreign firms were initially denied seats on the Tokyo Stock Exchange (TSE) and consequently had to do their trading though incumbent Japanese members, significantly raising their costs. After considerable high-level foreign pressure, the first foreign firms were admitted to the TSE in 1985, and more were added in 1987. Foreign firms now account for 22 of the 114 seats on the exchange, and while foreign firms continue to complain about prohibitions on buying and selling seats, the basic access issue appears to have been largely resolved.

The firms subsequently have encountered regulatory and private barriers to entry that are in some ways similar to those experienced in the bond market. Much of the market effectively does not trade, because of *keiretsu* cross-shareholding arrangements. As a consequence, trading is relatively thin, and relatively small trades can move share prices substantially.

This characteristic of the market has several important implications. The first is that it is relatively easy for Japanese firms to make money by ramping stocks and generating a high trading volume off a large base of retail clients. It has been alleged that the Big Four securities firms have used their influence over individual share prices to deter firms from using foreign firms for underwriting (*The Economist*, 22 December 1990). Foreign firms' access to the underwriting market has been further hindered by such regulatory measures as the 10,000-share rule, which limits the shares an underwriter can place with any client, and the 30 percent rule, which limits the percentage of shares that can be placed with certain classes of institutional investors (US Department of Treasury 1990). Again, both of these rules put a premium on large retail (versus small institutional) customer bases. An obvious tack would be to buy up the fringe of small, inefficient, domestic brokers. However, these investments are prohibited unless specifically approved by the Japan Fair Trade Commission. Although some foreign firms have reportedly considered expansion through this route, there have been no mergers or acquisitions to date. Merrill Lynch & Co., Inc., has been the only foreign firm to attempt to meet this challenge through the establishment of its own large retail client base.

Other firms have attempted to exploit their strengths in offering customized products and packages to an institutional clientele. The share of market capitalization accounted for by individual investors has been falling steadily, from around 60 percent in 1950 to just over 20 percent in 1990, with the implication that large retail networks are going to matter less and institutional investors more. Key to the foreign (mainly American) brokers has been futures arbitrage trading, both for their institutional customers and on their own accounts. The Osaka exchange began trading in stock market futures in 1987. The trade proved highly profitable both because investors wanted to hedge their positions for conventional risk management reasons, and because it was a way to arbitrage the large fixed commissions on the Tokyo market: foreign firms would sell futures contracts (at a low commission) to Japanese clients, then hedge by buying the underlying stock without the retail commissions.

Index arbitrage trading was blamed for increasing the volatility of the market, however, because with trading in many issues relatively thin, the program block trades could move prices considerably. The consequent volatility (and hence the potential gain to sophisticated program trading) has been exacerbated by the fact that the Nikkei index of Japanese stock prices is an *unweighted* index: small, lightly traded stocks count as much in the index as larger, more heavily traded shares. Even further opprobrium was heaped on the foreign program traders once the market began heading downward in January 1990 and they were blamed for accelerating the decline.

The Osaka exchange raised margin requirements four times, changed the settlement rules to make it more difficult to unwind positions, and introduced other rules designed to discourage program trading. The effect of this has been to move the market offshore to Singapore. The National Tax Administration has audited foreign firms (including Salomon Brothers and Kidder, Peabody), but not domestic firms, involved in index arbitrage trading. Ironically, the scrapping in 1992 of another 30 percent rule (a single broker could not account for more than 30 percent of trading in a particular stock in a day or a month), presumably done to enhance MOF's ability to prop up the market through administrative guidance, has made index arbitrage trading easier.

Perhaps more ominous for the Tokyo market was the revelation of financial scandals in 1991. As noted earlier, the large fixed commissions on stock trades effectively prevented firms from competing on the basis of price. The way that firms circumvented this was by guaranteeing rates of return (or compensating losses) for selected (generally large, corporate) clients. In July 1991, two of the Big Four, Nomura and Nikko, admitted that they had compensated clients for losses in 1990 of ¥17 billion and ¥16.5 billion, respectively. This angered MOF because they had specifically barred the practice after Daiwa and Yamaichi had been exposed using it in the wake of the 1987 crash. Later that month the two firms were forced to admit that they still had not discontinued the practice, and indeed, a number of the second-tier brokers also admitted guaranteeing losses to favored customers in order to remain competitive with the Big Four. All in all, it was revealed that the Big Four had compensated 231 clients a total of ¥128.3 billion, while the second-tier firms had paid

¥43.6 billion to another 386 customers. None of these compensated clients were small customers or foreigners.[80]

As the summer wore on, the scandal deepened, with MOF admitting complicity and Nomura admitting underworld links.[81] MOF officials testified before the Diet that the ministry had known of the practice for years, and had acted only when the National Tax Administration decided to tax the 1990 and 1991 payments. MOF then announced that it would make certain practices explicitly illegal, and prohibit the class of accounts most open to abuse. (The latter move was delayed, because officials feared the market would be pushed even lower as the accounts were unwound.) A number of commentators called for the creation of an independent securities regulatory agency along the lines of the US Securities and Exchange Commission. MOF successfully resisted this proposal, however, and securities oversight responsibility was ultimately vested in the MOF Securities and Exchange Surveillance Commission, which completed its first investigation (of a second-tier broker for illegally compensating clients) in December 1992.

The final area of conflict between Japan and the United States in the securities business is in funds management. Foreign firms are excluded from the investment trust (mutual fund) market through MOF's licensing policy. The mutual fund market in Japan has historically been monopolized by 15 licensed investment trust management companies, each of which is affiliated with one of the large Japanese securities firms. (Other national markets of comparable size typically have thousands of competing funds.) Rates of return on these managed funds' investments were abysmally low relative to comparable indexes (*The Economist*, 7 December 1991), giving the impression that the investment trusts were indeed living the quiet life of the oligopolist.[82] Foreign governments pressured MOF to liberalize the market, and regulations promulgated in December 1989 theoretically opened the business to foreign firms. The entry criteria were so stringent, however, that only four new firms applied (all foreign). One has the sense that, as in other cases examined in this book, the response to external pressure for greater market access has been to allow

---

80. Alerted by these revelations, the US Securities and Exchange Commission began its own investigation of Big Four activities in the United States. All four firms were found to be in violation of sundry rules and regulations, although only Yamaichi was found to have improperly compensated a client for stock trading losses.

81. Nomura confessed to lending large sums to gangsters for greenmail schemes and assisting in the plan by promoting targeted shares to customers, and several top executives resigned their positions. The slogan "*Sagi Nomura*" (Swindler Nomura) began appearing in street graffiti.

82. Japanese securities houses reportedly dump poorly performing shares and undersubscribed offerings into trusts managed by their subsidiaries (Tomkin 1990).

a select number of foreign firms into the oligopoly rather than to engage in wholesale liberalization.

Somewhat similar conditions exist in regard to pension management. Foreign firms historically were prohibited from managing pension funds, which were the special preserve of insurance firms and trust banks. Large corporate groups tended to steer their pension funds' management to their *keiretsu* affiliates. The market was gradually opened to foreign competition in the late 1980s, but regulations limited foreign firms to managing "new money" (as opposed to already existing pension funds), limited the amount of foreign currency–denominated instruments in which the funds could invest, and specified portfolio allocations by asset type. These restrictions kept foreign firms out of most of the business and constrained their ability to exploit their strengths where they were permitted to compete. Foreign firms also alleged that the failure of authorities to require Japanese firms to reveal their performance records, together with the absence of pension fund management rating firms, have limited foreign firms' ability to compete on the basis of their proven track records.

Under pressure from the US Treasury, MOF revised the rules in October 1991, raising the allowable foreign asset share for foreign, but not Japanese companies, and lowering the minimum size pension fund that foreign firms could manage. Foreign firms are still limited to managing "new money," however, and reportedly only account for 0.0025 percent of pension fund assets under management.

The themes that have emerged in the financial services sector are reminiscent of those seen in other industries: a concentrated and regulated Japanese industry encounters the challenge of technologically more advanced US firms. The US firms, facing entry barriers in the Japanese market, enlist the support of the US government. The US government adopts a policy of negotiating procedural changes, combined with monitoring of outcomes and threats of retaliation. This effort becomes entwined with the Japanese domestic politics of reform, and the Japanese government attempts to craft reforms that will satisfy both foreign pressure and domestic political exigencies. This may involve providing selective advantages to a foreign firm or firms.

US public policy faces two dilemmas at this point. It may no longer be in the interests of those US firms that have penetrated the cartel to see it dissolved. Hence, the US government must weigh the gains to its own incumbents against the potential gains of other US entrants to this market. Second, this being a service industry, the potential gains to the US domestic economy may be difficult to ascertain. This is particularly important in terms of establishing negotiating priorities. There is a paucity of estimates of what these gains may be. In the case of financial services, estimates reported by Bergsten and Cline (1985) put the gains to the US economy in the range of $150 million to $300 million. Arguably there could also be externalities associated with more open capital markets, such as facilitating inward foreign direct investment flows.

Conclusion

Foreign firms face a variety of access barriers in the Japanese market. The unusual nature of these barriers, and the tendency of the Japanese government to try to co-opt new entrants into existing cartels, creates special dilemmas for US policy. It is imperative, then, that US policymakers have a clear notion of both strategy and tactics when entering into sectoral trade negotiations. It is to these questions of priorities, strategies, and tactics that we now turn.

5

Assessment and Lessons

The policies and institutions described in the previous chapters clearly have an effect on trade flows in individual sectors. Their aggregate importance is subject to dispute, however. This chapter addresses the strategic issue of policy prioritization as well as the tactical issue of policy choice. It begins with an assessment of the overall impact of market access barriers in the Japanese economy and concludes with lessons for policymakers confronted with the dilemmas outlined in the previous chapters.

Assessment of Market Access Barriers

Estimation of the impact of the mostly overt barriers to trade in primary products, as detailed in the previous chapter, is straightforward. The story with respect to manufactures is far more controversial. By a variety of measures, Japan has a distinctive trade pattern. As noted in an earlier chapter, Japan has an unusually low share of manufactured imports in domestic consumption, an unusually low share of intraindustry trade, an unusually small share of domestic sales accounted for by foreign-owned firms, and an unusually high share of intrafirm trade.

The coincidence of a distinctive trade pattern and informal trade barriers does not establish a causal relationship, however. Indeed, the essentially hidden and arbitrary nature of these trade barriers poses very difficult problems for economists trying to assess their impact. Unlike with formal border measures, internationally accepted definitions and measures of their impact do not exist. Moreover, it is unclear whether they operate by raising import prices, as do tariffs, or by restricting import quantities, as do quotas. As a consequence, a veritable cottage industry of researchers has eschewed the strategy of attempting to measure the impact of these informal barriers directly, and instead has focused on inferring their impact indirectly.[1] The usual procedure followed in this literature is to estimate econometrically a model of international trade, and then to ascribe to trade policy the differences between actual and predicted trade flows. Since this amounts to an analysis of the error terms of the regression, the robustness of the underlying estimates is of crucial significance. Perhaps not surprisingly, these studies have reached a variety of conclusions as to the importance of Japanese trade policy.

Saxonhouse has argued that the informal barriers, however vexing, are ultimately of little quantitative significance. To substantiate this position, he regresses either net or gross trade flows against cross-national data on factor endowments, excluding Japan from the sample. He finds that, in the vast majority of cases, accounting for nearly all of Japan's trade, Japan's actual trade flows fall within statistical forecast bounds.[2] On this basis he concludes that, however unusual Japan's trade pattern, it can be explained on the basis of Japan's equally unusual factor endowments, without reference to trade policy, much less trade policy of a *sub rosa* sort.

These widely cited studies have been criticized on a number of grounds. First, their conclusions are at variance with what we know to be true about *formal* Japanese trade policies. Tests on data for 1964, for example, fail to indicate that Japan's trade pattern was distinctive (Saxonhouse 1983), yet it is a matter of historical record that Japanese border measures were unusually high prior to the Kennedy Round. In the same paper, Saxonhouse reports results for 1979 that indicate that Japan's trade pattern was not unusual in the rice sector—even though there was a complete import embargo. This inability to detect known instances of protection suggests that Saxonhouse's tests may have very low power against alternative explanations.[3]

---

1. Among the best known of these studies are those by Saxonhouse (1983, 1989, 1992, 1993), Bergsten and Cline (1985), Balassa (1986), Lawrence (1987, 1991b), Leamer (1988), Noland (1992b), and Harrigan (1992).

2. In a personal communication to the authors, Saxonhouse has indicated that, according to the model used in the 1989 paper, if Japanese global imports in 1979 were as expected they would have been $7.2 billion (or 7.2 percent) higher than they were in fact. According to the model used in the 1993 paper, Japanese global imports would have been $8.8 billion (or 7.7 percent) higher in 1983 than they were.

3. It should be recalled, however, that the tests measure whether the trade pattern is distinctive—so that if many other nations maintained barriers of a comparable importance the regressions would not identify Japan as an outlier, even though it was highly protected in absolute terms.

Balassa and Noland (1988) suggest one reason why this might be the case. The technique used to correct for possible errors in measurement of the factor endowments (or for variations in factor quality) is valid only if errors in the measurement (or variations in factor quality) and trade policies are unrelated. If trade protection is correlated with factor intensity (as basic political economy would suggest), Saxonhouse's approach will attribute to measurement error precisely the effects of trade policy that one is trying to detect. So, for example, although Japan protects arable land, the Saxonhouse technique would attribute low agricultural imports to superior land quality and find no evidence of protection.[4] Noland (1992b) imbedded the Saxonhouse model in a more general framework and confirmed the unreliability of the Saxonhouse approach, and using a model specification not used in Saxonhouse's papers, he found some weak evidence that Japan is indeed an outlier.

Noland then regressed the residuals of this first-stage regression against policy variables to investigate whether trade policies were correlated with these deviations from the expected trade pattern. His results indicate that Japan's unusual trade behavior is indeed related to both tariff and nontariff barriers in Japan, as well as to VERs applied to Japanese exports by Japan's trade partners.

Lawrence (1991b) and Harrigan (1992) both examined *bilateral* trade in the context of models based on the assumption that countries' trade in differentiated products is proportional to their shares of world output. Lawrence concluded that Japan imports fewer manufactured goods than would be expected on the basis of the model. Using a slightly different approach, Harrigan found that the United States, next to Australia, was the most open of the industrialized (OECD) economies. He also concluded that, while Japan's manufactured imports were unusually low, so were its exports. Bilaterally, Japan was somewhat more closed to the United States than the reverse, but both were more open vis-à-vis each other than was Europe to either.

Saxonhouse (1992) analyzed bilateral net exports and obtained results somewhat similar to Harrigan's. He found that in 1985 Japan's net exports of manufactured goods to Europe were lower than expected, and Japan's net exports to the United States were $13.2 billion higher than expected. He attributes it to trade diversion due to European barriers against Japanese exports, but this could also be due to Japanese import barriers against US exports. Noland (1992b) found that Japanese imports are

---

4. In fact, results reported in Saxonhouse (1989) suggest that this method generates implausible estimates of differences in international factor quality (e.g., the productivity of capital in Great Britain is nearly 11 times the world average; Icelandic labor is more than four times as productive as the world average; education in Cyprus is more than five times the quality of the world average).

unusually low in sectors in which Japan faces VERs; this could be interpreted as supporting Saxonhouse's export diversion argument. In any event, this Saxonhouse paper is subject to the same methodological criticisms elaborated earlier.

A number of studies have examined the possible impact of *keiretsu* on Japan's trade pattern. Kreinin (1988) surveyed the capital-goods procurement practices of the Australian subsidiaries of multinational firms. He found that the subsidiaries of Japanese firms used far less open procurement practices than did the subsidiaries of non-Japanese firms and were far more likely to purchase equipment from their home country.

Three other studies examined this question econometrically in a single-country, cross-industry framework. Petri (1991) found that import penetration was negatively related to the share of final purchases by business and government and the degree of oligopoly in distribution. If businesses and government were to achieve the same import propensity as households (controlling for differences in the composition of demand), Japanese manufactured imports would double. Lawrence (1991b) added variables relating to *keiretsu* affiliation to Petri's model and concluded that, while vertical *keiretsu* were efficiency-enhancing (reducing imports and promoting exports), horizontal *keiretsu* were not (they reduced imports only). Elimination of the *keiretsu* would lead to an initial increase in manufactured imports of $30 billion (or more than 100 percent from a 1985 base), which would then be partially offset by a depreciation of the yen. Fung (1991) found that the presence of *keiretsu* increased Japan's trade surplus with the rest of the world in general, and the United States in particular.

The fundamental problem with these three studies is that one cannot say anything sensible about the implications of Japanese practices for world welfare by examining cross-industry trade performance from the perspective of a single country. (One cannot devise an international norm with data on only one country.) Furthermore, the models may not fully account for comparative advantage. If *keiretsu* variables are positively correlated with the missing comparative advantage variables (e.g., inappropriable technological competence), then the effects of the omitted variables will be incorrectly attributed to the *keiretsu* variable.

One study, Noland (1992b), addresses this issue. First, a cross-national model of comparative advantage is estimated. The residuals from these regressions represent the component of actual trade flows that cannot be explained by factor endowments (i.e., unexplained deviations from comparative advantage). These residuals for Japan are then regressed cross-industry against trade policy and *keiretsu* variables. This approach provides a check on the other *keiretsu* studies and attempts to test the indirect inferences about trade policies made by the studies discussed above. These results broadly confirm the earlier results: *keiretsu* are consistently associated with higher than expected net exports and with lower than expected imports. Whether this is due to *keiretsu* enhancing their members' efficiency or acting as barriers to entry is not determinable.

All of these studies have shortcomings. They use fairly small samples (50 or fewer industries). It is also possible that the results are being driven by one or two industries with low imports and a high degree of *keiretsu* affiliation (e.g., automobiles). Nevertheless, the apparent consistency in these results, obtained independently by different researchers using differing models and data sets, suggest that *keiretsu* have a significant impact on the Japanese trade pattern.

The studies just reviewed attempt to estimate the impact of public policies and private preferences on trade quantities. Another approach is to examine price evidence. Numerous surveys have found that traded-goods prices are far higher in Japan than elsewhere (Economic Planning Agency of Japan 1989; US Department of Commerce 1989, 1991; Summers and Heston 1991; Union Bank of Switzerland 1991). Sazanami et al. (1993), using import and producer unit price data from the Japanese input-output table, have calculated the "tariff-equivalents" of Japanese nontariff barriers. Their results are astounding, indicating tariff-equivalents of more than 500 percent in some cases (table 5.1).[5] According to the authors, these price differences are due to government regulation in some cases (such as agriculture) and may simply be a statistical artifact in others (such as consumer electronics).[6]

Similar price differences have been discovered using bilateral data collected in the context of the SII negotiations. The joint survey conducted by the US Department of Commerce and MITI in 1991 found that two-thirds of the products covered were on average 37 percent more expensive in Japan than in the United States (tables 5.2 and 5.3; the survey done in 1989 obtained quantitatively similar results). Since unlike in the study by Sazanami et al. these data involve exact brand and model comparisons, the question immediately arises as to why arbitrage does not eliminate these price differences. The persistence of these differentials suggests that they are not simply due to short-run exchange rate

---

5. These results are discussed fully in the forthcoming volume edited by Hufbauer and Elliott.

6. Quality differences between imports and domestic production may account for some of the price differences that Sazanami et al. find. For example, Japan imports simple black-and-white televisions, while it produces sophisticated color models at home. Hence a comparison of import and domestic producer television prices reveals far higher prices for the domestically produced good.

Table 5.1   Japan: tariffs and estimated tariff-equivalents of nontariff barriers, 1989 (percentages ad valorem)

Product	Tariff	Tariff-equivalent
Milled rice	0.0	737.2
Citrus fruits	14.1	648.6
Oilseeds	0.0	625.8
Tea and roasted coffee	11.9	510.1
Wheat (domestic and import)	0.0	477.8
Soybeans (domestic and import)	0.0	423.6
Bread	6.5	346.5
Tobacco	0.0	316.8
Dairy products	17.6	242.0
Sparkling and still beverages	17.1	197.0
Beer	1.7	143.0
Confectionery	18.8	153.7
Leaf tobacco	0.0	119.7
Processed meat products	17.9	119.8
Canned or bottled vegetables and fruits	18.0	108.6
Whiskey and brandy	5.9	73.6
Other sugar and by-products of sugar manufacturing	63.8	0.0
Cosmetics, toilet preparations, and dentifrices	2.0	779.1
Clay refractories	1.2	578.7
Gasoline	5.5	488.5
Caustic soda	4.9	231.9
Methane derivatives	2.3	217.1
Soda ash	0.0	161.5
Copper ore	0.0	159.2
Natural gas	0.0	152.6
Nitric fertilizers	0.0	105.0
Other nonferrous metals	0.4	73.4
Oil- and fat-based industrial chemicals	0.8	72.5
Titanium oxide	4.1	48.9
Regenerated aluminum	0.8	31.8
Polyethylene (2041021-24)	5.7	35.2
Ferroalloys	3.5	26.3
Lead (incl. regenerated lead)	3.5	24.1
Crude petroleum	2.4	0.0
Medicaments	3.4	8.5
Heavy oil A	5.2	0.0
Radio and television sets	0.0	443.4
Communication equipment	0.1	337.7
Semiconductor devices and integrated circuits	0.0	107.0
Motor vehicles	0.0	70.2
Chemical machinery	0.1	61.1
Electric computing equipment	0.0	41.3
Medical instruments	2.1	32.7
Agricultural machinery	1.3	0.0
Wearing apparel	10.4	187.1
Foreign paper and Japanese paper	3.3	102.7
Leather footwear	6.4	51.6
Cotton yarn	5.3	43.5
Knit fabrics	14.3	44.5
Plywood	11.6	35.7
Paperboard	3.0	8.5

Source: Sazanami et al. (1993), who selected the listed products from approximately 500 product categories.

Table 5.2 Comparison of US and Japanese prices for selected goods by product group, 1991

Product group	Number of products surveyed	Japanese prices as a percentage of US prices	Number of products priced higher in Japan	Percentage of products priced higher in Japan
All goods	112	137.1	75	67.0
Electrical and optical goods	30	103.3	11	36.7
Auto parts	10	208.6	9	90.0
Liquor	10	167.1	10	100.0
Automobiles	7	104.5	4	57.1
Capital goods	20	117.0	11	55.0
Miscellaneous consumer goods	23	159.6	20	87.0
Food	12	146.6	10	83.3

Source: US Department of Commerce (1991).

Table 5.3 Comparison of US and Japanese prices for selected goods by country of manufacture, 1991

Country of manufacture	Number of products surveyed	Japanese prices as a percentage of US prices	Number of products priced higher in Japan
Total	112	137.1	75
Japan	40	98.6	12
United States	34	170.3	31
Other	20	165.9	19
Mixed	17	130.7	13

Source: US Department of Commerce (1991).

misalignment, but rather that they are the product of some type of market closure.[7]

A variety of hypotheses have been put forward to explain this phenomenon. One is that the high retail prices of traded goods in Japan are due to high costs in the retail sector. These include the notoriously high price of land, as well as alleged inefficiencies in the distribution system (Lawrence 1991b, Ito and Maruyama 1991, Itoh 1991). Another set of explanations emphasizes conventional resistance factors to international trade such as transportation costs and trade barriers. Bergsten and Cline (1987) estimate that the aggregate tariff-equivalent of nontariff barriers of all sorts imposed on US exports to the Japanese market is on the order of 25 percent. Lastly, some researchers have argued that the high prices in Japan are due to strategic decisions by oligopolistic firms: either rent extraction by foreign exporters or Japanese importers generating high prices in Japan (Cline 1990b), or exclusionary practices and dumping by members of the *keiretsu*, contributing to high prices at home and low prices abroad (Cheng and Kreinin 1991). *Keiretsu* domination of distribution channels is also alleged to contribute to the price differentials.

Noland (1992c) used the Department of Commerce–MITI survey data to test these hypotheses. The results of this paper indicate that these price differentials are associated with trade policies (in particular the presence of nontariff barriers) and the existence of *keiretsu*, suggesting, in confirmation of the trade quantity studies, that these are the main sources of market closure. (Indeed, these results would appear to tilt the explanation of the effect of the *keiretsu* on trade volumes toward the market closure hypothesis and away from the enhanced-competitiveness hypothesis.)

These results do not indicate, however, whether these entry barriers constrain foreign firms that are pricing at marginal cost in the Japanese market, or whether the existence of entry barriers permits Japanese and/

---

7. A distinct line of research has investigated the pricing strategies of Japanese firms in response to exchange rate changes (e.g., Loopesko and Johnson 1987, Marston 1991).

or foreign firms to price above marginal cost in the Japanese market. In either event, a conservative estimate is that elimination of these sources of market closure might lead to a more than 20 percent increase in the volume of manufactured imports into Japan.[8]

The results of this study along with six others are summarized in table 5.4. It is unsurprising that the results appear to be as divergent as these are: the question that they are trying to answer is an inherently difficult one. The studies can be broken down into three groups. The first group consists of Petri (1991) and Lawrence (1991b), who generate estimates of the potential increase in Japanese manufactured imports of 54.3 to 100.0 percent. For purposes of analyzing bilateral trade, these studies have two drawbacks. First, they were derived on the basis of single-country, cross-industry regressions, and so do not take into account the characteristics of countries other than Japan. Second, they refer to global, not bilateral, trade.

The Saxonhouse papers make up the next group. These figures are not directly comparable to the others: they refer to all imports, not just manufactured imports as do the other papers. Nonetheless, these results give the impression of implying somewhat less unusual importing behavior on the part of Japan—indeed that Japan's trade is as its factor endowments predict. This does not mean that Japan is a free trader, but only that its trade is not any more distorted than the world average. Saxonhouse (1992) interprets his finding that 1985 Japanese net exports were $13.2 billion higher than predicted as reflecting diversion of exports from Europe to the United States due to European trade restrictions. (This paper is not included in table 5.4 because it refers to *net* exports and is even less directly comparable to the other studies.) Putting the three papers together, one gets the impression that both Japanese imports and exports may be lower than expected. In any event, the previously detailed problems with the modeling approach used in these papers point to the unreliability of their results.

The final group of studies, by Bergsten and Cline (1987), Lawrence (1987), and Noland (1992c), generates estimates of potential increases in Japanese imports in a lower, narrower range than the Lawrence and Petri papers: 21.8 to 45.4 percent. Three things should be noted about

---

8. Applying the coefficients reported in this paper to the sample means (with the recognition that the sample may not be representative of the whole manufacturing-goods sector) yields the finding that elimination of the trade impediments would lead to a 32.5 percent fall in import prices. Noland (1989) reports a long-run price elasticity of demand for Japanese imports of -0.67. Presumably this is a lower-bound estimate for manufactured goods. Applying this elasticity to the price decline above, one obtains a 21.8 percent increase in import volume.

Alternatively, Bergsten and Cline's estimate of -1.16 for the Japanese import price elasticity of demand, applied to the price change noted above, yields an estimate of potential manufactured import growth of 37.7 percent.

Table 5.4 Alternative estimates of potential increases in Japanese manufactures imports under complete removal of trade barriers[a]

Study	Sample period	Potential increase (percentages)
Bergsten and Cline (1987)[b]	1985	45.4–24.4
Lawrence (1987)	1980	41.3
Saxonhouse (1989)[d]	1979	7.2
Petri (1991)	1985	100.0
Lawrence (1991a)[c]	1985	76.0–54.3
Noland (1992c)[b]	1991	37.7–21.8
Saxonhouse (1993)[d]	1983	7.7

a. Figures are percentage increases in imports from all sources except where noted otherwise.
b. Figure refers to US-Japan bilateral trade only.
c. Derived by applying general equilibrium offset factors of 0.5 (taken from Petri 1991) and 0.7 (taken from Lawrence 1987) to the initial increase of 108.5 percent.
d. Figures refer to all trade, not just manufactures, and thus are not directly comparable with the others. See the text for elaboration.

these studies. First, they are based on three different methodologies: industry-by-industry estimates in the case of Bergsten and Cline, cross-national regressions in the Lawrence study, and bilateral price regressions in the Noland study. Second, Bergsten and Cline, and Noland are based on US-Japan bilateral data. Third, some liberalization clearly occurred in Japan between 1980 and 1991; one should expect the potential manufactured import increases to decline. Using the estimates in the Bergsten and Cline, and Noland cases, this indeed occurs: the highest estimate, Lawrence's 41.3 percent, is based on data from 1980; the next highest, 34.9 percent (the midpoint of the Bergsten-Cline range), which is approximately 15 percent lower, is derived from 1985 data; and the lowest, 29.8 percent (the midpoint of Noland's range), calculated from 1991 data, is 15 percent lower still. All of this suggests that, from the standpoint of estimating current potential manufactured import increases in Japan, the greatest probability weight should be placed on the Noland (1992c) estimates.

These estimates pertain to manufacturing. In the case of agriculture, a lower-bound estimate derived from table 4.3 suggests that complete elimination of all barriers might increase the incomes of US producers by the equivalent of 28 percent of exports. (This would occur both through a combination of higher export volumes to Japan and through higher prices on exports to all markets.) The preferred manufactures estimate would conservatively put the potential increase in US manufactured export volumes to Japan at nearly 30 percent. Bergsten and Cline report estimates of potential export increases in fuels of 61 percent. Comparable figures for potential gains in nonfuel minerals and services are unavailable.

These estimates are by their very nature imprecise: complete liberalization in Japan would engender changes in economic behavior beyond the historical experience on which these models are based. Nonetheless, it may be instructive to summarize what they might imply for the bilateral trade imbalance. Applying the table 4.3 estimates to 1992 data and adjusting for sectors that have been liberalized since these studies were completed, one obtains estimates of $1.2 billion to $5.9 billion in increased US agricultural exports if the Japanese market were completely liberalized, with a mean estimate of $3.6 billion. The Office of the USTR (1993) gives an estimate of potential increases in wood products exports of $750 million. Applying the high-end Noland (1992c) estimate from table 5.4 to manufactures yields $10.9 billion in increased manufactured exports; the low-end estimate is $6.3 billion, for a mean estimate of $8.6 billion. Applying the Bergsten and Cline estimates for fuels to current data yields an estimate of $689 million in increased fuel exports. Thus, according to these estimates, if Japan were to eliminate all formal and informal barriers to trade, US exports to Japan would initially increase by somewhere in the range of $8.9 billion to $18.2 billion, with a central estimate of $13.6 billion.

Increasing market access in Japan would have an impact on the bilateral deficit, although by how much is difficult to say. The initial increase in Japanese imports would be accompanied by increased Japanese efficiency and by a depreciation of the yen. Both would tend to both dampen the import increase, as well as encourage more Japanese exports. In the end, the bilateral deficit would shrink by something less than the full $8.9 billion to $18.2 billion. In reality, liberalization would occur over an extended period of time, so that the reduction in the deficit due to liberalization would be intertwined with fluctuations in the balance due to macroeconomic developments. As a consequence, it could be very difficult to disentangle the effects of liberalization even in retrospect. None of these qualifications should detract from the desirability of gaining greater access to the Japanese market, however.

Improving access to the large Japanese market will increase opportunities for competitive US firms to capture economies of scale and scope, and would surely improve both the terms of trade for the United States and the real incomes of factors employed in the exporting sectors. (Indeed, Staiger et al. 1988 estimate that Japanese trade policies have a larger impact on factor returns in the United States than US trade policies do.) These are part of the traditional gains from trade and are worth pursuing regardless of the bilateral trade balance. Moreover, the removal of these access barriers would facilitate a more symmetrical interpenetration of the two economies and hasten the process of convergence.

Greater access is in the US economic interest. It would also contribute to reducing political tensions both by eliminating sources of sectoral trade disputes as well as by contributing to a reduction in the overall bilateral deficit. The chief questions are, What should the United States' strategic priorities be in pursuing greater access? And what tactics should the United States use to achieve them?

Lessons

The previous chapter surveyed the sectoral distribution of barriers to trade in the United States and Japan. Certain recurrent themes have emerged in plumbing the industry case studies. First, the Japanese government has pursued more obvious policies of industrial development than the United States. This is not to say that the United States has no industrial policies—it clearly does—but rather that Japanese policies have had a much more narrow industrial goal, without the national security emphasis that has played a major role in US policy formation. Consequently, in all of the cases studied, Japanese government action has played a significant role in how competition between US and Japanese firms has been conducted.

How this competition has played out has depended in large part on the fundamental competitive strengths of industries in the two countries. As a consequence, there are basically two typologies of conflict: the first arises where demands for trade action arise from import-competing sectors in the United States faced with a competitive Japanese industry (notably automobiles, and arguably semiconductors); the second where competitive US firms seek access to a restricted Japanese market (computers, telecommunications, securities, retailing, construction, and arguably semiconductors). The dynamics of the first type are relatively well-known: the US import-competing sector appeals to US authorities to impose some sort of protection, such as the VER on automobiles in the early 1980s, or domestic-content requirements masquerading as VIEs in auto parts more recently. The political dynamics of this are relatively well-understood (see Destler 1992), although recent proposals for a quota on Japanese cars, inclusive of the output of transplant factories in the United States, could significantly complicate domestic trade politics.

The second type of trade conflict, arising from the access problems encountered by US firms in the Japanese market, presents US policymakers with more difficult and subtle problems and choices. The recurrent pattern that emerges from the case studies is of competitive US firms denied access to the Japanese market by a combination of public policies and private behavior. In a number of cases, this takes the form of officially or informally sanctioned cartel behavior by Japanese oligopolists. The response of some firms is to seek US government assistance in prying open the market. (Presumably some firms, frustrated by their experiences, simply give up and are never heard from again.) If the US government takes up their case, and sufficient pressure is applied to Japan (including overt threats of retaliation in a number of cases), possibilities for change begin to appear.

The goals of the Japanese government (assuage foreign pressure) and Japanese business (maintain oligopoly profits) are obvious, as is the solution: buy off the foreign pressure. In practice this means allowing a particular foreign firm or firms into the domestic oligopoly and a share of cartel rents in exchange for a cessation of political pressure.

This solution, although perhaps satisfactory to the Japanese government, Japanese business, and the privileged foreign firm(s), creates a dilemma for US policymakers and those in third countries. Put starkly, should the United States be satisfied with certain of its firms gaining possibly privileged access to the Japanese market, or should it press for more fundamental liberalization to facilitate the entry of additional US and foreign firms on a competitive basis?

Although it is the structure of the Japanese economy that sets up this dilemma, it is the dynamics of US policymaking that makes the dilemma particularly vexing. The United States has a producer-oriented, complainant-initiated trade policy system. In colloquial terms, it's the squeaky wheel that gets the grease. Thus, US trade policymakers face two related problems: how to prioritize the myriad problems that they confront with Japan, and how to respond to co-optation opportunities presented by Japanese policies.

Priorities should be set on the basis of the likely payoff to the US economy and the likelihood of success. The obvious solution would be to calculate the present discounted value of prospective trade deals and prioritize them according to this ranking. One would want to take into account the stream of benefits to the US economy as well as the political costs and likelihood of successfully concluding a deal. The fact that one would regard the benefits as a stream extending into future years would tend to tilt the calculation toward rapidly growing markets. Focusing on the impact on the US economy (as distinct from the sales of US firms) would tend to tilt the prioritization toward activities with a large domestic component. While advocating the application of basic cost-benefit reasoning would seem singularly unoriginal, given the incentives facing US policymakers, this is not necessarily so.[9]

---

9. Recent trade deals, including the Semiconductor Trade Agreement and targets on auto parts purchases, have been specified in terms of corporate identities, not location of production. (To wit, a TI semiconductor produced in Kyushu counts as American, while a Hitachi chip produced in California counts as Japanese.) The proposed quotas on Japanese-maker automobiles, which would count the output of Japanese plants in the United States as Japanese, would extend this trend.

Table 5.5 Apparent and potential US gains from liberalization in Japan (millions of dollars)

Apparent gains from liberalizations implemented to date		Potential gains from future liberalizations	
Cigarettes	1,200	Computers[a]	1,075
Beef	500	Fuels	789
Semiconductors[b]	≤415	Wood products	750
Citrus	100	Retailing[c]	150
Fiber optics	33	Supercomputers	30

a. Does not include an estimated $1 billion in US firms' foreign-sourced products.
b. Does not include an estimated $715 million in US firms' foreign-sourced products.
c. Includes gains attributable to Toys'R'Us only.

To make these implications concrete, consider how some of the cases that have been examined in previous chapters might be ranked (table 5.5). (It should be emphasized that these cases are listed for purely illustrative purposes and are not comprehensive.) By far the largest impact from liberalization has been in cigarettes, where US exports increased by $1.2 billion, followed by beef ($500 million), the STA ($415 million as an upper bound), and citrus ($100 million).[10] The smallest apparent gains were in fiber optics ($33 million). On the basis of these admittedly crude calculations, it would take three fiber optics cases to have the impact on the US economy that the citrus deal did, 15 fiber optics cases to equal beef, or 36 fiber optics cases to match cigarettes.

The second column in table 5.5 reports some potential gains in sectors yet to be liberalized. To reiterate, these are by their very nature speculative estimates and subject to large errors. They are interesting nonetheless. The largest potential gain, more than $1 billion, comes from eliminating discriminatory public procurement practices in (nonsuper-) computers. (Again, this ignores the estimated $1 billion in estimated sales sourced outside the United States.) This is followed by liberalization in

---

This is fundamentally the wrong way to go. The US government should promote the interests of its citizens, which coincide most extensively with the interests of the internationally immobile factors of production. Consequently, issues should be prioritized according to their impact on the US economy, not the worldwide sales of US firms.

This has two immediate implications. First, trade pacts should be negotiated on the basis of benefits to the US economy rather than corporate identity. Second, deals that result in exports of goods and services from the United States would therefore tend to receive higher priority than deals that would result in higher sales for US firms, but where the production of goods and services would occur abroad.

10. In addition to exports, the STA may have increased the *sales* of North American firms in the Japanese market, generating additional benefits to the US economy in the form of remitted profits and increased headquarters activities in the United States. An upperbound estimate of the sales impact of the STA would be an increase of $1.1 billion. A similar issue arises with regard to potential gains in computers, where a significant share of the increased sales would be sourced outside the United States.

fuels ($789 million) and in wood products ($750 million), the entry of Toys 'R' Us into the Japanese retailing market ($150 million), and the elimination of discriminatory public procurement practices in supercomputers ($30 million). The listing of Toys 'R' Us is a bit misleading, since it was part of a broader effort to get retailers into the Japanese market, and the gains to other retailers have not been quantified. Nonetheless, the differences in magnitudes are striking: it would take 25 supercomputer deals to equal the potential gains in wood products, or 36 supercomputer public procurement agreements to equal one mainframe computer public procurement accord.

These comparisons should be qualified in three ways. First, they ignore any possible spillovers or externalities in the high-technology cases. Nonetheless, these figures suggest that there would have to be some extremely large externalities to a product such as fiber optics or supercomputers to compensate for the fundamental differences in export potential. The second qualification reinforces this caveat: these figures are the direct (not total) effects. If indirect effects on the rest of the economy through interindustry linkages are taken into account, the natural resource–based products will look even better, since they presumably have a lower import content.

Third, these estimates are static. As argued above, one would want to attach a greater priority to growing markets, both because the future payoffs are expected to be larger, and because new entrants in a growing market would presumably encounter less political resistance in Japan. These considerations might tilt the calculations toward high technology, where relatively small initial payoffs in manufacturing might also be parlayed into larger gains if they helped firms penetrate the "design-in" process.

More generally, our criteria will tend to favor cases involving products exported from the United States over those where a significant share of the products and/or services are sourced outside the United States (such as cellular telephones, semiconductors, and Toys 'R' Us, to name only three).

Having established some priority guidelines, we must next address the issue of tactics. US policymakers have essentially three options, in increasing order of difficulty in attainment: accept the entry of US firms into the Japanese oligopoly; go for a VIE, under which multiple firms (including foreign firms) can compete for market share; or aim for complete liberalization.

In sectors where there is one dominant producer (e.g., fiber optics, supercomputers), options 1 and 2 are in effect similar, and US policymakers may face overwhelming political incentives to adopt these approaches. Given the commitments of bureaucratic and political resources that attempting to achieve complete liberalization would require, satisficing with option 1 or 2 may not be a bad strategy.

As the number of US producers (or potential producers) increases, however, accepting co-optation or a VIE appears increasingly less attractive. Accepting co-optation, by pressuring the Japanese government until particular US firms have gained market access and then backing off, would imply a preferential disposal of rents that would be difficult to sustain politically. A VIE solution that facilitated more equitable access among competing firms would be more acceptable politically.

The question then becomes: When are VIEs preferable to traditional procedural liberalization efforts? We are very skeptical of the VIE approach for four related reasons. First, VIEs are likely to be captured politically. Producer groups in the exporting country will want the covered industries defined as narrowly as possible, to eliminate intergroup competition and to assure themselves that they will reap the prospective benefits. The importing country will also want to define them as narrowly as possible, to facilitate implementation. (Remember that the importing-country government ultimately has to ensure that the targets are attained.) Thus, there is a natural coincidence of interests between domestic producer groups and foreign governments to set up a patchwork of narrow VIEs. Indeed, the Japanese would make incumbents the recipients of VIEs, essentially "taking hostages" among US firms and turning them into allies against *all* new entrants, domestic or foreign.

Indeed, the ability of the importing-country government to implement and enforce such an agreement will be positively related to the degree of government involvement in the industry and inversely related to the number of firms. This suggests that the simplest case in which to implement a VIE would be that of a monopsonistic public corporation such as a national telecommunications monopoly. (In this case the obvious first-best solution is to negotiate the removal of public procurement preferences.) Implementation will grow increasingly difficult as the number of importing firms increases. Attempts to coordinate importing behavior across firms will inevitably contribute to the cartelization of the industry. Moreover, if the Japanese firms export to and produce in the United States, the US government runs the risk of encouraging cartelization and then importing the cartel behavior into its own market.

This raises the issue of third parties. A VIE must either include or exclude third parties. If it excludes them, it may shift rents to the *demandeur* country at the expense of third parties, and encourage emulation by other exporting countries elsewhere.[11] (Indeed, the VIE may set a precedent, and the original *demandeur* may find itself the object of VIE demands from others.) If instead the VIE includes third parties, it reduces

---

11. In the auto parts case, European and Australian officials have complained that purchases have been diverted from their exporters to US firms. Japanese officials have denied that any diversion away from third-party suppliers has occurred.

one of the avenues by which cartel behavior in the *demandeur*'s own market can be disciplined.

Second, the quantitative targets are fundamentally arbitrary. One can look at market shares in third-country markets, but these are little more than crude and debatable benchmarks. There is no consensus standard or methodology for judging what market shares ought to be, and one lesson of the sophisticated econometric literature surveyed above is that a significant amount of art as well as science is involved in these judgments. One observer's invisible barrier is another's superior competitiveness, and experience shows that market outcomes can vary greatly from the *a priori* estimates of knowledgeable observers; indeed, the negotiated outcomes could be far less desirable than those obtained by removing the trade barrier.[12]

Moreover, there is no obvious time dimension to the VIE (should they last for a fixed period? indefinitely?), nor is there any obvious way to determine how the quantitative target should evolve over time.

This leads to the third problem, namely, that in most of the cases surveyed, credible threats of retaliation have been important in achieving action in Japan. The VIE puts the exporting country in the position of making a decision whether to retaliate on the basis of factors outside either government's control, such as changes in the composition of demand or technological innovations (as in the case of the STA) or exchange rate changes. This would inevitably erode the credibility of enforcement of these agreements.

Lastly, it is always tempting for a large country to use its inherent market power to achieve its desired ends. It is almost assuredly true, however, that the adoption of a VIE strategy by the United States will create a precedent that will be adopted by other countries and will come back to haunt its originator.

---

12. A case in point is US cigarette exports to Japan, which faced multitudinous tariff and nontariff barriers prior to liberalization: annual US exports were $95 million, accounting for less than 1 percent of the Japanese market. Three contemporaneous studies addressed the potential increases in foreign market shares: Saxonhouse (1983) described such potential gains as "modest"; Bergsten and Cline (1985) estimated that, with liberalization, US exports might increase by $98 million; and the US Department of Commerce (in a study cited by Bergsten and Cline) estimated that the market might grow by $1.9 billion. In point of fact, US exports increased 13-fold, from less than $95 million in 1985 to more than $1.3 billion in 1990, after the market was opened. Similar is the case of beef: contemporary observers (e.g., the Department of Commerce, and Bergsten and Cline) predicted that US exports would increase by $280 million with liberalization. In fact, the increase in exports has been nearly twice this amount. Likewise, Bergsten and Cline, and the US Department of Commerce, predicted that citrus exports might increase by $40 million with liberalization; exports in fact grew by more than $100 million. In hindsight, it is very difficult to believe that trade officials could have obtained negotiated solutions in any of these cases that would have been nearly as advantageous to US interests as the market solution obtained through genuine liberalization.

Thus, for all of these reasons we remain skeptical of the VIE approach. In cases where there are clear instances of public impediments to imports (such as the discriminatory public procurement cases), it would be better to apply the first-best approach and negotiate the removal of the barrier. Similarly, in the cases of private entry barriers, it would be preferable to apply internationally agreed-upon competition policies, recognizing that in cases where there are only a few potential exporters, the cost-benefit calculation may indicate that the co-optation option may make sense. In the case of high-technology development programs it would be best to negotiate agreements on countervailing subsidies.

Nonetheless, VIEs do appear to be suited to a particular kind of problem that the United States sometimes faces in its dealings with Japan. Foreign providers of industrial intermediates or capital goods wanting to sell into the Japanese market (or even to the Japanese firms' subsidiaries outside of Japan) sometimes find that their entry is blocked by the contracting relationships of the vertical *keiretsu* system. This system may be efficiency-enhancing and may warrant emulation by non-Japanese firms, as some have already begun to do. At the same time, these long-standing relationships were developed in the context of what was essentially a closed system. Once these firms become major players in the international economic system, there is a clear political (and arguably an economic) rationale for developing a broader, more inclusive, *international* web of relationships.

Moreover, there may be cases, such as semiconductors and supercomputers, where the issues are such that internationally agreed-upon rules of competition are unlikely to be formulated in the politically relevant time frame. In these cases policymakers will be inevitably pushed toward second-best solutions. Once one has entered the world of the second best, evaluating the desirability of piecemeal policies becomes extremely difficult. Nevertheless, these are the choices that policymakers face in reality.

In these cases, VIEs may make some sense as a mechanism to force the adaptation of a system that was developed in the closed, policy-distorted environment of Japan in the 1950s and 1960s. A VIE could then be considered as a *temporary* compensatory policy to move the Japanese system closer to a free trade equilibrium. It may act as a prod to internationalize the *keiretsu*. It is precisely this encouragement to bring non-Japanese firms aboard in product development and the "design-in" phase that could be the avenue by which this inherently discriminatory structure is made compatible with an open international trade system. Once the process of inclusion begins, presumably some non-Japanese firms will succeed and some fail in developing stable and productive relationships with their Japanese counterparts; this is as it should be. At the same time, Japanese firms will have a positive incentive to find capable, efficient partners. Indeed, the goal of the exercise should be to build relationships that exceed the efficiency of the existing networks of Japanese firms. This too will promote the process of systemic convergence between Japan and the United States.

Yet in light of the potential pitfalls of the VIE approach, one should be very cautious in advocating them. It makes no sense to propose them for consumer products or final goods of any sort. They should only be considered in the case of industrial intermediates. They would make the most sense in rapidly expanding markets where new entrants could be accommodated without displacing existing domestic production. Even then, their application should be weighed carefully against first-best alternatives.

It is clear from our analysis that true market liberalization provides the greatest trade benefits in almost all cases of impeded market access in Japan. Every effort should therefore be made to identify government policies, or private practices (such as cartel behavior or the Japanese automakers' "genuine parts" requirement), that could be altered by government policies whose reform would enhance foreign access. The payoffs, as we have documented in several cases (including cigarettes, beef, and citrus), are likely to be much greater than in any "managed trade" deal.

In addition, however, this chapter has identified two types of second-bests that the United States has pursued in its dealing with Japan. One is the policy-assisted co-optation of US firms into Japanese cartels. The other is the pursuit of VIEs. These options may make sense where private arrangements growing out of previously policy-distorted environments impede foreign access in Japan, or where the political costs of pursuing true market liberalization are excessive. In such cases, co-optation may be least bad when only one or a few foreign firms are involved. Once there are more than a handful of potential entrants, however, the co-optation outcome will not be satisfactory from either a Japanese or a US perspective. In these cases it will be tempting—and may actually be beneficial—to settle for a VIE. Making the choice ultimately comes down to comparing the likelihoods of securing the first- and the second-best solutions.

6

Conclusions and Policy Recommendations

The analyses in this book have identified four sets of economic problems that the United States and Japan must address: the countries' trade imbalances, structural differences that reflect their alternative styles of capitalism and different institutional arrangements, sector-specific distortions that affect both the Japanese and the American market (and encompass investment and technology as well as trade), and the need for effective cooperation between the two economies—the world's largest—in pursuing their responsibilities for global leadership. We have devoted most of our attention to the structural and sector-specific issues, not because we believe they are more important than the macroeconomic and global leadership questions, but because they are now the most contentious and most difficult components of the equation. We begin this concluding chapter by summarizing our main analytical findings and then turn to our policy proposals.

Analytical Findings

Our first conclusion is that *both the aggregate imbalances and the structural and sectoral problems matter*. As long as the United States runs sizable global current account deficits, an important part of which consist of bilateral trade deficits with Japan, American output and employment will be transferred to the rest of the world under conditions of less than full employment. Increases in the deficit will increase American unemployment unless domestic demand is rising by an offsetting

199

amount. Servicing the accumulated foreign debt arising from these deficits will require additional transfers of American resources abroad. Continued secular depreciation of the dollar will adversely affect the United States' terms of trade and thus reducing its wealth and income.

In addition, the deficits inevitably generate pressures for protectionist trade policies. If implemented, such policies will reduce America's economic welfare still further (and hurt its foreign policy). Finally, if caused by disequilibrium exchange rates, as has frequently been the case, the deficits will distort investment and further impede the country's economic prospects.

The sharp increase in the Japanese global surplus in the face of sluggish world growth in the early 1990s, to a level well above its long-run equilibrium level of 1½ to 2 percent of its GDP (see chapter 2), represents a particularly significant problem. Occurring primarily via a reduction in imports, due to recession in Japan and the inappropriate depreciation of the yen in 1989–90, this increased surplus has depressed output in other countries around the world and intensified the global slowdown. The direct impact of Japan's increased surplus has fallen primarily on countries other than the United States, underlining the need to focus on Japan's global position (as well as that of the United States) rather than the bilateral imbalance between them.

The structural and sector-specific problems add to the level of the imbalances, as shown in chapters 3, 4, and 5, and hence contribute to the problems just cited. They also affect the composition of the US economy by disadvantaging particular industries. Denial of access to the Japanese market, the world's second largest and the most sophisticated in many high-technology products, can reduce the availability of economies of scale and scope to American firms that might otherwise generate important externalities for the economy as a whole. The United States may thus be hampered in developing those industries that will be disproportionately important, both quantitatively and qualitatively, to its economic future. Any effective policy strategy must address this full range of problems.

Our second key finding is that *Japanese market access limitations have a large and disproportionate impact on the United States because of the sectoral composition of the two economies and the interaction of their governments' policies.* Firms based in the two countries are the world's most competitive in a wide variety of high-technology sectors where economies of scale and scope are of critical importance. Hence access to global markets for high-technology products, especially in the largest and highest-income countries such as Japan, is particularly important to permit national realization of the externalities available in those sectors. The two governments, especially the Japanese but also the American (heretofore primarily for security reasons), thus tend to focus their government interventions in those sectors. The result is frequent clashes between both private- and public-sector efforts in the two countries, as Japan's access limitations tend to hit the United States harder than they hit other countries whose high-technology sectors are less important to their economies.

The United States also possesses clear comparative advantage in a number of agricultural products and in many services sectors in which Japan is less competitive and limits access to its markets. Similarly, the United States has tended to lose competitive advantage and erect import barriers in older manufacturing industries where Japan has remained highly competitive. Here too each country's trade policy has a disproportionate impact on the other's economy.

A third conclusion is that *these economic conflicts are magnified by major structural differences between the two countries.* "Difference" is frequently seen, at least on the US side, as "unfairness." The difficulty of achieving meaningful access to the Japanese market is viewed as a vindication of this thesis. Among the most important structural problems in Japan now are some aspects of its *keiretsu* system of corporate linkages and the lack of a potent competition policy to counter them, its approach to product liability and regulation, its inefficient distribution system, its land use policy, and elements of its policy toward intellectual property rights.

At the same time, however, Japan is clearly changing. The Japanese and American economies are converging, each toward the other, at a more rapid pace than is generally realized. Policymakers need to recognize that some of the most important differences between the two are thus already declining in significance, and that policy can—and must attempt to—broaden and speed that convergence. Convergence, however, will not resolve many of the problems confronting the two countries in the short to medium term.

Moreover, the two countries still differ vastly in their roles in the world economy. The United States, despite its economic problems of the past two decades or so, remains largely responsible for providing systemic leadership to promote global economic prosperity and stability. Japan, despite its enormous economic progress, and despite being the world's largest creditor country, remains very much a "free rider" in terms of both economic leadership and global security arrangements. Its failure to share a significant portion of the leadership role colors attitudes toward Japan among Americans (and Europeans and others), who believe that wealth and prosperity beget a responsibility for charity and leadership.

Fourth, we conclude that *the structural and sector-specific sources of market access problems in Japan require subtle and sophisticated policy responses by the United States* (and other foreigners). Where explicit barriers can be identified, the preferred approach is of course to seek to lower or eliminate them. In many industries, however, American firms face a multiplicity of access problems, due partly to private institutions and practices that grew out of an earlier, trade-distorted environment. In such cases, the United States has to choose: it can try to induce Japan (through governmental action or changes in the behavior of Japanese companies) to accept one or two American firms into an existing cartel (the "co-optation strategy"), or it can seek a voluntary import expansion (VIE) that would benefit a much larger number of outsiders. We have serious reservations about both courses of action, but we do not rule out either in certain circumstances.

The unique characteristics of the Japanese market interact with the American policymaking process to complicate the problem further. Rather than determine its sectoral priorities through objective analysis of the costs and payoffs of pursuing alternative initiatives, Washington tends to respond to the "squeaky wheel" that complains the loudest and plays the political game most effectively. Basic changes are called for in the way the United States chooses its negotiating targets and determines its strategies for pursuing them.

A fifth key conclusion is that *the sizable and ongoing trade imbalance between the countries is caused by microeconomic as well as macroeconomic factors*. The bilateral trade balance should not be an independent policy target in either country. But the analyses in chapters 3, 4, and 5 suggest that limitations on foreign access to the Japanese market due to structural and sector-specific considerations may be curtailing US exports by $9 billion to $18 billion annually. More than half of this total ($6 billion to $11 billion) relates to trade in manufactured products; much of the rest is in agriculture ($1 billion to $6 billion). Additional gains might be obtainable in service industries for which comprehensive estimates do not exist.

Full elimination of barriers in these sectors will obviously take time, if it can ever be achieved at all. There will be feedback effects that reduce the net impact of liberalization on the trade balance to a number considerably smaller than the predicted gross expansion in American exports. Nevertheless, significant resolution of the structural differences and liberalization in specific sectors could have an appreciable effect on the overall imbalance as well as strengthen the outlook for key US industries.

Sixth, *the countries' global and bilateral imbalances are primarily due to underlying macroeconomic conditions, notably the relationships between their underlying levels of saving and investment. Changes in the imbalances are clearly driven by macroeconomic factors*—notably changes in national fiscal policies as transmitted through large changes in exchange rates.

Estimates cited in chapter 2 suggest that policy-induced changes in the macroeconomic variables offer by far the largest "bang for the buck" in correcting the external imbalances. Every rise of 1 percent in the trade-weighted real exchange rate of the yen cuts Japan's global current account surplus by about $4 billion after two years, and every 1 percent rise in the real yen-dollar rate ultimately reduces the bilateral imbalance by about $1 billion. (Every 1 percent fall in the trade-weighted dollar exchange rate improves America's global current account position by about $10 billion.) More rapid growth of incomes also has a major impact: an increase of 1 percent per year in Japan's growth rate lowers its global surplus by $4 billion to $5 billion.

Chapter 2 also noted that we are currently in the fourth cycle of escalating trade imbalances in the last twenty-five years. Each of these escalations, which has sharply increased tensions between the two countries, has stemmed primarily from uncoordinated changes in macroeconomic policies and large resulting disequilibria in currency relationships. The time has clearly come to install new systemic arrangements, preferably at the global level through the Group of Seven (G-7) industrial countries and the International Monetary Fund (IMF), but by the two countries bilaterally if necessary, to avoid future repetitions of this cycle with their extremely damaging economic and political consequences.

Seventh, it is clear that *both countries must make major contributions to resolving all four elements of their economic conflict*. Most of the analysis in this book focuses on Japan, and particularly the structural and sector-specific factors that limit access to its markets. But the United States obviously must do its full part in addressing the problems: through domestic reforms that will strengthen its competitiveness and (at long last) correct its fiscal imbalances, by adopting elements of the Japanese economic model where that model is clearly superior to present American practices, and by a willingness to share leadership with Japan in managing the world economy. Symmetry and reciprocity are essential elements of any lasting, economically effective, and politically viable solution to the US-Japan economic conflict.

The Trade Imbalances

The Problem

It is clear that the repeated surges in the Japanese trade surplus and the American trade deficit, both global and bilateral, have caused significant economic problems in both countries and intensified tensions between them. The first postwar wave of serious US-Japan friction and broader protectionist pressure in the United States emerged when America slid into trade deficit for the first time since World War II at the beginning of the 1970s. Subsequent episodes occurred in the later 1970s and especially in the mid-1980s, when the imbalances reached unprecedented heights (Bergsten 1982). A new episode has been unfolding in the early part of the 1990s.

Three significant caveats must be noted, however. First, US-Japan tensions have been a constant throughout the past two decades—and have probably been rising on a secular basis—whatever the level of the global or bilateral imbalances. Although these macroeconomic developments clearly affect the intensity of the problem, in both economic and political terms, it is equally clear that they are no longer the chief cause of the tensions (Destler 1991).

Second, the rise of Japan's global surplus to record levels in the early 1990s (to perhaps $150 billion in 1993, eclipsing the pre-1992 high of $87 billion in 1987) has not generated as much concern in the United States as might have been expected. This may be partly because the surplus is smaller in relation to the overall Japanese economy than it was in the mid-1980s. It may be partly because much of the increase in the surplus stems from changes in Japan's terms of trade rather than volume shifts (Long Term Credit Bank of Japan 1993)—as it is the latter that determine market shares and hence output (and jobs) in a country's trade partners, and presumably thus drive industry complaints and trade policy. Most likely, it is because the surplus is now more diversified regionally: the bulk of the increase has been in trade with Europe and, especially, East Asia (see table 2.2 in chapter 2). Japan's bilateral surplus with the United States has risen very modestly since 1990 (less than 20 percent) compared with its global explosion (more than 300 percent).

Third, political attention in the United States focuses primarily on the bilateral imbalance between the two countries. We have stressed throughout this book that the bilateral balance is not a proper focus for policy in either country. We recognize, however, that this balance is in fact a focus—perhaps the most prominent single focus—of political and public attention in both countries.

Hence it is significant that the bilateral US-Japan imbalance has not risen as sharply as the Japanese global surplus in recent years. Neither, however, did it fall as precipitately as that surplus did after 1985. While Japan's global current account surplus dropped by almost 60 percent from 1986 to 1990, and America's current account deficit fell by an even greater percentage through 1991 (even if one excludes the one-time receipts from allies to help finance the 1991 Gulf War), the bilateral imbalance between the two countries dropped by less than half as much. The bilateral trade imbalance in fact accounted for more than half of America's entire trade deficit in 1991 and 1992—perhaps increasing rather than reducing concerns over the "Japan problem."[1]

---

1. In a speech at the Institute for International Economics on 10 September 1991, House Majority Leader Richard A. Gephardt (D-MO) declared that "America's trade balance problem is over except for Japan" (Gephardt 1991).

Japan thus received little credit in the United States for its huge positive adjustment of the late 1980s—the reduction of its global surplus from 4.3 percent of its GDP in 1986 to only 1.2 percent in 1990. It also received little credit for the dramatic turnaround in its bilateral position with the United States. American exports to Japan nearly doubled between 1986 and 1990 while American imports from Japan rose by less than 10 percent. This reversal was even more pronounced in volume terms. But the cut in the bilateral imbalance in dollar terms was modest because the starting point was so bad, with American imports triple the level of American exports as late as 1987. On the other hand, as just noted, the subsequent resurgence in Japan's global excess since 1990 has had only a modest impact on its bilateral balance with America, and, at least so far, Japan has taken relatively little heat in the United States for the renewed surpluses.

The Objectives

Nevertheless, correction of the aggregate imbalances must be a central component of any American strategy toward Japan. This element of the overall strategy has, of course, two components: American adjustment of its deficits and Japanese adjustment of its surpluses. Both countries must undertake effective initiatives to these ends.

A reasonable objective is to limit the American global deficit to about 1 percent of its GDP (although complete elimination or even restoration of a surplus would be desirable) and to limit the Japanese surplus to 1½ to 2 percent of its GDP. At current GDP levels, this would mean an American deficit of $60 billion or less (as achieved in 1991, even excluding the Gulf War receipts) and a Japanese surplus of about $60 billion to $80 billion. Imbalances at these levels should be easily financed and should be compatible with global stability.

It is important to recognize that achieving these global positions for the two countries would probably leave them with a considerable bilateral imbalance. This outcome stems partly from the sizable share of each country in the other's trade, coupled with continuing (albeit sharply reduced) global imbalances for each. But it also stems importantly from the triangular trade pattern of Japan, which must import huge quantities of primary products (hence running deficits with countries like Australia, Brazil, and Saudi Arabia) and thus must export like amounts of manufactured goods (to high-income areas such as Europe and the United States; see Bergsten and Cline 1987, 32–41). Zero bilateral balance between the two countries is therefore neither necessary nor feasible. Proposals to achieve bilateral balance over a five-year period, as incorporated in legislation proposed in recent years by House Majority Leader Richard A. Gephardt (D-MO) and Senator Donald W. Riegle, Jr. (D-MI), should be rejected.

The level of the trade imbalance between the United States and Japan is affected by trade barriers in the two countries.[2] The net impact on the overall imbalance of removing Japan's barriers to American products would certainly be less than the gross effect of $9 billion to $18 billion cited above, because the resulting trade liberalization would strengthen Japan's competitive position and because the increase in Japanese imports would lead to a weaker yen, and hence some offsetting changes in imports and exports. Moreover, it will take some time to achieve these gains under the best of circumstances. Nevertheless, enhanced market access in Japan could help reduce the bilateral imbalance and should be pursued for that reason as well as the other important reasons addressed throughout this study.

The aggregate trade imbalances, however, are primarily macroeconomic phenomena, and year-to-year changes in them are almost wholly macroeconomic in nature. Two elements are central: the growth of domestic demand in each economy and the exchange rate between their currencies. Changes in the bilateral US-Japan trade imbalance can be explained almost wholly by changes in the yen-dollar exchange rate, with the usual lag of two years, and differences in growth rates in the two countries.

Policy Recommendations

We can be confident that macroeconomic adjustments are effective in correcting these external imbalances (Krugman 1991). The dollar fell sharply from early 1985 through the end of 1987, retracing most of its earlier runup. The yen virtually doubled in value. The American budget deficit came down by over 2 percent of GNP. Japan enacted a substantial stimulus program to boost domestic demand (although it relied too heavily on monetary ease rather than fiscal expansion and triggered the subsequent "bubble economy"). As a result, the American global current account deficit fell from about 3½ percent of GDP in 1987 to less than 1 percent in 1991. The Japanese surplus fell from over 4 percent to just over 1 percent of its GDP in 1990. The bilateral imbalances also dropped, in direct relationship to the yen-dollar adjustment (see figure 2.3 in chapter 2), although by a smaller percentage, as just noted.

The renewed rise in the imbalances, particularly the Japanese surplus, in the early 1990s occurred primarily because both macroeconomic factors were permitted to get out of line once again. Fiscal adjustment in the United States stalled after a promising start, and the budget deficit was back to nearly record levels in 1992–93. Japan's excessively expansionary

---

2. These include American barriers to its own exports. "Export disincentives" may cut America's foreign sales by as much as $30 billion annually. See Richardson (forthcoming).

monetary policy of the late 1980s triggered a "bubble" in land and stock prices, which had to be burst by acute monetary tightening, pushing the economy into recession: in both 1992 and 1993, Japanese growth has been about 2 percentage points below its sustainable long-term norm of 3½ to 4 percent. Since every decline of 1 percent in Japan's annual growth rate below this norm increases its global account surplus by $4 billion to $5 billion (Cline 1993), this cumulative shortfall of 4 percentage points has raised Japan's external surplus by $15 billion to $20 billion.

Even more important was the renewed weakening of the yen. In 1989–90, the yen dropped in nominal value by about 15 percent from its 1988 average—and by about 20 percent from its end-1987 peak. During that period, moreover, Japan's underlying competitive position continued to improve; inflation was about 2 percent per year less than in the United States and most other industrial countries. Hence the *real* depreciation of the yen cumulated to 20 to 25 percent in 1989–90. Given the relationship between exchange rates and Japanese global trade balances noted above (about $4 billion for every 1 percent change in the yen), this set in motion a rise of $80 billion to $100 billion in the current account surplus in 1992–93.

Taken together, slowed Japanese growth in 1992–93 and the yen depreciation of 1989–90 fully explain (or slightly overexplain) the enormous surge in the global Japanese surplus in 1991–93. Responsibility for these increases rests on many shoulders. The Japanese authorities were unable to engineer a "soft landing" from the excesses of the late 1980s' bubble; instead their tight monetary policies produced a sharp slowdown in 1990–91. The United States failed (especially in the fiscal arena) to fully implement the needed and promised domestic adjustments. The G-7 failed to avoid the substantial yen depreciation of 1989–90 that sowed the seeds for most of the surge in Japan's surplus in the early 1990s.

The macroeconomic component of the needed policy package is thus clear, both for the short run and for the longer run. For its part, the United States needs to restore its underlying competitiveness and sharply reduce its budget deficit. The Clinton economic program seeks to do so. Its budget reduction effort, which aims to reduce the fiscal deficit by about $100 billion by fiscal year 1997, would if fully implemented cut the current account deficit substantially.

Japan needs to stimulate domestic demand sufficiently to restore sustained annual growth of 3½ to 4 percent of GDP. The stimulus should be achieved through expansionary fiscal policy to avoid the twin risks that could result from too much monetary ease, namely, of reflating the bubble economy and of a renewed weakening of the yen. Fortunately, Japan's consolidated government account is in surplus by 3 percent of GDP, so there is plenty of room for expansion without violating the fiscal prudence that Japan has worked so hard and so effectively to achieve. The programs announced in August 1992 and April 1993 mark important steps in the needed direction. American and Japanese fiscal adjustment, pursued simultaneously, will have a mutually reinforcing effect in reducing the countries' external imbalances.

One effect of fiscal stimulus would be to put upward pressure on Japanese interest rates, and thereby contribute to an appreciation of the yen. The yen has already risen by over 20 percent (to about 110 to the dollar) from its lows of 1989–90 as of this writing. A further increase of 5 to 10 percent, bringing the nominal appreciation to 25 to 30 percent, would restore the *real* yen-dollar rate to its end-1987 level—a level that produced sharp reductions in both countries' global imbalances, and a significant change in their bilateral position, by 1990–91. Fiscal stimulus and the attendant currency appreciation would encourage a shift in Japan toward domestic demand–led growth and away from reliance on increasing net exports. Together, the fiscal stimulus and currency correction could reduce Japan's current account surplus into the targeted range by 1994–95, while restoring overall economic growth in Japan. The latest yen appreciation will further *increase* Japan's surplus in 1993, and perhaps early 1994, because of the usual J-curve effect, but the subsequent improvement will be substantial. We saw in chapter 2 that this currency adjustment would also have a major impact in the key automobile sector.

It will be critical to *maintain* the yen-dollar exchange rate at or near this equilibrium level. Hence there is an urgent need to restore systemic arrangements that will limit the risk of new imbalances in the future. As already noted, on at least four occasions during the past twenty-five years a sharp rise in the two countries' external imbalances, triggered largely by currency overvaluations (America) or undervaluations (Japan) and underlying domestic disequilibria, have caused serious economic problems and intensified frictions between the two countries. Both countries have a major interest in avoiding replications of these events.

The United States and Japan should therefore adopt a yen-dollar target zone to limit their future current account imbalances. Under such a system, which we hope would be joined by at least the European G-7 countries, participants would agree on current account targets that are compatible with equilibrium in their domestic economies and with each other, and derive therefrom the exchange rates needed to achieve those targets (see Williamson and Miller 1987). As suggested above, the United States might aim to limit its deficit to 1 percent of its GDP, and Japan might shoot for a surplus of no more than 1½ to 2 percent of its GDP.[3]

---

3. The Clinton administration has proposed that Japan accept a target of 1 to 2 percent in the negotiations for a "new framework" between the countries without linking the concept to a new exchange rate regime. We do not believe that such an approach should be regarded as "managed trade," a term that is best reserved for sector-specific arrangements. We would note that it carries clear exchange rate implications, however, whether or not they are specified in the talks.

The countries would obligate themselves to maintain their exchange rates within the zones. They would accomplish this by "jawboning" (public statements, backed by the threat of intervention, about the desired level or direction of exchange rates), actual intervention (which is clearly effective in achieving official exchange rate goals—see Catte et al. 1992 and Dominguez and Frankel 1993), and, if needed, changes in monetary and fiscal policy. Because of the uncertainty inherent in estimating equilibrium exchange rates, the zones should be set fairly wide at the outset, perhaps in a range of 10 percent above and below the estimated optimum.

The zones would need to be adjusted over time, for two reasons. First, to maintain the *real* level of agreed exchange rates, *nominal* rates would have to be altered periodically—perhaps even annually—to offset differences in inflation rates between countries. In the past, this would have required steady nominal appreciation of the yen against the dollar, because Japanese inflation was consistently lower than American inflation. Indeed, gradual appreciation of the yen in 1988–90 instead of the sharp depreciation that actually occurred would have avoided most of the later runup in the Japanese surplus and the need for the rapid appreciation that occurred in early 1993, with traumatic effects on some Japanese industries. Second, the target zones would on occasion have to be changed in real terms to allow for real shocks, such as dramatic changes in oil prices, that have different effects on different countries.[4]

The United States and Japan in fact initiated a weak version of target zones, called "reference ranges," in October 1986.[5] Building on this "G-2" initiative, the G-7 as a group endorsed the idea at their Louvre meeting in February 1987 (Funabashi 1989). Unfortunately, the ranges were set before the dollar had completed its correction from its early-1985 peak. Thus their yen-dollar component had to be rebased almost immediately, in April 1987, and the ranges were violated toward the end of the year as the dollar plummeted to record lows.

Intervention by the G-7 in early 1988 both stopped the dollar's decline and restored confidence in the ranges. But there was inadequate follow-through on the necessary and promised domestic adjustments, particularly fiscal policy in the United States. Moreover, the ranges were set in nominal rather than real terms, and consequently no effort was made to promote the gradual yen appreciation that was needed to avoid new disequilibria. Worse yet, as noted above, the yen was permitted to depre-

---

4. For further details on the working of the target zone proposal see Williamson and Miller (1987). Interestingly, similar proposals have emerged from Japanese academic (Ito 1989b) and business quarters (Morita 1993).

5. Williamson and Miller (1987, 3) lay out the five major differences between target zones and reference ranges.

ciate in 1989–90 to levels well outside the ranges—even in nominal terms but especially in real terms. Despite this checkered history, a move to target zones could build on the experience already garnered by the G-7 in managing reference ranges and help prevent future recurrence of large US-Japan imbalances.

Structural Differences

Even a complete resolution of the current macroeconomic imbalances, and effective prevention of their recurrence, would leave in place major economic problems between the United States and Japan. As reiterated above, our analysis in chapter 5 concludes that a combination of economywide structural and sector-specific practices in Japan reduces US exports to that country by $9 billion to $18 billion annually from what they would otherwise be. More than half of the gap is in exports of manufactured products, where structural differences play a particularly significant role. Most of the remainder is in agriculture, where the restrictions consist largely of quotas and other traditional trade barriers.

Neither we nor other analysts have been able to quantify the "contribution" to these totals of specific structural features of the Japanese economy, such as the government's industrial policy, corporate *keiretsu* relationships and absence of aggressive antitrust policy, the distribution system, land use policy, or the product liability system. However, Japan appears to be different from other developed countries in the share of imported manufactures in consumption, the degree of intraindustry trade, the extent of intrafirm trade, and openness to inward foreign direct investment. Formal border protection is light, but there is a trove of anecdotal evidence suggesting that the government intervenes to limit imports of manufactures and sanctions limitations by the private sector. In chapter 3, moreover, we noted the sharp differences between these elements of the Japanese economy and most other market economies (including that of the United States). In chapter 4, we showed that some of these elements are related to the low levels of import penetration in specific sectors. In chapter 5, we summarized a number of studies that suggest that Japan's imports (both globally and from the United States) fall far short of what might be expected in the absence of structural and sector-specific access limitations.

Hence we believe that any comprehensive effort to address the US-Japan economic problem must include both structural and sector-specific components. This section will propose a course of actions on the structural issues. The next section will do the same for specific sectors.

Toward Structural Convergence

It is clear from chapter 3 that a number of US-Japan problems derive from differences in economic structure between the two countries. It is

also clear from chapter 1, however, that the structures of the two economies are converging. This convergence is likely to continue and will
probably accelerate with the increasing internationalization of both economies, in which business, labor, and governments on both sides of the
Pacific are all participating. Some of the problems posed for America
(and the world) by Japan's "differentness" will decline as a result. But
the pace of convergence is inadequate to resolve most of the current
problems in the near to medium term. Policy should therefore attempt
to speed the process of convergence and channel it in the right directions
wherever possible.

As we noted in chapter 1, the United States has adopted—or is in the
process of adopting—a number of steps that will improve its competitive
position. Significant changes are transpiring in Japan. Our policy recommendations focus on how change can be accelerated by new American
initiatives toward Japan, recognizing that even the best-laid efforts in
this area will take time to reach fruition, given the inertia that by definition inheres in structural economic problems.

The chosen vehicle for such efforts in the past was the Structural
Impediments Initiative (SII). In the initial round of SII talks in 1989–90,
the United States called for changes in the Japanese distribution system,
land use policies, investment policies, patent practices, discriminatory
pricing, and buying within corporate combines. Japan countered by
putting six US structural problems on the table: the low US saving rate,
the budget and trade deficits, high levels of consumption, the practice
of corporate raiding, and the short-term focus of businesses and financial
markets. There is an interesting difference between these two sets of
objectives: the United States argued that Japan's structural problems
both limited access to its market for foreigners and tilted Japan toward
external surpluses by increasing national saving and dampening national
investment, while Japan's complaints about the United States were
almost wholly targeted at its macroeconomic shortcomings—especially
its inadequate saving rate.

In the short run, Japan was generally credited with implementing its
side of the SII bargain—both the macroeconomic and the microeconomic
provisions—more faithfully than the United States. It began to open
its distribution system by amending the Large Scale Retail Store Law,
permitting Toys 'R' Us and a few other foreign mass marketers to begin
operating in Japan. It has begun to strengthen its antitrust capability.
Modest changes have been made in the taxation of land. Most important
among its SII commitments, Japan has fulfilled much of its pledge to
boost domestic government investment in public works as part of its
annual macroeconomic stimulus packages. Hence the SII has had at least
some modest payoffs in terms of Japanese policy. Now the United States
under the Clinton administration, as noted above, has begun to pursue

many of the structural reforms pledged by the Bush administration in the SII talks. The first round of these efforts has thus promoted, at least modestly, the convergence of the two economies.

We believe that it is desirable to resume the SII strategy, perhaps under a new name: the Structural Convergence Talks (SCT). That strategy is no substitute for macroeconomic policies, which continue to serve as the major vehicle for adjusting the countries' overall trade and current account imbalances. But, as noted, the needed structural changes in both countries can contribute importantly to reducing the imbalances. Moreover, the removal of market impediments will improve the effectiveness of macroeconomic measures, such as currency adjustments, by making each economy more responsive to price changes.

In addition, structural initiatives may on some occasions offer an alternative and more effective response to sector-specific trade problems than steps aimed at those sectors alone (although such steps will often be needed as well, as discussed in the next section). We reiterate that the impact of an SCT will probably take years—if not decades—to be realized fully, given that the problems it addresses are deeply rooted. Nor should there be any illusion, in either country, that total convergence is either feasible or desirable.

Even so, the economic impact of the structural differences between these two largest players in the world economy remains sufficiently great, as chapters 3, 4, and 5 have shown, that their governments must continue to address them as systematically as possible. Those who believe that sovereignty is violated by such intrusion in "domestic affairs" by foreigners ignore the fact that economic interdependence long ago destroyed much of the real autonomy of most nations. It is clearly more constructive to discuss key national differences openly, with an eye toward reducing them, than to ignore them. Their propensity to trigger real economic problems, and therefore disputes between the two countries, is too great. A renewal of structural talks must be part of any comprehensive new strategy to deal effectively with US-Japan economic relations.

The goal of the SCT should be to select and address those structural issues that meet three criteria. First, each issue covered must importantly affect the economic performance of the countries and especially their interaction in trade and investment. Second, the issues must in fact be susceptible to remedial action. In most cases, action will mean policy changes by one or both governments. Third, the United States should raise issues that will build public support for reform in Japan with groups such as consumers, and producers who are themselves excluded from *keiretsu* relationships, to enhance the prospect of long-run convergence as well as to help carry the day in the short term.

The SCT should also expand their scope to include the institutions and practices of the private sectors of both countries. These contribute mightily to some of the key structural differences, and certain business practices—notably those of the *keiretsu* in Japan, but also those of many American corporations that betoken a short-term orientation—are major sources of contention between the two countries at present. Inclusion of discussions on the two private sectors would both help the talks address the key issues and enhance the prospects for further meaningful harmonization of practices (and thus, eventually, convergence of outcomes).

Another key procedural issue is whether to multilateralize the SCT to include at least the European Community. This could diffuse some of the tensions that might be aroused by the bilateral context, since the Europeans would typically join with the United States in attacking Japanese structural problems. It could also add to the symmetry of the talks, because the EC negotiators would presumably join with Japan in attacking some of America's structural defects. Inclusion of the Europeans could also bring to the table a "third model" at which convergence could be aimed, as we advocate below for two specific structural issues. Against these gains, however, must be set the enormous complication of adding another party—with its own structural problems—to an already difficult process. (It would clearly be *too* complex to go beyond the G-3, e.g., to include all 24 of the industrial-country members of the Organization for Economic Cooperation and Development [OECD].) On balance, we come down against the idea of including the Europeans, but we would not reject such an expansion if Japan (or the Community itself) pressed for it.

Structural Issues in Japan

We would nominate four Japanese and four American issues for inclusion in the SCT, assuming that the talks proceed in a bilateral mode. First, the United States and Japan should explore *joint or at least parallel enforcement of their antitrust statutes* with respect to some aspects of *keiretsu* behavior and other potentially restrictive business practices that simultaneously occur in the two markets. As indicated in chapter 3, we believe that some aspects of *keiretsu* behavior are not only acceptable but worthy of emulation by American industry. In particular, long-term cross-holdings of corporate shares provide "patient" capital and encourage effective monitoring of management. Some aspects of vertical corporate integration, such as the "designing in" of components and just-in-time inventory deliveries, enhance efficiency.

On the other hand, control of distribution systems by dominant producers can lock out competing products—such as foreign automobiles, which Japanese producer-owned distributorships have blocked from entering Japan. Horizontal complicity among major firms can also restrain trade. These problems are among the thorniest in present US-Japan economic relations. The most appropriate remedy is antitrust policy.[6]

In early 1992, the US Justice Department attempted to resurrect an earlier doctrine whereby it would unilaterally apply American antitrust law to the behavior of foreign firms in foreign markets, if that behavior could be demonstrated to affect competition and prices within the United States. The main target was of course the *keiretsu* system. The Japanese authorities opposed any such initiative as an extraterritorial application of American law and indicated that they would implement blocking statutes, as Canada and Great Britain have done in the past, if the Justice Department pursued the effort.

A more appropriate approach would be joint prosecution by the US and Japanese antitrust authorities of collusive behavior that is occurring simultaneously in the American and Japanese markets (as initially proposed in Bergsten and Stern 1993). With the globalization of business, and especially the heavy engagement of Japanese firms in the United States, collusive buying practices or other restraints of trade by these firms may reduce competition in both countries rather than solely in one or the other. The two countries have a common interest in finding an effective joint response. Such an approach would be not only more palatable to the Japanese but probably more effective than a unilateral US effort, because the Japanese authorities are likely to possess far greater knowledge of the operations and impact of the targeted Japanese business combines.

The question, of course, is whether the two antitrust authorities could cooperative effectively. Such cooperation would have to begin with a firm commitment by the Japanese government that would rest on two premises: that such a "process-oriented" approach is superior to the likely alternative—a "results-oriented" resort to managed trade in the sectors affected by *keiretsu* behavior—and that the American authorities would be as balanced and objective in pursuing antitrust cases involving Japanese firms as those involving American firms (i.e., that US authorities would *de facto* observe a national treatment standard).[7]

---

6. Senators William V. Roth (R-DE) and Joseph I. Lieberman (D-CT) have proposed legislation that would create a bilateral consultative commission to address this issue.

7. Successful cooperation in this area might, over time, enable the two countries to harmonize related policies—such as antidumping duties and policies toward inward direct investment (including the Exon-Florio statute in the United States)—into a common approach toward competition policy broadly defined. Successful pursuit of such an approach could significantly accelerate convergence in an increasingly critical area.

A second Japanese candidate for the SCT is *product liability law*. As we noted in chapter 3, the absence of effective product liability law in Japan forces that country to rely heavily for product safety on an extensive system of standards, testing, and certification by the government bureaucracy. This process is readily subject to political capture and frequently produces significant barriers to imports. One possible remedy is to strengthen Japan's existing product liability laws. At present, Japanese law requires proof of producer negligence as well as of product defects. More generally, access to the court system is difficult. As a result, lawsuits are rare and few consumers even attempt the process.

We would *not* recommend that Japan adopt American product liability law, which goes much too far in the opposite direction by authorizing the award of sizable punitive damages. (It also generates considerable unpredictability by allowing the rendering of punitive awards by jury.) We would instead advocate a system like that in the European Community, which neither requires proof of negligence nor provides for punitive damages. Standards would still be required, but consumers could obtain effective redress through the courts. Hence product safety would not have to rely so heavily on detailed rules and bureaucratic monitoring thereof. The entire system would become much more transparent, less dominated by government and private interest groups, and less apt to discriminate against foreign products (as well as disfavored domestic products). Convergence would be promoted in an important area, with wide-ranging implications for trade between Japan and the rest of the world.

A third promising area for discussion is the paucity of foreign investment in Japan. The Japanese government has already made some moves, as noted in chapter 3, to increase inward direct investment. At least two other avenues remain to be explored.[8]

Mergers and acquisitions in Japan are relatively rare, because of crossholdings of stock and weak shareholder rights, which permit crossholders to dominate corporate decision making. Reforms to broaden corporate governance would ease this avenue of foreign investment.

With regard to greenfield operations there, the major complaint of foreign firms operating in Japan is the high cost of starting up a business. This in turn is related to the high cost of establishing distribution networks (which could usefully be addressed as part of the competition

---

8. Some observers suggest that yen appreciation, which we advocate to help correct the currently excessive Japanese external surplus, deters foreign direct investment in Japan and therefore runs counter to this proposal. It is true that a stronger yen increases the initial dollar costs of such investments. However, it also means that the earnings from such investment convert back into more dollars. Hence there should be no net effect of currency changes (in either direction) on foreign direct investment (in either direction; see Graham and Krugman 1991, 80–82).

policy discussions) and the high cost of land. The price of land in Japan is high both for reasons of natural scarcity and because of highly distorted land use policies.[9] The Japanese government has made some effort to reform tax policies that discourage efficient use of land, but these could be taken much farther. Such efforts would not only reduce the cost of entry to new foreign entrants to the Japanese market but improve living standards in Japan.

A fourth area for action is the *intellectual property rules*. As we noted in chapter 3, Japan has recently made some strides toward improving its intellectual property regime. Patent protection in Japan remains inadequate, however, and the reforms to date, although desirable, are unlikely to end intellectual property disputes between the United States and Japan. Indeed, with both countries increasingly specializing in activities with a high intellectual property component, disputes are likely to intensify without further action. As with competition policy, this appears to be an area in which both countries could gain by converging to something like the EC model. In the United States this would mean moving to a "first-to-file" patent system. In Japan it would mean eliminating the practice of pregrant challenges and greatly speeding up the approval process.

Structural Issues in the United States

Convergence from the American side could be promoted in four areas.[10] First, the talks could address reform of *the education system* at the elementary and high school levels. The test scores of American high school graduates are no better today than they were twenty to thirty years ago. The United States ranks at or near the bottom on all international comparisons of student performance. It is difficult to envisage a lasting restoration of America's international competitiveness without a sharp improvement in its human capital.

The central problem is that US elementary and high schools offer students few if any incentives to do well. Virtually all high school graduates can get into most colleges, regardless of their academic records. For those entering the work force directly, high school performance has virtually no impact, as employers seldom consider transcripts or teacher references. Reform will thus require building incentives into the system. These should include national standards, which high school graduates would have to meet to enroll in college, and rewards for teachers and other staff determined by the success of their students at meeting the new standards.

---

9. See Balassa and Noland (1988, chapters 4 and 5) for detailed descriptions of Japanese land use policies and recommendations for reform.

10. Details on all four can be found in Competitiveness Policy Council (1993).

Japan consistently ranks at or near the top of all international comparisons of attainment at the high school level. Hence it should be able to offer advice to the United States on how to improve its educational system. At the same time, however, there is dissatisfaction in Japan over the excessively routinized nature of its curricula and its young people's seeming lack of creativity. Japan also remains envious of America's higher education system and would like to import some of its virtues. Education, a critical foundation of national economic performance and international competitiveness, is thus a prime candidate for the new SCT. It is an area where convergence can be fostered simultaneously in both directions: toward Japanese norms at the elementary and high school level and toward American practices in higher education.

A second American structural problem for consideration under the SCT is the need to *increase private saving*. Despite much effort, no reliable methods have been discovered through which US policy could do so directly. However, there is one promising technique for doing so indirectly: shifting the focus of the American tax system from income to consumption, to induce Americans to save more by raising the price of consumption. Such measures could apply either to consumption across the board, through taxing spending rather than income or through the more limited variant of a value-added tax, or by taxing consumption of particular goods such as energy, alcohol, and tobacco. The new taxes could be enacted either at the margin, to provide additional revenues to help reduce the budget deficit, or more ambitiously to replace some or all current taxes. However implemented, they could raise national saving and hence reduce America's external deficits.

This is also an especially suitable topic for the SCT because Japan has recently enacted a national consumption tax. It experienced great political difficulty in doing so and thus could offer political as well as technical advice on the issue. More broadly, Japanese advice could be helpful because that country has maintained throughout most of the postwar period a tax system much more heavily oriented toward saving and investment than the tax system in the United States.

A third, related issue is *government support for private investment*. As noted in chapters 1 and 2, Japan's national investment rate has consistently been about twice as high as that of the United States. A modest share of the difference reflects government investment, but by far the greater part is due to private activity. Through tax incentives and other devices, the Japanese government has supported that process. The Clinton administration's initial proposals to spur private investment, notably for a new investment tax credit, failed to win congressional support, and little new legislation now seems likely on this crucial front. Japan has both a major interest in seeing better American investment performance and directly relevant experience that could be useful to the United States, so the issue could be usefully discussed in the SCT.

Fourth, the United States needs to *promote exports much more aggressively*. Many of its current policies, notably its export controls for national security and foreign policy purposes, in fact block or discourage billions of dollars worth of foreign sales annually. Its export credit mechanisms are less generous than those of most of its competitors, including Japan. Its export promotion programs are decidedly inferior to those of most other industrial countries. Its effort to promote export trading companies through legislation in the late 1970s, a conscious effort to emulate Japanese practice, has produced no notable successes to date. Japan, on the other hand, has been a successful exporting country for three decades or more. It should be able to help the United States meet one of the most important parts of its effort to correct its external deficit and strengthen its economy. Convergence in this area could pay high dividends both for the United States and for the relationship between the two countries.

Promoting Convergence

There are clearly a number of structural differences between the American and Japanese economies. Some of these differences have a significant impact on economic flows between the two countries. Thus, they affect the economies of both countries and the relationship between them. In a world of increasing interdependence, efforts to deal with these differences or at least their most salient effects need to be thoroughly discussed between the countries involved.

At a minimum, such discussions will enhance mutual understanding of how the two economies function and interact. This may dispel concerns that now exist out of ignorance or misunderstanding. More important, the discussions may illuminate opportunities for policy changes that can mitigate the adverse external (and perhaps internal) effects of the structural differences. They can thus reduce both real economic problems and the political tensions engendered by them.

The United States and Japan each believe that the other's economic performance is deeply rooted in its institutions and structural behavior. Even when efforts to correct macroeconomic imbalances and sector-specific trade problems have been successful, problems and tensions have merely declined rather than disappeared. There will always be some degree of trade friction between any two countries that interact as broadly and as deeply as these two. But this is especially true for the United States and Japan, given that they are the world's two largest economies, and given the inherent sectoral clashes we have documented.

Therefore the United States and Japan should renew the effort, begun promisingly in 1989–90 under the aegis of the SII talks, to address their structural differences and the economic impact thereof. Both countries are already undergoing structural change at a rapid pace, some of it induced by the market forces of globalization itself, and some consciously pursued through policy changes that seek to respond to those forces. A new round of Structural Convergence Talks will thus be leaning with the prevailing winds and may be able to accelerate the structural evolutions more effectively than did the original SII. The SCT also need to be more symmetrical and include a serious focus on America's structural problems such as those just outlined; this should be feasible now that an American administration has shown itself willing to recognize the problems of the past and begun its own effort to address many of the relevant issues.

The SCT should in fact become a continuous process, as the SII talks were originally envisaged to be in 1989–90, rather than a discrete set of one-time negotiations. They should be entered into with no illusions of achieving rapid diplomatic triumphs that would have immediate economic effects. The talks would rather aim to assist, and perhaps on occasion accelerate, the process of policy harmonization and economic convergence that is occurring already. Continuous joint discussion and periodic action could help resolve the economic problems between the United States and Japan and contribute to limiting the tensions that will remain between them for the foreseeable future. Such an effort must be part of any comprehensive strategy that the two countries adopt to deal with their economic relationship.

Sector-Specific Issues

It is clear from chapter 4 that, besides the broad structural differences just discussed, problems in specific industries and sectors also deter American (and other) imports into Japan. These too have an impact on the American economy, both on its aggregate trade balance and on its composition. We turn now to the policy responses we propose for this component of the problem.

The Problem

The Japanese pattern of comparative advantage has changed remarkably over the past twenty-five years. Its trade performance is built upon a rapid accumulation of skills and capital. Whatever policies it might have adopted, Japan could not have accomplished what it has without these fundamental strengths.

The unfortunate but central conclusion is that Japan's increasing specialization in high-technology manufacturing, together with its relative weakness in primary products industries and services, generate inherent conflict with the United States. Each area of US comparative advantage— primary products, high-technology manufacturing, and services—is an area of either emerging Japanese competitiveness, heavy Japanese government intervention, or both. Although Japan has steadily liberalized its international trade policies, they still have a disproportionate impact on the United States because of their sectoral composition—affecting both the internal US market (as in automobiles) and American export potential (as in many electronic products). With the exception of civilian aircraft, Japan has been central to most major US trade policy problems in the last fifteen years.

What is at stake in these disputes? Our analysis of merchandise trade in selected sectors concludes that there remain significant market access problems in Japan. As we indicated above, complete liberalization of these barriers—along with liberalization of Japan's structural impediments—could expand US exports by $9 billion to $18 billion annually. More than half of the gain would come in manufactured products and about a third in agriculture. (There could be additional gains from liberalization in services, but we have derived no quantitative estimates.)

Japanese trade liberalization could thus make a significant contribution to reducing the level of the US-Japan bilateral imbalance. As noted earlier, a resulting improvement in Japanese competitiveness and offsetting exchange rate movements would considerably diminish the potential net reduction. Moreover, full liberalization would, under the best of circumstances, take some time to accomplish. Nevertheless, trade liberalization in Japan could make an important dent in this aspect of the "Japan problem" that is the focus of so much concern.

Our survey also suggests that Japan's barriers, although still quite high, have come down markedly over the last decade. Their restrictive impact in the early 1990s appears to be about 25 percent less than in 1980. This implies both that Japan has been responsive to external (and perhaps internal) pressures to increase foreign access to its markets, and that liberalization measures work in enhancing market opportunities for higher import penetration. These results support two of the basic conclusions of this study: that Japan can change and in fact is changing, but that such change comes slowly and has much further to go.

Liberalization of Japan's markets should thus continue to be a central goal of American (and international) trade policy. Our analysis of a number of individual sectors, however, confirms the view that Japan's access problems represent a complex mix of public policies and private business practices. Government intervention is present in every case studied, and a share of each problem should thus be susceptible to traditional modes of international negotiation. However, restrictive corporate behavior, usually the expression of oligopoly practices of one type or another, is also omnipresent. This too could in some cases be addressed through changes in government policy, and in particular through more rigorous antitrust enforcement, but it frequently lies beyond the reach of official action.

In agriculture, Japan provides considerable protection of the traditional sort.[11] The research reviewed in this survey suggests that these policies have a substantial effect on trade volumes, prices, and incomes both in Japan and elsewhere. They cost the average Japanese family over $1,000 per year. Complete agricultural liberalization in Japan could increase global exports of agricultural goods to Japan by as much as $6 billion to $7 billion, of which $1 billion to $6 billion could come from the United States.

The problem of Japanese agricultural protection should be self-eradicating: the median age of Japanese farmers is 60, and the only group of farmers now growing in number is those over 65. The Ministry of Agriculture, Forests, and Fisheries has estimated that death and disability will reduce the number of farmers in Japan by one-third by 2000, providing scope for agglomerating landholdings and improving efficiency. A 1992 poll found that 31 percent of Japanese farmers wanted to quit farming, and another 13 percent wanted to scale down operations. Only 7 percent said that they were eager to expand their activities.

Furthermore, as Japanese incomes rise, the importance of rice in the diet will continue to fall. An optimistic adjustment scenario would envision fewer, more efficient, and less policy-dependent Japanese farmers producing higher-value-added products for domestic market niches. In fact, the government has been encouraging the consolidation of landholdings and the production of higher-value-added products as part of its income maintenance strategy for the farm sector.

In manufactures, the estimates are even less certain, because the less formal nature of Japanese protection makes reliable models more difficult to design and estimate. Studies attempting to indirectly infer the impact of restrictive Japanese policies on trade volumes have reached conflicting results. But the conclusion that Japan is an outlier with regard to its trade pattern, as elaborated in chapter 5, is bolstered by the observation that traded-goods prices are far higher in Japan than elsewhere and that this difference appears to be associated with the presence of nontariff barriers and the *keiretsu* in Japan. Indeed, a reasonable conclusion from the econometric studies reviewed in this book is that official policies and private arrangements—both structural and sector-specific—may reduce US manufactured exports by roughly $6 billion to $11 billion annually.[12]

---

11. The United States also protects agricultural sectors such as sugar and dairy products, but these are irrelevant to US-Japan relations.

12. The structure of protection can affect the commodity and partner composition of trade, even though the overall trade balance is determined primarily by the macroeconomic forces analyzed in chapter 2 and above. Thus, if the incidence of Japanese trade policies falls disproportionately on the United States, as we believe it does, it is possible that both US primary products and US manufactures could benefit disproportionately from Japanese trade liberalization.

The United States, too, protects (or has until recently protected) large manufacturing sectors such as textiles and apparel, steel, machine tools, and automobiles. In the case of automobiles, as discussed in chapter 4, the United States pressured Japan to adopt a system of voluntary export restraints (VERs) that cost US consumers billions of dollars and enhanced the competitiveness of Japanese producers. It is not clear, however, that these barriers currently have much real impact in limiting Japanese access to the American market.

The Options

The ultimate goal of any country's trade policy is to raise national welfare. In the simplest case, this requires alignment of the country's production according to comparative advantage through the adoption of free trade policies. This principle surely holds for most sectors where the United States and Japan engage in trade protection. It is very difficult to argue that the welfare of residents of Japan is raised by agricultural protection or that residents of the United States would be better off with a binding quota on the importation of Japanese cars.[13]

There are cases, however, in which the application of simple free trade precepts may be inadequate. In particular, losses to domestic industries subject to significant local externalities and targeting from abroad can more than offset the gains to domestic consumers from the enhanced availability of imported foreign products. These cases are extremely hard to document, however, and when they are documented it is difficult to design an effective policy response. But there clearly will be sectors, some of which we identified in chapter 4, where trade action is called for despite difficulty in pinpointing a specific access barrier. Such cases are typified by extremely low (or nonexistent) foreign shares of the Japanese market where the same foreign firms are clearly competitive internationally, as indicated by their shares of the global market and other highly competitive national markets.

For the United States and Japan, these issues are brought into bold relief in the high-technology and services sectors. Here it is plausible

---

13. We concluded in chapter 4 that an EC-style VER on automobiles that included sales by transplant Japanese automobile assembly plants in the United States would cost US consumers $3 billion to $8 billion annually. The competitive problems of the US automobile and auto parts industries should be addressed primarily by changes in domestic policy. This should include antitrust action against any identifiable *keiretsu* behavior of the Japanese industry in the United States that has the effect of blocking US parts suppliers from selling to the transplants. On the trade front, US negotiators should seek elimination of the Japanese automakers' requirement that prospective parts suppliers obtain "genuine parts" certification—a requirement that limits exports of US parts to Japan. US negotiators should also insist that the European Community continue to exempt imports from the US transplants from its VER in automobiles.

(although typically not demonstrated) that the sector under consideration is subject to scale economies or externalities that generate rents or efficiency gains for the domestic economy. This in turn can put a premium on domestic production.

The United States has to make a series of important choices in pursuing the trade policy component of its overall strategy toward Japan. Three stand out. First, which sectors or products should be emphasized? Second, which negotiating forums—multilateral, regional, or bilateral—are likely to be most effective? Third, particularly for cases that will inevitably be pursued through bilateral channels, which techniques are most promising among the three identified in chapter 5 as the real alternatives: true liberalization of an identifiable barrier to the market, co-optation of the complaining firm(s) into an existing Japanese oligopoly, or the use of "temporary quantitative indicators" including, in problems involving market access in Japan, VIEs?

We concluded in chapter 5 that two criteria should guide the choice of priorities. Primary focus should be on the magnitude of the potential payoff for the United States. This will often suggest an emphasis on sectors where Japanese liberalization will lead to expanded production in the United States (as opposed to sales by US firms sourced from non-US locations). Another element in choosing which sectors to address is the long-term growth potential of the market. Japan is planning a massive investment program in telecommunications over the next twenty years, for example, so access to that market for American firms is particularly important, even if parts of the market are modest in size at present. In contrast, rice and some other agricultural markets are unlikely to grow very rapidly.

Even without much (or any) increase in US production, however, Japanese liberalization may bring significant benefits to the American economy. The liberalization of Japan's distribution system, for example, could over time lead to a substantial market share for a number of American retail firms, such as Toys 'R' Us, and a very large increase in their total profits. These earnings contribute to the American economy and could render the negotiating effort quite worthwhile even if few American-made products are sold. As this instance suggests, specific cases should be taken up with an eye also to their precedent-setting impact—including the prospect of encouraging far broader structural reforms—as well as for their immediate payoff.

Hence any sensible US strategy toward Japan must begin with a careful evaluation of the potential payoff from the myriad sector-specific initiatives that could be undertaken. Up to now US policymaking has tended instead to respond to the "squeaky wheel": those firms or industries that complain the loudest, or that most effectively take advantage of US trade laws, have tended to emerge at the head of the negotiating queue.[14] A much more systematic comparative analysis is an essential starting point if US leverage is to be deployed effectively. That analysis should encompass all products that now have trouble entering the Japanese market, whether or not their firms have been pressing Washington for action.

The costs of pursuing liberalization in the different sectors are the second criterion to be considered. Some Japanese barriers may be more readily susceptible to change than others. In some cases domestic allies of liberalization in Japan are more readily identifiable: for example, as we observed in chapter 4, large Japanese retailers (as well as Japanese consumers) benefited from the US effort to liberalize the Large Scale Retail Store Law, and some Japanese financial institutions stood to gain from the liberalization of the financial markets sought by Citibank.[15]

Once that decision has been made, a second issue is to determine the most effective forum in which to proceed. The traditional choice is between the multilateral mechanism of the General Agreement on Tariffs and Trade (GATT) and bilateral negotiation. In the future, if an Asia Pacific Economic Community or a Pacific Free Trade Area (or PAFTA, on the model of the North American Free Trade Agreement or even the European Community) is negotiated, this regional forum may provide a third alternative venue.

The United States should use the GATT wherever possible to pursue market opening in Japan (and elsewhere). Other exporting countries can be mobilized to support most American efforts within that forum. Appeal can be made to existing rules, or new rules can be devised to cover problems not now addressed. Japan has a good record of implementing GATT decisions and in fact liberalized trade in 10 farm products in the late 1980s as a result of GATT actions initiated by the United States. Wide-ranging negotiating "rounds," such as the ongoing Uruguay Round, offer the prospect of intersectoral trade-offs that enhance the likelihood of Japanese cooperation. Less political tension is likely to be generated.

Some of the issues addressed in chapters 3 and 4 should be susceptible to the GATT approach. Government procurement policies are particularly important for computers construction, supercomputers, and telecommunications equipment; expanded coverage under the GATT pro-

---

14. The most notorious example was President Bush's decision to promote US automobile sales to Japan by taking the CEOs of the Big Three American automobile companies with him to Tokyo in January 1992. This gesture implied to Japan (and the world) that the United States placed automobile trade at the top of its negotiating agenda and had the practical effect of submerging some extremely constructive agreements that were reached on that occasion on both macroeconomic and other important issues.

15. Bayard and Elliott (forthcoming) stress the importance of finding and working with such allies.

curement code would provide a route to enhanced access to these markets in Japan. There is widespread agreement that one of the next orders of business for the GATT after the completion of the Uruguay Round, whether via another negotiating round or otherwise, is to forge a new code on competition policies. This could address at least certain aspects of Japan's oligopoly practices, such as those in the glass industry, and even some key aspects of the *keiretsu* system more broadly. Any new regional trade negotiations in the Pacific Basin, whether in pursuit of a comprehensive PAFTA or in a more evolutionary manner in the framework of the existing Asia Pacific Economic Cooperation, might be even more successful in pursuing such objectives because of the smaller number of countries involved and their geographical propinquity.

Whatever happens on the multilateral and regional fronts, the United States will inevitably pursue at least some of its trade interests with Japan through bilateral channels for at least the foreseeable future. Some of these initiatives may seek structural changes in Japan, as addressed in the previous section; some of these—for example, with respect to antitrust policy and the distribution system—could also make important contributions to resolving certain sector-specific issues. In addition, however, the United States will have to decide how best to use bilateral channels to pursue its sector-specific market access objectives with Japan.

Here the central question is whether to emphasize market-oriented process remedies or "results-oriented" managed trade. The latter option can in turn be pursued in either of two ways: by seeking entry of one or more specific American (or other foreign) firms into an existing Japanese oligopoly, or by establishing "temporary quantitative indicators" for an entire sector. The latter approach covers both VERs, to limit access to the US market, and VIEs, to increase US (or overall foreign) participation in the Japanese market.

Both variants of managed trade have been used by the United States in the past. Despite the emphasis of its rhetoric on process remedies and market approaches, the United States has resorted extensively to managed trade with Japan—including devices that aimed at quantitative outcomes. This was especially true under the Reagan and Bush administrations, which installed:

- automobile VERs in 1982;
- steel VERs in 1984;
- machine tool VERs in 1985;
- semiconductor VIEs in 1986;
- automobile VIEs in 1992; and
- auto parts VIEs in 1992.[16]

---

16. As noted in chapter 4, Japanese transplants in the United States are expected to account for about 80 percent of the anticipated increase in sales of American auto parts to Japanese automobile companies. Hence the bulk of this "VIE" seeks instead to increase the local content of the American production of the Japanese firms.

If one includes the traditional VERs in textiles and apparel (under the Multi-Fiber Arrangement) and Japan's administrative control of most of its agricultural imports, a substantial portion of US-Japan trade is already managed. Hence managed trade between the two countries would hardly be new or revolutionary. The key question is whether it has succeeded and what one means by "success." As chapter 4 documents, the record is mixed at best. In automobiles, steel, and probably machine tools and textiles, the VER technique promoted cartelization of the Japanese market, transferred substantial rents (several billion dollars annually in the automobile and steel VERs at the height of their protective impact in the mid-1980s) to the United States' major competitors, and encouraged product upgrading by Japanese firms that further eroded the market positions of the major American producers, while of course protecting their market share, for a temporary period. We strongly oppose a new automobile VER, especially one that would include the local transplants (as does the current EC arrangement with Japan).

On the other hand, the automobile VER promoted Japanese investment in the United States and spurred domestic firms to improve their performance. More recently, the semiconductor VIE can take substantial credit for the increased share of foreign companies in that Japanese market (although its original price floor provisions had decidedly unfavorable effects on the American computer industry and opened the door for Korean and other newer foreign competition). It is still too early to assess the results of the new VIEs on automobiles and auto parts.

The precise objectives of US excursions into managed trade with Japan have also shifted constantly, making it difficult to assess the impact of past efforts. In semiconductors, the target was stated in terms of sales in Japan by all foreign-owned firms—whether production was located in the firms' home countries, in third countries abroad, or in Japan. In auto parts, the target was sales to all Japanese firms—including their transplants in the United States—by American companies only. These two VIEs thus differ in two significant respects: whether all foreign firms or only US firms are to be the beneficiaries, and whether the target market is Japan itself or Japanese companies and their operations, wherever they are located.

Consideration of both the historical record and these critical distinctions is central in determining whether the United States should undertake additional efforts to manage its trade with Japan. The record reveals a typical pattern, which we described and documented in chapters 3 and 4. Action is instigated by one or a few American companies that feel aggrieved, sometimes legitimately, by impediments to their access to Japan's market. The US government embraces their case and presses Japan to liberalize. After much haggling, the Japanese government (in collaboration with the relevant Japanese companies) agrees instead to add the complaining American firm or firms to the domestic oligopoly.

The American complainants thus become entitled to share the rents—and typically find that their Japanese operations are among their most profitable in the world. As a result, even though other American (and other foreign) firms have no better access than before, the complainants stop pressing the US government to press Japan to liberalize. They may even urge the US government to halt any further efforts to enhance market access by attacking the oligopoly situation.

The question for US policy then becomes whether this seizure of a share of the oligopoly rents by American firms—the usual pattern in many recent sector-specific disputes and one that may often emerge in the future as well—is superior to the much less certain prospect of seeking genuine market opening for all foreigners, including Americans, or to the managed-trade alternative (a VIE) in which all American (and other non-Japanese) firms are allowed to compete for a negotiated market share. The best approach, from the standpoint of both American and Japanese welfare, is genuine market opening.[17] This should be possible where tangible barriers can be identified, such as Japanese government procurement practices in computers and supercomputers.[18]

The most difficult cases arise when the access problem centers on industrial organization and other opaque barriers in Japan. The real choice in such cases may be between co-optation into the existing oligopoly and competition for negotiated market shares. The preferred policy course is then unclear and has to be decided on a case-by-case basis.

In selecting which way to go at this point, the competitive situation within the United States is extremely important. If only one American firm is competitive or potentially competitive in the sector (e.g., Motorola, Inc. in cellular phone services or Corning Inc. in fiber optics), it may be more cost-effective simply to pursue its co-optation into the Japanese oligopoly structure. If, on the other hand, there are several American (or other non-Japanese) companies that could take advantage of enhanced market access, the negotiated VIE may be second-best to genuine market liberalization. In such cases it is essential that the VIE be truly temporary and maintained only long enough to achieve an outcome that would permit market forces to hold sway thereafter.

As we argued in chapter 5, however, there are four serious pitfalls in pursuing the VIE approach. First, the process is extremely susceptible to political capture in the United States. The "squeaky wheel" risk will

---

17. In some sectors in which the United States is uncompetitive, it might prefer that Japan manage the market and give US firms a greater share than they could obtain under free competition. Under the approach we propose, however, such firms would not qualify for government support in the first place.

18. For the details of our proposals regarding the computer, supercomputer, and other sectors, see chapter 4. As we pointed out there, in the case of supercomputers there are government procurement barriers in the United States as well as in Japan.

be high if the US government actively and enthusiastically pursues such a strategy (as opposed to using it reluctantly and as a last resort, as under the Reagan and Bush administrations). Producing firms or industries will also want to define the affected sector as narrowly as possible, to exclude competitors from the arrangement and thus maximize their gains. So will the Japanese firms that are the target of the effort. If a very narrow sector or a very few firms are involved, it may be better simply to negotiate entry into the existing cartel without the paraphernalia of a VIE.

Second, any minimum target for a VIE (such as the 20 percent goal for semiconductor sales in the 1986 Semiconductor Trade Agreement [STA]) is inherently arbitrary. There is no coherent basis for determining what would be the level of an expanded presence in a hypothetically liberalized market. Indeed, US negotiators may shoot too low and in practice create a ceiling rather than a floor. Our analysis in chapter 5 suggests that the actual results of market liberalization in beef, cigarettes, and citrus were far better than could have been anticipated (and hence negotiated) at the time they were addressed.

Third, the "success" of a VIE can depend on events totally outside the scope of the negotiation: growth rates in both countries, changes in exchange rates, structural changes in the industry, and the like. For example, the achievement of the targeted STA market share in the fourth quarter of 1992 derived at least partly from the shrinkage of the total Japanese semiconductor market, demand shifts within the sector, and technological innovations by non-Japanese firms.

Threats of retaliation are usually needed to ensure faithful implementation of a VIE. Given the importance of exogenous factors, however, retaliation in response to an unmet VIE target could easily be triggered by events totally outside the control of the target country. To refrain from retaliation in such instances—even though wholly justified by the facts—could lead to charges of "softness" and "inadequate enforcement." VIEs inherently give rise to such dilemmas.

Fourth, the United States will have to recognize that its use of VIEs could invite other countries to treat it in similar fashion. In supercomputers, for example, the United States as well as Japan restricts access to its public market.[19]

The Tactics

The final question is tactical: to what extent should the United States threaten and, if necessary, implement unilateral action to induce Japan

---

19. We believe that the United States should press Japan for mutual liberalization of procurement practices in this sector and pursue its sectoral goals through subsidization of consumption rather than production (as described in detail in chapter 4).

to liberalize? To some extent, this question pervades all aspects of the relationship. There have been numerous occasions, for example, when the United States has threatened to push down the dollar (or push up the yen) in the exchange markets to induce Japan to adopt domestic stimulus measures that would help reduce the macroeconomic imbalances. The question of American unilateralism nevertheless arises most frequently in the sector-specific context.

The most celebrated example is of course the Super 301 legislation of 1988, which was in effect during 1989 and 1990 and whose renewal is a topic of recurrent debate. But there are numerous variants. Under Title VII of the Omnibus Trade and Competitiveness Act of 1988, the US Trade Representative designated Japan in April 1993 as a country that discriminates against US firms in its government procurement practices (particularly regarding construction) and hence is subject to retaliation. That same month, under Section 306 of the 1974 trade act, the United States launched a "special review" of the US-Japan Supercomputer Agreement of 1990, with the threat of initiating a Section 301 action if Japan were deemed not in compliance. "Regular" Section 301 is the most prominent ongoing tool that authorizes unilateral US trade actions against Japan (and other countries).

Three interrelated factors unique to Japan combine to make these tactical questions both more important and more complicated with respect to that country than with other US trading partners. The first is the unique and pervasive nature of the market access problems documented in chapters 3, 4, and 5. Traditional market-opening and rules-based approaches have frequently failed to achieve their desired (and sometimes agreed) objectives. Hence unorthodox measures, such as VERs and VIEs, have been employed increasingly over the years. Given their unorthodoxy (and often their highly contentious nature as well), extraordinary tactics have been used to obtain Japanese acceptance of them.

Second, Japan's political decision-making system usually operates on the basis of widespread consensus, which is difficult to achieve and takes a long time to formulate. This is especially so in cases, such as many of these trade cases, that seek to disrupt traditional Japanese practices that are widely accepted throughout the country. Foreign pressure (*gaiatsu*) has thus frequently proved necessary to galvanize the system and has succeeded on numerous occasions. A forthcoming study (Bayard and Elliott) in fact suggests that the unilateral actions of the past, including those taken under Super 301 as well as under regular Section 301, have had considerable success in opening the Japanese market—particularly when they have found, and worked effectively with, Japanese groups that shared America's interests—and have never produced actual retaliation or closure of the American market. Japanese behavior has had the effect, whatever its intent, of inviting *gaiatsu*, because virtually all "successful" trade negotiations with Japan have been energized by at least a dose of such pressure.

From these two considerations, it might seem axiomatic that the United States would employ the maximum level of available unilateral pressure in virtually every sectoral negotiation. In practice, however, a third consideration applies: that Japan has now become a global economic superpower. This means *inter alia* that the United States has come to depend heavily on Japan for many of its own needs, including products that might otherwise be the targets of American retaliation. When the United States decided in 1987 to retaliate against Japanese noncompliance with parts of the STA, for example, a large number of *American* firms petitioned the US Department of Commerce to exempt from retaliation products for which they had no alternative sources of supply.

On the other side of the table, Japan has never counterretaliated against American exports, but there is an increasing possibility that it might do so. Another risk is that Japanese investors, fearing that trade conflict could lead to US action against their assets, could hurt the United States by withdrawing funds from key US markets, pushing up American interest rates and generating inflationary pressures by weakening the dollar excessively. Most likely, Japan will increasingly reject American demands, and stalemate will prevail in their negotiations—with the United States then announcing its "unilateral expectations" of Japanese behavior on both the macroeconomic and sector-specific issues. Tensions will rise as speculation mounts over whether the United States will in fact retaliate and what Japan would do in response.

Moreover, despite the end of the Cold War, the United States still has an important security and political stake in Japan. It cannot ignore the impact of trade actions on its overall relationship with that country. Some of America's efforts to induce Japan to cooperate more extensively in exercising global economic leadership, as described in the next section, could also be jeopardized by excessive unilateralism on the part of the United States (although judicious application of US pressure, including on specific sectors, could also promote systemic cooperation by Japan as an alternative to the direct remedies that are being sought). This may be especially true now that the Japanese government has adopted a strong position opposing any new agreements that set quantitative targets for trade outcomes, apparently ruling out future VIEs (and VERs) despite a possible further increase in American interest in such arrangements.

We believe that the traditional use of unilateral American *gaiatsu* on Japan has become anachronistic in a world in which Japan has joined the United States (and the European Community) as a global economic superpower. On the other hand, as we indicated throughout our discussion of the structural problems, we see considerable merit in each country's seeking to induce the other to improve its economic policies (and hence its performance). We also see merit in continuing efforts to promote convergence between the two countries through a steady process of policy harmonization. Such "reciprocal *gaiatsu*" could benefit both.

In the real world, however, Japan's domestic decision-making machinery and political system are clearly lagging its economic progress. Some form of external pressure continues to be needed to overcome political inaction and reluctance to liberalize. Indeed, Prime Minister Kiichi Miyazawa explicitly asked the United States to exercise such pressure before his meeting with President Bill Clinton in April 1993.[20] *Gaiatsu* must therefore remain a central feature of US-Japan economic relations for the foreseeable future.

This does not mean, however, that Super 301 should be renewed. The passage of Super 301 in 1988 reflected lagged concerns over the huge macroeconomic imbalance of the mid-1980s and the inaction of the administration that had permitted it to develop, and the frustrations of internal political and bureaucratic debates over trade policy within the United States (Destler 1992). Super 301 was in part an effort by a Democratic Congress to force a Republican President to take a "tougher" approach to trade policy, especially on sector-specific issues and especially with Japan; it also represented an effort to strengthen the hand of those agencies with responsibility for trade issues (the Office of the US Trade Representative and the Department of Commerce) vis-à-vis the foreign policy agencies (the departments of State and Defense and the National Security Council). Such legislation should be unnecessary now that the macroeconomic imbalances have been at least somewhat reduced, the same party controls both the White House and the Congress, and the administration itself has decided that trade is its major policy priority in relations with Japan and that it will seek to coordinate all its policies effectively through the new National Economic Council. Anything that can be accomplished in any event under Super 301 can be accomplished under regular Section 301, which will probably be more effective with Japan in the future because of its less emotional history and rhetoric.

We also oppose the passage of legislation that would mandate an elimination of Japan's bilateral surplus with the United States. As already noted, the bilateral balance should not be an independent target of policy action. Such a goal would be both unnecessary and infeasible in any event, because the United States would almost certainly still run a sizable bilateral deficit with Japan even if it were to eliminate its global current

---

20. "Japanese Invite Trade Hard Line: Tough U.S. Stance Could Spur Change, Prime Minister Says." *Washington Post*, 13 April 1993, A-1.

account deficit and successfully resolve its structural and sector-specific problems with Japan. Given the triangular nature of Japanese trade, it is unclear how Japan could go about eliminating its bilateral surplus with the United States without massively increasing total governmental control (i.e., by MITI) over the economy and diverting large amounts of trade from other countries.

We doubt the need for any new legislation toward Japan. All of the trade policy proposals made in this book can be fully implemented under existing statutes.[21] If the Congress should feel compelled to act, the most constructive approach would be to embody in law the procedural proposals laid out earlier in this section: a systematic prioritization of American concerns over market access in Japan, encompassing both quantitative analysis of the benefits of liberalizing each candidate sector and an assessment of the most effective means for doing so. Such an effort would build on the National Foreign Trade Estimates that are now prepared annually to identify impediments to trade in all foreign countries, but call for much more in-depth analysis of the merits and possibilities of alternative policy courses in the special case of Japan.

With or without new legislation, the United States will have to apply substantial continuing pressure to achieve its negotiating objectives with Japan. In as many instances as possible, it is desirable to do so through multilateral institutions such as the GATT (on specific trade issues) and the G-7 (on macroeconomic topics). As noted above and elaborated in the next section, new regional instruments could become available for these purposes over the next few years.

The United States will also have to determine its priorities clearly and resist the tendency to try to pursue all issues with equal vigor at the same time. It will have to carefully calibrate the extent of pressure on a given negotiation to the potential payoff from succeeding. It must keep in mind that Japan *is* now a global economic superpower that can effectively defend its interests if pushed too hard, that continued friendship with Japan is central to the United States for broad economic but also security and political reasons, and that excessive pressure could backfire in light of the domestic weakness of Japan's contemporary political leadership. But both countries must understand that aggressive American trade initiatives must be part of the ongoing policy landscape, both to provide a basis for resolving the real economic problems emphasized throughout this book and to manage the relationship in a sufficiently activist manner to preclude much more disruptive interventions by the Congress. Such intervention would surely result if the "benign neglect" of the early

---

21. Extensive legislation is, of course, required to implement the domestic reforms needed to correct the budget deficit and improve the underlying competitive position of the United States, as discussed in chapters 1 and 2.

1980s—on either the macroeconomic front or specific trade issues—were ever to return.

Cooperative Leadership of the Global Economic System[22]

The fourth component of a stable US-Japan economic relationship in the future is close cooperation in managing the global economic system. The United States and Japan together account for 30 to 40 percent of world output. They are the acknowledged leaders in most of the world's critical technologies. The United States is the world's largest debtor country and Japan the largest creditor. They are the two largest democracies in the Pacific.

Effective cooperation between these two giant competitors is essential for global prosperity and stability.[23] The erosion of the global trading system, throughout the 1980s and to a lesser extent in earlier periods, was accelerated by US-Japan trade frictions and the inability of the GATT to deal with them effectively. The dollar overvaluation that precipitated the breakdown of the Bretton Woods system of fixed exchange rates in 1971–73, pushing the United States into a trade deficit for the first time in the postwar period and raising the first fears in modern times of American economic decline, was most pronounced against the yen. Japan's external surplus in the mid-1980s was the largest single counterpart to America's huge current account deficit. And the Japanese surplus was clearly the major source of the surging protectionist pressure in the US Congress that was the proximate trigger for the Plaza Agreement in 1985 and the adoption of a "tough" trade policy by the Reagan administration at the same time (and that produced the Super 301 legislation in 1988).

The global economic system will be at risk as long as US-Japan economic relations are in conflict. Part of the answer of course lies in their bilateral responses to the problems described in the previous sections of this chapter. Hence our recommendations there are important for systemic as well as bilateral reasons. But the two countries will also need to collaborate closely at the systemic level to exercise their responsibilities for its successful conduct.

---

22. Much of this section was originally presented in Bergsten (1991).

23. American foreign policy in the post–Cold War era must find a way to reconcile tough competition among the economic superpowers with effective systemic cooperation among them (see Bergsten 1992).

Moreover, effective systemic cooperation between the United States and Japan could contribute to resolution of their bilateral problems. Better global arrangements would reduce, perhaps significantly, the likelihood of new or heightened problems and tensions between them. For example, an international monetary system that avoided substantial currency misalignments would prevent or at least limit the replication of the large trade imbalances that emerged in 1969–71, 1977–78, and 1983–87 and are now recurring. An effective GATT dispute-settlement mechanism that addressed the major sources of US-Japan tensions, such as the objectionable parts of Japan's *keiretsu* system and industrial targeting, would be enormously valuable. New agreements within the GATT on antitrust and other instruments of competition policy could provide a handle on the *keiretsu* problem, and an expanded GATT subsidies code and an improved government procurement code might do the same for Japanese industrial targeting.

There is thus a crucial two-way feedback between the management of the bilateral relationship between the United States and Japan, on the one hand, and their cooperation in managing the multilateral economic system, on the other. Improvements in the bilateral relationship improve the prospects for successful systemic performance. Systemic improvements, which require cooperation between the United States and Japan (and, in most cases, the European Community), will create a much healthier climate for dealing effectively with the two countries' bilateral problems. Systemic cooperation must therefore play a central role in any overall US-Japan strategy.

Two historic transformations intensify this need (Bergsten 1990). First, the end of the era of American economic dominance means that collective leadership must replace US hegemony in the provision of such essential international public goods as open markets, foreign lending, and defense of the system's rules and institutional moorings. Ideally, the uniting European Community and Japan would join the United States in a new tripolar structure to provide this leadership. In practice, however, Europe's unification is faltering, and its economic outlook is extremely uncertain for at least the medium term. Hence the United States and Japan may have to exercise "G-2" leadership, an issue to which we return below.

The second historic transformation is the end of the Cold War. Although the Cold War will not be over in Northeast Asia until Japan and Russia resolve their dispute over the southern Kurile Islands and stability is ensured in the Korean peninsula, the demise of the Soviet Union as a global superpower has ended the primary insecurity faced by all nations outside the old Soviet bloc. Hence Japan's need for American defense, including the nuclear umbrella, has declined sharply, and America's leverage over Japan is reduced correspondingly. Likewise, the United States has less military need for its alliance with Japan.

Both historic shifts sharply heighten the possibility of economic conflict between the United States and Japan. The Cold War no longer provides a comprehensive security blanket to smother disputes on economic (and other) issues between the two countries. Japan's ascension as a global economic superpower, one on which the United States has come to depend in several important senses, renders it much more able to conduct independent policies and even to confront the United States on occasion. Old habits die hard, and America still dominates the bilateral relationship on most occasions. But American leverage has declined, and Japanese cooperation must now be sought and won, rather than dictated, on most key issues.

A cooperative relationship on systemic issues is very difficult to achieve, however, because Japan and the United States start from very different points on the spectrum of international leadership. The United States has been the clear leader of the international economic and security systems throughout most of the postwar period. Japan, meanwhile, has been the quintessential free rider, with its strategic interests defended by someone else and benefiting enormously from an economic order created and nurtured by someone else. Both countries and global systemic interests require a fundamental change in this "leadership imbalance."

This leadership difference may in fact be the most important difference between the United States and Japan and may explain much of the underlying antagonism toward Japan in the United States. Most Americans believe that wealth and prosperity carry an obligation to provide leadership, whether at the local or the global level. Hence the growing dichotomy between Japan's economic success and its insular policies has produced increasing American frustration and charges of ingratitude. Japanese assertion of a full partnership role in managing the world economy, in expanding world trade through completion of the Uruguay Round and restoring its own domestic growth, and in picking up an appropriate share of the cost of international public goods, could go far to ease US-Japan tensions. It would be far better if such contributions could be made without the torturous process of *gaiatsu*, which leaves Japan's foreign audiences remembering the initial resistance rather than the eventual generosity, as in the case of Japan's $13 billion contribution to the Gulf War.

For both countries, collective leadership will require an unprecedented willingness to share international power and decision-making responsibility. As the previously dominant country, the United States will have to accept partnership with Japan (and Europe). For example, it might accept (or even propose) Japanese nationals to fill top leadership posts at key international economic organizations such as the IMF or the World Bank. As the previous free rider on the system, in both security and economic terms, Japan will have to accept unaccustomed responsibilities. The two countries must join in global management from opposite ends of the leadership spectrum—a task of enormous psychological and historic complexity.

A central question is whether the United States and Japan should pursue collective leadership on their own via a G-2 arrangement or rely on multilateral approaches. There are at least three arguments for starting with a G-2. First, the intensity of US-Japan tensions requires that the two countries move ahead as rapidly as possible to construct systemic arrangements that will help them deal with their problems. Second, bilateral negotiations (such as the SII talks or our proposed successor the SCT) are simply more practical and likely to succeed than three-way efforts on such complex and contentious issues. Third, it will be some time before Europe can complete its economic and monetary union (EMU) and thus be able to play a full global role.

G-2 leadership has already occurred on several occasions. Secretary of the Treasury James A. Baker III and then–Minister of Finance Kiichi Miyazawa agreed in October 1986 to initiate the reference range system for currencies, which the Europeans joined four months later in the Louvre Accord. A contribution of $10 billion of Japanese money permitted the launch of the Brady Plan for Third World debt in 1989 (and some of the provisions of that plan were part of an earlier Miyazawa Plan). Any new G-2 efforts would presumably leave the door open for subsequent partnership with Europe and full participation by other countries prepared to accept the new obligations. The two largest economies, however, should begin the process on their own if necessary.

The broader point is that the US-Japan relationship in the future should flow from a shared vision of the need to install effective collective management of the world economy. While continuing to deal with bilateral problems as they arise, as do any pair of countries with intense economic interactions, the United States and Japan should seek to identify areas of common global concern and then launch joint initiatives in as many of them as necessary to construct and maintain a stable global economic order for the 1990s and beyond. This will speed the convergence between them and between Japan and the world as a whole. It will, as already noted, create a more hospitable and effective framework for resolving the bilateral disputes that will inevitably arise. Finally, it will clearly promote American economic interests as well as improve the prospects for global growth and stability, and that would itself help limit the intensity of future bilateral conflicts.

Cooperation in International Monetary Affairs

One important area for such an initiative is the international monetary system. As noted earlier in this chapter, current account imbalances caused by disequilibrium exchange rates and divergent macroeconomic policies have severely hurt the American economy and deeply intensified US-Japan frictions during four separate periods in the last twenty-five years—including much of the 1980s. Macroeconomic imbalances and currency misalignments large enough to distort economies and bring on severe protectionist pressures could be largely avoided through the effective implementation of a system of currency target zones, like that described in the section on trade imbalances above.[24]

International monetary affairs are the most natural, as well as the most needed, domain for leadership by the United States and Japan. The international role of the yen is rising steadily, and along with the deutsche mark, or perhaps in future the ecu, the Japanese currency will steadily pick up market share from the dollar. Japan's international net asset position now exceeds $500 billion. The United States has net international liabilities close to $500 billion. Both countries have a massive stake in international financial stability and in a system that would prevent large new misalignments.

Hence systemic reform in this area should be high on the American agenda. This has been a fruitful area for US-Japanese collaboration in the past, and there is reason to believe that Japan might be quite willing to share leadership on it now.

Cooperation in Trade Policy

In the trade area, the immediate task is successful completion of the Uruguay Round. A failure of the round would discredit the global trading system and the GATT, thereby escalating tendencies toward protectionism and bloc formation. Japan would be a major target of such pressures, and numerous issues (such as rice) that have been bottled up by the round would immediately produce bilateral confrontation. It is noteworthy that Japan, which often talks of "shared leadership" and has much to gain from successful completion of the round (and much to lose from its collapse), has displayed little initiative to break the logjam that has perpetuated the negotiations for almost seven years.

Beyond a successful Uruguay Round, two trade policy objectives must be pursued: to maintain momentum toward liberalization by avoiding the typical postround hiatus and backsliding, and to undertake new efforts to deal with the view that Japan is an unfair trader and a free rider in the present system. These goals can be pursued by US-Japan

---

24. It would definitively end the risk that Japan would be charged with "manipulating" its exchange rate, a practice that requires a US response under the Omnibus Trade and Competitiveness Act of 1988. Japan did engage in such practices in 1976–77 (Bergsten 1976) and is still accused of doing so from time to time.

agreement, preferably joined by the European Community and others, to negotiate a number of further trade steps for implementation by 2000:

- elimination of all tariffs;

- maintenance of quotas or other restrictions only in full accord with the safeguard provisions of the GATT;

- a sharp expansion of the mandate accorded to the GATT to police the system, including more rapid and effective dispute-settlement techniques.

The "Japan problem" and the US-Japan differences described above go far beyond the traditional overt trade barriers, however. Hence the United States and Japan should take the lead in urging the GATT, as soon as practicable after the conclusion of the Uruguay Round, to develop new rules that would govern issues of particular relevance to the Japanese market as discussed in chapters 3, 4, and 5. Examples include competition policy and further improvements in the GATT subsidies and government procurement codes. In light of the continuing proliferation of "voluntary" trade distortions, now including VIEs as well as VERs, these gray-area measures should also be subjected to international discipline in the GATT.

Cooperation in Investment Policy

The G-2 should also take the lead in seeking to create a "GATT for investment" (Bergsten and Graham, forthcoming). Such an institution would aim to contain governmental interference in the international economic activities of business, as does the GATT itself, but would also authorize governmental responses to distortive practices by private firms. For example, it would tighten the disciplines on such trade-related investment measures as investment incentives and performance requirements, but go far beyond them to address such issues as taxation and transfer pricing (and, if it were not by then covered by the GATT itself, competition policy).

All these microeconomic issues are central to concerns over alleged unfair practices and collusive behavior by Japanese companies, including through their investments in the United States. Competition policy is especially important because of the centrality of the *keiretsu* issue and the clear need to increase the transparency and openness of that system. Convergence in the direction of norms prevailing in America and most other countries—in a way that does not eliminate the efficiencies of *keiretsu* but makes them more internationally compatible—should be one goal of the exercise. For example, it might pave the way for the proposed joint action by the Justice Department and the Fair Trade Commission of Japan against exclusionary practices of *keiretsu* in their home and foreign markets.

Since these corporate practices have now supplanted government policies as the leading sources of tension in the US-Japan relationship to an important extent, there would be major advantages in such an initiative on investment issues. It would indicate that Japan is willing to take the lead in dealing with some of the most vexing aspects of the current problem. It would indicate Japanese readiness to open its own market substantially to inward direct investment and to conform some of its relevant policies (such as antitrust) to international norms. It would build on recent proposals by Akio Morita, Chairman of Sony Corp., that Japanese companies conform their practices toward those of companies based in other OECD countries (Morita 1992).

Moreover, international agreement on these issues should help Japan achieve such policy changes domestically by subsuming its protectionist forces in an agreed global effort. It would thus help deal with some of the sharpest criticisms now levied against Japan: its lack of reciprocity on direct investment, its tolerance of corporate oligopolies, and alleged tax underpayments by its firms' subsidiaries in the United States.

Cooperation in the Pacific Basin

One other trade (and perhaps investment) issue requires joint systemic leadership by the United States and Japan, namely, economic relations around the Pacific Basin. The Pacific Rim is the most dynamic area of the world economy. Its economies, particularly those on the Asian side, have been the world's fastest growing for the past two decades and seem likely to retain that distinction for the foreseeable future. Their shares of world output and trade have grown steadily.

US trade with East Asia now greatly exceeds its trade with Europe or any other region. Nevertheless, there is widespread concern in Asia that the United States is abandoning the area. This view is clearly incorrect and may be a product of three (mis)perceptions: that Japan's overwhelming presence, especially its extensive investment throughout the region, will discourage further American investment; that America's (involuntary) military withdrawal from the Philippines, coupled with the end of the Cold War and the sharp reduction of the traditional security threat to the region, will presage an economic withdrawal as well; and that the negotiation of the North American Free Trade Agreement (NAFTA) and its proposed extension throughout the Western Hemisphere suggest that the United States is looking south rather than across the Pacific.

Most Asian countries would be extremely unhappy with the prospect of American withdrawal. None of them want the region to be dominated by Japan. Most fear the uncertainty that would result from continued rapid development of China and the possible security problems that could come in its wake with the elimination of the Soviet presence. Some, such as Korea and Taiwan, have historically close ties to the United States that they wish to maintain or even strengthen. Most countries in the region are decidedly unhappy that the United States has pursued the NAFTA initiative and seems likely to extend it to other countries in the Western Hemisphere; this raises fears both of trade diversion in the traditional sense and diversion of American attention to its south rather than westward across the Pacific.

East Asia is in fact an arena of growing interaction, and perhaps future conflict, between the United States and Japan. There have already been some skirmishes between them, such as over how quickly to resume normal economic activity with China following the events at Tiananmen Square. Japan has usually deferred to the United States when such conflicts loomed. For example, Japan politely but pointedly ignored Malaysia's proposal for an East Asian Economic Group (EAEG) that would have excluded the United States (and Australia, Canada, and New Zealand), instead favoring strengthening the Asia Pacific Economic Cooperation (APEC), in which the English-speaking countries of the Pacific Rim are fully represented. As Japan becomes increasingly independent of the United States in both the economic and the security area, however, the potential for another confrontation between the two countries will rise steadily.

The United States and Japan should therefore work closely together, along with the other countries of the region, in institutionalizing cooperation in the Pacific Basin. Despite its enormous economic success, this is the one major part of the world economy that, except for the nascent APEC and a few subregional arrangements (the Association of South East Asian nations [ASEAN], the Closer Economic Relations [CER] between Australia and New Zealand, and now the NAFTA), has no intergovernmental machinery to facilitate its expansion and settle the inevitable disputes among its members.

Building on APEC, the United States and Japan should make sure that both sides of the Pacific Rim remain closely linked. Each should avoid any exclusive arrangements, like the EAEG, that would discriminate against the other (and provide an excuse for reciprocal discrimination by the excluded party), and the United States should keep the NAFTA from itself becoming exclusionary. This means that the United States, Canada, and Mexico should either take advantage of NAFTA's open accession clause to offer membership to qualifying countries around the Pacific Basin (as proposed by Stern 1993), or agree to launch a parallel negotiation—probably based on APEC and its current membership of 15—to create a new Pacific Free Trade Area (PAFTA) or an Asia Pacific

Economic Community. Any such arrangement would of course need to be fully consistent with the GATT in light of the paramount global interests of all its members.

From the standpoint of US-Japan relations, such an arrangement would represent valuable insurance against the risk that the tensions in their bilateral relationship would be extended into regional affairs. Creation of a meaningful regional association might even help resolve some of those bilateral tensions, as the other countries of the region might side with either the United States or Japan against the other on individual cases and thus help reach an amicable outcome (Krause 1991).

On the other hand, a bilateral US-Japan Free Trade Agreement, as proposed by some Japanese in the late 1980s, is both undesirable and highly unlikely to materialize. It is undesirable because it would divert a large volume of trade away from other countries, and it is unlikely given widespread American perceptions that any opening of markets under it would be one-sided: that is, that Japan's opaque barriers would resist effective liberalization while the United States would eliminate its more transparent restraints (see Kuroda 1989 and the comments thereon by Robert Z. Lawrence and Clyde V. Prestowitz, Jr., in Schott 1989). The same disparity would represent a significant hurdle to new trade arrangements in the Pacific Basin as a whole, but such arrangements would avoid much of the diversion of a bilateral accord, and the disparity might be more amenable to solution in that context, both because of the larger stakes involved for both countries and because of the more modest (and certainly more gradual) nature of any regional liberalization effort.

Institutionalizing Cooperation

It will not be easy for either Japan or the United States to make the psychological and political adjustments required to achieve joint leadership of the world economy as proposed here. Both will have to change many ingrained habits and learn to share power and responsibility across a wide range of issues.

The United States will have to accept Japan as a full partner and accommodate some of its practices and policy preferences, including when Japan disagrees with its erstwhile patron. Japan will have to accept the responsibility that goes with full partnership; this means being willing to initiate policy ideas and proposals rather than reacting belatedly and defensively. In practice, convergence and sharing of responsibility are virtually certain to emerge over time, either as a result of crisis responses or as a well-thought-out strategy implemented in stages. The latter course is clearly preferable.

In addition to all the merits cited above, the strategy of shared US-Japan leadership could help deal with two key underlying problems for the future. One is America's sense of decline (at least in relative terms) and its resultant tendency to lash out at Japan, whose success is the most visible external manifestation of that decline. The other is Japan's frustration that its economic success has not produced any clear Japanese vision of what to do with that success, nor has it led the world to accord to Japan the rightful fruits of its progress. Both these problems would be addressed, if not fully resolved, by joint adoption of the global vision and courses of action proposed here. The governments of the two countries should adopt that vision as a central element in managing their economic (and perhaps their overall) relationship in the 1990s and beyond. The results could help immeasurably in dealing with the differences between the countries' economic systems, in speeding the convergence of those systems, and thus in promoting the economic goals of both countries as well as a smoother bilateral relationship and a more stable and prosperous world economy.

Implementing the Strategy

A four-part strategy is thus required to deal effectively with the US-Japan economic relationship in the years and decades ahead.

First, the United States and Japan must take a series of macroeconomic steps to cut their global current account imbalances to no more than 1 to 2 percent of their GDPs. For the United States, this will require substantial reduction in the budget deficit, to which its trade deficit is linked, and the series of steps to bolster domestic competitiveness described earlier. For Japan, reducing its growing current surplus means undertaking enough fiscal stimulus—including full implementation of the program launched by Prime Minister Miyazawa in April 1993—to restore sustained growth in domestic demand of 3½ to 4 percent annually. For both countries working together, reducing the imbalances means modest further appreciation in the real value of the yen, to about 100 yen to the dollar in nominal terms.

For the longer run, the United States and Japan must prevent the recurrence of yet another cycle of huge macroeconomic imbalances—after the four of the past twenty-five years. The single most effective technique would be to institute a system of target zones to avoid renewed misalignments in the real exchange rate between the dollar and yen. Given Japan's propensity to experience lower inflation and higher productivity growth than the United States, this will probably require small annual appreciations of the *nominal* yen-dollar rate. Installation of target zones will induce a degree of coordination of monetary and other macroeconomic policies between the two countries, which would also help them move toward more effective exercise of cooperative leadership of the world economy. It would be desirable to manage such a system in cooperation with the European members of the G-7 and perhaps other countries.

Second, the United States and Japan need to resume the discussion of their structural differences by launching a series of Structural Convergence Talks. The goal of this exercise would be to accelerate the process of performance convergence and policy harmonization that is already under way. Over the long run, this may be the most promising avenue for dealing with the underlying problems in the relationship. In the short run, the issues to be given highest priority include joint antitrust policy; Japanese product liability law, patent policy, shareholder rights, and land use policy; and the American elementary and high school education system, new tax incentives to promote private saving and private investment, and a coherent export promotion program.

Third, sector-specific negotiations will be needed to deal with the inevitable problems that arise over trade in individual industries and products. The preferred goal should always be to eliminate practices in either country that clearly impede trade with the other. In cases where Japan maintains cartel-like arrangements that seem unlikely to dissolve anytime soon, and where only one or a very few American (or foreign) firms are competitive, an appropriate goal might be simply the acceptance of those firms into the cartel.

In cases involving intermediate industrial products where cartels or other structural problems limit foreign access, and where a variety of American (or foreign) firms can compete, but full liberalization is unlikely, negotiation of temporary voluntary import expansions (VIEs) should be considered. Policymakers must, however, recognize several dangers in this approach: it is inherently susceptible to political capture in the United States (and perhaps in Japan as well); it tends to reinforce rather than break up the cartel structure in the importing country; it is inherently arbitrary in setting its numerical market targets; and it can succeed or fail in meeting those targets because of events wholly outside the parties' control, such as changes in the countries' aggregate economic growth rates, exchange rates, or composition of demand.

Fourth, the United States and Japan need to forge a new collective leadership of the world economy to replace the unilateral American leadership of the past. Such leadership would preferably be exercised in cooperation with the economically uniting European Community, but it should be done within a G-2 framework if Europe is not yet ready. Early priority areas for collaboration include:

- reform of the international monetary system through adoption of target zones;

- completion of the Uruguay Round and the launch of new postround initiatives to sustain the momentum of trade liberalization and deal explicitly with some of Japan's access problems (e.g., through new rules on competition policy, and improvements in the GATT subsidies and government procurement codes); and

■ institution of a "GATT for investment" to deal with the wide range of international investment problems that have been ignored by, or lie outside the scope of, the GATT and other existing international arrangements.

This four-part strategy will have to be implemented in a variety of international forums and tightly coordinated within the governments of the two countries. The macroeconomic and currency elements of the package will be addressed primarily within the G-7, with occasional recourse to the IMF and perhaps other bodies of broader membership such as the OECD. These issues should be managed operationally by the Department of the Treasury in the United States and the Ministry of Finance in Tokyo, in close cooperation with the two countries' central banks in matters concerning the conduct of monetary policy and intervention in the exchange markets.

The structural and sector-specific components of the strategy are, as we have stressed throughout, closely connected and thus should be considered together to some degree in the new SCT. Sectoral cases that illustrate generic structural problems should be deliberately included in these talks in an effort to make headway on both simultaneously. We reject the proposal for multilateralizing the SCT as too unwieldy, despite its attractions, and instead opt for a renewed bilateral effort. A large number of departments and ministries will inevitably be involved, as was the case with the SII talks. To ensure that positions taken within each government are carefully coordinated, we recommend that the negotiating teams be led from within the White House (presumably by the National Economic Council) and the Prime Minister's office.

The sector-specific negotiations must include both multilateral and bilateral dimensions. As suggested earlier, as many issues as possible should be channeled into the GATT for resolution. A successful conclusion to the Uruguay Round would greatly enhance this prospect in three ways: by increasing the scope of issues covered by the GATT, by improving the dispute-settlement mechanism itself, and by providing the foundation for an early follow-on negotiation to address some of the most critical aspects of the Japan problem (such as competition policy). On the other hand, a failure of the round would inevitably push a much larger portion of the US-Japan debate into bilateral channels.

In any event, many of the sector-specific negotiations will continue to be conducted bilaterally. The main issue here, as we have noted, is for each country to choose its priorities carefully among the large number of sectors that could be discussed. The Office of the US Trade Representative must have the clear responsibility for the effort in the United States, with the Department of Commerce playing a supporting role. Japan needs to resolve its traditional bifurcation of authority, in which MITI has been in charge of bilateral negotiations but the Ministry of Foreign Affairs has continued to chair the country's participation in the GATT.

The systemic cooperation issues will also play out in a series of different venues. The international monetary reforms, like the currency and macroeconomic issues, should be centered in the G-7 and the IMF and managed by the countries' finance ministries. Negotiation of the trade issues will take place primarily within the GATT, although perhaps in the future within APEC to some degree, with some of the initial intellectual spadework perhaps done in the OECD. These negotiations should be led by the trade ministries.

Our proposed strategy is exceedingly far-reaching and will require unprecedented coordination across a range of international institutions and domestic governmental agencies. To succeed, it will have to be tightly managed by the heads of the two governments—the President of the United States and the Prime Minister of Japan. Management from the very top would have two major advantages: it would ensure that the top officials of each country devote continuing attention to the issues, and it would enhance the ability of each to impose a consistent and prioritized strategy on the numerous governmental agencies that must be involved in executing it. The former virtue is particularly important in the United States, some of whose presidents tend to ignore economic issues of this type, while the latter might especially help Japanese prime ministers forge the consensus necessary for Japan to participate effectively in the relationship.

For both substantive and symbolic reasons, the heads of the two governments should meet twice annually to monitor and, as necessary, energize the process. One of these meetings should occur, as in July 1993, at the time of the annual G-7 summit—whose agenda will to an important degree overlap and be affected by the bilateral agenda of the United States and Japan. The United States and the European Community have already begun to meet on a semiannual basis, so there could be no basis for the charge that the United States and Japan are attempting to create a new condominium or in any way dominate world economic management.

We recommend a two-phase process to launch the new strategy. The two countries have already been engaging in active discussion of their trade imbalances, particularly the surging Japanese surplus, and have taken a number of steps to correct them. More clearly needs to be done, however, as laid out above. Both the short-run adjustment and long-run systemic components of these issues can and should be pursued immediately, both bilaterally and in the broader G-7 forum. This is particularly important because we know that the benefits of currency adjustment take two to three years to reach full fruition, and no time should be wasted in getting that process under way.

The new structural and sector-specific initiatives, however, will take time to prepare properly. As noted above, it is essential that each country—but especially the United States—undertake a careful prioritization of its concerns in these areas and how it plans to seek redress of them. This requires a good deal of analytical work, consultation with the private sector, and considered policy judgments—including with respect to mobilization of potential allies in Japan. Linkages between the structural and sectoral issues need to be evaluated in order to maximize their potential synergy.

Hence we recommend that the two governments set a date in early 1994 to begin the actual negotiating process in the structural and sector-specific areas. The intervening six months or so would be used to carry out the preparatory work just described (and to complete the macroeconomic adjustments and policy coordination initiatives that are already well in train). The heads of government could launch these talks at their semiannual meeting in early 1994 and instruct the negotiators to report back to them with initial results in mid-1994 and definitively in early 1995.

This four-part strategy would substantially reduce the global imbalances of the two countries. Japan's combination of domestic fiscal stimulus and yen appreciation should cut its global surplus sharply. Effective trade liberalization would, over time, reduce the surplus still further. America's global deficit would fall as a result of the Japanese measures and drop markedly with full implementation of the fiscal adjustment proposed by President Clinton and others. The bilateral imbalance would drop as well, especially as a share of the countries' GDPs and the level of their trade, but would probably remain substantial in nominal terms and represent a much larger share of the remaining global imbalance of each country.

In addition, the proposed strategy would continue the painstaking but essential process of restoring America's international competitiveness and opening Japan to the world economy. Its structural component would accelerate the convergence of the two economies and societies. Its sector-specific steps would reduce the list of industry and product problems that continue to cause economic difficulties and political problems.

This strategy is highly preferable to several alternative proposals. It rejects the view that macroeconomic measures alone will deal with the problem. It also rejects the converse view that such measures are hopeless (or irrelevant) and that all efforts should be directed to specific industry problems—perhaps through "managed trade." It rejects protectionism and exclusionary regionalism (e.g., an EAEG or the extension of NAFTA to the rest of the Western Hemisphere while shutting out East Asia). It also rejects the notion of a US-Japan Free Trade Agreement.

The proposed strategy in fact maintains a high degree of continuity with past initiatives. Each component has been pursued in the past, often successfully. There have already been extended periods of cooperation on macroeconomic policy and exchange rates, such as those surrounding the Bonn summit in 1978 and the Plaza-Louvre period of 1985–87. Structural issues were addressed in the SII talks in 1989–90. Sector-specific negotiations have taken place consistently for over twenty years—only the products under scrutiny have changed. There have been instances of cooperative systemic leadership—for example, on international monetary affairs in the mid-1980s and Third World debt in the late 1980s. None of the major constituencies in either country should therefore be surprised by our approach.

Our proposal differs in two major respects from its predecessors, however. The first is to see each of its four components as part of an integrated strategy in which priorities are set consciously and the separate elements are pursued as part of a coherent whole. The second, symbolized and propelled by the semiannual meetings of the President and Prime Minister, is to conduct the strategy on an ongoing and consistent basis with a focus on long-term goals—such as maintenance of currency equilibrium and structural convergence—rather than the episodic and even erratic pattern of the past. Successful implementation of the strategy could thus radically transform the US-Japan economic relationship.

The proposed strategy ultimately rests on four fundamental premises. First, the United States and Japan, as the world's two largest economies, must and can resolve cooperatively and effectively the economic problems between them—and build mechanisms to limit the reemergence of such problems in the future. Second, their economies are converging and their policies (in both the public and the private sector) are in the process of harmonizing—so that the intensity of their problems and disputes, despite a steady further increase in the level and breadth of their economic transactions, will ultimately decline rather than rise. Third, the basic remedies to each country's problems—and especially to the problems between them—lie primarily with internal reforms rather than dramatic new mechanisms for managing their international economic relations; hence key elements in the proposed strategy, such as the SCT and the reforms of the international monetary and trading systems, seek to encourage and intensify the pace of those internal reforms. Fourth, however, the importance of the problems and the intensity of the tensions are such that mishandling of the relationship by either country could initiate a period of extreme hostility and disruption—so that conscious adoption of a strategy as proposed here is absolutely essential.

For the United States, the proposed approach represents the Japanese component of the strategy of "competitive interdependence" suggested by one of the authors several years ago (Bergsten 1988). That strategy counsels a twofold approach by the United States: a comprehensive effort to restore its competitive position through budget correction and other far-reaching domestic reforms, and a set of international initiatives to improve the functioning of the global economic system by recognizing and building on the acute interdependence now experienced by all countries. Because of its potent competitive position and its unique background, Japan represents both the most important and the most difficult aspect of the implementation of this strategy. But the strategy will succeed only if its Japanese dimension can be successfully navigated.

For Japan, the proposed strategy embodies numerous virtues. It offers the possibility of stabilizing relations with its chief trading partner and political ally. It could provide at least one element of the new world role that Japan is seeking—and one that would play to Japan's comparative advantage of economic prowess. By providing Japan with central global and regional roles to play, it would cater to Japan's desire to broaden its participation in international affairs at the same time that it strengthens its basic bilateral tie with the United States.

The time has clearly come for the United States and Japan to take a comprehensive, long-term look at their economic relationship and to put in place a strategy that accurately reflects both countries' economic priorities and political realities. We believe that our proposed four-part program meets these criteria. We commend it to the leadership of the two countries.

References

Advisory Committee for Trade Policy and Negotiations (ACTPN). 1993. "Major Findings and Policy Recommendations on U.S.-Japan Trade Policy." Washington: Advisory Committee for Trade Policy and Negotiations (January).

Advisory Group on Economic Structural Adjustment for International Harmony. 1986. *Report of the Advisory Group on Economic Structural Adjustment for International Harmony* (the Maekawa Report).

American Chamber of Commerce in Japan. 1991. *Trade and Investment in Japan: The Current Environment*. Tokyo: American Chamber of Commerce in Japan (June).

Anchordoguy, Marie. 1989. *Computers Inc: Japan's Challenge to IBM*. Cambridge, MA: Harvard University Press.

Anderson, Kym, and Rod Tyers. 1987. "Japan's Agricultural Policy in International Perspective." *Journal of the Japanese and International Economies* 1, no. 2: 131–46.

Aoki, Masahiko. 1987. "The Japanese Firm in Transition." In Kozo Yamamura and Yasukichi Yasuba, eds., *The Political Economy of Japan, Vol. 1: The Domestic Transformation*, 263–288. Stanford, CA: Stanford University Press.

Aoki, Masahiko. 1990. "Toward an Economic Model of the Japanese Firm." *Journal of Economic Literature* 28 (March): 1–27.

Aoki, Masahiko. 1991. "The Japanese Firm as a System: Survey and Research Agenda." Paper presented at the Japan Economic Seminar, New York: Columbia University (16 November).

Ariga, Kenn, Yasushi Ohkusa, and Hisashi Namikawa. 1991. "The Japanese Distribution System." *Ricerche Economiche* 45, no. 2-3: 185–230.

Asako, Kazumi. 1991. "The Land Price Bubble in Japan." *Ricerche Economiche* 45, no. 2-3: 167–84.

Auerbach, Alan J., and Lawrence J. Kotlikoff. 1989. "Demographics, Fiscal Policy, and U.S. Saving in the 1980s and Beyond." *NBER Working Papers* 3150. Cambridge, MA: National Bureau of Economic Research.

Auerbach, Alan J., Lawrence J. Kotlikoff, Robert Hagemann, and Giuseppe Nicoletti. 1989. "The Dynamics of an Aging Population: The Case of Four OECD Countries." *NBER Working Papers* 2797. Cambridge, MA: National Bureau of Economic Research.

Balassa, Bela. 1986. "Japan's Trade Policies." *Weltwirtschaftliches Archiv* 122: 745–90.

Balassa, Bela, and Marcus Noland. 1988. *Japan in the World Economy*. Washington: Institute for International Economics.

Balassa, Bela, and Marcus Noland. 1989. "The Changing Comparative Advantage of Japan and the United States," *Journal of the Japanese and International Economics* 3: 174–88.

Bayard, Thomas O., and Kimberly Ann Elliott. 1993. *Reciprocity and Retaliation: An Evaluation of Tough Trade Policies*. Washington: Institute for International Economics (forthcoming).

Beltz, Cynthia A. 1991. *High-Tech Maneuvers*. Washington: American Enterprise Institute.

Bergsten, C. Fred. 1976. "Let's Avoid a Trade War." *Foreign Policy* 23 (Summer): 24–31.

Bergsten, C. Fred. 1982. "What to Do About the US-Japan Economic Conflict." *Foreign Affairs* (Summer): 1059–75.

Bergsten, C. Fred. 1988. *America in the World Economy: A Strategy for the 1990s*. Washington: Institute for International Economics.

Bergsten, C. Fred. 1990. "The World Economy After the Cold War." *Foreign Affairs* (Summer): 98–101.

Bergsten, C. Fred. 1991. "The World Economy After the Cold War: The Implications for the Economic Relationship Between the United States and Japan." Paper presented to the KAMPO International Economic Symposium, *An Age of Transition, the World Economy, and Japan*. Tokyo (14 February).

Bergsten, C. Fred. 1992. "The Primacy of Economics." *Foreign Policy* (Summer): 3–24.

Bergsten, C. Fred, and William R. Cline. 1987. *The United States-Japan Economic Problem*. POLICY ANALYSES IN INTERNATIONAL ECONOMICS 13, rev. ed. Washington: Institute for International Economics.

Bergsten, C. Fred, and Edward M. Graham. 1993. *The Globalization of Industry and National Governments*. Washington: Institute for International Economics (forthcoming).

Bergsten, C. Fred, and Paula Stern. 1993. "A New Vision for United States-Japan Economic Relations." In *Harness the Rising Sun: Managing Japan's Rise as a Global Power*. An Aspen Strategy Group Report. Cambridge, MA: Aspen Institute (forthcoming).

Bhagwati, Jagdish. 1982. "Directly Unproductive, Profit-Seeking (DUP) Activities." *Journal of Political Economy* 90, no. 5: 988–1002.

Bhagwati, Jagdish. 1988. *Protectionism*. Cambridge, MA: MIT Press.

Blinder, Alan S. 1992. "More Like Them?" *American Prospect* (Winter): 51–62.

Bloom, Justin. 1991. "Survey of Direct U.S. Private Capital Investment in Research and Development Facilities in Japan." Washington: National Science Foundation (January).

Boltuck, Richard, and Robert E. Litan. 1991. *Down in the Dumps*. Washington: Brookings Institution.

Boone, Peter, and Jeffrey Sachs. 1989. "Is Tokyo Worth Four Trillion Dollars? An Explanation for High Japanese Land Prices." Paper presented to the Japan Economic Seminar, New York (18 November).

Borrus, Michael, James Millstein, and John Zysman. 1983. "US-Japanese Competition in the Semiconductor Industry." *Policy Papers in International Affairs* 17. Berkeley, CA: Institute for International Studies, University of California.

Borrus, Michael, Laura D'Andrea Tyson, and John Zysman. 1986. "Creating Advantage: How Government Policies Shape International Trade in the Semiconductor Industry." In Paul R. Krugman, ed., *Strategic Trade Policy and the New International Economics*, 91–114. Cambridge, MA: MIT Press.

Brander, James, and Paul Krugman. 1983. "A 'Reciprocal Dumping' Model of International Trade." *Journal of International Economics* 15: 313–21.

Brock, Philip L. 1992. "External Shocks and Financial Collapse: Foreign-Loan Guarantees and Intertemporal Substitution of Investment in Texas and Chile." *American Economic Review* 82, no. 2: 168–79.

Catte, Pietro, Giampaolo Galli, and Salvatore Rebecchini. 1992. "Concerted Interventions and the Dollar: An Analysis of Daily Data." Paper presented at the Rinaldo Ossola Memorial Conference, sponsored by the Banca d'Italia, Perugia, Italy (9–10 July).

Cheng, Leonard K. 1993. "Are Distributional Costs Equivalent to Tariff Barriers?" Department of Economics, Hong Kong University of Science and Technology (mimeographed, March).

Cheng, Leonard K., and Mordechai E. Kreinin. 1991. "Supplier Preference and Dumping: An Analysis of Japanese Corporate Groups." East Lansing: Michigan State University (mimeographed, December).

Cline, William R. 1990a. *The Future of World Trade in Textiles and Apparel*, rev. ed. Washington: Institute for International Economics.

Cline, William R. 1990b. "Japan's Trade Policies." Washington: Institute for International Economics (mimeographed, May).

Cline, William R. 1993. "How Undervalued Is the Yen?" Washington: Institute for International Economics (mimeographed, 4 February).

Cohen, Stephen D. 1991. *Cowboys and Samurai: Why the United States Is Losing the Battle with the Japanese, and Why It Matters.* New York: Harper Business.

Competitiveness Policy Council. 1992. *Building a Competitive America: First Annual Report to the President and Congress.* Washington: Competitiveness Policy Council.

Competitiveness Policy Council. 1993. *A Competitiveness Strategy for America: Second Report to the President and Congress.* Washington: Competitiveness Policy Council.

Cooper, Richard N. 1986. "Industrial Policy and Trade Distortion." In Dominick Salvatore, ed., *The New Protectionist Threat to World Welfare.* New York: North-Holland.

Council on Competitiveness. 1991. *Gaining New Ground: Technology Priorities for America's Future.* Washington: Council on Competitiveness.

Dekle, Robert. 1989. "The Unimportance of Intergenerational Transfers in Japan." *Japan and the World Economy* 1: 403–13.

Dekle, Robert. 1992. "Market Value Estimates of Japanese Saving and Comparisons with the U.S.: Can Capital Gains to Land Be Included in 'Saving'?" Boston: Boston University (mimeographed).

Dekle, Robert, and Lawrence Summers. 1991. "Japan's High Saving Rate Reaffirmed." *Bank of Japan Monetary and Economic Studies* 9, no. 2: 63–78.

deMelo, Jaime, and David Tarr. 1992. *A General Equilibrium Analysis of US Foreign Trade Policy.* Cambridge, MA: MIT Press.

Destler, I. M. 1991. "The United States and Japan: What Is New?" Paper presented to the 32nd annual convention of the International Studies Association, Vancouver, BC (March).

Destler, I. M. 1992. *American Trade Politics*, rev. ed. Washington: Institute for International Economics.

Dinopolous, Elias, and Mordechai Kreinin. 1988. "Effects of US-Japan Auto VER on European Prices and U.S. Welfare." *Review of Economics and Statistics* 70: 484–91.

Dinopolous, Elias, and Mordechai Kreinin. 1990. "An Analysis of Import Expansion Policies." *Economic Inquiry* 28: 99–108.

Dollar, David, and Edward N. Wolff. 1993. *Competitiveness, Convergence, and International Specialization.* Cambridge, MA: MIT Press.

Dominguez, Kathryn, and Jeffrey A. Frankel. 1993. *Does Foreign Exchange Intervention Work?* Washington: Institute for International Economics (forthcoming).

Dornbusch, Rudiger. 1992. "US-Japan Relations at the Cross Roads." Cambridge: Massachusetts Institute of Technology (mimeographed).

Economic Planning Agency of Japan. 1989. "Commodity Price Report." Tokyo: Economic Planning Agency of Japan.

Economic Strategy Institute. 1992."The Case for Saving the Big Three." Washington: Economic Strategy Institute (mimeographed).

Elliott, Kimberly Ann, and Gary Clyde Hufbauer. 1992. "The Costs of Protecting the US Auto Industry: Analysis of Various Proposals." Washington: Institute for International Economics (mimeographed).

Encarnation, Dennis J. 1992. *Rivals Beyond Trade*. Ithaca, NY: Cornell University Press.

Fecher, Fabienne, and Sergio Perelman. 1992. "Productivity Growth and Technical Efficiency in OECD Industrial Activities." In Richard E. Caves, ed., *Industrial Efficiency in Six Nations*, 459–88. Cambridge, MA: MIT Press.

Flamm, Kenneth. 1990. "Semiconductors." In Gary Clyde Hufbauer, ed., *Europe 1992: An American Perspective*, 225–92. Washington: Brookings Institution.

Flamm, Kenneth. 1993. "Forward Pricing vs. Fair Value: An Analytical Assessment of 'Dumping' in DRAMs." In Anne O. Krueger and Takatoshi Ito, eds., *Trade and Protectionism*, 47–94. Chicago: University of Chicago Press.

Flath, David. 1989. "Vertical Restraints in Japan." *Japan and the World Economy* 1, no. 2: 187–203.

Frankel, Jeffrey A. 1984. *The Yen/Dollar Agreement: Liberalizing Japanese Capital Markets*. POLICY ANALYSES IN INTERNATIONAL ECONOMICS 9. Washington: Institute for International Economics.

Funabashi, Yoichi. 1989. *Managing the Dollar: From the Plaza to the Louvre*, rev. ed. Washington: Institute for International Economics.

Fung, K. C. 1991. "Characteristics of Japanese Industrial Groups and Their Potential Impact on U.S.-Japan Trade." In Robert Baldwin, ed., *Empirical Studies of Commercial Policy*, 137–68. Chicago: University of Chicago Press.

General Agreement on Tariffs and Trade. 1990. *Trade Policy Review: Japan*. Geneva: GATT.

Gephardt, Richard A. 1991. "Proposals for United States Trade Policy." Speech delivered at the Institute for International Economics, Washington (10 September).

Gerlach, Michael. 1989. "*Keiretsu* Organization in the Japanese Economy." In Chalmers Johnson, Laura D'Andrea Tyson, and John Zysman, eds., *Politics and Productivity*, 141–176. Cambridge, MA: Ballinger.

Goto, Akira, and Ryuhei Wakasugi. 1986. "Technology Policy." In Ryutaro Komiya, Masahiro Okuno, and Kotaro Suzumura, eds., *Industrial Policy of Japan*, 183–204. San Diego: Academic Press.

Graham, Edward M. 1992. "Japanese Control of R&D Activities in the United States: Is This Cause for Concern?" In Thomas S. Arrison et al., eds., *Japan's Growing Technological Capability*, 189–206. Washington: National Academy Press.

Graham, Edward M., and Paul R. Krugman. 1991. *Foreign Direct Investment in the United States*, rev. ed. Washington: Institute for International Economics.

Grossman, Gene M. 1990. "Explaining Japan's Innovation and Growth: A Model of Quality Competition and Dynamic Comparative Advantage." *Bank of Japan Monetary and Economic Studies* 8: 75–100.

Harrigan, James. 1992. "Openness to Trade in Manufactures in the OECD." Pittsburgh: University of Pittsburgh (mimeo).

Hartzell, Jon K. 1990. "Japanese Financial Deregulation: What's *Really* Happening?" Paper presented to the International Monetary and Economic Research Institute, Tokyo (1 June).

Hayashi, Fumio. 1990. "Japan's Saving Rate: New Data and Reflections." Paper presented to the Japan Economic Seminar, New York (22 September).

Hayashi, Fumio. 1991. "Rejoinder to Dekle and Summers." *Bank of Japan Monetary and Economic Studies* 9, no. 2: 79–89.

Hayashi, Fumio. 1992. "Explaining Japan's Saving: A Review of the Recent Literature." *Bank of Japan Monetary and Economic Studies* 10, no. 2: 63–78.

Hillman, Jimmye S., and Robert A. Rothenberg. 1988. "Agricultural Trade and Protection in Japan." *Thames Essays* 52. London: Trade Policy Research Centre.

Horioka, Charles Yuji. 1989. "Why is Japan's Private Saving Rate So High?" In Ryuzo Sato and Takashi Negishi, eds., *Developments in Japanese Economics*, 145–78. Tokyo: Academic Press.

Horioka, Charles Yuji. 1990. "Why Is Japan's Household Saving Rate So High? A Literature Survey." *Journal of the Japanese and International Economies* 4, no. 1: 49–92.

Horioka, Charles Yuji. 1991a. "The Determinants of Japan's Saving Rate: The Impact of the Age Structure of the Population and Other Factors." *Economic Studies Quarterly* 42, no. 3: 237–53.

Horioka, Charles Yuji. 1991b. "Saving in Japan." In Arnold Heertje, ed., *World Saving*. Oxford: Basil Blackwell (forthcoming).

Horioka, Charles Yuji. 1992a. "Future Trends in Japan's Saving Rate and the Implications Thereof for Japan's External Imbalance." *Japan and the World Economy* 3, no. 4: 301–30.

Horioka, Charles Yuji. 1992b. "Japan's Consumption and Saving in International Perspective." *Economic Development and Cultural Change* (forthcoming).

Horioka, Charles Yuji. 1992c. "The Determinants of Japan's Household Saving Rate: A Cointegration Analysis." Osaka: Osaka University (mimeographed, June).

Horioka, Charles Yuji. 1992d. "The Household Saving Rate and the Age Structure of the Population: The Case of Japan." *Institute for Social and Economic Research Discussion Papers* 271. Osaka: Osaka University (August).

Horioka, Charles Yuji. 1992e. "The Impact of Capital Gains on Household Consumption and Saving in Japan: A Cointegration Analysis." *Institute for Social and Economic Research Discussion Papers* 276. Osaka: Osaka University (September).

Hufbauer, Gary Clyde, and Jeffrey J. Schott. 1993. *NAFTA: An Assessment*. Washington: Institute for International Economics.

Hufbauer, Gary Clyde, Diane E. Berliner, and Kimberly Ann Elliott. 1986. *Trade Protection in the United States: 31 Case Studies*. Washington: Institute for International Economics.

Ichioka, Osamu, and Toshiaki Tachibanaki. 1989. "General Equilibrium Evaluations of Tariffs, Nontariff Barriers, and Subsidies for Agriculture in Japan." *Economic Studies Quarterly* 40, no. 4: 317–35.

Imai, Ken-ichi. 1990. "Japan's Business Groups and *Keiretsu* in Relation to the Structural Impediments Initiative." Tokyo: Hitotsubashi University (March). Mimeographed.

Ishihara, Shintaro. 1989. *The Japan That Can Say No*. New York: Simon & Schuster.

Ito, Takatoshi. 1989a. "Japan's Structural Adjustment: The Land/Housing Problem and External Balances." Mimeographed, (February).

Ito, Takatoshi. 1989b. "Was There a Target Zone?" Policy Studies Series 14. Tokyo: Japan Center for International Finance (June).

Ito, Takatoshi, and Masayoshi Maruyama. 1991. "Is the Japanese Distribution System Really Inefficient?" In Paul R. Krugman, ed., *Trade with Japan*, 149–174. Chicago: University of Chicago Press.

Itoh, Motoshige. 1991. "The Japanese Distribution System and Access to the Japanese Market." In Paul R. Krugman, ed., *Trade with Japan*, 175–190. Chicago: University of Chicago Press.

Japan Research Institute. 1992–93. "A Special Report: The Japanese Economy in 1993." Tokyo: Japan Research Institute.

Johnson, Chalmers. 1982. *MITI and the Japanese Miracle*. Stanford, CA: Stanford University Press.

Julius, D., and S. Thomsen. 1988. "Foreign-owned Firms, Trade, and Economic Integration." *Tokyo Club Papers* 2. London: Royal Institute of International Affairs.

Kleidon, Allan W., and Kenneth J. Singleton. 1989. "Liberalization in the Japanese Financial Markets." Paper prepared for the Japan Advisory Committee of the New York Stock Exchange.

Kodama, Fumio. 1986. "Technological Diversification of Japanese Industry." *Science* 233: 291–96.

Komiya, Ryutaro, and Motoshige Itoh. 1988. "Japan's International Trade and Trade Policy, 1955–1984." In Takashi Inoguchi and Daniel I. Okimoto, eds., *The Political Economy of Japan, Vol. 2: The Changing International Context*. Stanford, CA: Stanford University Press.

Krause, Lawrence B. 1991. "Can the Pacific Save the United States-Japan Relationship?" In *Preparing for a Pacific Century: Exploring the Potential for Pacific Basin Cooperation—*

Perspectives from an International Conference. 17–35. Washington: Commission on United States-Japan Economic Relations for the 21st Century (November).

Kreinin, Mordechai E. 1988. "How Closed Is Japan's Market?" *The World Economy* 7: 529–41.

Krishna, Kala. 1989."Trade Restrictions as Facilitating Practices." *Journal of International Economics* 26 (May): 251–270.

Krueger, Anne O. 1974. "The Political Economy of the Rent-Seeking Society." *American Economic Review* 69, no. 3: 291–303.

Krugman, Paul R. 1986. "Targeted Industrial Policies: Theory and Evidence." In Dominick Salvatore, ed., *The New Protectionist Threat to World Welfare.* New York: North-Holland.

Krugman, Paul R. 1991. *Has the Adjustment Process Worked?* POLICY ANALYSES IN INTERNATIONAL ECONOMICS 34. Washington: Institute for International Economics (October).

Kuroda, Makoto. 1989. "Strengthening Japan-US Cooperation and the Concept of Japan-US Free Trade Arrangements." In Jeffrey J. Schott, ed., *Free Trade Areas and U.S. Trade Policy,* 121–41. Washington: Institute for International Economics.

Laird, Sam, and Alexander Yeats. 1990. *Quantitative Methods for Trade Barrier Analysis.* Houndsmill, England: Macmillan.

Lawrence, Robert Z. 1987. "Imports to Japan: Closed Markets or Closed Minds?" *Brookings Papers on Economic Activity* 2: 517–54.

Lawrence, Robert Z. 1988. "The International Dimension." In Robert E. Litan, Robert Z. Lawrence, and Charles Schultze, eds., *American Living Standards: Threats and Challenges,* 23–56. Washington: Brookings Institution.

Lawrence, Robert Z. 1991a. "How Open Is Japan?" In Paul R. Krugman, ed., *Trade With Japan,* 9–50. Chicago: University of Chicago Press.

Lawrence, Robert Z. 1991b. "Efficient or Exclusionist? The Import Behavior of Japanese Corporate Groups." *Brookings Papers on Economic Activity* 1: 311–41.

Lawrence, Robert Z. 1992. "Is Japan's Trade Regime Different?" Cambridge, MA: John F. Kennedy School of Government, Harvard University (mimeographed, March).

Leamer, Edward E. 1987. "Paths of Development: the Three-Factor-n-Good General Equilibrium Model." *Journal of Political Economy* 95, no. 5: 961–99.

Leamer, Edward E. 1988. "Measures of Openness." In Robert Baldwin, ed., *Trade Policy Issues and Empirical Analysis,* 147–200. Chicago: University of Chicago Press.

Leamer, Edward E. 1991. "Empirical Studies of Trade Issues: The Structure and Effects of Tariff and Non-Tariff Barriers in 1983." In Ronald Jones and Anne Krueger, eds., *Political Economy of International Trade: Essays in Honor of Robert E. Baldwin.* Cambridge, MA: Basil Blackwell.

Lee, Hiro. 1989. "Quantitative Assessments of Japanese Industrial Policies During the 1960s." Irvine: University of California at Irvine (mimeographed, October).

Lee, Hiro, and David Roland-Holst. 1993. "Cooperation or Confrontation in U.S.-Japan Trade? Some General Equilibrium Estimates." Irvine: Department of Economics, University of California—Irvine (mimeographed, March).

Lincoln, Edward J. 1990. *Japan's Unequal Trade.* Washington: Brookings Institution.

Long Term Credit Bank of Japan. 1992. *LTCB Economic Analysis* (September/October). Tokyo: Long Term Credit Bank of Japan.

Long Term Credit Bank of Japan. 1993. "Survey of the Japan-U.S. Merchandise Trade Imbalance: A Report." Tokyo: Long Term Credit Bank of Japan (mimeographed, 22 March).

Loopesko, Bonnie E., and Robert A. Johnson. 1987. "Realignment of the Yen-Dollar Exchange Rate: Aspects of the Adjustment Process in Japan." *International Finance Discussion Papers* 311. Washington: International Finance Division, Board of Governors of the Federal Reserve System.

Marris, Stephen. 1987. *Deficits and the Dollar: The World Economy at Risk.* POLICY ANALYSES IN INTERNATIONAL ECONOMICS 14. Washington: Institute for International Economics (August).

Marston, Richard C. 1991. "Price Behavior in Japanese and U.S. Manufacturing." In Paul R. Krugman, ed., *Trade with Japan,* 121–148. Chicago: University of Chicago Press.

Mason, Mark. 1992. *American Multinationals and Japan*. Cambridge, MA: Council on East Asian Studies, Harvard University.

Masson, Paul R., and Ralph W. Tryon. 1990. "Macroeconomic Effects of Projected Population Aging in Industrial Countries." *IMF Staff Papers* 37, no. 3: 453–85.

McKinsey Global Institute. 1992. "Service Sector Productivity." Washington: McKinsey and Co. (October).

McMillan, John. 1991. "*Dango*: Japan's Price Fixing Conspiracies." *Economics and Politics* 3, no. 3: 201–18.

Ministry of International Trade and Industry. 1993. "Report on Unfair Trade Policies by Major Trading Partners." Tokyo: MITI (mimeographed, 11 May).

Miyao, Takahiro. 1991. "Japan's Urban Economy and Land Policy." *Annals of the American Academy of Political and Social Science* 513: 130–138.

Morgan, James C., and J. Jeffrey Morgan. 1991. *Cracking the Japanese Market*. New York: Free Press.

Morita, Akio. 1992. "Turning Point for Japanese Managers?" *International Economic Insights* (May/June): 2–10.

Morita, Akio. 1993. "Toward a New World Economic Order." *Atlantic* 271, no. 6 (June): 88–98.

Mowery, David C., and David J. Teece. 1992. "The Changing Place of Japan in the Global Scientific and Technological Enterprise." In Thomas S. Arrison et al., eds., *Japan's Growing Technological Capability*, 106–135. Washington: National Academy Press.

Mutoh, Hiromichi. 1988. "The Automotive Industry." In Ryutaro Komiya, Masahiro Okuno, and Kotaro Suzumura, eds., *The Industrial Policy of Japan*, 307–332. San Diego: Academic Press.

Nakatani, Iwao. 1992. "The Asymmetry of the Japanese-Style vs. American-Style Capitalism as the Fundamental Source of Japan-U.S. Imbalance Problems." National Bureau of Economic Research and Japan Center for Economic Research. Background paper for the U.S.-Japan Economic Forum (February).

Nakauchi, Isao. 1989. "The Yoke of Regulation Weighs Down on Distribution." *Economic Eye* 10, no. 2: 17–19.

National Critical Technologies Panel. 1991. *Report of the National Critical Technologies Panel*. Washington: National Critical Technologies Panel (March).

Nishimura, Kiyohiko G. 1991. "The Distribution System of Japan and the United States: A Comparative Study from the Viewpoint of Consumers." Paper presented to the Japan Economic Seminar, New York (16 November).

Noguchi, Yukio. 1989. "Macroeconomic Implications of Population Aging." Paper presented at the Conference on the Economics of Aging, Tokyo (8–9 September).

Noland, Marcus. 1989. "Japanese Trade Elasticities and the J-Curve." *Review of Economics and Statistics* 71, no. 1: 175–79.

Noland, Marcus. 1990a. "Prospective Changes in Japan's Trade Pattern." *Japan and the World Economy* 2: 211–38.

Noland, Marcus. 1990b. *Pacific Basin Developing Countries: Prospects for the Future*. Washington: Institute for International Economics.

Noland, Marcus. 1991. "Macroeconomic Policy Coordination and the U.S.-Japan Trade Problem." *Ricerche Economiche* 45, no. 2-3: 329–38.

Noland, Marcus. 1992a. "Industrial Policy and Japanese Trade Specialization." *Review of Economics and Statistics* (forthcoming).

Noland, Marcus. 1992b. "Public Policies, Private Preferences, and Japan's Trade Pattern." Washington: Institute for International Economics (mimeographed, January).

Noland, Marcus. 1992c. "Why Are Prices in Japan So High?" Washington: Institute for International Economics (mimeographed, May).

Noland, Marcus. 1992d. "Research and Development Activities and Comparative Advantage in Japan." Washington: Institute for International Economics (mimeographed, August).

Noland, Marcus. 1993. "Asia and the NAFTA." Paper presented at the Asia Society Conference on "Korea and East Asia: Trade Relations and Investment in the Pacific Rim." Hong Kong, 22–24 February.

Nye, Joseph. 1992–93. "Coping with Japan." *Foreign Policy* 89 (Winter): 96–115.

Office of Technology Assessment. 1991. *Competing Economies: America, Europe, and the Pacific Rim*. Washington: Government Printing Office (October).

Office of the US Trade Representative. 1989. *Foreign Trade Barriers*. Washington: Government Printing Office.

Office of the US Trade Representative. 1990. *Foreign Trade Barriers*. Washington: Government Printing Office.

Ogura, Seiritsu, and Naoyuki Yoshino. 1988. "The Tax System and the Fiscal Investment and Loan Program." In Ryutaro Komiya, Masahiro.

Okuno, and Kotaro Suzumura, Eds. *Industrial Policy in Japan*, 121–54. San Diego: Academic Press.

Ohtake, Fumio. 1991. "Bequest Motives of Aged Households in Japan." *Ricerche Economiche* 45, no. 2-3: 283–306.

Okita, Saburo. 1992. "Transition to Market Economy." Mimeographed.

Okumura, Hirohiko. 1991. "Financial Fragility in Japan and Its Impact on the World Economy." Paper presented to the United States-Japan Economic Policy Group, Tokyo (23–24 April).

Okuno-Fujiwara, Masahiro. 1992. "The Japanese Government's Relationship with Industry." National Bureau of Economic Research and Japan Center for Economic Research. Background paper for U.S.-Japan Economic Forum (February).

Organization for Economic Cooperation and Development. 1991. *Agricultural Policies, Markets, and Trade*. Paris: OECD.

Peters, Lois S. 1993. "Technology Strategies of Japanese Subsidiaries and Joint Ventures in the United States." In Mordechai E. Kreinin, ed., *International Commercial Policy*, Washington: Taylor & Francis.

Petri, Peter A. 1991. "Japanese Trade in Transition: Hypotheses and Recent Evidence." In Paul R. Krugman, ed., *Trade With Japan*, 51–84. Chicago: University of Chicago Press.

Porges, Amelia. 1991. "U.S.-Japan Trade Negotiations: Paradigms Lost." In Paul R. Krugman, ed., *Trade With Japan*, 305–27. Chicago: University of Chicago Press.

Prestowitz, Clyde V., Jr. 1988. *Trading Places: How We Are Giving Our Future to Japan and How to Reclaim It*. New York: Basic Books.

Reich, Robert B. 1990. "Who Is Us?" *Harvard Business Review* (January–February): 53–64.

Richardson, J. David. 1993. *Sizing Up U.S. Export Disincentives*. Washington: Institute for International Economics (forthcoming).

Roningen, Vernon O., and Praveen M. Dixit. 1991. "Reforming Agricultural Policies: The Case of Japan." *Journal of Asian Economics* 2, no. 1: 87–111.

Rosenbluth, Frances McCall. 1989. *Financial Politics in Contemporary Japan*. Ithaca, NY: Cornell University Press.

Rosovsky, Henry. 1985. "Trade, Japan, and the Year 2000." *New York Times* (6 September).

Sakakibara, Eisuke. 1992. "Japan: Capitalism Without Capitalists." *International Economic Insights* 3, no. 4 (July–August): 45–47.

Sato, Kazuo. 1990. "The Paradox of Japan's Distribution System." Paper presented to the Japan Economic Seminar, New York (22 September).

Saxonhouse, Gary R. 1983. "The Micro- and Macro-Economics of Foreign Sales to Japan." In William R. Cline, ed., *Trade Policies in the 1980s*, 259–304. Washington: Institute for International Economics.

Saxonhouse, Gary R. 1989. "Differentiated Products, Economies of Scale, and Access to the Japanese Market." In Robert C. Feenstra, ed., *Trade Policies and International Competitiveness*. Cambridge, MA: National Bureau of Economic Research.

Saxonhouse, Gary R. 1992. "Trading Blocs, Pacific Trade and the Pricing Strategies of East Asian Firms." In Jeffrey A. Frankel and Miles Kahler, eds., *Regionalism and Rivalry: Japan and the US in Pacific Trade.* Chicago: University of Chicago Press (forthcoming).

Saxonhouse, Gary R. 1993. "Economic Growth and Trade Relations: Japanese Performance in Long-Term Perspective." In Takatoshi Ito and Anne O. Krueger, eds., *Trade and Protectionism,* 149–79. Chicago: University of Chicago Press.

Sazanami, Yoko, Shujiro Urata, and Hiroki Kuwai. 1993. "Trade Protection in Japan." In Hufbauer, Gary, and Kimberly Elliott, *Comparing the Costs of Protection: Europe, Japan, and the United States.* Washington: Institute for International Economics, (forthcoming).

Schlesinger, Jacob M. 1993. "Japan's Trade Surplus with the US Likely Is Wider if Output Elsewhere Is Included." *Wall Street Journal,* 22 March 1993.

Schott, Jeffrey J., ed. 1989. *Free Trade Areas and US Trade Policy.* Washington: Institute for International Economics.

Scott, Bruce R. 1987. "U.S. Competitiveness in the World Economy: An Update." Paper presented at the Workshop on Competitiveness, Harvard Business School, 12–18 July.

Shigehara, Kumihara. 1992. "Causes of Declining Growth in Industrialized Countries." In *Policies for Long-Run Economic Growth.* Federal Reserve Bank of Kansas City.

Shinjo, Koji. 1988. "The Computer Industry." In Ryutaro Komiya, Masahiro Okuno, and Kotaro Suzumura, eds., *Industrial Policy of Japan,* 333–368. San Diego: Academic Press.

Shinohara, Miyohei. 1982. *Industrial Growth, Trade, and Dynamic Patterns in the Japanese Economy.* Tokyo: Tokyo University Press.

Smitka, Michael. 1993. "The Decline of the Japanese Auto Industry: Domestic and International Implications." Paper presented at the Japan Economic Seminar, New York (20 February).

Staiger, Robert W., Alan V. Deardorff, and Robert M. Stern. 1988. "The Effects of Protection on the Factor Content of Japanese and American Foreign Trade." *Review of Economics and Statistics* 70, no. 3: 475–83.

Steinmuller, W. Edward. 1988. "Industry Structure and Government Policies in the U.S. and Japanese Integrated Circuit Industries." In John B. Shoven, ed., *Government Policy Towards Industry in the United States and Japan.* Cambridge, England: Cambridge University Press.

Stern, Paula. 1993. "U.S. Economic Policy in Asia at a Crossroads: The Challenge Facing the New Clinton Administration." Paper presented at a meeting of the US-Thai Leadership Council, Bangkok (7 March).

Summers, Robert, and Alan Heston. 1991. "The Penn World Table (Mark 5): An Expanded Set of International Comparisons, 1950–1988." *Quarterly Journal of Economics* 106, no. 2: 327–68.

Takagi, Keizo. 1989. "The Rise of Land Prices in Japan: The Determination Mechanism and the Effect of the Taxation System." *Bank of Japan Monetary and Economic Studies* 7, no. 2: 93–139.

Tarr, David. 1989. *A General Equilibrium Analysis of Quotas on US Imports.* Washington: Federal Trade Commission.

Tomkin, Robert. 1990. "Fund Managers to Assume Limelight as Investment Trusts Take Center Stage." *Japan Economic Journal* Special Report on Financial Markets (Winter).

Torii, Akio, and Richard E. Caves. 1992. "Technical Efficiency in Japanese and U.S. Manufacturing Industries." In Richard E. Caves, ed., *Industrial Efficiency in Six Nations,* 425–58. Cambridge, MA: MIT Press.

Trefler, David. 1993. "Trade Liberalization and the Theory of Endogenous Protection: An Econometric Study of U.S. Import Policy." *Journal of Political Economy* 101, no. 1: 138–60.

Tyson, Laura D'Andrea. 1992. *Who's Bashing Whom? Trade Conflict in High-Technology Industries.* Washington: Institute for International Economics.

Union Bank of Switzerland. 1991. *Prices and Earnings Around the Globe.* Zurich: Union Bank of Switzerland.

Urata, Shujiro. 1993. "Changing Patterns of Direct Investment and Implications for Trade and Development." In C. Fred Bergsten and Marcus Noland, eds., *Pacific Dynamism and the International Economic System,* 273–98. Washington: Institute for International Economics.

US Department of Commerce. 1989. *The Joint DOC/MITI Price Survey: Methodology and Results.* Washington: US Department of Commerce (December).

US Department of Commerce. 1991. "Results of the 1991 DOC/MITI Price Survey." *U.S. Department of Commerce News* (ITA 91-32, 20 May).

US General Accounting Office. 1991. *U.S. Business Access to Certain Foreign State-of-the-Art Technology.* Washington: US General Accounting Office (September).

US Department of the Treasury. 1990. *National Treatment Study.*

US Trade Representative Office. 1993. *National Trade Estimates.*

VanDenBerg, Jan. 1993. "The Gift Horse's Mouth." Mimeograph.

Van Wolferen, Karel. 1989. *The Enigma of Japanese Power.* New York: Knopf.

Verleger, Philip K., Jr. 1993. *Adjusting to Volatile Energy Prices.* Washington: Institute for International Economics (forthcoming).

Vincent, D. P. 1988. "Effects of Agricultural Protection in Japan: An Economy-wide Analysis." Paper prepared for the Global Agricultural Trade Study, Centre for International Economics, Canberra, Australia.

Weinstein, David E. 1992. "Competition and Unilateral Dumping." *Journal of International Economics* 32, no. 3/4: 379–388.

Williamson, John. 1983. *The Exchange Rate System.* POLICY ANALYSES IN INTERNATIONAL ECONOMICS 5. Washington: Institute for International Economics (September).

Williamson, John, and Marcus H. Miller. 1987. *Targets and Indicators: A Blueprint for the International Coordination of Economic Policy.* POLICY ANALYSES IN INTERNATIONAL ECONOMICS 22. Washington: Institute for International Economics (September).

Womack, James P., Daniel T. Jones, and Daniel Roos. 1990. *The Machine That Changed the World.* New York: Harper.

Vogel, Ezra. 1985. *Comeback. Case by Case: Building the Resurgence of American Business.* New York: Simon and Schuster.

Vogel, Ezra. 1979. *Japan as Number One.* Cambridge, MA: Harvard University Press.

Yamamura, Kozo. 1990. "Will Japan's Structure Change? Confessions of a Former Optimist." In Kozo Yamamura, ed., *Japan's Economic Structure: Should It Change?* 13–64. Seattle: University of Washington Press.

Yoshitomi, Masaru. 1990. "*Keiretsu:* An Insider's Guide to Japan's Conglomerates." *International Economic Insights* 1, no. 2 (September–October): 10–15.

Index

Advanced Display Manufacturers of America
139
Advanced Research Projects Agency (ARPA)
139, 148
Advisory Committee on Trade Policy and
Negotiations (ACTPN) 19, 66, 120
AEG-Westinghouse 164
Agriculture. *See also specific products*
costs of protection in 100
disproportionate effect of Japanese policies
on US 201
estimates of impact of trade liberalization in
101–03, 188, 189, 202, 220
in GATT 20, 100
in Japan 100, 221, 223
in US 69–70
land prices and 47
managed trade in 226
quotas in 70, 100
subsidy-equivalents in 100–01
American Chamber of Commerce 80, 81
American Electronics Association 156
American Telephone and Telegraph Co.
(AT&T) 124, 148, 151
Anchordoguy, Marie 126, 128
Anderson, Kym 100
Annunzio, Rep. Frank 170
Antidumping
harmonization of policies in 214
in automobiles 116, 117
in Japan 71
in LCDs 139
in semiconductors 129–30, 132

in STA 132
in supercomputers 149
in US 17, 70, 139
Antitrust. *See* Competition policy
Aoki, Masahiko 8, 9, 11, 74
Apple Computer, Inc. 127, 129
Applied Materials 141
Ariga, Kenn 76
ARPA (Advanced Research Projects Agency)
139, 148
Asako, Kazumi 47
Asia Pacific Economic Community, proposed
224, 241
Asia Pacific Economic Cooperation 17, 225,
240, 245
Asset prices, in Japan 43, 46–53, 216
AT&T (American Telephone and Telegraph
Co.) 124, 148, 151
Auerbach, Alan J. 42
Auto parts
employment in 112
"genuine parts" certification for 113, 121,
222
GM procurement policy on 112
in MOSS talks 116
Japanese transplants' sourcing of 112, 117,
225, 226
US exports to Japan of 112
VIE in 16, 18, 113, 117, 121, 194, 225, 226
Automobiles
antidumping in 116, 117
Big Three US manufacturers of 104, 114,
115, 118, 121–23, 224

comparisons of US and Japanese industries 108–11
competition policy in 114, 121, 222
costs of protection in 118
distribution system for 76, 114, 121
employment in 112
evaluation of proposed quotas in 119
exchange rates and trade in 106–07, 123
foreign direct investment in 105, 111, 120. *See also* Transplant Japanese automobile plants in US
history of Japanese industry 105–06
Japan Development Bank funding of FDI in 120
Japanese imports of 114
joint ventures in 111
keiretsu in 111
luxury 108, 114
minivans 116, 121–22
nontariff barriers in 113–15
off-road vehicles 116
policy recommendations for 118–24
tariffs in 105
US-Japan competition in 1
VERs in 16, 19, 70, 106–08, 116, 118, 119, 222, 225, 226
VIEs in 16, 115, 120–21, 225
worldwide excess capacity in 119

Baker, James A., III 236
Balassa, Bela 38–40, 46, 47, 50, 54, 61–62, 64, 66, 72, 73, 82, 84, 85, 152, 180, 216
Bank for International Settlements (BIS) 51, 171
Bank of Japan 53, 54, 168, 171
Banking 51, 167, 168, 70–72
Banking Act of 1982 168
Bastion markets 81, 148, 159, 170
Bayard, Thomas O. 123, 224, 229
Beef 100, 161, 192, 195, 228
Beeper-pagers 151
Beltz, Cynthia A. 156
Bentsen, Lloyd 84, 140
Bergsten, C. Fred 3, 7, 13, 15, 33, 36, 127, 177, 180, 186–89, 195, 204, 205, 214, 233, 234, 237, 238, 248
Bhagwati, Jagdish 72, 100, 132
Bid-rigging 78, 162. *See also Dango*
Big Four Japanese brokerages 173–75
Big Three US automakers 104, 114, 115, 118, 121–23, 224
Bilateral US-Japan trade balance
causes of imbalance in 23, 205
econometric analysis of 181–82
economic growth and 206
effects of trade liberalization on 189, 202, 206, 246
exchange rates and 30, 55, 206, 220
impact of fiscal policy on 54–55

in high-technology industry 33
in services 158
inappropriateness of policy targeting of 5, 57, 202, 231
political preoccupation with 5, 20, 55, 204, 205
recent dramatic turnaround in 205
relative stability of 17, 33, 204
secular trend in 54
Southeast Asian subsidiaries and 33
triangular trade and 35
BIS (Bank for International Settlements) 51, 171
Blockbuster Video 161
Bloom, Justin 93
Blue Bell Dairy 84
Bond underwriting 173
Bonn economic summit 15, 17, 247
Boone, Peter 47, 50
Borrus, Michael 79, 128
Bovetti, Keith 166
Brady Plan 17, 236
Brander, James 70
Brock, Philip L. 51
Brokerages, Big Four Japanese 173–75
Brooks Brothers 161
"Bubble economy" 3, 46–53, 61, 81, 118, 206–07
Budget deficit, US. *See* Fiscal policy, US
Bush administration, economic policies of 10, 18, 78, 220, 225,
Bush, George, 1992 trip to Japan 113, 115, 117, 121, 127, 160, 224, 228
Buy American Act 69
"Buy American" policy in supercomputers 149

Canada 71, 117
Canada-US Free Trade Agreement 117
Canon 141
Capital per worker, estimates of, in Japan and US 61, 62
"Capitalism of the latecomer" 7
Cartelization. *See also* Co-optation
association of regulatory barriers with 72
countervailing subsidies to undermine 142
in banking 170
in construction 162–63
in declining sectors 64
in semiconductors 130
penalties for illegal 77
under STA 136–38
VERs and 226
VIEs and 194
Carter administration 106
"Catch-up capitalism" 7
Catte, Pietro 209
Caves, Richard E. 75
CBO (Congressional Budget Office) 53
Cellular telephones 151–55

Central banks. *See* Bank of Japan; Federal Reserve; Monetary policy
CFIUS (Committee on Foreign Investment in the United States) 96
Cheng, Leonard K. 76, 186
China 13, 32, 33, 71, 150, 160, 240
Chrysler Corp. 105, 111
Cigarettes 161, 192, 195, 228
Citibank 169, 171, 224
Citrus fruits 100, 192, 195, 228
Cline, William R. 36, 54, 55, 70, 127, 177, 180, 186–89, 195, 205, 207
Clinton administration
  aggressive trade policy stance of 3, 19
  economic program of 3, 5, 10, 18–19, 54–56, 207, 217, 246
  implementation of SII commitments by 211
  negotiating credibility of 18
  proposed current account targets of 208
  sectoral policies of 18–19
Clinton, Bill, statement on minivan decision 122
Cold War, implications of end of 3, 13, 230, 234–35
Collective global leadership 13, 16, 234–36, 241–42. *See also* Leadership of global economy
Color televisions 70, 157
Committee on Foreign Investment in the United States (CFIUS) 95, 96
Compaq Computer Corp. 139
Competition policy
  extraterritorial application of 78
  FDI and 82
  GATT and 225, 234, 238, 244
  harmonization of 11, 196
  in automobiles 114, 121, 222
  in Japan 9, 16, 77–78, 211, 243
  in proposed GATT for investment 238
  in SCT 243
  in SII 77
  in US 78–79
  joint US-Japan enforcement of 78–79, 213, 214
  keiretsu and 213, 238
  policy recommendations for 78–79, 213–14
Competitive interdependence, strategy of 3, 248
Competitiveness Policy Council 10, 216
Composition of output and trade 1, 6, 24–27, 33, 59, 92, 200, 220
Computer software 90, 149–50
Computers. *See also* Supercomputers
  early history of 124–26
  effects of STA on 226
  government procurement of 125, 126, 224, 227
  in Japan 90, 91, 124–25
  joint ventures in 126
  personal 127

Concentration of industry, in Japan 74
Congress 10, 95, 106, 117, 122, 131, 163, 169, 171, 231–233. *See also specific legislation*
Congressional Budget Office (CBO) 53
Construction industry 78, 161–67, 229
Convergence of US-Japan economies and policies 8, 9–12, 189, 201, 210–13, 236, 238, 241, 246
Cooper, Richard N. 69
Co-optation
  dilemma for US policy posed by 60, 99–100, 155, 190–91, 194, 226–28, 243
  in banking 172
  in construction 161, 166
  in financial services 177
  in supercomputers 147
Copyright 84
Corning Inc. 84, 154
Cost of capital, in Japan 9
Council on Competitiveness 94, 95
Countervailing duties 70
Countervailing subsidies 142, 143, 149
Cray Research, Inc. 144–49
"Critical technologies" lists 93–94
Cross-shareholding 46, 74, 75, 77, 80, 82, 174, 213, 215
Cross-subsidization 126, 134, 148, 149, 172
Currencies. *See* Exchange rates
Current account balance. *See also* Trade balance
  definition 34
  in Europe 20
  in Japan 1, 17, 20, 30, 35
  in US 1, 2, 4, 35, 199-200
  relation to merchandise trade balance of 34
  saving and investment and 5
  targets for 35, 57, 208, 242

Daini Denden 153
Daiwa Securities 173, 175
Dango 78, 162–64, 166–67
Debt, US foreign 1, 5, 200, 233
DeConcini, Sen. Dennis 84
Dekle, Robert 38, 40, 51
DeMelo, Jaime 106
Demographics of Japan 40, 43, 56, 115
Designated bidder system 161, 163, 167
"Design-in" R&D 11, 196
Destler, I. M. 70, 190, 204, 231
"Developmental state," Japan as 7
Diem, Carl 144
Dingell, Rep. John D. 116
Dinopolous, Elias 106, 132
Direct foreign investment. *See* Foreign direct investment
"Directly unproductive activities" 100
Dispute settlement 166, 234, 238, 244
Distribution system
  in automobiles 76, 114, 121

in Japan 9, 16, 72, 75–77, 114, 134, 159–61, 186, 211, 213–15, 223
keiretsu and 75–77, 134, 186
proposed reforms 77
Dixit, Praveen M. 100
Dollar. *See* Exchange rates
Dollar, David 61
Domestic allies of liberalization in Japan 14, 212, 224, 229
Dominguez, Kathryn 209
Dornbusch, Rudiger 66

EAEG (East Asia Economic Group), proposed 240, 247
East Asia, US-Japan conflict over 239–41
East Asian Economic Group, proposed 240, 247
EC. *See* European Community
Economic growth
bilateral imbalances and 206
contributors to 43–46
impact on trade imbalances of 28, 203
in Japan 9, 12, 53, 207–08
in US 3–5, 9, 46, 5
sluggish worldwide 5
Economic Planning Agency (Japan) 74, 183
Economic Strategy Institute (ESI) 118, 121, 122
Economies of scale 6, 81, 200, 223
Education 10, 11, 16, 216–17, 243
Efficiency of industry 60–61
Elliott, Kimberly Ann 118, 183, 224, 229
Employment 8, 64, 92, 112, 199
Encarnation, Dennis J. 79, 80, 126, 128
Endaka 47
Endo, Yukihiko 171
Enhanced-definition television 157
ESI (Economic Strategy Institute) 118, 121, 122
ETA Systems 145, 146
European Community
competition policy of 78, 79
inclusion in SCT talks of 213
labor productivity in 10
"mutual recognition" of differences within 8
objections to STA of 131
participation in global economic leadership by 243
patent system of 83
product liability system of 74, 215
subsidies in 148
supercomputers in 148
support for HDTV by 156
VER in automobiles of 19, 119, 222, 226
Exchange controls 105
Exchange rates
asset prices in Japan and 50
automobile trade and 106–07, 123
effects of disequilibrium 200
government intervention in 209, 244
impact on FDI 215

impact on global trade imbalances 4, 28–32, 46, 55, 202, 207, 208, 246
manipulation of 237
real effective 28, 30
systemic arrangements for 15, 208–10, 273
US-Japan bilateral imbalance and 30, 55, 206, 220
Exon, Sen. J. James 95
Exon-Florio amendment 95, 214
Export controls 69, 148, 218
Export credits 218
Export disincentives 69, 148, 206, 218
Export-Import Bank (Japan) 68
Export promotion 218, 243
Export volumes 28–32, 46
External debt, US 1, 5, 200, 233
Externalities 6, 93, 134, 178, 193, 222
Extraterritoriality 78, 120, 214

Factor endowments 180, 182, 187
Fair Trade in Financial Services Act 169
Fairchild Industries 95, 124, 127
FDI. *See* Foreign direct investment
Fecher, Fabienne 94
Federal Reserve 54, 169
Fiber optics 192
Fifth Generation Computing Project 143
FILP (Fiscal Investment and Loan Program) 68
Financial scandals, in Japan 170, 174–76
Financial services
co-optation scenario in 177
deregulation of 168–69
externalities in 178
in Japan 167–78, 224
in US 167
reciprocity in 169
Financial systems in Japan and US 167–69
"First-to-file" patent system 83–85, 216
"First-to-invent" patent system 83
Fiscal Investment and Loan Program (FILP) 68
Fiscal policy
impact on trade imbalances of 54–55, 202
in Japan 3, 43, 44, 46, 53–56, 206–07, 242, 246
in US 10, 18, 43–44, 53–54, 56, 123, 206–07, 242, 246
Fish products 104
Flamm, Kenneth 129, 131, 138, 139
"Flash" memory chips 139
Flath, David 76
Florio, James 95
Food processing 68
Ford Motor Co. 105, 106, 108, 111, 115, 116
Foreign debt, US 1, 5, 200, 233
Foreign direct investment (FDI)
competition policy and 82
encouragement by MITI of 81
greenfield 80, 82
harmonization of policies in 214

impact of exchange rate changes on 215
in automobiles 105, 111, 120. *See also*
Transplant Japanese automobile plants in
US
in banking 170
in computer software 150
in computers 125
in high-technology industry 92–93
in SCT 215
in semiconductors 128
in SII 82
inward, in Japan 8, 67, 79–82, 105, 125–26,
210, 215, 239
inward, in US 80
Japanese investment boom and 51
Japanese restrictions on 79–80, 105, 111, 125
keiretsu and 79
land prices and 82
legal services for 82
outward, by Japan 10, 92
outward, by US 79–80
national security and 95, 143
policy recommendations 82, 215–16
political influence and 82
R&D and 93–94
securities markets and 178
transplant-inclusive VER and 118
Foreign exchange allocations 125
Forward pricing 139
Forward rate agreements 169
Frankel, Jeffrey A. 17, 168, 209
Free rider, Japan as 3, 201, 235, 237
Fuels, trade in 72, 104, 189, 193
Fuji Bank 171
Fujita 161
Fujitsu Ltd. 95, 126, 145, 147
Funabashi, Yoichi 15, 50, 209
Fung, K. C. 182
Futures arbitrage trading 174–75

"G-2" initiatives 17, 209, 234, 236, 238, 243
G-7 (Group of Seven) 15, 17, 32, 203, 209, 232,
243–45
Gaiatsu 3, 13, 18, 60, 169, 229–31, 235
Garn, Sen. Jake 169
Gasoline 72
"GATT for investment" 238–39, 244
General Agreement on Tariffs and Trade
(GATT). *See also* Uruguay Round
agriculture in 20, 100
as forum for US-Japan negotiations 17, 232
competition policy in 225, 234, 238, 244
discipline over VERs and VIEs, proposed
238
dispute settlement in 234, 238, 244
enforcement powers of 238
government procurement in 126, 224, 234,
238

Japanese accession to 71
Japanese implementation of decisions of 224
post–Uruguay Round agenda for 225,
237–38
regional trade arrangements and 241
ruling on STA by 131
sectoral issues in 224–25, 244
services in 20
subsidies in 234, 238
General Motors 105, 108, 111–13, 115
General Motors–Suzuki joint venture 117
Generalized System of Preferences 71, 72
"Genuine parts" certification 113, 121, 222
Gephardt, Rep. Richard A. 20, 117, 204, 205
Gerlach, Michael 74
Germany 20, 32, 35, 92, 114
Glass industry 76
Global trade balances. *See also* Bilateral US-
Japan trade balance; Trade balance
economic growth and 28, 203
influences on 28–32, 43, 46, 54–56, 202, 207
Japanese surplus 1, 5, 17, 20, 28–32, 200–04,
206, 208
reasons not to expect zero 35
strategy to correct imbalances in 205–07
US deficit 24–25, 28–29, 31–32, 34–36
Globalization of business 9, 214
Goto, Akira 79
Government procurement
harmonization of policies in 11
in computers 125–26, 192, 227
in GATT 126, 224, 234, 244
in Japan 67, 72
in supercomputers 145, 147, 193, 224, 227,
228
in telecommunications 151, 224
in US 69, 227
VIEs and 194
Graham, Edward M. 92, 93, 143, 215, 238
Gross domestic product, growth in. *See*
Economic growth
Grossman, Gene M. 85
Group of Seven (G-7) 15, 17, 32, 203, 209, 232,
243–45
Growing markets, better prospects for trade
initiatives in 193
Growth, economic. *See* Economic growth
Gulf War 13, 204, 205, 235

Harada, Shozo 164
Harmonization of policies 11, 196, 214, 219,
231, 243
Harrigan, James 180, 181
Hartzell, Jon K. 169
Hayashi, Fumio 38, 43
HDTV (high-definition television) 156–58
Heads of government, role in proposed
USJapan strategy 245–46
Health care reform, in US 10, 54, 122

Heston, Alan 9, 183
Hicks, Sir John R. 105
High-Definition Display Manufacturing
    Consortium 140
High-definition television (HDTV) 156–58
High technology
    access of US firms to Japanese 94–95
    bilateral trade balance and 33
    countervailing subsidies for 196
    externalities in 222
    FDI in 92–93
    joint ventures in 157–58
    nature of government intervention in 59
    revealed comparative advantage in 85–90
    scale economies in 223
    US-Japan leadership in 200
    US-Japan rivalry in 1, 85–96
Hillman, Jimmye S. 100
Hills, Carla A. 138, 164, 166
Hiraguchi, Toshio 144
Hitachi Ltd. 126, 129, 139, 145
Honda Motor Co. 108, 115, 117, 124
Horioka, Charles Yuji 40, 43, 51
Households, Japanese, saving by 38–40
Housing and housing policy 11, 40, 68
Housing Loan Corporation (Japan) 68
Hufbauer, Gary C. 70, 117, 118, 183
Hysteresis 70

IBM (International Business Machines Corp.)
    124, 125, 127, 139, 148
Ichioka, Osamu 101
IDO 153
Imai, Ken-ichi 126
IMF (International Monetary Fund) 203, 235,
    244, 245
Import penetration 66–67, 182, 210
Import promotion 72
Import volumes 28–32, 46
Industrial Bank of Japan 171
Industrial policies. See also Sectoral issues;
    Structural differences; specific industries
    in Japan 67–69, 105, 126, 128, 190
    in US 69, 190
    trade specialization and 64
Inflation 209, 242
Infrastructure and public works 10, 16, 56, 211
Intel Corp. 135, 139
Intellectual property protection 72, 82–85, 94,
    216–17, 243
Interest rates 15, 50, 51, 53, 55, 68–69, 118,
    167–70
International Business Machines Corp. (IBM)
    124, 125, 127, 139, 148
International Monetary Fund (IMF) 203, 235,
    244, 245
International monetary system, reform of 15,
    208–10, 236–37, 242–45
International Motor Vehicle Program 108–11

International net asset positions 2, 237
Internationalization of US and Japanese
    economies 11, 211
Intervention in foreign exchange markets 209,
    244
Intrafirm trade 66, 67, 80, 210
Intraindustry trade 64–66, 210
Investment. See Foreign direct investment;
    Saving and investment
Investment boom, in Japan 51
Investment incentives, in SCT 217
Investment tax credit, proposed 123
Ishihara, Shintaro 14, 150, 162
Israel 71
Isuzu 108, 111, 118, 119
ITC (US International Trade Commission) 106,
    116, 122, 140
Ito, Takatoshi 76, 186, 209
Itoh, Motoshige 71, 76, 186

J-curve 32
Japan. See also specific sectors and institutions
    advantages of proposed strategy for 248
    as creditor 1, 233
    as "developmental state" 7
    as economic superpower 3, 230, 232, 235
    as "free rider" 3, 201, 235, 237
    disproportionate impact on US of market
        access limitations in 200
    domestic allies of liberalization in 14, 212,
        224, 229
    emphasis on production 7
    failure to accept global leadership role 4, 201
    financial exposure in US 14
    geographic composition of trade in 26–27
    government interventionism in 8
    implementation of international agreements
        by 211, 224
    inherent economic conflict with US 219
    issues for SCT negotiation 213–16
    opposition to further managed trade 14, 20,
        230
    postwar technological catch-up 61
    public support for R&D by 90, 92, 156
    regulatory barriers in 72–73, 215
    that can say "no" 14
    trade with Southeast Asia 34
Japan Center for International Finance 169
Japan Development Bank 68, 81, 90, 113, 141,
    154
Japan Electronic Computer Company (JECC)
    125
Japan Fair Trade Commission 77, 78, 174, 239
Japan Patent Office 85
Japan Research Institute 53
JECC (Japan Electronic Computer Company)
    125
JESSI 143
Johnson, Chalmers 7, 67, 105

Johnson, Robert 186
Joint ventures 111, 117, 126, 128, 132, 157, 162
Just-in-time inventory system 10, 11, 105, 213

Kaifu, Toshiki 166, 171
Kajima Engineering 163
Kansai International Airport 162–65
KDD 152
Keatley, Robert 76
Keidanren 82
Keiretsu
  as source of structural differences 8
  competition policy and 213, 238
  definition and characteristics of 8, 74–75
  econometric analysis of trade impact of
    182–83, 186
  extraterritorial measures aimed at 214
  FDI and 79, 80
  financial 9, 75
  impact on Japanese prices of 221
  in automobiles and parts 111–12, 124
  in banking 170
  in computers 126
  in distribution system 75–77, 134, 186
  in semiconductors 129, 134
  in SII 16
  in supercomputers 145
  Japanese failure to obviate adverse effects of
    18
  trade specialization and 64
  use of GATT to address 234
  vertical 75, 111
  VIEs and 196
KIA (Kansai International Airport) 162–65
Kia Motors Co. 111, 114
Kilby, Jack 124
Kleidon, Allan W. 173
Kodama, Fumio 90
Komiya, Ryutaro 71
Korea 13, 20, 32, 72, 140, 234, 240
Kotlikoff, Lawrence J. 42
Krause, Lawrence B. 241
Kreinin, Mordechai E. 106, 132, 182, 186
Krishna, Kala 136
Krueger, Anne O. 100
Krugman, Paul R. 69, 70, 143, 206, 215
Kurile Islands 13
Kuroda, Makoto 145, 241

Labor productivity in Japan and US 10
Labor relations 8, 112
Laird, Sam 73
Land, prices of, in Japan 46–50, 52, 82, 216
Land use policy, in Japan 11, 47, 82, 211, 216,
  221, 243
Large Scale Retail Store Law 16, 78, 160, 211,
  224

Lawrence, Robert Z. 5, 64, 67, 73, 180-182,
  186, 187, 241
Leadership of the global economy
  collective 13, 16, 234–36, 241–42
  EC participation in 243
  "imbalance" in 235
  Japanese failure to assume proper role in 4,
    201
  policy recommendations on 233–41
Leamer, Edward E. 64, 73, 180
"Lean production" 105
Leather products 71
Lee, Hiro 14, 69, 96–97
Legal system, access to, in Japan 73
Liberal Democratic Party 53
Liberalization, estimates of trade impact of
  in agriculture 101–03, 188, 189, 202, 220
  in manufactures 221
  in retailing 161
  in securities industry 177
  overall 187–89, 192, 202, 206, 220
  versus optimal tariff 96–97
Licensing 76, 162
Lieberman, Joseph I. 214
Lifetime employment, in Japan 8, 64, 92
Lincoln, Edward J. 64, 66, 72
Liquid crystal displays 139–40
Locomotive theory 15
Long Term Credit Bank of Japan 33, 53, 204
Loopesko, Bonnie 186
Louvre Accord 15, 209, 236
LTV Corp. 95

Machine tools 16, 18, 70, 71, 225
Macroeconomic policies. *See also* Fiscal policy;
    Monetary policy; Saving and investment
  impact on saving and investment of 43
  impact on semiconductor trade of 143
  impact on trade balance 56
  in Japan 43–53
  in US 53–54
  past initiatives in 15–16
  policy recommendations for 56–57, 206–10,
    217–18, 242–43
Maekawa Report 9, 35
Major Projects Agreement (MPA) 163, 165, 166
Mamco Manufacturing Co. 95
Managed trade
  current account targets and 208
  differing US objectives in 226
  in agriculture 226
  Japanese opposition to further 14, 20, 230
  joint antitrust enforcement as alternative to
    214
  past US examples of 225
  process remedies versus 225–28
  to address structural differences 7
  under Bush administration 225
Manipulation of exchange rates 237

Manufactures, estimates of impact of
  liberalization in 202, 221
Market-oriented, sector-specific (MOSS) talks
  16, 17, 116, 145, 151, 152, 155
Marris, Stephen 50
Marston, Richard C. 186
Maruyama, Masayoshi 76, 186
Mason, Mark 79, 126, 128
Masson, Paul R. 42
Mazda Motor Corp. 108, 111, 115, 116
McDonald's Japan 161
McMillan, John 162
Merchandise trade balance. See Trade balance
Merrill Lynch & Co., Inc 174
Micron Technology 129
Miller, Marcus H. 208, 209
Ministry of Agriculture, Forests, and Fisheries
  221
Ministry of Finance (MOF)
  co-management of proposed
    macroeconomic strategy by 244
  indirect subsidization of industry by 68
  involvement in financial scandals of 176
  liberalization of financial services by 169
  licensing of mutual funds by 176
  pension fund regulation by 177
  regulation of bond underwriting by 173
  regulation of securities market by 172
  relations with Citibank 171
  resistance to foreign bank takeovers 170
Ministry of Foreign Affairs 245
Ministry of International Trade and Industry
  (MITI)
  control over the Japanese economy 131
  encouragement of FDI by 81
  foreign exchange allocation by 125
  intervention in automobile industry 105,
    113, 116
  intervention in computer industry 126
  intervention in retailing industry 160
  intervention in semiconductor industry 127,
    128, 130–31
  price survey with US Department of
    Commerce 183
  Sixth Generation Computing Project 148
  support of HDTV research 156
Ministry of Posts and Telecommunications
  151, 152, 153, 156
Minivans 116, 121–22
MITI. See Ministry of International Trade and
  Industry
Mitsubishi Corp. 108, 111, 115
Mitsui Group 74
Miyao, Takahiro 50
Miyazawa, Kiichi 231, 236, 242
MOF. See Ministry of Finance
Monetary policy 50–53, 56, 207, 244
Moore Special Tool Co. 95
Morgan Stanley Group Inc. 173

Morita, Akio 9, 209, 239
MOSS (market-oriented sector-specific) talks
  16, 17, 116, 145, 151, 152, 155
Motorola, Inc. 127, 140, 152–54, 155
Mowery, David C. 93
MPA (Major Projects Agreement) 163, 165, 166
MPT (Ministry of Posts and
  Telecommunications) 151, 152, 153, 156
Multi-Fiber Arrangement 70
Murkowski, Sen. Frank 163, 165
Mutoh, Hiromichi 105
Mutual funds 176
"Mutual recognition" of structural differences
  11

NAFTA (North American Free Trade
  Agreement) 71, 117–19, 239, 240, 247
Nakatani, Iwao 7, 11
National Aeronautics and Space
  Administration 147
National Critical Technologies Panel 94, 95
National Economic Council 231, 244
National Foreign Trade Estimates 126, 232
National Institute of Fusion Science (Japan)
  146
National Science Foundation 147
National security 12, 13, 230, 234, 240
National Security Council 231
National Tax Administration (Japan) 175
Nationality question in semiconductors 130
Natural resources, US comparative advantage
  in 60, 64
NEC Corp. 126, 128, 145–48
"Network capitalism," in Japan 7
NHK 156
Niigata Engineering 164, 165
Nikkei index 47, 175
Nikko Securities 173, 175
Nikon 141
Nippon Telegraph and Telephone Corp.
  (NTT) 124, 125, 151, 153, 154
Nippondenso 112
Nishimura, Kiyohiko G. 76
Nissan Motor Co. 108, 112, 113, 115, 119
Noguchi, Yukio 42, 50
Noland, Marcus 38, 40, 46, 47, 50, 54–55,
  61–62, 64, 66, 68–69, 72, 73, 82, 84, 85,
  90, 92, 152, 180–82, 186–89, 216
Nomura Securities Co., Ltd. 173, 175, 176
North American Free Trade Agreement
  (NAFTA) 71, 117–19, 239, 240, 247
Noyce, Robert 124
NTT (Nippon Telegraph and Telephone
  Corp.) 124, 125, 151, 153, 154
NTT Procurement Procedure Agreement 151
Nye, Joseph 12

OECD (Organization for Economic
   Cooperation and Development) 213, 244,
   245
Off-road vehicles 116
Office of Technology Assessment (OTA) 124,
   125, 126, 145, 146, 149
Office of the US Trade Representative 146,
   154, 163–64, 189, 231, 244
Ogura, Seiritsu 68
Ohtake, Fumio 40
Oki Electric 130
Okita, Saburo 7
Okumura, Hirohiko 50
Okuno-Fujiwara, Masahiro 11
Omnibus Trade and Competitiveness Act of
   1988 169, 229, 237
Onoue, Nui 171
Optical fibers 154–55
Optical Imaging Systems 140
Optimal tariff argument 96
Orderly marketing agreements 71
Organization for Economic Cooperation and
   Development (OECD) 213, 244, 245
OTA (Office of Technology Assessment) 124,
   125, 126, 145, 146, 149

Pacific Basin regional relations 239–41, 247
Pacific Free Trade Area (PAFTA), proposed
   224, 225, 240
Patents 83–87, 94, 216
Pension fund management 177
Per capita income, in Japan and US 9
Perelman, Sergio 94
Peters, Lois S. 93
Petri, Peter A. 182, 187
Petroleum, trade in 104
Philippines 239
Plaza Agreement 15, 233
Policy recommendations
   as integrated strategy 247
   continuity with past initiatives 247
   in automobiles 118–24
   in construction services 167
   in HDTV 157
   in semiconductors 141–43
   in supercomputers 148–49
   in telecommunications 155
   on choice between process remedies and
      managed trade 225–28
   on choice of negotiating forums and tactics
      193–97, 224–25, 228–33, 244–45
   on competition policy 78–79, 213–14
   on distribution system reform 77
   on exchange rate management 208–10, 237,
      242, 243
   on export promotion 218
   on FDI policy 82, 215–16
   on incentives for saving and investment
      217–18
   on intellectual property protection 85,
      216–17
   on international investment issues 238–39
   on international monetary reform 208–10,
      236–37, 242
   on leadership of the global economy 233–41
   on macroeconomic issues 56–57, 206–10,
      217–18, 242–43
   on management of proposed US-Japan
      strategy 245–48
   on Pacific Basin regional relations 239–41
   on prioritizing trade initiatives 191–93,
      223–24
   on product liability system reform 74, 215
   on strengthening global trading system
      237–38
Poling, Harold A. 116
Political decision making, in Japan 3, 14, 229,
   231
Porges, Amelia 167
Postal saving system, in Japan 167
President, US, role in proposed strategy 245
Prestowitz, Clyde V., Jr. 7, 69, 146, 151, 241
Price differences, US-Japan, econometric
   analysis of 183–87
Primary products. See Agriculture; Fish
   products; Fuels; Wood products
Prime Minister, Japanese, role in proposed
   strategy 245
Prioritization of trade initiatives 191–93, 202,
   223–24, 232, 244
Procurement. See Government procurement
Product liability systems 73–74, 215, 243
Productivity, US-Japan differences in 60, 62,
   94
Protection, costs of 100, 104, 118

Quantitative import restrictions 70, 71, 100,
   119, 238
Quasi-public organizations, in Japan 69
Quotas 70, 71, 100, 119, 238

RCA 127
Reagan administration 10, 106, 116, 131, 163,
   225, 228, 233
Real effective exchange rates 28
Reciprocity 163, 169, 171
Reference ranges 15, 17, 209–10, 236
Regional relations 239–41, 247
Reich, Robert B. 130
Relative efficiencies of industry 60–61
Research and development (R&D) 10, 90–94,
   123, 148, 196
Retailing 75–77, 159–61, 224. See also
   Distribution system
Retaliation 155, 195, 228–30
Revealed comparative advantage 62–65, 85,
   88–90

Ricardian equivalence doctrine 38
Richardson, J. David 69, 206
Riegle, Sen. Donald W., Jr 20, 169, 205
Robotics 90
Roland-Holst, David 14, 96–97
Roningen, Vernon O. 100
Rosenbluth, Frances McCall 168
Rosovsky, Henry 79
Roth, Sen. William V. 214
Rothenberg, Robert A. 100
Russia 13, 234

Sachs, Jeffrey D. 47, 50
Sakakibara, Eisuke 7
Sakamoto, Misoji 166
Sato, Kazuo 76
Saving and investment
    causes of US-Japan differences in 40
    convergence of US and Japan in 11
    impact of macroeconomic policy on 43
    in industrialized countries 39, 42
    in Japan 9, 16, 36–41, 217
    in SCT 217, 243
    in US 10, 15, 18, 36–38, 41–43, 211, 217, 243
    inadequacies of statistics on 36–38
    trade balances and 5, 36–43, 56, 202
Saxonhouse, Gary 68, 69, 180–81, 187, 195
Sazanami, Yoko 104, 183
Scale economies 6, 81, 200, 223
Scandals, financial 170, 174–76
Schlesinger, Jacob M. 33
Schott, Jeffrey J. 117
Schultz, George P. 151
Schumer, Rep. Charles E. 167
Scott, Bruce R. 64
SCT. See Structural Convergence Talks,
    proposed
Sears Roebuck & Co. 161
Section 301 (of 1974 trade act) 71, 117, 129,
    163, 231
Section 306 (of 1974 trade act) 229
Sectoral issues. See also specific sectors
    bilateral negotiations on 225
    choice of forum for 224–25
    choosing priorities among 223–24, 232, 244
    costs of pursuing 224
    evaluation of benefits of agreements on
        223–24
    goals for US in 243
    history of US-Japan conflict over 16
    importance of 200
    in GATT 224, 244
    past initiatives in 16
    policy recommendations for 219–33
    salience in political debate of 6
    structural initiatives and 212
    tactical questions concerning 228–33
    timing of 246

Securities 172–78
Securities and Exchange Commission 176
Securities and Exchange Surveillance
    Commission 176
Security issues 12, 13, 230, 234, 240
Sematech 10, 91, 140, 142, 143
Semiconductor Industry Association 129
Semiconductor manufacturing equipment
    140–42
Semiconductor Trade Agreement (STA)
    alternatives to 142–43
    antidumping under 132
    as VIE 132
    cartelization under 136–38
    effect on market entry of 138
    effect on semiconductor users of 139
    estimate of US gains from 136, 141, 192
    evaluation of 132–42
    GATT ruling on 131
    impact on market efficiency of 141
    innovativeness of 132
    interest in similar initiatives 19
    market access provisions of 132
    1991 extension of 132
    objectives of 226
    price floor provisions of 132, 141, 226
    product nationality under 135, 191
    retaliation to violation of 17, 131, 230
Semiconductors
    access to Japanese technology in 94–95
    antidumping in 129–30
    cartelization in 130
    FDI in 128
    foreign participation in research consortia in
        143
    impact of capital market imperfections in
        129
    impact of macroeconomic policy on 143
    Japanese industrial policy in 128–29
    joint ventures in 132
    keiretsu in 134
    policy recommendations 141–43
    pricing incentives in 128
    sales in Japanese market of 137–38
    US Department of Defense support of
        research in 143
    US exports of 135
Services. See also specific service industries
    bastion markets in 159
    disproportionate effect of Japanese policies
        on US in 201
    externalities in 222
    in GATT 20
    nature of government intervention in 59
    scale economies in 223
    trade in 34–35, 158–78
Shareholder rights 82, 215, 243
Sharp 140
Shinjo, Koji 124

Shinohara, Miyohei 67
Short-term orientation of US business 80, 213
Siemens AG 148
SII. *See* Structural Impediments Initiative
Silk, trade in 71
Singleton, Kenneth J. 173
Sixth Generation Computing Project 148
Ski equipment, trade in 72
Small Business Finance Corporation (Japan) 90
Smithsonian Agreement 15
Smitka, Michael 119
Socialization of Big Three benefits packages, proposed 121–22
Software 90, 149–50
Sony Corp. 128
Sound recordings, copyright protection of 84
Southeast Asia, Japanese and US trade with 34
Sovereignty, national, structural initiatives and 212
Special 301 85, 153
Staiger, Robert W. 189
Standards, testing, and certification 70, 72–74, 104, 151–52, 156, 215
Steel 16, 70, 225
Steinmuller, W. Edward 124, 128
Stern, Paula 7, 214, 240
Stock market, in Japan 47–48, 52, 168, 173–76
Structural Convergence Talks (SCT), proposed
  as continuous process 219
  competition policy in 214, 243
  criteria for inclusion of issues in 212
  education in 216–17, 243
  export promotion in 218, 243
  foreign direct investment in 215
  inclusion of third countries in 213, 236, 244
  intellectual property protection in 216, 243
  investment incentives in 217
  issues for Japan in 213–16, 243
  issues for US in 216–18, 243
  land use policy in 243
  need for symmetry in 219
  potential benefits of 218–19
  private-sector issues in 212
  product liability law in 215, 243
  saving and investment in 217, 243
  sectoral issues in 244
  shareholder rights in 243
  taxation in 217, 243
  timing of 246
Structural differences, US-Japan. *See also* Composition of output and trade; *specific policies and institutions*
  and economies of scale 200
  economic impact of 200–01, 210
  history of US-Japan initiatives in 16
  industrial policy and 67–68
  in competition policy 74–79
  in FDI policy 79–82

  in manufactures 210
  in industrial organization 74–79
  in intellectual property protection 82–85
  in product liability systems 73–74
  national sovereignty and 212
  orthodox and revisionist views on 7
  policy recommendations for 210–19, 243
  relation between sectoral issues and 212
Structural Impediments Initiative (SII)
  Clinton administration implementation of commitments to 211
  competition policy in 77
  FDI in 82
  implementation of agreement by Japan 211
  intellectual property protection in 83
  Japanese public attitudes toward 9, 14
  keiretsu in 16
  macroeconomic initiatives in 15
  retailing in 160
Subaru 108, 118
Subcontracting 75
Subsidies
  countervailing 142, 143, 149, 196
  GATT code on 234, 244
  in EC 148
  in Japan 68–69, 71, 90–91, 124–25
  in supercomputers 148
  in US 69
  indirect, by MOF 68
  to computer industry 124–25
  to R&D 90–91
Subsidization 228
Subsidy-equivalents 100
Sumitomo Corp. 111, 164, 165
Summers, Robert 9, 38, 183
Super 301 16, 71, 146, 117, 229–31, 233
Supercomputer Agreement of 1990 229
Supercomputers
  antidumping in 149
  bastion markets in 148
  co-optation in 147
  definition and characteristics of 144–45
  government procurement of 145, 147, 149, 224, 227, 228
  in EC 148
  in MOSS talks 145
  keiretsu and 145
  market shares in 147
  policy recommendations for 148–49
  R&D in 148
  subsidies to 148, 149
  Super 301 and 146
  US-Japan agreement on 146, 147, 193
Suzuki 111

Tachibanaki, Toshiaki 101
Tactical issues in trade negotiations 17, 96–97, 193–97, 228–33
Taiwan 32, 138, 160, 240

Takagi, Keizo 47
Tanaka, Kakuei 47
Tandy Corp. 139
Target zones for currencies, proposed 208–10, 237, 242, 243
Tariff-equivalents 104, 183, 186
Tariffs 69, 71, 96, 105, 122–23, 125, 184, 238
Tarr, David 106
Taxation. *See also* Fiscal policy
    alleged underpayment by Japanese subsidiaries in US 239
    in proposed GATT for investment 238
    in Japan 43, 68, 71, 79, 90–91, 105, 121, 169, 211, 216
    in SCT 217
    in US 10, 19, 69, 122–23, 217
    incentives to industry 91, 123, 125, 243
Teece, David J. 93
Telecommunications 150–55, 223–24
Temporary quantitative indicators (TQIs) 19, 121, 123, 225
Texas Instruments, Inc. 70, 84, 124, 128, 139
Textiles and apparel 16, 70, 104, 226
Third parties in VIEs 194
Third-party radio 153
Tokyo Round 71
Tomkin, Robert 176
Topix index 47
Torii, Akio 75
Toshiba 124, 139
Tourism 34
Tower Records 161
Toyo Shinkin 171
Toyota Motor Corp. 105, 106, 108, 111, 113, 115, 119
Toys 'R' Us, Inc. 160–61, 193, 211, 223
TQIs (temporary quantitataive indicators) 19, 121, 123, 225
Trade Act of 1974 229
Trade balance. *See also* Bilateral US-Japan trade balance; Current account; Global trade balances
    demographics and 56
    economic growth and 203
    emergence of imbalances in 1970s 203
    exchange rates and 46, 55, 202, 207, 246
    fiscal policy and 54–55, 202
    policy recommendations to rectify imbalances in 206–10
    relation to current account balance of 34
    saving and investment and 36–43, 56
Trade Enhancement Act 117
Trade preferences, US and Japanese 71
Trademark protection 84
Transfer pricing 238
Transparency, in banking 170
Transplant Japanese automobile plants in US as response to VER 108

auto parts procurement by 112, 117, 225, 226
benefits to US auto industry of 111
exports to Japan by 115
inclusion in EC VER of 19, 190, 222, 226
quality and productivity of 108
Trefler, David 71
Triangular trade 35, 55, 57, 205, 232
TRON 150
Tryon, Ralph W. 42
Tulips 72
Tyers, Rod 100
Tyson, Laura D'Andrea 67, 70, 128, 129, 131, 132, 134, 138, 143, 146, 149, 151–53, 156

Uenohara, Michiyuki 149
Unilateral trade policy initiatives 228, 230
Union Bank of Switzerland 183
United Auto Workers 106
United Nations Conference on Trade and Development 73
United States. *See also specific sectors and institutions*
    advantages of proposed strategy for 248
    comparative advantage in natural resources of 60, 64
    disproportionate impact of Japanese market access limitations on 200
    emphasis on consumption in 7, 12
    export-led growth in 46
    geographic composition of merchandise trade of 24–25
    global leadership role of 201
    imitation of Japanese business practices by 10
    inherent conflict with Japan 219
    need for domestic reforms in 12, 203
    negotiating clout of 13–14
    recent gains in competitiveness by 10
    regulatory regime of 70, 85, 89
    role in Pacific regional relations of 239
    sense of decline in 242
    trade with Southeast Asia 34
Urata, Shujiro 34
Uruguay Round. *See also* General Agreement on Tariffs and Trade
    consequences of possible failure of 1, 20–21, 237, 244
    Japanese role in success of 235, 237
    potential for intersectoral trade-offs in 224
    problems left unresolved by 4
    sectoral issues in 244
US minivan tariff in 123
US Department of Commerce 129, 147, 183, 195, 231, 245
US Department of Defense 91, 131, 143, 231
US Department of Justice 78, 129, 162, 214, 239

US Department of State 231
US Department of the Treasury 172, 174, 244
US Federal Communications Commission 156
US Federal Trade Commission 117
US General Accounting Office 94, 140
US General Services Administration 147
US International Trade Commission 106, 116, 122, 140
US-Japan Free Trade Agreement, evaluation of proposed 241, 247
US Memories consortium 143
US Trade Representative 146, 154, 163–64, 189, 231, 244

Value-added networks 152
VanDenBerg, Jan 53
Verleger, Philip K. 104
VERs. *See* Voluntary export restraints
Vertical foreclosure 76, 121
Vertical integration 75–76, 111, 134
Very Large Scale Integration Research Association 91
VIEs. *See* Voluntary import expansions
Vincent, D. P. 101
Volkswagen 105
Voluntary export restraints (VERs)
  as alternative to co-optation 100
  EC-Japan 19, 119, 222
  GATT discipline over, proposed 238
  in automobiles 16, 19, 70, 73, 106–08, 116, 118, 119, 222, 225, 226
  in color televisions 70
  in machine tools 16, 18, 70, 225
  in steel 16, 70, 225
  in textiles and apparel 16, 226
  inclusion of Japanese transplants in 19, 190, 222, 226
  Japan-Korea 71
  transplants as response to 108
Voluntary import expansions (VIEs) *See also* Semiconductor Trade Agreement
  and government procurement 194
  arbitrariness of targets of 195, 228
  as temporary compensatory policy 196
  cartelization and 194
  enforcement problems of 120

GATT discipline over, proposed 238
greater appropriateness for intermediate goods of 196–97
greater effectiveness in growing markets of 135
impact of exogenous factors on 228
importance of time limitation on 227
in auto parts 16, 18, 113, 117, 121, 194, 225, 226
in automobiles 16, 115, 120–21, 225
keiretsu and 196
precedent-setting nature of 195
retaliation for violation of 195, 228
risk of political capture of 120, 194, 227
STA as first US 132
third parties in 194
versus managed trade 197
welfare effects of 132
when to pursue 194–97, 227–28, 243

Wakasugi, Ryuhei 79
Watanabe, Tadashi 148
Wealth effect of high yen 50
Weinstein, David E. 70
Williamson, John 35, 208, 209
Wolff, Edward 61
Womack, James P. 105, 108
Wood products 104, 189, 193
Woods, Peter J. 120
Worker training 11, 123
World Bank 235

Yamaichi Securities 173, 175, 176
Yamamura, Kozo 11
Yanase 115
Yeats, Alexander 73
Yen, international role of 237. *See also* Exchange rates
Yen-dollar talks 17
Yokosuka Naval Base 78, 162, 165
Yokota Air Force Base 78, 162
Yoshino, Naoyuki 68
Yoshitomi, Masaru 8

Zenith 157

Other Publications from the
Institute for International Economics

POLICY ANALYSES IN INTERNATIONAL ECONOMICS Series

1   The Lending Policies of the International Monetary Fund
    John Williamson/*August 1982*
                        ISBN paper 0-88132-000-5   72 pp.

2   "Reciprocity": A New Approach to World Trade Policy?
    William R. Cline/*September 1982*
                        ISBN paper 0-88132-001-3   41 pp.

3   Trade Policy in the 1980s
    C. Fred Bergsten and William R. Cline/*November 1982*
    (out of print)   ISBN paper 0-88132-002-1   84 pp.
    Partially reproduced in the book *Trade Policy in the 1980s.*

4   International Debt and the Stability of the World Economy
    William R. Cline/*September 1983*
                        ISBN paper 0-88132-010-2   134 pp.

5   The Exchange Rate System, Second Edition
    John Williamson/*September 1983, rev. June 1985*
    (out of print)   ISBN paper 0-88132-034-X   61 pp.

6   Economic Sanctions in Support of Foreign Policy Goals
    Gary Clyde Hufbauer and Jeffrey J. Schott/*October 1983*
                        ISBN paper 0-88132-014-5   109 pp.

7   A New SDR Allocation?
    John Williamson/*March 1984*
                        ISBN paper 0-88132-028-5   61 pp.

8   An International Standard for Monetary Stabilization
    Ronald I. McKinnon/*March 1984*
                        ISBN paper 0-88132-018-8   108 pp.

9   The Yen/Dollar Agreement: Liberalizing Japanese Capital Markets
    Jeffrey A. Frankel/*December 1984*
                        ISBN paper 0-88132-035-8   86 pp.

10 Bank Lending to Developing Countries: The Policy Alternatives
    C. Fred Bergsten, William R. Cline, and John Williamson/*April 1985*
                        ISBN paper 0-88132-032-3   221 pp.

11 Trading for Growth: The Next Round of Trade Negotiations
    Gary Clyde Hufbauer and Jeffrey J. Schott/*September 1985*
                        ISBN paper 0-88132-033-1   109 pp.

12 Financial Intermediation Beyond the Debt Crisis
    Donald R. Lessard and John Williamson/*September 1985*
                        ISBN paper 0-88132-021-8   130 pp.

13 The United States-Japan Economic Problem
    C. Fred Bergsten and William R. Cline/*October 1985, 2d ed. January
    1987*
                        ISBN paper 0-88132-060-9   180 pp.

14 **Deficits and the Dollar: The World Economy at Risk**
Stephen Marris/*December 1985, 2d ed. November 1987*
ISBN paper 0-88132-067-6   415 pp.

15 **Trade Policy for Troubled Industries**
Gary Clyde Hufbauer and Howard F. Rosen/*March 1986*
ISBN paper 0-88132-020-X   111 pp.

16 **The United States and Canada: The Quest for Free Trade**
Paul Wonnacott, with an Appendix by John Williamson/*March 1987*
ISBN paper 0-88132-056-0   188 pp.

17 **Adjusting to Success: Balance of Payments Policy in the East Asian NICs**
Bela Balassa and John Williamson/*June 1987, rev. April 1990*
ISBN paper 0-88132-101-X   160 pp.

18 **Mobilizing Bank Lending to Debtor Countries**
William R. Cline/*June 1987*
ISBN paper 0-88132-062-5   100 pp.

19 **Auction Quotas and United States Trade Policy**
C. Fred Bergsten, Kimberly Ann Elliott, Jeffrey J. Schott, and
Wendy E. Takacs/*September 1987*
ISBN paper 0-88132-050-1   254 pp.

20 **Agriculture and the GATT: Rewriting the Rules**
Dale E. Hathaway/*September 1987*
ISBN paper 0-88132-052-8   169 pp.

21 **Anti-Protection: Changing Forces in United States Trade Politics**
I. M. Destler and John S. Odell/*September 1987*
ISBN paper 0-88132-043-9   220 pp.

22 **Targets and Indicators: A Blueprint for the International Coordination of Economic Policy**
John Williamson and Marcus H. Miller/*September 1987*
ISBN paper 0-88132-051-X   118 pp.

23 **Capital Flight: The Problem and Policy Responses**
Donald R. Lessard and John Williamson/*December 1987*
ISBN paper 0-88132-059-5   80 pp.

24 **United States-Canada Free Trade: An Evaluation of the Agreement**
Jeffrey J. Schott/*April 1988*
ISBN paper 0-88132-072-2   48 pp.

25 **Voluntary Approaches to Debt Relief**
John Williamson/*September 1988, rev. May 1989*
ISBN paper 0-88132-098-6   80 pp.

26 **American Trade Adjustment: The Global Impact**
William R. Cline/*March 1989*
ISBN paper 0-88132-095-1   98 pp.

27 **More Free Trade Areas?**
Jeffrey J. Schott/*May 1989*
ISBN paper 0-88132-085-4   88 pp.

28 **The Progress of Policy Reform in Latin America**
John Williamson/*January 1990*
                        ISBN paper 0-88132-100-1   106 pp.

29 **The Global Trade Negotiations: What Can Be Achieved?**
Jeffrey J. Schott/*September 1990*
                        ISBN paper 0-88132-137-0   72 pp.

30 **Economic Policy Coordination: Requiem or Prologue?**
Wendy Dobson/*April 1991*
                        ISBN paper 0-88132-102-8   162 pp.

31 **The Economic Opening of Eastern Europe**
John Williamson/*May 1991*
                        ISBN paper 0-88132-186-9   92 pp.

32 **Eastern Europe and the Soviet Union in the World Economy**
Susan M. Collins and Dani Rodrik/*May 1991*
                        ISBN paper 0-88132-157-5   152 pp.

33 **African Economic Reform: The External Dimension**
arol Lancaster/*June 1991*
                        ISBN paper 0-88132-096-X   82 pp.

34 **Has the Adjustment Process Worked?**
Paul R. Krugman/*October 1991*
                        ISBN paper 0-88132-116-8   80 pp.

35 **From Soviet disUnion to Eastern Economic Community?**
Oleh Havrylyshyn and John Williamson/*October 1991*
ISBN paper 0-88132-192-3   84 pp.

36 **Global Warming: The Economic Stakes**
William R. Cline/*May 1992*
                        ISBN paper 0-88132-172-9   128 pp.

37 **Trade and Payments After Soviet Disintegration**
John Williamson/*June 1992*
                        ISBN paper 0-88132-173-7   96 pp.

BOOKS

IMF Conditionality
John Williamson, editor/*1983*
                        ISBN cloth 0-88132-006-4   695 pp.

The Policy in the 1980s
William R. Cline, editor/*1983*
                        ISBN cloth 0-88132-008-1   810 pp.
                        ISBN paper 0-88132-031-5   810 pp.

Subsidies in International Trade
Gary Clyde Hufbauer and Joanna Shelton Erb/*1984*
                        ISBN cloth 0-88132-004-8   299 pp.

International Debt: Systemic Risk and Policy Response
William R. Cline/*1984*
                        ISBN cloth 0-88132-015-3   336 pp.

Trade Protection in the United States: 31 Case Studies
Gary Clyde Hufbauer, Diane E. Berliner, and Kimberly Ann Elliott/*1986*
                    ISBN paper 0-88132-040-4   371 pp.

Toward Renewed Economic Growth in Latin America
Bela Balassa, Gerardo M. Bueno, Pedro-Pablo Kuczynski, and Mario Henrique
Simonsen/*1986*
(out of stock)   ISBN paper 0-88132-045-5   205 pp.

Capital Flight and Third World Debt
Donald R. Lessard and John Williamson, editors/*1987*
(out of print)   ISBN paper 0-88132-053-6   270 pp.

The Canada-United States Free Trade Agreement:
The Global Impact
Jeffrey J. Schott and Murray G. Smith, editors/*1988*
                    ISBN paper 0-88132-073-0   211 pp.

World Agricultural Trade: Building a Consensus
William M. Miner and Dale E. Hathaway, editors/*1988*
                    ISBN paper 0-88132-071-3   226 pp.

Japan in the World Economy
Bela Balassa and Marcus Noland/*1988*
                    ISBN paper 0-88132-041-2   306 pp.

America in the World Economy: A Strategy for the 1990s
C. Fred Bergsten/*1988*
                    ISBN cloth 0-88132-089-7   235 pp.
                    ISBN paper 0-88132-082-X   235 pp.

Managing the Dollar: From the Plaza to the Louvre
Yoichi Funabashi/*1988, 2d ed. 1989*
                    ISBN paper 0-88132-097-8   307 pp.

United States External Adjustment and the World Economy
William R. Cline/*May 1989*
                    ISBN paper 0-88132-048-X   392 pp.

Free Trade Areas and U.S. Trade Policy
Jeffrey J. Schott, editor/*May 1989*
                    ISBN paper 0-88132-094-3   400 pp.

Dollar Politics: Exchange Rate Policymaking in the United States
I. M. Destler and C. Randall Henning/*September 1989*
                    ISBN paper 0-88132-079-X   192 pp.

Latin American Adjustment: How Much Has Happened?
John Williamson, editor/*April 1990*
                    ISBN paper 0-88132-125-7   480 pp.

The Future of World Trade in Textiles and Apparel
William R. Cline/*1987, 2d ed. June 1990*
                    ISBN paper 0-88132-110-9   344 pp.

Completing the Uruguay Round: A Results-Oriented Approach to the GATT Trade
Negotiations
Jeffrey J. Schott, editor/*September 1990*
                    ISBN paper 0-88132-130-3   256 pp.

Economic Sanctions Reconsidered (in two volumes)
  Economic Sanctions Reconsidered: History and Current Policy
    (also sold separately, see below)
  Economic Sanctions Reconsidered: Supplemental Case Histories
  Gary Clyde Hufbauer, Jeffrey J. Schott, and Kimberly Ann Elliott/*1985, 2d ed.*
    December 1990

	ISBN cloth 0-88132-115-X	928 pp.
	ISBN paper 0-88132-105-2	928 pp.

Economic Sanctions Reconsidered: History and Current Policy
Gary Clyde Hufbauer, Jeffrey J. Schott, and Kimberly Ann Elliott/*December 1990*

	ISBN cloth 0-88132-136-2	288 pp.
	ISBN paper 0-88132-140-0	288 pp.

Pacific Basin Developing Countries: Prospects for the Future
Marcus Noland/*January 1991*

	ISBN cloth 0-88132-141-9	250 pp.
	ISBN paper 0-88132-081-1	250 pp.

Currency Convertibility in Eastern Europe
John Williamson, editor/*October 1991*

	ISBN cloth 0-88132-144-3	396 pp.
	ISBN paper 0-88132-128-1	396 pp.

Foreign Direct Investment in the United States
Edward M. Graham and Paul R. Krugman/*1989, 2d ed. October 1991*

	ISBN paper 0-88132-139-7	200 pp.

International Adjustment and Financing: The Lessons of 1985-1991
C. Fred Bergsten, editor/*January 1992*

	ISBN paper 0-88132-112-5	336 pp.

North American Free Trade: Issues and Recommendations
Gary Clyde Hufbauer and Jeffrey J. Schott/*April 1992*

	ISBN cloth 0-88132-145-1	392 pp.
	ISBN paper 0-88132-120-6	392 pp.

American Trade Politics
I. M. Destler/*1986, rev. June 1992*

	ISBN cloth 0-88132-164-8	400 pp.
	ISBN paper 0-88132-188-5	400 pp.

Narrowing the U.S. Current Account Deficit
Allen J. Lenz/*June 1992*

	ISBN cloth 0-88132-148-6	640 pp.
	ISBN paper 0-88132-103-6	640 pp.

The Economics of Global Warming
William R. Cline/*June 1992*

	ISBN cloth 0-88132-150-8	416 pp.
	ISBN paper 0-88132-132-X	416 pp.

U.S. Taxation of International Income: Blueprint for Reform
Gary Clyde Hufbauer, assisted by Joanna M. van Rooij/*October 1992*

	ISBN cloth 0-88132-178-8	304 pp.
	ISBN paper 0-88132-134-6	304 pp.

Who's Bashing Whom? Trade Conflict in High-Technology Industries
Laura D'Andrea Tyson/*November 1992*

	ISBN cloth 0-88132-151-6	352 pp.
	ISBN paper 0-88132-106-0	352 pp.

Korea in the World Economy
Il Sakong/*January 1993*

	ISBN cloth 0-88132-184-2	328 pp.
	ISBN paper 0-88132-106-0	328 pp.

NAFTA: An Assessment
Gary Clyde Hufbauer and Jeffrey J. Schott/*February 1993*

	ISBN paper 0-88132-198-2	92 pp.

Pacific Dynamism and the International Economic System
C. Fred Bergsten and Marcus Noland, editors/*May 1993*

	ISBN paper 0-88132-196-6	424 pp.

Economic Consequences of Soviet Disintegration
John Williamson, editor/*May 1993*

	ISBN paper 0-88132-190-7	664 pp.

Reconcilable Differences? United States–Japan Economic Conflict
C. Fred Bergsten and Marcus Noland/*June 1993*

	ISBN paper 0-88132-129-X	296 pp.

SPECIAL REPORTS

1 **Promoting World Recovery: A Statement on Global Economic Strategy by Twenty-six Economists from Fourteen Countries/** *December 1982*
(out of print)   ISBN paper 0-88132-013-7   45 pp.

2 **Prospects for Adjustment in Argentina, Brazil, and Mexico: Responding to the Debt Crisis**
John Williamson, editor/*June 1983*
(out of print)   ISBN paper 0-88132-016-1   71 pp.

3 **Inflation and Indexation: Argentina, Brazil, and Israel**
John Williamson, editor/*March 1985*
                         ISBN paper 0-88132-037-4   191 pp.

4 **Global Economic Imbalances**
C. Fred Bergsten, editor/*March 1986*
                         ISBN cloth 0-88132-038-2   126 pp.
                         ISBN paper 0-88132-042-0   126 pp.

5 **African Debt and Financing**
Carol Lancaster and John Williamson, editors/*May 1986*
(out of print)   ISBN paper 0-88132-044-7   229 pp.

6 **Resolving the Global Economic Crisis: After Wall Street**
Thirty-three Economists from Thirteen Countries/*December 1987*
                         ISBN paper 0-88132-070-6   30 pp.

7 **World Economic Problems**
Kimberly Ann Elliott and John Williamson, editors/*April 1988*
                         ISBN paper 0-88132-055-2   298 pp.

Reforming World Agricultural Trade
Twenty-nine Professionals from Seventeen Countries/*1988*
                         ISBN paper 0-88132-088-9   42 pp.

8   Economic Relations Between the United States and Korea: Conflict
    or Cooperation?
    Thomas O. Bayard and Soo-Gil Young, editors/*January 1989*
                              ISBN paper 0-88132-068-4   192 pp.

FORTHCOMING

Reciprocity and Retaliation: An Evaluation of Tough Trade Policies
Thomas O. Bayard and Kimberly Ann Elliott

The Globalization of Industry and National Economic Policies
C. Fred Bergsten and Edward M. Graham

The New Tripolar World Economy: Toward Collective Leadership
C. Fred Bergsten and C. Randall Henning

The United States as a Debtor Country
C. Fred Bergsten and Shafiqul Islam

The Dynamics of Korean Economic Development
Soon Cho

Third World Debt: A Reappraisal
William R. Cline

Does Foreign Exchange Intervention Work?
Kathryn M. Dominguez and Jeffrey A. Frankel

Equilibrium Exchange Rates for Global Economic Growth
Rudiger Dornbusch

Global Competition Policy
Edward M. Graham and J. David Richardson

International Monetary Policymaking in the United States, Germany, and Japan
C. Randall Henning

The New Europe in the World Economy
Gary Clyde Hufbauer

The Costs of U.S. Trade Barriers
Gary Clyde Hufbauer and Kimberly Ann Elliott

Comparing the Costs of Protection: Europe, Japan, and the United States
Gary Clyde Hufbauer and Kimberly Ann Elliott, editors

Toward Freer Trade in the Western Hemishpere
Gary Clyde Hufbauer and Jeffrey J. Schott

A World Savings Shortage?
Paul R. Krugman

Migration and Trade: The Case of NAFTA
Philip Martin

Sizing Up U.S. Export Disincentives
J. David Richardson

Adjusting to Volatile Energy Prices
Philip K. Verleger, Jr.

The Future of the World Trading System
John Whalley

Trading and the Environment: Setting the Rules
John Whalley and Peter Uimonen

Equilibrium Exchange Rates: An Update
John Williamson

The Politics of Economic Reform
John Williamson

For orders outside the US and Canada please contact:

Longman Group UK Ltd.
PO Box 88
Harlow, Essex CM 19 5SR
UK

Telephone Orders: 0279 623925
Fax: 0279 453450
Telex: 817484